3495

$ 17⁵⁰

6/2

D0960654

Between Friends

Between Friends

The Correspondence of
Hannah Arendt and Mary McCarthy
1949–1975

EDITED AND WITH AN
INTRODUCTION BY CAROL BRIGHTMAN

HARCOURT BRACE & COMPANY
New York   San Diego   London

Copyright © 1995 by the Literary Trust of
Hannah Arendt Bluecher, Lotte Kohler, Trustee
Copyright © 1995 by The Literary Trust of Mary McCarthy West,
Margo Viscusi and Eve Stwertka, Trustees
Introduction and editorial notes
copyright © 1995 by Carol Brightman

All rights reserved. No part of this publication may be reproduced or
transmitted in any form or by any means, electronic or mechanical, including photocopy, recording, or any information storage and retrieval
system, without permission in writing from the publisher.

Requests for permission to make copies of any part of the work should
be mailed to: Permissions Department, Harcourt Brace & Company,
6277 Sea Harbor Drive, Orlando, Florida 32887-6777.

Library of Congress Cataloging-in-Publication Data
Arendt, Hannah.
Between friends: the correspondence of Hannah Arendt and Mary
McCarthy, 1949–1975 / edited with an introduction by Carol
Brightman. — 1st ed.
p.   cm.
Includes bibliographical references and indexes.
ISBN 0-15-100112-X
1. Arendt, Hannah—Correspondence. 2. Political scientists—
Germany—Correspondence. 3. McCarthy, Mary—Correspondence.
4. Authors, American—20th century—Correspondence.
I. McCarthy, Mary. II. Brightman, Carol. III. Title.
JC263.A69A3 1994
320.5'092—dc20   93-47425
[B]

Designed by Lori J. McThomas
Printed in the United States of America.
First edition
A B C D E

Contents

Introduction:

An Epistolary Romance

"One can't say how life is, how chance or fate deals with people, except by telling the tale."
—HANNAH ARENDT,
May 31, 1971

They first met at the Murray Hill Bar in Manhattan in 1944. Mary McCarthy, then married to Edmund Wilson, was accompanied by the critic Clement Greenberg, whose brother Martin was a co-worker of Hannah Arendt's at Schocken Books. Arendt, whose reviews and essays, initially published in *Menorah Journal* and *Contemporary Jewish Record*, were beginning to appear in *Commentary, Partisan Review*, and *The Nation*, was being introduced to the larger circle of New York intellectuals that lay beyond the German Jewish émigré community of which she was a part. She was not yet the figure she would become, but already, three years off the boat, she conveyed a sense of authority—"of speaking for something older and deeper that she understood as European culture," a contemporary, William Barrett, recalled[1]—which fascinated her new American friends.

In 1944, Mary McCarthy was struck by Arendt's skeptical wit, a breezy "Szee here" insouciance that she shared with her Berlin-born husband, Heinrich Blücher, which reveled in refugee jokes like the one about the émigré dachshund who bemoans his previous life as a Saint Bernard. "She was full of vitality," McCarthy recalled in an interview with me in 1985, "an extraordinary electric vitality. . . .

---

1. *The Truants* (1982), 99.

She filled me with delight and wonder." America, Arendt said glee-fully at the Murray Hill Bar, hadn't "jelled" yet. It was still a nation of shopkeepers and peasants, more Old World than New, whose social vision seemed as narrow as the political vision of the country's Founding Fathers was broad.

The observation was echoed in an essay McCarthy wrote in September 1947, but with a different twist. Trying to account for the nomadic character of life in the United States, and for what she saw as "the ugliness of American decoration, American entertainment, American literature," she wondered, in "America the Beautiful," if this "vulgarity" was not "the visible expression of the impoverishment of the European masses, a manifestation of all the backwardness, deprivation, and want that arrived here in boatloads from Europe?" Pointing to the immense popularity of U.S. movies abroad, she suggested that "Europe is the unfinished negative of which America is the proof."

This Europe was the home, as well, of "a stable upper class," whose absence in the United States, McCarthy reasoned, was "responsible for much of the vulgarity of the American scene."[2] It was not Hannah Arendt's Europe. Nor for that matter did Arendt's "republic," as she often referred to her adopted country, much resemble the postwar United States that McCarthy described. Arendt saw something else. Writing to the philosopher Karl Jaspers in 1946, she noted, approvingly, the lack of a "national state" and a "truly national tradition" in the United States.[3]

Fantasy was at work here, fantasies of considerable creative potential for both women, not only for their friendship, which grew by leaps and bounds after an early misunderstanding, but also for their work, much of which was inspired by ideals attached to the other's traditions. One thinks of Arendt's critical engagement with the political principles embodied in the Constitution and the Bill of Rights in On Revolution and Crises of the Republic; and of McCarthy's Venice Observed, The Stones of Florence, and Birds of America, the last haunted by the moral philosophy of Kant. Even The Group, with its all-American cast from Vassar's Class of '33, gives the last word to the girl who got away: "Lakey," who sails for Europe and re-

---

2. "America the Beautiful," On the Contrary (1961), 18.
3. Hannah Arendt and Karl Jaspers, Correspondence: 1926–1969 (1992), 30.

turns on the eve of war with the mannish Baroness d'Estienne, a German.

In later years, Mary McCarthy viewed her friendships with both Hannah Arendt and the Italian critic Nicola Chiaromonte, whom she also met in 1944, as a kind of conversion experience. "Probably that was Europe! You know I've never thought of that until this minute," she told me in the fall of 1980, recalling the unforgettable summer she had fallen under Chiaromonte's influence. It was the summer of 1945, on the beach in Truro, after she had separated from Edmund Wilson. She and Chiaromonte had talked about Tolstoy and Dostoevsky, "and the *change* from someone like Edmund and his world . . . and most of the *Partisan Review* boys," she exclaimed, "was absolutely stunning."

McCarthy had previously reviewed plays for *Partisan Review* and had written the autobiographical fiction collected in *The Company She Keeps.* In 1945, she was translating Simone Weil's essay "l'Iliad, ou le poème de force" for Dwight Macdonald's *politics,* and reading Russian novels for her first academic appointment, at Bard College. Change was in the air, especially after Hiroshima brought an end to politics as usual, including her brief flirtation with Trotskyism. "We were feeling very quick in the biblical sense," she remembered of the little group in Truro, which also numbered James Agee, Niccolo Tucci, and Chiaromonte's wife, Miriam. But the "absolute awakening" of which she spoke involved not much more than "thinking about what these writers [Weil and the Russians] were *saying!*"

Edmund Wilson, whose monumental study of the revolutionary tradition in Europe, *To the Finland Station,* had appeared only six years before, represented "an empty literary point of view in comparison," McCarthy believed. It wouldn't have occurred to him to look at Tolstoy and Dostoevsky as "anything but two writers," to observe "that Tolstoy was of course a much better stylist and Dostoevsky wrote bad Russian and so on . . . . It never occurred to any of those people that there should be some connection with their own lives, how they were living and what they believed in."[4] Such a connection was vital to McCarthy. It was as if the personal losses of her early life had left her peculiarly vulnerable to literature's power to endow those "ragged claws" of self, "scuttling across the floors of

---

4. "Mary, Still Contrary," interview by Carol Brightman, *The Nation,* May 19, 1984, 619, 614.

silent seas," of which Eliot speaks in "The Love Song of J. Alfred Prufrock," with purpose and meaning.

Chiaromonte and Arendt were different, as much from each other as from the New York intellectuals McCarthy knew. But they were both Europeans—"Platonists too," McCarthy noted in 1980, "or Socratics, rather"—who shared a fundamental concern for personal and political morality which excited her in a way that ideologically driven politics did not. The injunction in Hannah Arendt's credo, *amor mundi*, to substitute love for the world in place of an excessive concern for the self, for example, returned to political life some of the redemptive power that Mary McCarthy, in childhood, drew from religion.

It is not hard to imagine what she saw in Hannah Arendt, who "possessed the gift of thinking poetically amid the ruins of modernity's dark times," as one of Arendt's Jesuit admirers has written.[5] Their friendship, however, had to overcome a hapless remark McCarthy made at a party in New York in 1945. In a conversation about the hostility of French citizens to the Germans occupying Paris, she said she felt sorry for Hitler, who was so absurd as to want the love of his victims. It was pure Mary McCarthyism, a remark calculated to offend pious antifascists, not Hannah Arendt. But Arendt was incensed. "How can you say such a thing in front of me—a victim of Hitler, a person who has been in a concentration camp!"[6] she snapped. McCarthy was unable to make amends. Three years later, after they found themselves in a minority at a meeting to discuss the future of *politics*, Arendt, according to McCarthy, turned to her on a subway platform and said: "Let's end this nonsense. We think so much alike." McCarthy apologized for the Hitler remark, and Arendt admitted she had never been in a concentration camp, only an internment camp in France. And to a degree unmatched among modern intellectuals, their friendship prospered ever after.

Born in Seattle in 1912, orphaned at six, and raised by Catholic, Protestant, and Jewish guardians, Mary McCarthy grew up a willful,

---

5. James W. Bernauer, S. J., ed., "The Faith of Hannah Arendt," in *Amor Mundi: Explorations in the Faith and Thought of Hannah Arendt* (1987), 1.
6. Quoted in Elizabeth Young-Bruehl, *Hannah Arendt: For Love of the World* (1982), 196–97.

headstrong girl who bowed to no one but the intellectual women she met at school. These appeared first among the *mesdames* of the Sacred Heart convent in Seattle, later at Annie Wright Seminary in Tacoma, and then at Vassar. Hannah Arendt, who was born in Hannover in 1906, and raised in Königsberg, East Prussia, the only child of educated Jewish parents, became, in a sense, the most distinguished of McCarthy's teachers. Her authority, as much moral as intellectual, did not prevent McCarthy from questioning Arendt's thought, however, both when it seemed obscure and when it violated her sense of reality.

Thus, after praising *The Origins of Totalitarianism* as "a truly extraordinary piece of work, an advance in human thought of, at the very least a decade," McCarthy couldn't resist noting, in the first letter she wrote to Arendt, "a ,ew barbarisms, such as the use of 'ignore' to mean 'be ignorant of' that . . . might be corrected in another edition." When she offered her "larger criticism" of Arendt's view of totalitarianism—namely, that it emerged as "a scheme in the minds of certain displaced men to rob other men of their sense of reality"—she touched on an interesting difference between them, one that enlivens their twenty-five-year correspondence and gives its several disputations the quality of a *conte philosophique*.

Arendt, McCarthy proposed, scanted "the element of the fortuitous" in totalitarianism. By this she meant the possibility "that certain features have been incorporated into [totalitarian regimes] simply because they worked." Arendt seemed to think there were "laws of political conduct . . . that the Nazis and Stalin [had] special access to," McCarthy wrote in April 1951. One often did get that impression, she conceded, but Arendt had failed to demonstrate it. Instead, she sometimes seemed to entertain the opposite view: "that man is not interpreter or *artiste* to a rational universe, but a creator without a model to draw from."

This view, in which both chance and choice enter into the making of a life—chance rather more than choice—was of course McCarthy's own. The drama of creation, of making something new out of the torn cloth of family, convention, history, crops up everywhere in her prose. Not only does it appear in memoirs and letters, where you might expect a writer to test her inventions and flex her personae, but also in historical reflections. In *Venice Observed*, the city itself, with its polyglot heritage, serves to mirror McCarthy's ironic apprehension of the mixed blessings of orphanhood. "Venice, as a city, was a foundling, floating upon the waters like Moses in his basket," she declares. "It was therefore obliged to be inventive, to steal and improvise."

At bottom, her differences with Arendt centered on the question of change—not political change, to which both women subscribed in times of crisis (Vietnam, Watergate), though Arendt's knowledge of totalitarianism left her more pessimistic, but personal change, especially in close encounters with the opposite sex. Some kind of personal transformation, McCarthy believed, was not only possible but very likely the only justification for falling in love. (Hence, perhaps, her propensity for doing so. Love, in McCarthy's middle years, helped fuel an absolutely relentless program of self-improvement.) Arendt, who was more comfortable with Nietzsche's dictum to become "what one is" against whatever conventions of thought and society hem one in, adhered to a darker view, more European, yet romantic in a different way.

"You know I believe that one ought to trust one's senses, and I don't think, therefore, that you can have been wrong," Arendt wrote of a doomed affair McCarthy had started with a London critic in 1956; but she was glad that Mary had decided not to try to see the man again. Later, she commiserated with her over his lying, which she called *pseudologia phantastica*, the lies of a boaster, and therefore not to be believed (a typical Arendtian paradox, drawn from the Latin roots of our sawed-off modern speech). To "lie about one's origin and play the aristocrat in England" was as much a satire on the English, she suggested, as it was imposture. Such lies concern only facts which are bound to come out anyway, whereas "if one lies about his 'feelings,' he is really safe; who can find out?" There was "some supreme defiance in this," Arendt thought, and what one fell for was "among other things this defiance."

Brecht is evoked, with his warning "Here you have somebody upon whom you can*not* rely"; and Heidegger, Arendt's teacher in 1925, with whom she had a youthful affair (*"the* great love affair of her life," McCarthy told me in 1985). With men like that, talent overruled unreliability, or compensated for it, Arendt suggested. For the rebel without genius, however, whose value is nowhere recognized in society, life becomes pointless. Thus, "to destroy oneself and become 'self-destructive' can be a time-consuming and rather honorable job. More honorable and probably less boring than to save oneself. The only thing which is really not permissible is to drag other people into one's own amusements." So Mary had to be frightened away. "Certainly, there is a great deal of cruelty in all this," Arendt observed, "but then you can't expect somebody who loves you to treat you less cruelly than he would treat himself."

These pronouncements on love reveal an unexpected side of Hannah Arendt, one prompted no doubt by McCarthy's consuming entanglements. Arendt's misgivings about her friend's readiness to throw up everything for a new man resurfaced in 1960 when McCarthy embarked on a hectic transcontinental affair with James West, the public affairs officer at the U.S. Embassy in Warsaw who became her fourth husband.

Arendt had been "frightened" that McCarthy "might get hurt," and McCarthy wrote back in May 1960 to tell her not to worry — "I *got* hurt," she said, after treating Arendt to a lovers' tour of Zurich, where she and West had spent a stolen weekend. McCarthy had foolishly told him about an earlier affair; he had reacted with disbelief and anger, and she had broken into tears. He repented, acknowledging a "wicked strain" in his nature; McCarthy had not felt free of guilt, but consoled herself that the "wicked" trait could be "cured."

"The story about [the earlier affair] sounded very funny," Arendt replied, chuckling over "how long some chickens take to come home to roost." But she hadn't meant "this kind of getting hurt — which is only another way of being alive." Meanwhile, she hoped McCarthy was not fooling herself: "Nobody ever was cured of anything . . . by a mere woman, though this is precisely what all girls think they can do. Either you are willing to take him 'as is' or you better leave well enough alone."

This deflating touch — not to be confused with indifference — can be heard in the story *Partisan Review* editor William Phillips tells about meeting Simone de Beauvoir in 1947, and complaining to Hannah Arendt afterward about the "endless nonsense" Beauvoir talked about America. "The trouble with you, William, is that you don't realize that she's not very bright. Instead of arguing with her," Arendt advised, "you should flirt with her."[7]

---

7. Quoted in Carol Brightman, *Writing Dangerously: Mary McCarthy and Her World* (1992), 330.

Despite Arendt's warning that "nobody ever changes for a mere woman," McCarthy thought they would "both change a little. What's the use of falling in love," she replied, "if you both remain inertly as-you-were?" Very soon, she was safely married again (this time for twenty-eight years). Yet Arendt never could understand the rush to get divorced and remarried. "Why can't you just live together?" McCarthy, in 1985, remembered Hannah asking. "She wanted this thought to be seriously entertained," she told me. "And probably wherever she is she's still shaking her head that we didn't do it that way."

Arendt, who was aware of McCarthy's restlessness with her third husband, Bowden Broadwater, and even helped persuade him to accede to the divorce, aired her disapproval only once. When Broadwater threatened to delay the divorce until West obtained his, McCarthy wrote her on October 7, 1960 that she was "tremulous with anger, disappointment, and incredulity." It struck her, she said darkly, that Bowden had somehow persuaded Hannah that he was right. "I am more deeply in love with Jim than ever and vice versa, and it is simply too ridiculous for us to be the passive foils of other people," she proclaimed a few weeks later. Arendt simply reasserted certain facts. Broadwater was "utterly powerless" in the matter, she wrote on November 11, 1960. She had talked to him "as a friend," honestly, "without any threats," because, thanks to McCarthy, that is what he was ("not a personal friend . . . but a friend of the house"), and because it appeared she had some influence. As for its being "simply too ridiculous" for McCarthy and West to be "passive foils," as McCarthy had written, it seemed to Arendt "rather obvious that you both are the victims of your own, self-chosen past. This may be inconvenient but it is not ridiculous, unless you wish to say that your whole past was not only a mistake, but a ridiculous one."

Such commentaries on the "crooked corkscrews of the heart" (Auden's phrase, a favorite of Arendt's) recur throughout the correspondence, which differs from the published exchanges of other writers in that it retains, alongside its loftier reflections, an over-the-counter immediacy of women talking shop—not gossip, though there is that, and not all of it Mary McCarthy's. Arendt's 1960 sketches of "little Podhoretz, already soooo 'tired' like the proverbial Jewish waiter" and Alfred Kazin, who resembles (as Harold Rosenberg suggests to her) "in walk and posture an arrogant Camel," are not easily forgotten. What sets McCarthy's and Arendt's letters apart, and gives them a rare dramatic force, is the immediacy of their voices, an immediacy that is sometimes frankly theatrical. Even the commentaries on personal affairs read like dialogue—dialogue, that is, which conveys thought.

Thought, as it functions in these letters (this "thinking-business," Arendt called her favorite pastime), is not to be confused with ideas or opinions, which may or may not result from thought. Arendt's and McCarthy's many reflections on the *idées reçues* of twentieth-century intellectual life are exercises in critical thought, but this, too, differs from the *activity* of thinking that one discovers in the letters. Pure thought, it might be called, if the adjective didn't violate the spirit of Arendt's "thinking ego." In the *act* of thinking—whether about affairs of the heart, crime in the streets, student revolts, or Black Power—Arendt, in particular, shuttles back and forth across a gap that ordinarily separates the experience of everyday life from the contemplation of it. The essence of this kind of thinking is its power to bring the world into sharper focus, and not just our experience of the world, but the world itself; to strip it of superstition, sentiment, and the drapery of theory.

In this sense Arendt, in her political essays as well as in her correspondence, does resemble Socrates, who wanted to bring philosophy *down to earth*, to examine the invisible measures by which we judge human affairs. When I asked Jerome Kohn, Arendt's teaching assistant in the 1970s, whether Judging, the subject of the unwritten third volume of *The Life of the Mind*, might have been a stumbling block, he said, "Far from it," and pointed to something that will be readily apparent to readers of this correspondence. "Hannah practiced judgment throughout her life. Judging events, grasping their consequences for other people," he observed, "was an exercise of common sense for her."

This kind of thoughtfulness—not to be confused with *being good*—is the opposite of the traditional elevation of *thought* into an exit visa from the petty world of appearances. Reading Hannah Arendt on the "feebleminded thoughtfulness of intellectuals," one may wince over an ungainly Germanic sentence (English was Arendt's *third* language, after German and French), but the effort, here and elsewhere, is frequently rewarded with a fresh insight into how we think about the world. A metaphor for Arendt's kind of thinking is suggested by the little train she liked to ride in the Swiss Alps. She named it "Bimmel-Bammel," and took it from Tegna, her summer retreat high in the mountains, to Locarno, where she went to the circus or the movies. "Surrounded by friends, she rode like a solitary passenger on her train of thought," McCarthy writes, in "Saying Good-bye to Hannah," of Arendt's desolation after Heinrich Blücher's death in 1970; and this quieter image evokes the uncanny sense one has, when reading Arendt, of a mind traveling.

In Germany, according to Gordon A. Craig, a passenger who recently boarded the Frankfurt-Hamburg train was greeted with the announcement, "I welcome you on board the InterCity Express *Hannah Arendt* —whoever that was—and wish you a pleasant journey." A bit later the voice returned: "Hannah Arendt was a *Dichterin* [poet or author]." And, finally: "Incidentally, I have meanwhile learned— Hannah Arendt was a *Philosophin*."[8] An amusing anecdote, it suggests that a certain justice has been done. (In the United States we do not name trains after poets or philosophers, but NASA scientists mapping Venus are naming that distant planet's craters after famous women: Pearl Buck, Margaret Mead, Clare Boothe Luce, Lillian Hellman, Gertrude Stein, and Mary Stuart, Queen of Scots. Arendt and McCarthy have been spared the honor.)

McCarthy liked to watch her friend *"think."* "Watching [Hannah] talk to an audience was like seeing the motions of the mind made visible in action and gesture," she told the mourners at Arendt's funeral in 1975. And she drew a vivid image of Arendt's kinetic relation to ideas: "Hannah was a conservationist; she did not believe in throwing anything away that had once been thought. A use might be found for it," she began. "Thought, for her, was a kind of husbandry, a humanizing of the wilderness of experience—building houses, running paths and roads through, damming streams, planting windbreaks. The task that had fallen to her, as an exceptionally gifted intellect and a representative of the generations she had lived among," McCarthy continued, "was to apply thought systematically to each and every characteristic experience of her time—*anomie*, terror, advanced warfare, concentration camps, Auschwitz, inflation, revolution, school integration, the Pentagon Papers, space, Wa-

---

8. "Letters on Dark Times," *The New York Review of Books*, May 13, 1993, 14.

tergate, Pope John, violence, civil disobedience—and, having finally achieved this, to direct thought inward, upon itself, and its own characteristic processes."[9]

Not all these weighty subjects are treated in the correspondence, but a great many are, as they were in conversation. Philosophy gave Arendt a way of thinking about politics and the social world that, in a quite practical sense, was important to McCarthy and is to us today, for it counters both the demagoguery of ideological thinking and the sectarian faith of "theoretic intellectuals" (McCarthy's term for President Kennedy's academic advisers) in the factuality of the social sciences. For contemporary readers, Arendt's dialogues with classical philosophers (dead white men, a multiculturalist might call them) offer a blessed release from current academic debates over what constitutes intellectual tradition in a pluralistic universe. Unabashedly Eurocentric, her readings in Western history and philosophy, scattered throughout her letters, are pertinent today precisely because they challenge us to think for ourselves: Not *by* ourselves— "I always thought that one has got to start thinking as though nobody had thought before, and then start learning from everybody else," Arendt once proposed[10]—but *for* ourselves. *Denken ohne Geländer:* thinking without a banister, she called it.

This was no existential conceit; the banisters *are* gone, long gone. Tocqueville was right: "Since the past has ceased to throw its light onto the future, the mind of man wanders in obscurity" (a favorite quotation of Arendt's). But the obscurity, in Arendt's view, holds promise—not unlike the darkness Dante enters in the middle of the "dark wood." Deliverance comes if first the traveler dares to tell the fearful things that he has seen.

Both by accident and by choice, Hannah Arendt was schooled in a German tradition of exalted solitude that sometimes baffled her American friends. She had lost her father at six, the same age McCarthy was when her parents died. And even before she left Hitler's Germany and became a refugee in Paris, acquiring the sense of "homelessness" of which she often spoke, she had impressed her fellow students at the University of Marburg as exceptional: "shy

9. "Saying Good-bye to Hannah," *Occasional Prose* (1985), 37–38.
10. Quoted in *Hannah Arendt: The Recovery of the Public World*, Melvyn Hill, ed. (1979), 337.

and withdrawn, with strikingly beautiful features and lonely eyes," she stood out immediately," her friend the philosopher Hans Jonas remembered after Arendt's death in 1975. "Brightness of intellect was no rare article there," he recalled of Marburg in the mid-twenties. What Arendt possessed "was an intensity, an inner direction, an instinct for quality, a groping for essence which cast a magic about her." [11]

Her aloofness was untouched by misanthropy. It went hand in hand with a genius for the kind of friendship in which much is given, little demanded. With fellow intellectuals Arendt sometimes felt "intoxicated with agreement against a world of enemies," [12] as she wrote to Randall Jarrell in the mid-forties. With McCarthy, who thrived on a sense of embattlement, all the more when it involved other writers (notably, other women writers), Arendt was moved to temper the impulse. Still, her loyalty and unbroken affection for her closest American friend gave McCarthy a home, emotionally speaking, to which she returned again and again.

There was a filial component to this relationship. Another fantasy perhaps, though no less real for that, it allowed McCarthy to enlist Hannah Arendt in the service of a conscience that never slept, even in the midst of writing. "My novel is going ahead, but I have you horribly on my conscience every time sex appears," she wrote in December 1954, midway through *A Charmed Life*. "You are tugging at my elbow saying 'Stop' during a seduction scene I've just been writing. And your imagined remonstrances have been so effective that I've rewritten it to have it seen from the man's point of view, instead of the heroine's." The revision was fortunate; the hilarious seduction of Martha Sinnott (as in sin not) by the Edmund Wilson character, Miles Murphy, rescues an otherwise talky roman à clef from sententiousness.

McCarthy never spoke to me of the filial aspect of her relationship with Hannah Arendt, but she was sensitive to the quality when it appeared in Arendt's prose. "This book is very maternal, Hannah—*mütterlich*, if that is a word," she wrote of *Men in Dark Times* in December 1968. Its portraits of contemporary poets, philosophers, and revolutionaries reminded her of "fairy tales of the Northern for-

---

11. Quoted in Young-Bruehl, 468.
12. Ibid., 194.

ests." Their "funny animistic magic . . . comes partly from the terror you surround them with, the dark times," she suggested. Thus, their "lone enterprises" took on the quality of "hand-carved, home-made destinies." It was the only work of Arendt's that she "would call 'German,' " McCarthy added, referring not only to the "runic" aspect of the tales but also to "the role friendship plays in it, workmanly friendship, of apprentices starting out with their bundle on a pole and doing a piece of the road together."

Arendt, who professed not to know why McCarthy found the book "German," agreed with her "about the fairy tale quality of the portraits," which she called "silhouettes." And she was touched by the perception of friendship's role in the book, "in the sense of 'do-ing a piece of the road together'—as distinguished from intimacy." The distinction is revealing. Intimate exposure is not something one finds in Arendt's writing, not even in her letters to Mary McCarthy. Intimate experiences, one suspects, were not insignificant to her, but their sufferance, being well-nigh universal, was not worth writ-ing about. Or, if the experience struck a chord in the psyche, the less said the better, until one wove a story out of it.

"Chutzpah Hannah," an old friend used to call Arendt, "because she would take on anyone and remake him in her image."[13] Anyone, that is, whose life and work had pierced the curtain of failed revolu-tions, war, and genocide that hung like a shroud over her genera-tion. These included the subjects of *Men in Dark Times*, among them Rosa Luxemburg, literary critic Walter Benjamin, Karl Jaspers, Ber-tolt Brecht, Isak Dinesen, and Angelo Roncalli (Pope John XXIII). In truth, they are not remade in her image, but something of the revolutionary, the critic, the philosopher, the poet, the writer, and the churchman in Hannah Arendt enters into her illumination of them.

"Hannah Arrogance," a less friendly epithet, came from the "boys" at *Partisan Review*. "Who does she think she is? Aristotle?" Arendt reported William Phillips as saying. In this 1964 letter, she lamented the insidious tendency of American intellectuals to compare them-selves to one another, to compete. It was something Arendt never did, perhaps because she really stood (as she observed of her politi-cal ideas) "between all schools." Or more likely because she knew

---

13. Quoted in Anthony Heilbut, *Exiles in Paradise* (1983), 398.

better. "She was humble," Jerome Kohn reflects, "but she wasn't modest."

"Envy *is* a monster," Arendt assured McCarthy in October 1965, after Alfred Kazin had attacked McCarthy's character and writing in his *Starting Out in the Thirties*, which was published after *The Group* had made Mary McCarthy a household name. It was Arendt's contention that the drubbing Mary got from New York intellectuals after publication of *The Group* was sparked by jealousy and fanned by group-think. The quality of the novel—which she regarded as a swan song to McCarthy's "former life" in the thirties, "beautifully written" and "often hilariously funny"—was not, for her, at issue; though the book was not to be taken all that seriously. Referring, in June 1964, to some "propaganda material" McCarthy's German publisher had circulated on *The Group*'s behalf, she found the criticism full of "flattering and complicated theories" that missed "most of the points. It is as though these people"—"Serious animals," Arendt called the critics—"have forgotten how it is to *laugh*."

Such commentaries on life among the literati are a leitmotif of their letters to one another. In March 1952, when Arendt, who had arrived in New York in 1941, was still a relative newcomer, McCarthy introduced her to the fine art of decoding literary politics in the United States. Pondering the obsession with Stalinism that kept the American Committee for Cultural Freedom from challenging Senator Joseph McCarthy, she told Arendt that she could not believe that its members, many of them former comrades at *Partisan Review*, "seriously think that stalinism [*sic*] on a large scale is latent here, ready to revive at the slightest summons; but if they don't think this," and they were not simply "victims of momentum," she wondered, "what *do* they 'really' think?"

The fear was genuine but localized, McCarthy decided. And she went on to treat Arendt to an insider's account of the splitting apart of the American left after the Moscow purge trials in 1936–38, which still isn't taught in school. Of the Cultural Freedom stalwarts, McCarthy writes: "They live in terror of a revival of the situation that prevailed in the Thirties, when the fellow-travelers were powerful in teaching, publishing, the theatre, etc., when stalinism was the gravy-train and these people were off it and became the object of social slights, small economic deprivations, gossip and backbiting. These people, who are success-minded," she continued (offering

Hannah an account that was "rather on the petty side, but at any rate human"), "think in terms of group-advancement and cultural monopoly and were really traumatized by the brief stalinist apogee of the Thirties . . . In their dreams, this period is always recurring; it is 'realer' than today."

McCarthy's sensitivity to the hunger for "cultural monopoly" among the intellectuals of her generation rings a contemporary bell. Substitute "male chauvinists" for "fellow-travelers" in the first sentence of her exposition, and you have a fair approximation of the conditions that have contributed to the paranoid streak in American feminism. For the generation of career-minded women who were traumatized by the discrimination they experienced in graduate school and the professions in the 1950s, 60s, and 70s, this period, too, remains "realer" than today.

In McCarthy's comments on the private, often venal impulses behind ideological thinking and "group-advancement" are found what she called the "gifts of observation and analysis, the social gifts that women develop almost as a species from their historic position of having to get their way without direct confrontation."[14] Arendt, who went her own way without confrontation, direct or indirect, brings quite different gifts to the dissection of twentieth-century intellectual life.

Referring, on August 20, 1954, to the "feebleminded thoughtfulness or thoughtful feeblemindedness of intellectuals," whose craving for argument substitutes for real thought, she draws on Socrates to answer a hypothetical question McCarthy raised in a letter of August 10: "Why shouldn't I murder my grandmother if I want to?" McCarthy had paraphrased Dostoevsky's question in *Crime and Punishment* as an example of the modern obsession among "bohemianized people" with the question "Why not?" " 'How do you *know* that?' one of the characters [in *A Charmed Life*] keeps babbling about any statement in the realm of fact or aesthetics," she continued, and added: "I feel I have got hold of a subject that I'm not equipped to deal with." Arendt, who found this eager letter "a real joy," responded with the "philosophic answer."

"Since I have got to live with myself, am in fact the only person from whom I never shall be able to part, whose company I shall

14. "Mary, Still Contrary," 616.

have to bear forever, I don't want to become a murderer," she stated. She had already disposed of both the "religious answer" (fear of hell) and the "common sense answer" (fear of death) as no longer binding on the modern sensibility. The statement is a personal canon. It is Socrates' answer, and it, too, has lost its force for the "bohemianized people" of their generation. Why? Because "this life by oneself, on which it is based," Arendt explains, "is the life of the thinker par excellence: in the activity of thought, I am together with myself—and neither with other people nor with the world as such, as the artist is. Our friends, craving for philosophic 'information' "—Dwight Macdonald, a chronic debater, is mentioned—"are by no means 'thinkers' or willing to enter the dialogue of thought with themselves."

The passage might stand as proof of Hannah Arendt's arrogance if it were not for one of those sudden insights into the nature of modern alienation that enliven her ruminations. The "root of modernity"—namely, the "ritual of doubt" that began with Descartes, she observes—resides in "distrust in the senses." In her August 1954 letter, which anticipates the treatise on Thinking in *The Life of the Mind*, Arendt traces this distrust to the "great discoveries of the natural sciences which demonstrated that human senses do not reveal the world as it is, but on the contrary lead men only into error. From this followed the perversion of common sense." "Le bon sens," Arendt writes, "is a kind of sixth sense through which all particular sense data, given by the five senses, are fitted into a common world." After the scientific revolution, it was changed into a form of reasoning which Hobbes called "reckoning with consequences." Common sense, no longer a distillation of a sentient being's experience of the world, much less of collective experience, became merely a faculty of mind—a "logical faculty," which guaranteed a common answer to the question of two plus two, but was "entirely incapable of guiding us through the world or of grasping anything at all."

The letter is a jumble of notes whose underlying theme concerning the importance of the senses to clear thought and action was no doubt the subject of numerous conversations with McCarthy. Common sense, Mary McCarthy told me in 1989, was something she and Hannah had aplenty, contrary to what most people might think, "because strangely enough it is very unconventional. Conventional people," she insisted, "usually have absolutely zero common sense."

Careful exposition, in any event, was not Arendt's forte; something she knew herself, and tolerated to a degree that sometimes made McCarthy uncomfortable. Her carelessness was forgivable in correspondence, where her mea culpas for writing "hastily and impatiently" or for delivering "a few remarks in shorthand—perhaps to be talked about when we see each other" could be accepted with good grace. More disturbing was to find her "disregard for words," as McCarthy saw it, in print. A sentence such as "The human condition of work is worldliness," appearing on the first page of *The Human Condition*, bothered McCarthy greatly. With its uncertain use of the word *worldly*, it could not help but offend a writer whose commitment to clear and accurate expression in whatever she wrote was *her* way of humanizing the wilderness of experience.

When Arendt sent unpublished manuscripts for comment and correction, as she did on numerous occasions, they often elicited McCarthy's "protests" against what she thought "Hannah was trying to do to language—a kind of violation that it wouldn't take," she once told me. " 'Thoughtlessness.' It doesn't mean what you want it to mean in English, not any more," McCarthy wrote her in June 1971, after receiving a "thinking lecture" that appeared in essay form as "Thinking and Moral Considerations," and was ultimately incorporated into *The Life of the Mind*. It seems a "mistake," McCarthy argued, "to force a key word in an essay to mean what it doesn't normally, even when the reader understands what you are trying to say with it." The meaning would invariably be read as "*heedlessness, neglect, forgetfulness,* etc." She suggested that Arendt "find not *a* substitute— another abstract noun—but substitutes," such as she had done earlier with "inability to think." "But maybe *this* reader doesn't understand," McCarthy continued, moving into deeper waters, which is where such questions of definition frequently led.

She was disturbed by Arendt's reference to Eichmann's "thoughtlessness." Ten years earlier, seated in the Israeli courtroom, Arendt had been astonished by the glibness with which Adolf Eichmann admitted his crimes. " 'Of course' he had played a role in the extermination of the Jews; of course if he 'had not transported them, they would not have been delivered to the butcher,' " she recalled him saying, in *Eichmann in Jerusalem*, whose subtitle, *A Report on the*

Banality of Evil, was almost as controversial as the book's findings. " 'What,' he asked, 'is there to "admit"?' Now, he 'would like to find peace with [his] former enemies.' "

The latter sentiment, expressed by Eichmann with an " 'extraordinary sense of elation' " had been shared by Himmler at the end of the war, along with another leading Nazi, Robert Ley, who proposed the establishment of a "conciliation committee" to be made up of Nazis responsible for the massacre of Jews and Jewish survivors. The "outrageous cliché," as Arendt called the reconciliation notion, circulated among ordinary Germans after the war; no longer dictated from above, "it was a self-fabricated stock phrase, as devoid of reality as those clichés by which the people had lived for twelve years."

Watching Eichmann's cross-examination in 1961, Arendt had noticed an interesting pattern. Whenever the judges appealed to his conscience, they were met with an "elating cliché." Clichés and conventional sentiments functioned as armor, blocking the consciousness of the accused at just those junctures where painful intrusions of reality threatened. Eichmann himself, meanwhile, remained unperturbed by the startling contradictions in his statements.

At the end of the war he had declared: "I will jump into my grave laughing, because the fact that I have the death of five million Jews"—"enemies of the Reich," he claimed he'd said—"on my conscience gives me extraordinary satisfaction." But in Jerusalem he told the court: "I shall gladly hang myself in public as a warning example for all anti-Semites on this earth." The former, utterly damning, statement had been repeated to anyone who would listen, even in Argentina, Arendt noted, because the vision of himself "laughing" had given Eichmann " 'an extraordinary sense of elation to think that [he] was exiting from the stage in this way.' " The later sentiment, delivered in starkly different circumstances, fulfilled the same purpose of giving him a "lift." [15]

He was a macabre Dr. Feelgood; and with this insight of Arendt's (though she doesn't call him that), Mary McCarthy seems to have had little quarrel. In "General Macbeth," McCarthy had reckoned with another famous murderer, Shakespeare's king, who was also a kind of organization man, "not a monster, like Richard III or Iago or Iachimo." Indeed, the gruesome paradox posed by the "blackness

---

15. All these quotations are from *Eichmann in Jerusalem* (1963), 47, 52–54.

of his deeds" and the petty self-interest of the perpetrator was astonishingly similar, something Arendt noticed immediately when she read McCarthy's essay, with delight, while writing *Eichmann in Jerusalem*.

In 1971, in *Thinking*, Arendt had taken her analysis of Eichmann's "elating clichés" one precipitous step further. As in 1961 she was struck by a "manifest shallowness in the doer that made it impossible to trace the incontestable evil of his deeds to any deeper level." Eichmann had betrayed no symptoms of insanity, no ideological interests, no base motives beyond the usual careerist ambitions of a petty official. He professed respect for the Jews, or at least for the Jewish functionaries he had dealt with in the early years of the war. As one of the Reich's designated "Jewish experts," he had read Theodor Herzl's *Der Judenstaat*, a Zionist classic, and it had made a lasting impression on him. So had the "idealism" (Eichmann's word) of the Zionists with whom he had briefly worked to negotiate a "political solution" to the "Jewish question"—expulsion, for the privileged few versus the "physical solution" (extermination) about whose imminence he claimed to have been unaware. Remembering this courtroom spectacle years later in the *Thinking* volume, Arendt found one "notable characteristic" that set Eichmann, the man, apart from ordinary mortals, and that was "something entirely negative: it was not stupidity but *thoughtlessness*."

The word was a "mistake," McCarthy argued, not only because "usage" relegated it to petty crimes, but also because in saying that Eichmann differed from the rest of humanity in being incapable of reflection, Arendt had, in effect, made him a "monster," though in a sense different from what was commonly believed. McCarthy preferred to think of him as "profoundly, egregiously stupid," which was "not the same as having a low I.Q." Here she agreed with Kant, "that stupidity is caused, not by brain failure, but by a wicked heart. Insensitiveness, opacity, inability to make connections, often accompanied by low 'animal' cunning. . . . If you allow [Eichmann] a wicked heart," she observed, "then you leave him some freedom, which permits our condemnation."

McCarthy's objection echoes a charge that was leveled at *Eichmann in Jerusalem* in 1963: that Arendt's analysis of Eichmann's "banality" took him off the hook. Her failure to supply a villain equal to the death of millions of Jews was, in fact, converted in the furor unleashed by the book (about which *Between Friends* has much to say) into the preposterous claim that Arendt had written Eichmann's defense. The accusation left her speechless; a year passed before she would issue even a letter to the editor in protest.

Writing McCarthy in September 1963, shortly after the Anti-Defamation League sent a letter to rabbis urging them to preach against *Eichmann in Jerusalem* on the Jewish New Year, Arendt gave her reasons for remaining silent. The attacks against her in review after review were part of a "political campaign" to create an absurd "image" of the book to hide the real one. There was nothing she could do about it, she argued, "because an individual is powerless by definition and the power of the image-makers"—who have "money, personnel, time, connections"—"is considerable." "My position is that I wrote a report," she said, "and that I am not in politics, either Jewish or otherwise."

McCarthy was sympathetic but unconvinced. "Hannah always scolded me for reacting to criticism," she commented in 1985; "she pretended that she paid absolutely no attention to it. But it was *not true.*" Arendt had "behaved foolishly" in remaining silent during the Eichmann controversy, McCarthy believed. "I think it was her duty to answer—her duty to *herself*, to her *material*," she told me, "but it was her stubbornness and hurt feelings, and pride, that kept her from answering. I *know* that she reacted," McCarthy added, "but self-knowledge was not Hannah's strong point."

McCarthy rushed to her defense in *Partisan Review,* as did a smattering of other friends, mostly non-Jews, in other periodicals and in conversation. It was left to young Jewish radicals such as Norman Fruchter, writing in *Studies on the Left* in 1964, to appraise the larger significance of Arendt's work for "Jewish identity." In Arendt's account of the role the Jewish Councils had played in cooperating with Eichmann's office—perhaps the most controversial section of the book—Fruchter found a release from "the myth of the victim which Jews tend to substitute for their history." The culpability of officialdom argued, as well, he wrote, for a fresh understanding of "citizen responsibility [which is] necessary in every modern state to prevent the reemergence of the totalitarian movement which ravaged Germany."[16] Don't follow leaders, in other words; watch the parking meters, as Bob Dylan said.

---

16. Quoted in Young-Bruehl, 360.

Hannah Arendt's profile of Eichmann was to prove immensely useful to antiwar activists in the 1960s, who were confronted with another historic paradox in the spectacle of a liberal administration launching a bloody intervention in a tiny backward country in the name of nation-building. Whether or not Vietnam-era radicals read Arendt, and most did not, the ideas she unleashed with *Eichmann in Jerusalem* gave form to a perception of "the men who now engineer that war," as Carl Oglesby presented them at the first big antiwar march on Washington in 1965. These were the men "who study the maps, give the commands, push the buttons, and tally the dead: Bundy, McNamara, Rusk, Lodge, Goldberg, the President himself. They are not moral monsters," Oglesby asserted. "They are all honorable men. They are all liberals." (Perhaps that is why they got away with it; no Nuremburg or Jerusalem for them. Instead, liberalism took a nosedive after Vietnam, and still wanders, dazed and bloodied, outside history.)

Arendt never questioned the enormity of Eichmann's crimes, or the execution that awaited him. Her assessment of his "banality" may be gathered from the lines of Brecht she chose for *Eichmann in Jerusalem*'s dedication:

> O Germany —
> Hearing the speeches that ring from your house,
>   one laughs.
> But whoever sees you, reaches for his knife.

Her absorbing interest in Eichmann's cliché-ridden inability to think from the standpoint of anybody but himself was no idle inquiry, but a pledge to the future to learn from the past. She was fascinated and horrified by the possibility that evil deeds on such a massive scale could be committed not only without "intent" (in the legal sense), but also without consciousness. It might be easier to ascribe such crimes to a "wicked heart"; and the public, especially the American public, is usually content to attribute official wrongdoing to an invisible chain of command or, as with Vietnam, to a "mistake." The Eichmann case was different, however.

Kant, Arendt declared in *Thinking*, "once observed that 'stupidity is caused by a wicked heart.' This is not true," she contended. "Absence of thought is not stupidity; it can be found in highly intelligent people, and a wicked heart is not its cause; it is probably the other way round, that wickedness may be caused by absence of thought."

Arendt, Kohn suggests, "actually believed that thinking conditions people to resist evildoing." This novel view sets her apart from contemporary moral theorists, as well as from her beloved Kant. It suggests why the philosopher J. Glenn Gray, speaking of *The Life of the Mind* shortly before his death in 1972, told Kohn that "this book is at least a hundred years ahead of its time." It suggests, too, why someone might find in Arendt's meditations on Thinking, Willing, and Judging a spirit of inquiry more contemporaneous with Plato's *Apology.*

The furor over *Eichmann in Jerusalem* did not pass easily into memory's good night. ("Hannah Eichmann," the literary historian Alan Wald inadvertently let slip at an October 1993 conference on Mary McCarthy at Bard College, entitled "Truth Telling and Its Cost.") And Arendt's "hurt feelings" and "pride" proved resilient. Meeting her at a party for the poet Frederick Seidel toward the end of the 1960s, the late Irving Howe remembered approaching her "with hand extended." In 1963, he had been aligned with Lionel Abel, whose "The Aesthetics of Evil: Hannah Arendt on Eichmann and the Jews," published in *Partisan Review,* had led the attack on "the Rosa Luxemburg of Nothingness," as Abel called Arendt. But years before, Arendt had gotten Howe his first job, as a reader for Schocken Books, and he didn't want to lose their friendship. "At the party," he told me in 1986, "very dramatically, she cut me."

Arendt was probably right in not stepping into the ring to defend herself and her "material." If anything is ever learned from history, it is nearly always over the bruised bodies of those who speak truth to power; and then only after the issues have been thrashed out in public. Pride, if it dictated her silence, did not, in any event, presage her fall. And history seems to have lent weight and nuance to her perceptions of Eichmann and the Jewish elite, and to have justified her courage in setting them out at a time when, as she surely knew, American Jews were still wrestling uneasily with their wartime removal from the terrible events in Europe, and Jewish patriotism ran deep.

An epistolary romance, I have called the correspondence between Mary McCarthy and Hannah Arendt, because it frames the tale of a passionate friendship that was improbable on the face of it. "The wonder was that these two women kept on together," remarks their publisher William Jovanovich (who emerges in these letters as a somewhat romantic figure himself). "Hannah," Jovanovich wrote me in December 1992, "did not really comprehend the American-ness of Mary's comportment." As examples, he points to her amazement over the money McCarthy spent on her teeth, adding, "I didn't dare explain I'd spent far more"; and to the abruptness of Arendt's departures, which were often misunderstood by McCarthy, who was unfamiliar with the European style of not lingering over good-byes.

The tenderness found in their letters, however, bespeaks a friendship that borders on romance; not sexual romance, but not entirely platonic either. A longing for one another's physical presence runs throughout the correspondence of the 1960s, after McCarthy had settled in Europe. Mary to Hannah, Rome, 1960: "I am writing you this note for purely selfish reasons: because my heart is full of emotion and I want to talk. As if we were in your apartment." Hannah to Mary, New York, 1969: "God knows why I write only today. I wrote you countless letters—thanking you, missing you so much, thinking of you with a new closeness and tenderness. The trouble is that in order to write you must stop thinking; also, thinking can be done so comfortably, writing is so troublesome. Forgive me."

Arendt was drawn to qualities in McCarthy that transcended their cultural differences, and transcended, as well, the political and literary affinities that bound her to most of her American friends. Chief among these was McCarthy's openness to experience, an openness verging on the naive, which was not unlike a quality Arendt admired in Rahel Varnhagen, the subject of one of her most unusual books, *Rahel Varnhagen: The Life of a Jewish Woman*. Varnhagen, whose Berlin salon became a meeting place for Romantic poets at the dawn of the nineteenth century, impressed Arendt, when she first wrote about her in 1929, for her "effort to expose herself to life so that it could strike her 'like a storm without an umbrella.' "

Mary McCarthy, exactly. But it was her "American-ness"—which seemed to intensify the longer Mary lived abroad—that set McCarthy apart from Arendt's world, and gave their friendship a fabulous quality. In her foreword to McCarthy's *Intellectual Memoirs: New York 1936–1938*, Elizabeth Hardwick imagines, correctly, I think, that Arendt "saw Mary as a golden American friend, perhaps the best the country could produce, with a bit of our western states in her, a bit of the Roman Catholic, a Latin student, and a sort of New World, blue-stocking salonnière like Rahel Varnhagen."

In another sense, more like a tale of two travelers than a romance, the conversations Arendt and McCarthy sustained with each other, across oceans and continents, served as lifelines in the storms of controversy in which they engaged. They were a party of two, seeking in friendship a refuge from those other parties whose failures beset their generation. These included Communism and anti-Communism, in neither of which they placed much stock, and also the parties of progress and social control embedded in the behavioral sciences, and the parties of derision and doubt endemic to their own cramped corner of the left.

The result is a survivors' tale: uplifting, not because it has a happy ending—there is no *ending* to a tale—but because of the pleasure each woman so patently takes in the profusion of talents at her disposal. If Mary McCarthy and Hannah Arendt sometimes seem like two schoolgirls, arms entwined, voices low, buzzing with gossip about the silly antics of the boys (and girls) on the playground, this concession to the social ground of their lives is what lends credibility to everything else. We follow them down remote, barely navigable rivers of speculation about the intellectual life of our times, because we know that these two scouts keep their matches dry.

— CAROL BRIGHTMAN

Editor's Foreword

The correspondence between Hannah Arendt and Mary McCarthy is presented here in its entirety, with the exception of a few post-cards and notes written to establish dates and addresses, and two memoranda.

The first memorandum, from Arendt, is a single-spaced, four-page document entitled "Ad Lionel Abel's review in PR," and is of considerable historical interest as an unpublished rejoinder to Abel's famous broadside against Arendt's *Eichmann in Jerusalem* in the Spring 1963 *Partisan Review*. Because of its length and level of detail, however, it is not included here; readers will find its main points recapitulated in Arendt's letters of September 20 and October 10, 1963. The original document can be found in the Arendt-McCarthy correspondence on deposit with the Mary McCarthy papers at Vassar College.

The second memorandum I have omitted is a note McCarthy prepared for Arendt in the spring of 1973 on the etymology and usage of the word *intellect*, probably in connection with the first of the Gifford Lectures on "The Life of the Mind," which Arendt delivered later that year in Aberdeen, Scotland.

The correspondence contains several references to letters, mostly Arendt's, which appear to have been lost, and these are duly noted.

There may have been more, especially during the 1950s when Arendt's voice is heard only intermittently. McCarthy herself suspected that a handful of Arendt's letters were missing from the early years of their friendship, and searched her files, unsuccessfully, in the summer of 1989 when I began to consult with her on the editing of the correspondence. (As Hannah Arendt's co-executor, with Lotte Kohler, she had already inventoried Arendt's papers at the Library of Congress.)

"You needn't apologize to me for slowness of writing," McCarthy wrote on June 27, 1951, referring either to a missing letter of Arendt's or a telephone conversation. "I am a frightful correspondent, having never learned to communicate in a brief style." McCarthy, of course, was an ardent, one might say irrepressible, correspondent, whose letters served both her autobiographical impulse and her delight in writing as a way of bringing order to the onslaught of experience. Arendt was more likely to pick up the phone when the urge to communicate overtook her, or wait for one of McCarthy's frequent overnight visits with her in New York.

In the few weeks we worked together during the summer before her death on October 25, 1989, McCarthy and I reached an understanding about the editorial protocols that would apply to the letters. There were to be minimal cuts. Those permitted could be made for three reasons: to eliminate obscure and/or unimportant references; to reduce repetition, especially in greetings and salutations; and to remove material which might be deemed injurious to persons still living. In the text, all such cuts are indicated by ellipses inside brackets. Ellipses without brackets are the correspondents'.

Naturally, the most troublesome category is the third. How to interpret it? It was McCarthy's wish not to reproduce remarks damaging to people she knew. "We can't go into print saying that so-and-so is a drunk!" she exclaimed one morning, over coffee at our work station on the living room couch in Castine, Maine. But surprisingly, in some thirty sheets of correspondence from the 1950s that we managed to review, she found only one comment she thought should be dropped.

So I have cut sparingly, sometimes resisting an impulse to protect someone from a remark that will surely hurt. I have depended on the good judgment of Margo Viscusi, one of McCarthy's literary trustees, and Lotte Kohler, each of whom read the manuscript, answered queries, made corrections, and offered editorial suggestions.

Margo Viscusi, in particular, exercised a restraining influence on my initial tendency to cut more material than was necessary. I am grateful to her for taking the time to follow each ellipsis back to its source, and then, in many cases, to present reasons for restitution.

In general, when a derogatory remark is tossed off in jest, or says more about the author than the subject, or makes a philosophical or political point, it remains. McCarthy, of course, would have dismissed her more biting characterizations as simply "overexuberant analysis." The exchange of gossip she regarded as a kind of sport and, in knowledgeable hands, even useful, as was a "gossipy and *mondain*" report on the Chilean coup in the French press, she wrote Arendt on October 4, 1973: "Like a lot of gossip, it tells you rather revealing things that the 'serious' journalists don't know about or don't think worth mentioning."

When cuts have been made, as in the case of McCarthy's unrelenting criticism of James West's previous wife, whom he divorced in 1961, I have tried to make them judiciously, to remove the potentially damaging material without losing either the sense of McCarthy's feelings (or lack of feeling) for her subject, or the complicated sequence of events leading to the divorce. In some instances, material has been removed on legal advice.

Arendt's letters, with their quirky departures from standard English, raise different questions. When should errors in spelling, grammar, and punctuation be corrected, and when not? McCarthy herself had "Englished" a number of Arendt's essays, to the latter's evident satisfaction; when she edited *The Life of the Mind* after Arendt's death, however, she took it on herself to tidy up some street slang that Arendt (like Brecht) was fond of using. Thus, the poker player's "When the chips are down" ("Ven de cheeps are down, you must make some choices," her students recall her saying) became "When the stakes are on the table."

What would she have done with Arendt's "Thanks God!" in the letters, or "Shall now [be] returning my running nose to the grindstone"? Would McCarthy have changed "whig" to *wig*, and corrected the repeated misspelling of the name of Mary's other dear friend, Nicola Chiaromonte? I never found out, but I believe she would have agreed to leave such signature errors alone. That, in any event, is what I have done, correcting only those orthographic and syntactic mistakes which appear accidental, and supplying missing accents to foreign words.

Misspelled surnames remain misspelled, with the correct spelling bracketed, or footnoted, when it first appears, on the assumption that such errors, especially in the case of names often seen in print, tell us something about the correspondent's awareness of her subject. When a dead author's name is spelled idiosyncratically (e.g. Dostoivesky), however, it is flagged with a *sic* the first time, then brought into accord with current practice in subsequent letters. Missing words and names are inserted in brackets.

McCarthy saw the letters as documents, and documents are not subject to revision. As a dialogue, moreover, the correspondence serves to memorialize her relationship with Hannah Arendt (her real aim in publishing it, I think) only if the drama in which readers are now invited to join retains its tie to actual speech—in Arendt's case, speech whose occasional malapropisms bring her gruff, tender voice to life on the page.

Personal names mentioned in the letters are given a brief identification in the footnotes, usually on first occurrence. The identifying page appears in boldface in the index. Allusions to historical events and public figures are also explained in the notes, which contain bibliographic information for books and articles cited in the letters, as well.

The correspondence is partitioned somewhat arbitrarily, to give readers a pause for reflection, but also to mark significant turning points. Short introductory paragraphs convey the biographical facts the reader needs to know in order to clarify the context of certain letters. I have tried to keep such explanatory passages—including the footnotes—brief, so they can be presented alongside the text (rather than in the back of the book) without interrupting the narrative flow of the letters themselves.

The task of annotating the letters would have been easier with McCarthy on hand to consult. As it was, I set the correspondence aside after her death to finish *Writing Dangerously*, and when I resurfaced in 1992, I had, of course, traversed much of the ground covered in the correspondence. Still, the letters bristled with allusions to persons, places, events (both current and ancient), books, articles, and manifestoes that remained unfamiliar to me. Having moved to Maine in 1987, I no longer had access to New York libraries or the New York grapevine. And here is where Margo Viscusi stepped in—canvassing libraries, preparing memos on historical references, tracking down bibliographical information, with the sort of meticulous attention to detail that McCarthy esteemed.

I am grateful to others who not only answered factual questions but shared their personal experiences of one or the other correspondents—or both, as in the case of their publisher, editor, and friend, William Jovanovich. As Hannah Arendt's close friend, Lotte Kohler, of course, was the principal source of information concerning Arendt's letters and the one person who could decipher her sometimes illegible handwriting. Professors Joan Stambaugh and Jerome Kohn helped clarify philosophical points, and Kohn filled me in on events at the New School for Social Research during the years Arendt taught there. Both Alfred Kazin and William Phillips provided me with vivid accounts of Arendt's and McCarthy's friendship, one that baffled them even as it impressed them as the real thing. Elizabeth Hardwick was also moved by this relationship, and saw it at closer quarters; and I am indebted to her for helping me understand its romantic component.

Further insights, useful to me in writing the introductory essay, were provided by McCarthy's good friends Carmen Angleton and Kot Jelenski (deceased), whom I interviewed in Paris in 1985 when I was researching the biography. McCarthy's second literary trustee, Eve Stwertka, is to be thanked for her critical reading of the Introduction (which Kohler, Viscusi, and Kohn also reviewed), and for her spirited encouragement all along the way.

McCarthy's last editor at Harcourt Brace Jovanovich, Julian Muller, must be credited with proposing the book's title to McCarthy, who embraced it immediately. When he retired shortly after drawing up the contract, he invited me to consult with him by telephone whenever necessary—an offer I didn't refuse. Other helpers were Robert Silvers and Arthur Schlesinger, who supplied identifications for obscure personages; and Nancy MacKechnie, curator of Special Collections at the Vassar College Library, who provided information about both McCarthy's and Arendt's scheduled visits to the college. I am grateful to them all, and to McCarthy's husband, James West, who after Mary's death was generous with his recollections of Hannah Arendt's many visits.

It was in the Special Collections room at Vassar, in September 1985, that I first discovered the letters, and started whispering them into a tape recorder, my voice hoarse with excitement and the injunction not to disturb the other readers. Back home, when I turned on the tape to transcribe them, I could barely hear myself. ("And then *dash* well *comma* to tell the rest *comma* I must confide to you that I am pregnant *period*." Back-pedal to *confide*, or was it *confess?* etc.) Later, I was permitted to type passages directly on a borrowed Radio Shack laptop in a Special Collections alcove. I don't remember when I started submitting pages for Xeroxing, but by then I knew some paragraphs by heart.

McCarthy had suggested that I might find the correspondence useful for the biography—an understatement. Right away, I sensed there was a book in the letters themselves; reading them was like reading a good novel. I first asked McCarthy about the possibility of publishing them in October 1985, during an interview session in the New York apartment of her old Vassar classmate Frani Blough Muser. She said she would have to talk it over with Bill Jovanovich, and then we both put it on hold until the fall of 1988, when the plans for this volume were finally laid.

Copyediting a manuscript of this size and complexity requires an expert, and no one could have done it better than Roberta Leighton, who has copyedited the work of both Hannah Arendt and Mary McCarthy over the past thirty years at Harcourt Brace. I am especially indebted to her fact-checking of the footnotes, something that most copyeditors don't do anymore, and appreciative of her good judgment in trimming back some notes, expanding others.

—C. B.

Part One
March 1949 – *November* 1959

March 10, 1949

Dear Mary:

I just read the Oasis and must tell you that it was pure delight. You have written a veritable little masterpiece. May I say without offense that it is not simply better than The Company She Keeps, but on an all together different level. [1]

> Very cordially yours,
> Hannah

1. *The Oasis* (1949) is a short satirical novel about the utopian intellectuals of McCarthy's generation; *The Company She Keeps* (1942), a collection of largely autobiographical stories.

Newport RFD 2
Rhode Island
4/26/51

Dear Hannah:

I've read your book [*The Origins of Totalitarianism*], absorbed, for the past two weeks, in the bathtub, riding in the car, waiting in line in the grocery store. It seems to me a truly extraordinary piece of work, an advance in human thought of, at the very least, a decade, and also engrossing and fascinating in the way that a novel is: i.e., that it says something on nearly every page that is novel, that one

1

could not have anticipated from what went before but that one then recognizes as inevitable and foreshadowed by the underlying plot of ideas. I liked particularly the South African section—the highest point, to my mind, of the writing—the section on Disraeli, on the elite and vice and crime, on the modern nihilists, on the structure of the totalitarian movement, with the fellow-travelers representing "reality" to the members, the members to the cadres, and so on. My remarks on the style at lunch (which were largely second-hand) I utterly withdraw; there are a few barbarisms, such as the use of "ignore" to mean "be ignorant of" that are of no consequence but might be corrected in another edition. I would make one larger criticism: the implication you make, through the sheer exuberance of explaining its functioning, that totalitarianism is a scheme in the minds of certain displaced men to rob other men of their sense of reality seems to me to scant the element of the fortuitous in the development of this whole phenomenon, that is, the fact that certain features have been incorporated into these movements, without anyone's cleverness, simply because they worked. In other words, you sometimes suggest that [there] are laws of political conduct, comparable to the laws governing aesthetic matters, that the Nazis and Stalin have special access to, that they have understood and interpreted the meaning of their epoch as a great *maître* would have done, i.e., that something existed prior to them, of which they are the Platonic shadows or eidolons. This may very well be true; it certainly is often the impression one gets; and yet it is not demonstrably true here, in the text, for at other times you appear to take an opposite view, that is, that man is not interpreter or *artiste* to a rational universe, but a creator without a model to draw from.

I don't think I express this very well, and I haven't the book to consult, having already lent it, but perhaps you will see what I mean. It is why the Concluding Remarks follow a little oddly on the text, and why, I think, you lean perhaps a little too heavily on paradox (a formalist truth) in the opening chapters where factual evidence is slight or balky. But all this is of very minor import and perhaps results from an amateur's innocence (I mean mine, not yours). I thought David Riesman's strictures and pious exceptions terribly stupid; it seemed to me that he understood the book and the marvel of its construction very little ("How did the treatment of the natives by the Boers influence Hitler?" or words to that effect).[1]

Other great admirers of the book are the Schlesingers [Arthur and Marian],[2] who are very eager to meet you. Could you and Heinrich [Blücher, Arendt's husband] come up to stay with us for the weekend after this one or any weekend in May? They would like to come down and have lunch and talk to you whenever you can come.

Bowden [Broadwater, McCarthy's third husband] sends greetings to you both. And many thanks to you as an author. I must say, as a fellow one, I stand in awe, among other things, of your energy. What a tremendous job that must have been!

Yours,
Mary

P. S. Come on Friday, on the one o'clock train, departing at Providence, where we'll meet you.

P. P. S. Where would you situate D. H. Lawrence? Much more to say on this point, on the anti-semitism [sic] of modern prophetic types, Lawrence, Pound, Dostoeivsky [sic]. Will save it for your visit.

1. David Riesman's "strictures" must have been delivered in conversation or in a panel discussion, for there is no record of his having reviewed Arendt's book.
2. Arthur Schlesinger, Jr., then teaching at Harvard, had recently published *The Vital Center*, whose appearance had elicited a congratulatory note from McCarthy not unlike Arendt's overture to McCarthy after *The Oasis*.

Newport RFD 2
Rhode Island
6/27/51

Dear Hannah:

You needn't apologize to me for slowness in writing; I am a frightful correspondent, having never learned to communicate in a brief style. I've been delaying over writing to you for the past ten days, to ask you whether you and Monsieur [Heinrich Blücher] would like to spend a week with us in August, very simply, without compulsive cooking on my part.[1] I say this so that you won't think it will be "trouble"; it won't, I promise you, and I should be awfully happy to have you; likewise Bowden. We've fixed up an outside studio (I can't remember whether this was done when you were here), and with Reuel gone everything is very quiet and there are three typewriters. We're living on native chickens and fish and shell-fish and fresh fruit and vegetables. The weather so far is not very brilliant, but it should improve.

Dwight [Macdonald] is coming up for a night on Tuesday with [Nicola] Chiaromonte, and there should be a discussion of a revived *politics*.[2] It seems to me now that item a should be the question of raising money. Dwight, whom we saw on the Cape, seems more at ease and less bellicose from his psychiatry. Whether this will bear later fruit it's hard to say. I thought his review of your book far too relaxed and offhand-dogmatic; it was as though he were looking for a way (*three* books, pricing, style, etcetera) of making the book his own.[3]

My own book [*The Groves of Academe*] is going along. I find it harder and harder to blend the action with the opinion of the action and yet don't feel sympathetic with the talk-novel where the characters discuss the ideas—*while* they are being enacted. This seems to me a bit too packaged, like the spaghetti and the sauce and the cheese all in one box *for your convenience*. In reference to our conversation, I'd say that mercy was simply administrative pity; I can't take a distinction farther than that. I'd say also that pity was not really an emotion in its own right but an adulterant of some opposite emotion; Graham Greene, for example, tries to treat it as a major emotion and source of action and gets into the mess of identifying himself and his pity-inhibited heroes with God-in-His-Infinite-Understanding, etc., etc.

In any case, please do come and stay with us. There are very few people whom I should feel at liberty to ask this summer, but you and Heinrich are a spur and an incentive in yourselves to hard work and thought.

Our best to you both,
Mary

1. Arendt and her husband had visited in May, when the "compulsive cooking" took place.
2. These were old friends. Dwight Macdonald (1906–1982) published *politics* (the *p* was lower-case) from 1943 to 1947, with both McCarthy and the Italian critic Nicola Chiaromonte (1905–1972) as frequent contributors; and all three organized the Europe-America Groups in 1948 to send books and money to isolated intellectuals in Europe.
3. Dwight Macdonald, "A New Theory of Totalitarianism," *The New Leader*, May 14, 1951.

Newport RFD 2
Rhode Island
3/14/52

Dear Hannah:

Just a note of thanks and *bon voyage*.[1] I enjoyed my stay so much, too much, I fear, from your point of view: your house is becoming a regular magnet to me. Here we are rather quiet. I'm writing a story on the first Waldorf conference and the Cultural Freedom counter-conference, calculated to make new enemies—this is confidential.[2] The March 29 topic has been changed from "The Witch Hunt" to "Who Threatens Cultural Freedom in America?" This seems to me quite a difference; unless one defines "culture" anthropologically, one can hardly say that Senator McCarthy and his cohorts threaten it directly. From Fred Dupee, who was up here on a tour of Newport with two Columbia [University] colleagues,[3] I got an intimation of the [Sidney] Hook[4] group's line, which seems to be that the goings-on of McCarthy, Budenz,[5] etc., are not within the province of a committee for *cultural* freedom. Fred also indicated that the Committee, acknowledging that there is really no Communist menace here, is principally interested in raising funds to fight Communism in Western Europe, or, rather, to fight neutralism, which is taking first place as a Menace. This was proffered [to] me as "between ourselves."

On the other hand, he said, echoing others (he's not at all political), that the great thing to be combated was a relapse into neutralism over here. That if Hook and Co. relaxed their efforts for a moment, stalinism [*sic*] would reassert itself in government and education, culminating in appeasement abroad. I couldn't tell whether this was a genuine fear (it seems so fantastic) or a rationalization. I can't believe that these people seriously think that stalinism on a large scale is latent here, ready to revive at the slightest summons; but if they don't think this what *do* they "really" think or are they simply the victims of momentum? My impression is that the fear is genuine, but so to speak localized. They live in terror of a revival of the situation that prevailed in the Thirties, when the fellow-travelers were powerful in teaching, publishing, the theatre, etc., when stalinism was the gravy-train and these people were off it and became the object of social slights, small economic deprivations, gossip and backbiting. These people, who are success-minded, think in terms of group-advancement and cultural monopoly and were really traumatized by the brief stalinist apogee of the Thirties, when they suspected that their book, say, was not being pushed by their publishers because of stalinist influences among the salesmen or even the office-workers. In their dreams, this period is always recurring; it is "realer" than today. Hence they scarcely notice the deteriorating actuality and minimize Senator McCarthy as not relevant, and indeed he is not as relevant to *them* as Harold Taylor [then president of Sarah Lawrence College] or a [Party] worker who is a proofreader at Viking Press.

What do you think of this explanation? It is rather on the petty side, but at any rate human. We saw a perfect madman, Varian Fry (ex-IRR man), at Westport, on our way back, at our friends' house. He was fulminating about the necessity of "protecting our society from dangerous elements" and proposing that the *New Yorker* magazine be investigated by Congress. He himself, ironically, had been investigated for nine months, having been denounced to the military as an "open Communist," and had the greatest difficulty getting cleared, despite letters from Alfred Kohlborg, Sol Levitas, William Green, John Chamberlain,[6] attesting his anti-Communism. (Bowden said to him, "All you lacked was a letter from Hitler.") But he accepted his ordeal with graceful heroism. "It was right that I should suffer," he said, "if our society can be safe."

Well, have a very nice trip. I so envy your going to Greece, or, rather, I wish that we too could be there this summer. What has happened about the magazine?[7] In my desk drawer, I have dozens of suggestions for articles, drawn up on previous occasions, for a new magazine. They're mostly all still good; they remain to be done by someone. Doubtless, Dwight has a regular morgue of them too. [. . .] My love to Monsieur, ditto to you and best wishes, in which Bowden joins.

Yours,
Mary

1. Arendt was leaving for a lecture tour of European universities and a pleasure trip to Greece.
2. McCarthy, Dwight Macdonald, Elizabeth Hardwick, and Robert Lowell spoke up as dissidents at the "first Waldorf conference," the pro-Soviet Cultural and Scientific Conference for World Peace at the Waldorf-Astoria on the weekend of March 25–27, 1949. Three years later, at the Waldorf "counter-conference," sponsored by the American Committee for Cultural Freedom, McCarthy was also in the opposition. Clashing with Sidney Hook and Max Eastman, she argued that the real threat to cultural freedom in 1952 came from the paranoid anti-Communism of Senator Joseph McCarthy rather than from any so-called Communist conspiracy. McCarthy's story, "On The Eve," was never finished to her satisfaction, and remained unpublished.
3. Dupee's Columbia colleagues were Richard Chase and John Thompson. F. W. Dupee, a *Partisan Review* editor in the late 1930s and 40s, chaired the English Department at Bard College when McCarthy taught there in 1945–46.
4. Sidney Hook was the former Marxist theoretician who chaired the militantly anti-Communist American Committee for Cultural Freedom.
5 A leading Communist Party cadre in the 1930s, Louis Budenz served both the House Un-

American Activities Committee (HUAC) and the Subversives Activities Control Board as a cooperative witness.
6. All outspoken anti-Communists of the period.
7. This may be an early reference to the magazine McCarthy tried to launch the following year.

Newport RFD 2
Rhode Island
9/22/52

Dear Hannah:

Many, many thanks for the gravures; they've intensified my travel yearnings. Are you and Heinrich, one or both, going to be able to come up here for a stay? I should have written sooner; the summer has slipped by without my noticing. The last weeks have been a final demi-idyl with Reuel,[1] before sending him off to boarding-school, a self-possessed youth. We went to Maine, all three of us, and looked at some marvelous silent scenery and then came back and equipped him frantically: sheets, bureau-covers, towels, blankets, suits to be let out by the tailor, and hundreds of name-tapes to be sewed on. He left Saturday. Meanwhile, we suddenly sold our house, though we'll be in it until Christmas, and decided to go to Europe in January. I hope that you can come here in the next weeks; after the storms of the fall equinox, the weather gets very beautiful and blue all through New England. We have a half idea of going to Cape Cod, to use Dwight's house on a pond, some time between now and the 18th of October, when Dwight comes up by himself, but we shan't stay there more than a week and can fix our plans to your convenience, if you can come.

My law-hopes have been blighted by a federal judge of the Court of Appeals who came up from Delaware to warn me against the undertaking.[2] It seems that there is a period of apprenticeship required by law, plus the three years in law school; you have to pass one or two years in a law-office as a clerk before you can practice, *after* you have your law-degree. In addition to this, you would need several years courtroom experience, trying petty cases, before you would be of any use to a client; good trial lawyers are very rare, it appears, and come out of the crucible, usually, of criminal practice, after a very long simmering—there are only about three in the country, all veterans. To assist, on the other hand, in preparing a brief in a civil-liberties case, say, you don't need a law degree and could be useful without going [through] the mill. My legal friend recommends that I take some courses in constitutional law and do some reading, which would fit me to write on those subjects and even to assist, if it became urgent, on the preparation of cases and appeals. Rather sadly, I've accepted this advice; the judge is an important figure, a former novelist himself, and a liberal of the Roosevelt circle, very much concerned about these matters. He assures me that I would be blunting my arrows by following the course I'd planned. This has left me feeling rather deflated and foolish. Also, my novel [the first chapters of *The Group*] hasn't been going well, perhaps because of this setback.

How are you? What are you doing? I'm glad your trip was happy; we've all missed you enormously. What do you think of the campaign? Arthur (Schlesinger), as you probably know, is working with [Adlai] Stevenson, and is on leave of absence from Harvard. If Stevenson is elected, he'll probably be an Assistant Secretary of State, which I think would be very exhilarating—too good to be true, really. We've seen his wife in Cambridge and been commissioned to send on "constructive" suggestions for the campaign. I find Stevenson quite fascinating, at least on the radio—a strange personality, with something of the Roundhead in him and something of the headmaster. He's the only political figure who's awakened my curiosity in years; I don't know quite what I think of him but my breath is bated to see what he would do in office. Women are swooning over him (Dorothy Thompson is positively in *love*), but he seems to me quite impervious to women. The wit is not very good, but the sarcasms are alive; a rather saturnine man. Whether a campaign that's really based on the *rebuke* can succeed, I can't guess; it's a call to austerity, behind the quips, which are like a doctor's humor or a minister's, an assurance that he is human. The Nixon thing is appalling; we've just heard him on the radio.[3] On a lower level, he reminds me of my character, Mulcahy,[4] in cheap mass-production—there's a sort of groveling sense of justification and threatening inferiority.

I must stop or I shall never get this letter mailed. Please drop a line if you can come. Much love to you and Heinrich from both of us.

Mary

1. Reuel Wilson, McCarthy's son by her second husband, Edmund Wilson, was fourteen when he went to the Brooks School in North Andover, Massachusetts, in 1952.
2. The judge was John Biggs, whom McCarthy had met through Edmund Wilson. In 1952, responding to the lack of effective political resistance among American intellectuals to Senator McCarthy and HUAC, Mary McCarthy had briefly contemplated embarking on a new career as a constitutional lawyer.
3. Eisenhower's running mate, Richard Nixon, spoke of "Adlai the Appeaser," who lacked "backbone training" because he was a "Ph.D. graduate of Dean Acheson's cowardly college of Communist containment" (Walter LaFeber and Richard Polenberg, *The American Century*, 1975, 360).
4. Professor Henry Mulcahy is the villain of McCarthy's *The Groves of Academe* (1952).

Wellfleet, Massachusetts
10/7/52

Dear Hannah:

The 28th would be fine, or any time earlier, from the 11th on. We've come up here to Dwight's shack sur pond and are staying till the 10th; it's extraordinarily beautiful, wild and woodsy, with steel-blue ponds mirroring each other and the pine trees—an arcadia at this season when the summer Pans have fled. This rustic life is a sort of compensation for the real estate we're losing, an assurance that far fields are greener. Perhaps we shall end by buying something here,[1] for when we come back from Europe. Anyway, we go home on the 10th, and I'm greatly excited at the prospect of your coming. I think Stevenson speaks in Providence on the 28th, and we might combine that, if it seems feasible, with meeting your train in Providence—would you like to do that? I've never been to a political meeting, not counting the good old Left protest meeting, that is. To my mind, Stevenson has a good chance, but it's clear that all his experts are worried. Some newspaper man the other day remarked that Stevenson had political chic, that he figured for his admirers as a discovery, like an art-object or some old-fashioned herb newly marketed, exciting a sentiment of gourmandisme; this is certainly true, but do such factors count here in politics? The Nixon success, if it's really serious, is too horribly Orwellian to contemplate; it would mean that mass society is a reality, which nobody here, even those who have denounced its symptoms, really has ever believed except in talk. The idea that people are influenced, not by their passions or interests, but by advertising techniques, i.e., by mass-conditioning, blows all my conceptions of U.S. life sky-high. If this is true, if Nixon actually "put it over," it seems to me in a way more terrifying than any of the successes of Nazi or Soviet propaganda, which after all are based on *something*, on deteriorated ideologies, national interests, primitive mysticism, and on the *fact* of a dictatorship. But the Nixon formula simply evoked certain images whose power was based merely on their familiarity: people had heard or seen them on the air. In short, do the reflexes that send people out to buy a certain box of soap-flakes, where the choice is really a matter of indifference, all brands being more or less alike, now work in politics, where there have always been supposed to be differences? There remains of course the possibility that the people who were "moved" by Nixon and wept real tears for him were already on his side anyway; even this would be bad enough. If you've read the [Whittaker] Chambers book [*Witness*], you know that he and Esther and "Dick" and "Pat" Nixon are bosom friends, which is quite interesting, since the parallel with the friendship with the Hisses completes the totalitarian picture and includes, along the line, Mr. Luce, Mrs. Luce, Fulton J. Sheen, etc.[2] As Lawrence (D. H.) saw, the notion of the little couple and the marriage is the beginning of mass-society. One gets, or used to get, a glimpse of this in the [Philip and Nathalie] Rahvs'[3] drawing room, with the favored couples arrayed on the Bauhaus furniture.

Well, I must stop. If I don't hear from you, I'll expect you on the 28th, but if you can come sooner, please do. Both halves of this couple long to see you. . . .

Much love,
Mary

1. The Broadwaters had just seen the red colonial house in Wellfleet they took possession of the following spring.
2. Henry R. Luce, whose wife was playwright Clare Boothe Luce, founded the *Time, Life, Fortune* empire; Bishop Fulton J. Sheen was a popular television personality in the 1950s.
3. Philip Rahv (1908–1973), who was McCarthy's lover in 1937, later married her Vassar classmate Nathalie Swan. From 1934 to 1969 he was co-editor, with William Phillips, of *Partisan Review*.

Newport RFD 2
Rhode Island
12/2/52

Dear Hannah:

I was so glad to get your letter today.[1] I've kept intending to write *you* a thank-you note for my stay, but you've anticipated me. The election results [Eisenhower and Nixon won] have held me in a state of bitter exaltation for nearly a month; it was a queer, abrading experience to get them at Arthur Schlesinger's and I feel almost treacherous for having anticipated them. Arthur (whom we saw again two days ago) is still in a galled, almost uncomprehending, angry, defiant mood; he says he lacks the rebel's temperament which can respond to defeat as to a natural state of affairs. I don't know whether anything will be done to keep the [Stevenson] Volunteers alive; it was talked of the morning-after, but I didn't have the heart to ask this weekend whether anything were being done. I agree; it's an excellent idea.

What I've been trying to push is the idea of a magazine.[2] Apparently, Dick Rovere has had the same thought and has been talking to Alfred [Kazin],[3] I think, among others. He [Rovere], Arthur and I had a three-corn[er]ed long-distance conversation about it on Sunday. Their notion, currently, is to try to move in on the *Reporter*,[4] with a nucleus of people (all ourselves, Dwight, etc.) who want to make a new political medium. [*Reporter* editor Max] Ascoli, they say, is desperate—mainly for money reasons—and will listen to any proposal. I regard this idea as definitely second-best, chiefly because of my own experience with the *Reporter*, but I think perhaps it ought to be tried, if only to create a sense of confidence among the participants. Basically, nobody wants to do anything, and perhaps this includes me too, though I'm under the impression that I'm ready, if anyone else will do anything. There's a lot of listless talk about how it would take a million dollars to start a new magazine (nonsense!) and little gusts of idle energy that die down like a post-luncheon breeze. Would *you* write for the *Reporter* under some arrangement to be agreed upon in which six to ten of us would try to concentrate fire there? I do have the sense, myself, that a concerted attack of some sort is necessary—an attack, in particular, on the new intellectual Right: [James] Burnham, the *Freeman*, the *Mercury*.[5] I think there's a need for analysis, above all, of this phenomenon, which I see without understanding, except as an example of Repetition in history: I mean the curious amalgam of left elements, anarchist elements, nihilist elements, opportunist elements, all styling themselves conservative, in a regular *Narrenschiffe* [ship of fools]. To reduce it to its simplest, the final word certainly remains to be said about [Whittaker] Chambers; he can't be treated simply as a book, among other books, to be reviewed. The great effort of this new

Right is to get itself accepted as *normal,* and its publications as a *normal* part of publishing—some opinions among others, all equally worthy of consideration—and this, it seems to me, must be scotched, if it's not already too late. What do you think? I know you agree about the fact; the question is how it's to be met.

At the moment, yes, we're still going to Europe, but I'd give it up like a shot if there were any hope of doing anything here that required my presence. I expect to come down December 9, to go to a party to meet Sonia Brownell, [George] Orwell's widow, and to talk this over with Dick Rovere. Are you going to the party and could you meet with us on the magazine question? Probably you knew all about the *Reporter* business, but if you don't, I imagine it's fairly confidential. In any case, I'm awfully anxious to see you. We're not leaving here permanently until December 26, when we'll come to New York and take an apartment until January 14, when the Ile de France sails. Meanwhile, I'm negotiating with Isaiah Berlin[6] to get some sort of speaking engagement at Oxford—too many irons and not enough fire. [They did not sail for Europe.]

> Much, much love to you and Heinrich
> and many thanks for a happy stay,
> Mary

1. This letter is lost.
2. The new magazine was to be called *Critic.*
3. Richard Rovere was a political columnist for *The New Yorker,* and Alfred Kazin was best known in the 1950s for his study of nineteenth-century American literature, *On Native Grounds.*
4. *The Reporter* was a liberal magazine whose anti-Communist preoccupations kept it from challenging McCarthyism.
5. The *Freeman* and the *American Mercury* were lively organs of reaction to internationalism abroad and New Deal social programs at home.
6. Isaiah Berlin is a Russian-born British political philosopher and historian who taught for many years at Oxford.

Newport RFD 2
Rhode Island
12/23/52

Dearest Hannah:

Well, there's nothing in the Ascoli proposition—nothing, that is, but some articles he would agree to order. I think he would like to treat with each of us, individually, on that basis, but that's all. The only thing gained that I can see is that, for the time being, one could place pieces with the *Reporter* without the usual petty arguments and haggling. I spoke to him about an article you would like to do (possibly) on the falsifications in [Chamber's] *Witness*; he was interested and said he himself had noted a mass of internal contradictions when reading the book. I said I would speak to you about it further.[1]

Would you and Heinrich feel receptive to my coming to stay with you the 26th and 27th, Friday and Saturday? Don't say yes if it's at all inconvenient. I'll just telephone you Friday sometime and find out. I don't know yet, for sure, when I'll get in but probably around noon. Our plans keep shifting under us like a bucking bronco. Currently, Reuel is being dispatched to his father in Princeton Friday afternoon, and Bowden is coming down on Sunday. The combination of Christmas and moving has got my head reeling, Christmas being Reuel's birthday also. Everything is assuming a disordered, unreal aspect, to which the Ascoli conference contributed. He's really impossible. One can't talk to him straightforwardly for two sentences running; he lives in a kingdom of words and debaters' points. He told me four times in three hours that he was "a monotheist of freedom." A car and chauffeur meet him, with a lap rug, to take him seven blocks to lunch and back.

Will you tell Harold [Rosenberg],[2] if you see him or talk to him on the phone that nothing came of the discussions? I haven't heard a word from Arthur, so I presume that nothing is coming of the independant magazine too. . . .

Anyway, merry Christmas and much love to you both. Bowden and Reuel send greetings.

Yours,

Mary

1. Arendt's article, "The Ex-Communists," eventually appeared in *Commonweal*, March 20, 1953.
2. Critic Harold Rosenberg, a *Partisan Review* contributor who was also interested in the new magazine venture, was close to Arendt.

Wellfleet, Massachusetts

4/10/53

Dearest Hannah:

Long, long ago, I should have written you. But there never seems to be any time, now particularly, when in the evenings we huddle with our books around the sitting room fire and the outlying rooms are arctic. [The Broadwaters had moved to Wellfleet.]

Did you (confess) send me a wonderful French casserole from the Pottery Barn? I think it must have been you or else it was my sister-in-law, who lent me one like it last winter that I returned to her very grudgingly when we left New York. In this case, I can say with literal precision: *it is just what I wanted*—an unparalleled utensil.

The weather is so enchanting (in the daytime) that we don't leave. We swim and walk and go mushrooming in the afternoons and pick wild grapes and even get sunburned. We've eaten four varieties of mushroom and I'm hovering, dubitant, over a fifth. We're coming down definitely on the 15th, if a cold spell doesn't displease us earlier.

What happened about Princeton?[1] I finished the story I was writing; I didn't make it into a novel.[2] I've been having a long tussle with *Harper's* about the memoir, which I've renamed My Confession, courtesy you. They wanted to publish it, with cuts that made it into a sort of bloomer-joke about the thirties. I refused and cut it my own way, repossessing the manuscript; now they want it back. This affair has consumed over a month.[3]

Have you seen *Encounter*?[4] It is surely the most vapid thing yet, like a college magazine got out by long-dead and putrefying undergraduates.

Mr. [Joseph] McCarthy's marriage surely portends some new political step—like a warrior's ritual purification. Among the mighty, there is grave talk about a new depression, the interest rate, farm prices, tottering small banks. We saw Arthur [Schlesinger, Jr.] (the last sentence doesn't refer to him) in Cambridge when we took Reuel up to school; Arthur seems to have recovered his balance; he and Marian are at peace again; the children are happier. Isaiah Berlin was there; you would like him, really, I think—a serpentine dove, moralistic, familial, perhaps not very brave.

I'm eager to see you, otherwise not very eager to come to New York. I'm becoming very dubious about the magazine, or perhaps hopeless is the word. Rovere has an assignment from the *New Yorker* to go to Europe for six months with his whole family. That means he and Arthur, for all practical purposes, are out of the picture. It seems to me that we might as well give up altogether or abandon hope of a coalition and try to do something on a small scale with Dwight, if Dwight were willing. . . . Which would mean finding new backers. For myself, I can't give time to the magazine, in any form, until my finances are replenished. If the *New Yorker* takes my new story. I'll be all right for a little while; otherwise, I shall have to keep writing commercially until *something* sells. What I'd *really* like to do, I think, is start a new novel or start afresh on my old one [*The Group*]. But that would mean goodbye magazine.

Forgive me; I'm not as gloomy as this sounds. In fact, I'm in rather good spirits, primed for something, but not sure what it should be. The weather and the walks and the solitude are very invigorating; every morning, you feel it is really a New Day dawning. We look back with great happiness on your stay—a beautiful island in the summer.

See you in about ten days.

Much love,
Mary

1. In October 1953 Hannah Arendt became the first woman to be invited to lecture at Princeton under the auspices of the Christian Gauss Seminars in Criticism.
2. This was probably "Appalachian Revolution," which was published by *The New Yorker* on September 11, 1954.
3. McCarthy's "My Confession" appeared in *The Reporter*, December 22, 1953, and in *Encounter*, February 1954; it is reprinted in *On the Contrary* (1961).
4. *Encounter*, then edited by English poet Stephen Spender (1909–) and the American writer Irving Kristol (1920–), was a British publication funded by the Congress for Cultural Freedom until 1964, when reports from London of the Congress's ties to the CIA led the magazine to seek new financing.

Pensao Bela Vista
9 Rua Ataide
Lisbon, Portugal[1]
January (?) 1954

Dearest Hannah:

It's snowing cats and dogs here, the first time, they say, in either a hundred or ten years—I can't make out which. Hence, an afternoon that can be given to letter-writing; every other day, after lunch, we've been walking our shoes off. We've done most of the churches, the Alfame [the Alfama, Lisbon's oldest neighborhood], the Botanical Gardens, which are enchanting, I think—a real national expression—the American library, the English library, shops, hotels, coffee-houses. The first night we walked to the Rossio [a downtown plaza] and tried to find the cafe that you and Heinrich would have had coffee at. But I don't think we succeeded.

We're in a pension, where we seem to be the only guests, though other lodgers are alluded to. The former proprietress, recommended by Leonid [Berman], the painter, went mad some years ago, it seems, and the place is Under New Management. I fear it is a sinking ship. But we have two rooms, one very large, with a balcony and a wonderful view over the harbor. The new Madame is a Mlle. Carole, in her late thirties, smoking a perpetual cigarette and wearing a red bolero jacket and a little English shirtwaist buttoned up at the neck. She has a certain Marlene Dietrich melancholy grace that indicates, I think, that she is about to be ruined financially. She is half French, half Swedish, with a fat French *maman* in a black dress and a look of powdered resignation. They keep listening to the French radio and talking in four languages: German, French, English, and Portuguese. They despise and despair of the Portuguese, i.e., the help. The cooking is very fitful, like the weather; when the Portuguese cook cooks, it's very mediocre; when Madame cooks, it's good; when Maman cooks, it's superb. Like all people in an insecure situation, they seem to have the power of mind-reading. They know exactly the moment when we're deciding to try another place, and Maman proceeds to the kitchen: that night the dinner is worthy of La Pérouse [sic].[2] But there's a general air of hovering creditors, help leaving, confusion, fuses blowing; in short, I find it very sympathetic and Bowden has now been placated by a tour of the other pensions, and the location here is awfully convenient, high up, just above and west of the Chiado. Naturally, we're being overcharged, by Portuguese standards, but we console ourselves with the fact that we have only to express a wish and the whole boarding-house springs into action. This is because, I know, we're Americans. And Americans, to these people, are like some primitive deity, a cluster of unforeseeable and mysterious Wants that have to be gratified and if possible anticipated. They have some of the strangest ideas of what we might be likely to want, timid, hopeful ideas, like offerings. At present, we have a gas-heater in our room, but the boy keeps coming up with an electric heater too, though it's the only one in the house and we don't need it in the least.

I don't know how long we'll stay here. They say the Algarve, in the south, where we plan to go eventually, is completely covered with snow, though the mimosa is supposed to be out. Did I tell you the New Yorker has asked me to do a Letter from Portugal?[3] Yesterday I went to see our press attache, who seems quite decent and spoke of Plato. To me, the most striking thing here is the phenomenon of Americanization. American business interests, Ford, Buick, International Telephone, TWA, are very active; there are thousands of new cars on the streets and in the shop windows radios, frigidaires, pressure cookers, baby bathinets, many of American make. The strangest thing is to see along the Rua Garrett—the principal shopping street—boxes of Ritz crackers enshrined in red velvet, a whole window devoted to them; and another window to Tootsie Rolls. There's a kind of childlike or primitive pathos in this; their own confections and cakes are so charming—you must remember. And everywhere, in the suburbs, and even in the city itself, Housing Projects are springing up. I must say, they do them better than we do.

I don't know anything about the country politically yet. It seems quite puzzling on the economic level, a strange mixture of prosperity and poverty. The prosperity must be quite widespread throughout the city middle-class, but I can't figure out where it's coming from. The tea and coffee-houses are jammed with well-dressed men and women, whom you'd take for business people in the U.S. or even secretaries and salesmen; all the middling-class younger people, in fact, look very American, as if they'd modeled their gestures and expressions on the movies—it's only the aristocracy and the poor who look what I would call Portuguese. (I find this very different from Italy or France.) On the other hand, the factory-made products in the shop windows, even on the best streets, are very shoddy—I mean shoes, bags, dresses, men's shirts. Everything has a sort of Gimbel's basement or fire sale look. And there seem to be no handicrafts at all—only some very cheap gaudy peasant stuff, very inauthentic, the kind of thing you might buy in the railroad station for a souvenir. On the back streets and in the Alfame, there is plenty of medieval poverty, like Africa, as you say, or like the most graphic pages of Les Misérables or the Hunchback of Notre Dame.

Well, I must stop. It's getting dark and one thing I've not been able to secure in this pension is a good reading or writing light. I'll send you another report before long. If you have a minute, drop me a line here. [. . .] We both talk of you constantly. Where did you stay in Lisbon, I wonder. In what quarter?

Tomorrow I see the number two man in the Ministry of Propaganda.[4] The only other native we've met is a male ballet-dancer, also recommended by Leonid, who is going to take us tomorrow night to hear the Fado [Portuguese folk songs] in the Alfame.

Much, much love to you both,

Mary

1. Early in 1954, the Broadwaters spent three months in Portugal.
2. Lapérouse was then a first-rank restaurant in Paris.
3. Mary McCarthy, "Letter from Portugal," *The New Yorker*, February 5, 1955.
4. The encounter is memorialized in "Mister Rodriquez of Lisbon," *Harper's*, August 1955.

Wellfleet, Massachusetts
August 10, 1954

Dear Hannah:

This is the second letter I've written you; the first I discarded as too boring. Are you and Heinrich coming up, the first part of September? I hope so. I'm awfully eager to talk to you. At the moment, I'm dead beat with the social chatter of the Cape midsummer, gasping for air. Our defenses have somehow been breached and we've yielded to the relentless give-and-take of invitations. The early part of the summer was wonderful, but for the last three weeks we've been responding like invertebrates to the mysterious call of social duty. There are huge parties for a hundred people, outdoors. One can hear the noise and, literally, smell the fumes of alcohol half a mile off. One decides not to go, and then somehow, at the last minute, one finds oneself there, for fear of missing something. They're not even especially dissipated; they exhale a noxious boredom. We're struggling free again this week, except for the fact that we now "owe" dozens of people, whom we supposedly have to have back. You are wise to go to Palenville,[1] though I'm sure, if you were here, you would resist the trend. Anyway, it all ends, abruptly, on Labor Day, like a record stopped in the middle. September will be golden and peaceful again.

I've been working on my novel [*A Charmed Life*], fairly well, up till three weeks ago, when I began having visitors whom I felt I had to entertain. One thing I'm anxious to talk to you about is a problem connected with the novel, which is about bohemianized people and the dogmatization of ignorance. Or about the shattered science of epistemology. "How do you *know* that?" one of the characters keeps babbling about any statement in the realm of fact or aesthetics. In morals, the reiterated question is "Why not?" "Why shouldn't I murder my grandmother if I want to? Give me one good reason," another character pleads. This is Raskolnikov's old problem [in *Crime and Punishment*], but in a kind of grotesque parody; the questioner is not serious but in a kind of mental fret, like a child begging for answers, which it doesn't expect to understand. This pseudo-questing or stupid "thoughtfulness" is getting more and more general in modern society, I think; the average man, mistrustful and cunning, is an intellectual, of sorts. He doubts, like a burlesque of a philosopher, and has a craving for information that's like the craving for sugar. I see this and am trying to describe it, but what I don't know—and would like to talk to you about—is how and when it happened, historically. I feel I have got hold of a subject that I'm not equipped to deal with. When did this ritualistic doubting begin to permeate, first, philosophy and then popular thinking? I presume that in its modern form it goes back to Kant. Or would you say Hume? My own ignorance and incapacity appal me when I consider trying to trace this thread back through the labyrinth. I want to begin reading but I don't know where to start. I would think Nietzsche was crucial, and that nothing really had been done since him to meet the problem. Aren't all modern philosophies—logical positivism, existentialism, neo-Thomism, philosophical relativism, whatever that is, exactly—evasions or attempts to circumscribe the epistemological question, like the return to religion, which is depressing chiefly because nobody really believes in it; it is just another form of doubt[?] In this sense, Marxism, surely, is an anachronism as a political philosophy; it has nothing to do with modernism, at least that I can see.

Philip Rahv was here and left me your manuscript,[2] which I've been reading and which I find not only very alive, like all your articles, but curiously pertinent to this topic that's oppressing me. I've also been thinking about your piece about Ideology and Terror—the section about logic, particularly.[3] The use of logic as the prime tool of understanding is also characteristic of the "thoughtfulness" I've mentioned above. One sees this very clearly in Dwight's thinking and his sexual morality, which is eminently "logical." This again makes me want to talk to you. There's nobody else I know who seems to be concerned with this matter, which appears to me crucial. Rahv's Marxist assurance strikes me as antediluvian; it's like talking with some fossilized mammoth. I don't agree with you that he's interesting on the subject of politics—at least not on the basis of his recent visit. I like him best when he's soliloquizing about literature, not current writing, which he regards from a polemical or strategic standpoint, but the old authors, Russian and German, who thrill his imagination. On all the other topics, he made me horribly nervous, as if we were screaming at each other on the Tower of Babel. Not unfriendly; just estranged and mutually watchful. Probably it was my fault.

Alfred [Kazin] was here and cutting me dead, for some reason. It upset me at the time, quite unjustly, since I don't like him. On the other hand, I don't dislike him so *totally*. Saul Bellow was here too, with son and dog, not very friendly, either. In short, last month was rather paranoid, which got me rattled. That's the worst of places like this; your value is continually being called into question and you shiver at social slights, even from people you don't care for. And all your friends are eager to tell you, on the beach, about parties you aren't invited to. You can't avoid knowing just what your current status is, unless you stay in the house with the door locked. Even then you would have to emerge to buy groceries and in the store you meet Mrs. Kazin, Mrs. Levin, Mr. Bellow, Mrs. Wechsler, etc.[4]

I miss Dwight, I must say. Arthur Schlesinger was here, working mornings in our studio, writing a piece on the Oppenheimer case.[5] He had the transcript and I read it. What do you think about the case? For my part, I can't see him as a security risk at all, though I don't precisely admire him. He is queer, eerie in a way, and it's that he's being punished for, plainly. People talk resentfully about his "arrogance," as if that were treasonable in a democracy. I myself wished he had been a little more arrogant during the proceedings; he was too *serviable* and deferential, too conformist to current opinion. He lacked political courage. And yet it makes my blood boil to hear beefy, middle-aged sultans like Herbert Solow and Allen Strook of the AJC [American Jewish Committee] condemn him for political "immaturity," like sententious pigs. I wish you would write something about it. I thought of it and laid the idea aside; my ideas weren't clear enough. Rahv, as an old Marxist, opined that the case proved that intellectuals should not work for the government; it will first corrupt you and then degrade you. I rather agree with this. He says he had a terrible fight with Greenberg[6] about the case,

20

Greenberg claiming that Oppenheimer ought to be jailed. But Danny Bell,[7] amazingly, sent a telegram to the [American] Committee for Cultural Freedom nominating Oppenheimer for Chairman. It seems to boil down to a sort of puritan envy. Old hacks like Greenberg and Solow grudge Oppenheimer his lunch in Paris with [Haakon] Chevalier[8] as if they were faithful husbands watching a colleague have an affair with an actress.[9]

Well, I must stop. Please do come if you can. You don't know how I long to see you. Bowden sends his best to both of you. He drew a rather funny picture, last night, arguing with Solow, of Sidney Hook deserting [. . .] to the Soviet camp and beginning to issue pamphlets: *Conspiracy, Yes! Heresy, No.*[10]

Much love to you both,
Mary

1. Palenville, NY, in the Catskills, is where Arendt and her husband rented a bungalow for many summers.
2. The manuscript may have been "The Concept of History, Ancient and Modern," an essay which appeared in *Partisan Review*, January–February 1957, as "History and Immortality." It was one of several written as part of a larger study Arendt planned of Marxism's paradoxical relation to the "Great Tradition" of Western thought, as she called it, and the rise of modern totalitarianism. She never finished the study; the essays were collected in *Between Past and Future* (1961).
3. "Ideology and Terror," originally chapter four of the unfinished book on Marxism, was first published in *Review of Politics*, July 1953. In the second edition of *The Origins of Totalitarianism* (1958), it appears as the book's epilogue.
4. Mrs. Levin and Mrs. Wechsler were the wives of Harvard critic Harry Levin and newspaper editor James Wechsler.
5. In the summer of 1954, the Atomic Energy Commission, after hearings, denied a security clearance to J. Robert Oppenheimer, director of the Institute for Advanced Study at Princeton. An expert in nuclear and quantum physics, he had been the director of the Los Alamos Science Laboratory who coordinated the production of the atomic bomb, 1942–45. The AEC considered him a security risk because of early associations with leftwing groups, and particularly with Haakon Chevalier (see n. 8), but also because of his lack of support for developing the hydrogen bomb.
6. This was the critic Clement Greenberg's brother, Martin Greenberg, who edited *Commentary*.
7. Sociologist Daniel Bell was a member of the executive committee of the American Committee for Cultural Freedom.
8. Haakon Chevalier was a well-known French translator, a friend of Oppenheimer's, and a key player in the "Oppenheimer case." Talking with Oppenheimer after the start of the atomic program at Berkeley, he said he had a friend who wanted to arrange for Oppenheimer to talk with people at the Soviet consulate about scientific matters. Oppenheimer reported the conversation to security officers but said he had heard it take place with someone else. On being questioned later, he admitted he had lied. That he had had lunch with Chevalier in Paris also brought sharp criticism at his security hearing before the AEC.
9. McCarthy used the "affair with an actress" metaphor in the 1942 story "Portrait of the Intellectual as a Yale Man," in *The Company She Keeps* (1942).
10. In 1953, Sidney Hook issued a pamphlet called *Heresy, Yes; Conspiracy, No.*

Chestnut Lawn House
Palenville, N.Y.
August 20, 1954

Dearest Mary—

Your letter was a real joy. Only when I got it, did I notice that I had been expecting it. Let me go into the midst of it, and leave the ends and odds for later.

The feebleminded thoughtfulness or thoughtful feeblemindedness of intellectuals—Your Example: why should I not kill my grandmother if I want to? Such and similar questions were answered in the past by religion on one side and common sense on the other. The religious answer is: because you will go to hell and eternal damnation; the common sense answer is: because you don't want to be murdered yourself. Both answers don't work any longer, and this not only because of these specific replies—nobody believes in hell any longer, nobody is so sure if he does not want to be killed or if death, even violent death is really so bad—but because their sources, faith on one hand and common sense judgements don't make sense any more. The philosophic answer would be the answer of Socrates: Since I have got to live with myself, am in fact the only person from whom I never shall be able to part, whose company I shall have to bear forever, I don't want to become a murderer; I don't want to spend my life in the company of a murderer. This answer is no longer good because hardly anybody nowadays lives by himself; if he is alone, he is lonely, i.e. not together with himself. (If under such circumstances one is able to be together with other people, is a different matter.)

I am in complete agreement with you that all these people behave like burlesque philosophers because they have been put into a situation into which only philosophers throughout our history ever dared to risk themselves. The Socratic answer never worked really because this life by oneself, on which it is based, is the life of the thinker par excellence: in the activity of thought, I am together with myself—and neither with other people nor with the world as such, as the artist is. Our friends, craving for philosophic "information" (something which does not exist) are by no means "thinkers" or willing to enter the dialogue of thought with themselves. The Socratic answer would not help either. Help means here only: Cut short the argument.

As to the kind of argument that is being put up, it depends more than this general attitude on different national traditions, upbringings and so forth. I'd think Dwight is as good an example for the Anglo-Saxon-American type that anybody could reasonably be expected to be. It is among English philosophers that modernity showed up in the disguise of common sense *arguments*, i.e. that one distorted common sense and its sensual quality into a very specific form of reasoning which Hobbes, the greatest master of them all, called "reckoning with consequences." That is what Dwight does: he proceeds from some assumption which he usually will not reveal, and could not for that matter, and then proceeds to "reckon the consequences." The result at the end is what he thinks truth is. The fallacy is simple: any fool can point out to him the assumption and start himself from a different hypothesis and arrive at a different kind of "truth." The doubt which you mention is in this tradition only a fake; it is not the doubt at all that starts the argument but the assumption. This is very different with the French brand of modernity where the Cartesian doubt dominates and penetrates whatever follows. What both the French and the English tradition have in common and what I think is the root of modernity is the distrust in the senses which probably was the immediate result of the great discoveries of the natural sciences which demonstrated that human senses do not reveal the world as it is, but on the contrary lead men only into error. From this followed the perversion of common sense, or rather the misgivings about it in its sensual quality, which is that common sense (le bon sens) is a kind of sixth sense through which all particular sense data, given by the five senses, are fitted into a common world, a world which we can share with others, have in common with them. Common sense in other words was the control-instance for the possible errors of the five other senses. The average life is led in a world given by senses and controlled and guided by common sense. If this common sense is lost, there is no common world any longer, not even that world from which the philosopher will temporarily insist on absenting himself and to which he always must return. The perversion of common sense started when it was assumed that it is not a sense which constitutes the common world, but a faculty which we all have in common. This faculty is the logical faculty, the fact that we all shall say unanimously: 2 plus 2 equals 4. But this faculty, though we may have it all in common, is entirely incapable of guiding us through the world or of grasping anything at all. It underlines only the utter subjectivization, even though we may assume (wrongly of course) that all subjects are the same. In the line of this development you must arrive at the idea of "normal man," who for lack of a world they could have in common are all the same. And since this is of course impossible, you get a situation in which everybody is "not normal" and needs some psychoanalyst or God knows what to make him like "everybody else"— i.e. like somebody who is nobody in the most literal sense of the word.*

Now, historically: The ritual of doubt started with Descartes and only in him will you find the original motives: the real anxiety that not God but an evil spirit is behind the whole spectacle of Being. In Hobbes you will find the consistent development of the modernistic argumentation. Kant: tried already to escape this predicament. He asked: What are the conditions of our experience. Crucial for Kant is that for him, and him alone, the highest faculty of man is Judgment (and not reasoning, as for Descartes, nor the drawing of conclusions after conclusions as for Hegel). (Hume, I feel, is not so interesting.) —Nietzsche: of course, especially everything from the late manuscripts published under the misleading title: Will to power. But also the Zarathustra. —Then of Kierkegaard a small, little-known treatise about the Cartesian doubt, De omnibus dubitandum est. —Last not least, Pascal. —Among modern philosophers, Heidegger I think is the most interesting one, because he tries to think Nietzsche through in all his consequences while, at the same time, he keeps the whole tradition of philosophy in mind and alive. A few translations into English will appear shortly, and many things were translated into French.

If I may add a word of my own, independent of historical situations: The chief fallacy is to believe that Truth is a result which comes at the end of a thought-process. Truth, on the contrary, is always the beginning of thought; thinking is always result-less. That is the difference between "philosophy" and science: Science has results, philosophy never. Thinking starts after an experience of truth has struck home, so to speak. The difference between philosophers

---

*A normal man would be somebody who could say only in endless repetition: 2 plus 2 equals four. [Arendt's note was inserted at the top of the page.]

and other people is that the former refuse to let go, but not that they are the only receptacles of truth. This notion that truth is the result of thought is very old and goes back to ancient classical philosophy, possibly to Socrates himself. If I am right and it is a fallacy, then it probably is the oldest fallacy of Western philosophy. You can detect it in almost all definitions of truth, and especially in the traditional [one] of ae[de]quatio rei et intellectus [the conformity of the intellect to the thing known]. Truth, in other words, is not "in" thought, but to use Kant's language[,] the condition for the possibility of thinking. It is both, beginning and a priori.

Enough of all this—which I feel is strictly not permitted me at this moment. Palenville is wonderful as ever and I was very much amused about your report on Wellfleet's society. Nothing of the sort here. Rahv: You are probably right, I had difficulties myself in recent months, but I sort of like him, and so do you. (Bowden's quip about Hook is wonderful. Except that I always think that reality may always overtake even the best witticism and simply make it come true. You will see, Sidney in three years, publishing another book, repenting on this one . . . etc.) Alfred: Rose [Feitelson][1] told you, I think, what happened. I am afraid he is acting on orders. I am rather sad and also surprised. Would not have thought it possible.[2] Danny Bell is generally behaving better than those around him; he is the only one who has got a conscience that bothers him once in a while. He is also a bit more intelligent than the others.

Wellfleet: Mary, I don't yet know. Heinrich goes back to college after Labor day already,[3] we shall stay here almost to the end, the only solution because of work etc. I am going to [the University of] Chicago on the 8th and shall be back around the 12th. Let us see how things work out and maybe telephone—all right? How is it with you? How long do you stay there? Don't you think you would rather like to come to NY and stay with us?? I don't have to repeat that I shall always be happy to have you. Think it over! Another possibility would be that you come here; Heinrich goes home on the 29th and I'll stay the following week until Friday. Maybe you want to combine that with a trip to New York. I have a little bungalow here and we could have a wonderful time. [. . .]

Oppenheimer: I dislike him thoroughly, but of course he is not a security risk and the whole thing is a shame, though rather serious. In 10 years, America will have fallen behind in science and that can be a catastrophe in our age. Rahv on this point is not so wrong; one should really not work for the government. But if natural scientists wise up to this wisdom, it will be a catastrophe, and not a minor one.

I am glad you liked the essay on History. All this are odds and ends and I publish them maybe for no good reason. At the moment, translating the old book [*The Origins of Totalitarianism*] into German, I am unhappy and impatient to get back to what I really want to do—if I can do it.[4] But that is minor, I mean whether or not I am capable of doing what I want to do. Heinrich has a wonderful advice to give to his students when they talk about studying philosophy: he tells them you can do it only if you know that the most important thing in your life would be to succeed in this and the second most important thing, almost as important, to fail in precisely this.

I am very eagerly looking forward to seeing whatever you have of your novel [*A Charmed Life*] and would care to show. Needless to say, I think the subject fascinating. And let's get together soon, one way or another.

Love to both of you. Yours,
Hannah

1. Rose Feitelson was a close friend of Arendt's who served as one of her chief "Englishers" (Hannah's term) in the editing of *The Origins of Totalitarianism*.
2. According to Feitelson, Kazin's coldness toward McCarthy resulted from his wife's, Ann Birstein's, anger over disparaging remarks that the Broadwaters made about the Kazins' apartment in New York after they sublet it early in 1953.
3. Blücher taught humanities at Bard College.
4. The "Great Tradition" essays written during this period were intended for Arendt's unfinished analysis of Marxism, but what she "really want[ed] to do" may have been the reflections on labor, work, and action which grew out of these essays and later became *The Human Condition* (1958).

Wellfleet, Massachusetts
September 16, 1954

Dearest Hannah:

Again I have to beg forgiveness for not writing sooner. I've been quite sick for the past week, with something, bronchitis, pleurisy— I don't know; anyway I've been in bed with fairly high temperatures and an aching rib cage, the result of a two weeks' bad cold that I *didn't* go to bed with. Everything has been out of joint, hurricanes, illness, streams of visitors, and the house at sixes and sevens because

Bowden is painting the dining-room. I should have written anyway, but just before I finally succumbed I was trying to get a block of work [on *A Charmed Life*] finished and kept putting off the letter till then. I couldn't have come to Palenville; for one thing, Reuel is here and being got ready to go off to school Saturday; the other thing was the work, which I did somehow manage to finish—only a section.

At the moment, the weather here is so cold and gloomy and the house so dismantled that I don't want to ask you to come. The trouble is I don't know when, if ever, before Christmas, I shall get to New York. I'm trying to get my book finished by the first of the year, and at this point in the writing a regular work schedule of five to eight hours a day, without days off, seems to make all the difference. (Also, I've just lost ten days or more, with the illness, and have to spend the next two taking Reuel to school.) After the 15th of October and perhaps before, if this awful weather continues, we've taken a house near Newport [the Wellfleet house was unheated]. Could you come and see us there? It has the advantage of being much more accessible than the Cape. The house itself is very nice, eighteenth century with quantities of twentieth century bathrooms, and it is situated fairly near the coast, high, with big trees, in the midst of a bird sanctuary. I'm very glad of this decision because we'll be near a library, and Newport really is quiet. We'll stay there till the book is finished. If you can possibly come, that would be wonderful. [. . .]

Hannah, your letter was a joy, an act of munificence. Bowden went off immediately to the library in Newport and came back with stacks of Kant and Kierkegaard and Nietzsche. The only profit of this illness is that I read them all day long, my brain benumbed with fever, which was rather good, in that it made the thought seem easier. It's the first time I've ever had any luck in understanding either Kierkegaard or Kant. Now I understand (I think) much more of this whole matter than when I wrote you. I've also been reading Plato again. I would question one thing in your letter: what you gave as Socrates' answer to the question of why not murder one's grandmother: because I don't want to spend the rest of my life with a murderer. Isn't this really a *petitio principi?* The modern person I posit would say to Socrates, with a shrug, "Why not? What's wrong with a murderer?" And Socrates would be back where he started. It seems to me that Kant's demonstration (in Practical Reason) is watertight, as far as it goes, but of course it assumes the worth of ethics, which is just what the twentieth century clown wishes to have *proved* to him, which is impossible.

Did you see Lizzie Hardwick's piece in the current PR on Riesman?[1] And what did you think of it? It seems to me completely demolishing, in a way that will be utterly ruinous to a man like that—a total loss of face. I think this is a good thing, even though some of Lizzie's premises are a little peculiar, a little Riesmanesque themselves, in their way.

Dwight has been here, with his new wife [Gloria]. I finally see the point. The girl is a nitwit, but she's feminine in a positive way, flirtatious with him, lively, full of to him mysterious little graces and unaccountable opinions and mental vagaries. The contrast with poor Nancy [Dwight's first wife] is very striking. Nancy represented the negative femininity—caution, conscience, moral worth, lugubrious economies. It came to me suddenly that Dwight had never had any fun with Nancy; if he enjoyed himself in her company he was really alone and she was watching him dubiously, meting out a concessive laugh now and then, like a hygienic cookie. He *had* to escape from her, I now think. Nicky, curiously enough, seems delighted with this new arrangement; he's all chirpy, like a cricket. Mike is gloomy[2] [. . .].

This letter is getting very stupid and I'll stop; I'm still feeling rather wan and vague. Hannah, I've just made a cursory search of my outside study, which is like some icy cavern, and I can't find your letter to me. What was it you asked me about Rachel Bespaloff's[3] daughter? Was it the name of a literary agent? If that was the question, I think I'd recommend Russell and Volkenning [*sic*], in the phone book. My own is Brandt and Brandt, but they're better, I think, for fiction than for serious non-fiction; I don't use any agent for non-fiction. If that wasn't the question, please excuse this answer, and ask me again. If it was a question of reading a manuscript, I'd be glad to. Or anything else.

Please give my love to Heinrich; also to Rose [Feitelson]. There's a boy up here named Tony Tuttle, who's going to Bard as a junior this year (a transfer from Kenyon), whom I recommended to Heinrich. He's ambitious to write and has at least a funny kind of nervous sincerity.

Oh yes, one more thing. Dwight was talking vaguely of reviving Politics [*sic*], as his personal organ, not as a group thing. I encouraged him and told him I'd try to help raise money for him. Perhaps you won't agree, but I think a small, individualistic, eccentric magazine, run by one person, is somehow in order again.[4] Anyway, he feels a sort of urge for it, for the first time in years.

Much, much love to you,
Mary

1. Elizabeth Hardwick, "Riesman Considered," *Partisan Review*, September–October 1954. Hardwick (1916–), a novelist and critic, was a close friend of McCarthy's.
2. Nicky and Mike were Nancy and Dwight Macdonald's sons.
3. Rachel Bespaloff was a French critic whose *On the Iliad* (1970), an inquiry into the common ground of Greek and Biblical thought, was introduced by Hermann Broch, a friend of Arendt's, and translated by Mary McCarthy.
4. *politics* was not revived.

Paradise Farm
Newport, Rhode Island
December 8, 1954

Dearest Hannah:

Please forgive me for not writing sooner. I had a wonderful time, staying with you, as always. You've been in my thoughts constantly, but something always seems to intervene between the idea and the letter: just as I wrote this, for instance, twenty minutes ago, all the lights blew out—high winds from the sea and bitter cold, like the cold one remembers from childhood. I love it here, with fires burning or ready to burn in seven fireplaces and a view of snow-covered fields and pale-blue ocean out the windows. We've been having a lot of guests; it's easy to have guests in this commodious snuggery. But that's why I haven't written, chiefly.

Among others, we had the Rahvs and Dwight and Gloria. Dwight is positively besotted with happiness, shaking his head over it like a sad clown. He must have been really wretched with Nancy all these years and not realized it, so that now he's like a man who wakes up after a ten years' sleep in fairyland and pulls his grey beard in astonishment. [. . .]

The Rahvs, on the contrary, seemed to me in a very poor state. They seemed so *old* and in Philip's case sour, like two ancient beasts in a zoo staring out at the children throwing peanuts. There's something awfully wrong, with Nathalie, at least. I don't think it's alcohol, unless she's become a secret drinker and keeps a bottle in her room and takes things to scent her breath. Except on one occasion, she didn't drink much when they were here; in fact, she drank puzzlingly little. But she was in a state of stupor; her skin looked grey and coarse, like some material woven in a prison. I had to use all my force of character to meet her eye or even to look at her directly, the way one looks at a friend. Either she's ill or unbalanced or both, or else she's unhappy beyond belief. And Philip took no notice whatever. My conclusion was that he is terrified, like a child coming on death or a dreadful accident, and playing dumb, so to speak—petrified. Bowden was startled out of his wits by the whole thing. Somebody, I think, will have to speak to Philip, and I will try, if I dare, the next time I see him. Nathalie is too far gone to communicate with, and she has tremendous pride, which appears to be all that keeps her in motion. You couldn't say to her "What's the matter?" or at least I couldn't. [. . .]

Aside from this bad news, everything is fine. I've been reading Pascal but don't seem to be getting much for my purpose from him, except the part about the impossibility of *knowledge* in matters of religion. But perhaps I'm reading the wrong work. The *Pensées?* I don't find him very interesting, really, except as a sort of "period" curiosity. And the writing is very pure, like a child's, though that's perhaps just the seventeenth century spelling. The translation, brought out by Pantheon, is execrable. But all the *vanitas vanitatum* doesn't move me; it seems somehow a formalistic lament and too close to the weary "wit" of La Rochefoucauld.

My novel [*A Charmed Life*] is going ahead, but I have you horribly on my conscience every time sex appears. You are tugging at my elbow saying "Stop" during a seduction scene I've just been writing. And your imagined remonstrances have been so effective that I've rewritten it to have it seen from the man's point of view, instead of the heroine's. But you still won't like it, I'm afraid. I'm not joking, altogether; I have misgivings about the taste of this novel, which localize around your anticipated or feared reaction. It has a "personal" note that troubles me, even though I assure myself that many of the great novels had that too. Tolstoy is almost embarrassingly *there*, in the character of Levin, and in many other of his works, like *The Kreutzer Sonata*. And Dostoevsky with Stavrogin's "Confession." And George Eliot's heroines have an ungainly, almost mawkish likeness to the author. Well, one doesn't have to rehearse the history of literature to know that there are precedents, but precedent is a poor rallying-point for works of art; the appeal to authority doesn't convince here.

Well, I won't bore you further with my anxieties. "Why do you do it if you don't want to?" says one of the characters to the heroine. The answer is, heavily: "I don't know."

Much love to you and Heinrich. I'm going to be in town, with Bowden, for exactly eighteen hours next week, doing Christmas shopping and going to a publisher's party. I'll call you up and say hello. I wish you and Heinrich would come up over New Year's. We have a whole separate house, we've discovered, that we rented without knowing it—I mean that was included in the rent. It has a huge studio, two bedrooms, bath,* and kitchen, and is heated by its own furnace. You could stay as long as you liked and not feel you were troubling me in any way—not that you would be, if you stayed here in the main house, but you might think so. Reuel is going to be here over Christmas and perhaps over New Year's; I'm not sure yet of his plans. Please think about this and let me know, if I don't reach you next week by phone. I'll also be down one night—the 28th—to chaperone Reuel for a dance. [. . .]

Love again,
Mary

*two baths, I learn from Bowden, who enthusiastically supports this plea, adding that you wouldn't have to have *any* social activities. On second thought, can't you come for Christmas as well?

Paradise Farm
Newport, Rhode Island
January 20, 1955

Dear Hannah:

Just a hurried note to ask if you can or would like to have me to stay the nights of the 26th and 27th, next week? It occurs to me that it might be a bad time for you—so near your departure date.[1] If so, please say frankly. In any case, I want to see you before you go. I have your key, by the way, and will return it.

The purpose of this trip is to see Shaw's *The Doctor's Dilemma*, which I'm going to write about for PR. Would you like to go with me? I have two tickets, for the night of Thursday, the 27th. If you don't feel like going, I might ask Rose. The weather is terrible up here, bitter winds. I've had a poor month, so far, being in bed for a week with pneumonitis (a lung infection) and too doped with opium cough-medicine to be able to read much or think. There's been an awful lot of sickness this winter, according to the doctor, who attributes it all to bugs that were swept up here by the hurricanes!

I can't think of any news. Did you see that Riesman drivel in PR?[2]

I think of bringing part of my novel with me to show you, but I fear you will be too busy.

Much love,
Mary

1. Arendt was preparing for her first full-time teaching position, at the University of California, Berkeley.
2. David Riesman, "The Intellectuals and the Discontented Classes," an exchange with Nathan Glazer, *Partisan Review*, January–February 1955.

[In February 1955, the Broadwaters set sail for Capri, where Mary hoped to finish *A Charmed Life*. After side trips through southern Italy, they stopped in Rome to visit Nicola and Miriam Chiaromonte, and pick up a former girlfriend of Bowden's, an attractive expatriate named Carmen Angleton. In May, the three of them planned to tour Greece in a borrowed jeep, an objective which was not to be reached.

This trip to Europe was a turning point in McCarthy's life. By its end, she had established a beachhead in Europe, one to which she would return again and again.]

Rome, Italy
June 4, 1955

Dear Hannah:

I've been putting off writing to you for months, till I could write a letter adequate to you. But I despair of that time's coming, so I'll simply send a few words. Our trip has been very chequered. We had five weeks in Capri; I finished my book and we swam and took walks. It is just another bohemian place with an overlay of tourists — a great many Germans and Swedes and American airborne Rotarians. (Two million Germans are supposed to have crossed the Italian border at Eastertime.) We saw Pompeii and Naples, i.e., we saw more tourists, more cameras, more guides, and souvenir sellers. Then we spent two weeks in Rome, which I find enchanting this time; we had a wonderful trip through Umbria to see all the Pieros and the Giottos; and later a marvelous trip through the Abruzzi. I met Silone, Moravia, etc. [1]

We were supposed to go to Greece by boat, taking a jeep with us. The jeep broke down and had to be abandoned in Bari; we went without it, al ponte, under conditions of inutterable squalor, sleeping, perforce, in the hold, next to a manure pile, our faces covered with flies. (We had had a romantic vision of sleeping on deck, in the moonlight, wrapped in army blankets.) Out of all this horror, at dawn, the Greek islands materialized, like poetic metaphors. Ithaca was marvelously beautiful and absolutely Homeric—like the virgin west of the world, green, with mysterious inlets and coves, swathed in faint mists and with rose-pearl clouds reflected in still waters. Corfu was rather good too, very Eastern, with brilliant vegetable bazaars and straight-backed old women in Albanian-looking costumes.

And then—well, to tell the rest, I must confide in you that I am pregnant. I came to Greece only half-aware of this fact, disbelieving it, rather like St. Elizabeth when she got the news. But in Athens, it made itself felt, chiefly in the form of doctors' prohibitions—i.e. no climbing, no buses, no trains, a minimum of walking. So that I was able to see very little, the museums, which are beyond parallel, the Acropolis by moonlight, Daphne, Sunium. (I had managed to get those in before I saw the doctor.) But despite these precautions, I started to have a miscarriage on the Island of Myconos, in the Aegean, where we had settled down for ten days. It was averted; that is, the bleeding was arrested, thanks to the fact that the Madame of the hotel there was a Red Cross nurse who had a veritable passion for gynecology. But after that, I had to stay in bed until we finally dared venture the trip back to Athens. The Greek boats are terrifying and the roads equally so. In fact, for anyone in my circumstances, Greece is sheer terror. We stayed in Athens while tests were made to find out whether the baby was dead (it isn't). I was half in, half out of bed, but confined to the hotel, with the doctor's telephone number clutched in my hand. He moved during the course of these events—this is typical of Greece—and for a day he could not be found. I won't harrow you with the details. Anyway, I was finally told I could leave Athens, by plane only, and given some hormones to take—corpus luteum. We've been here in Rome since last Tuesday and next Tuesday, the day after tomorrow, we fly to Paris, where we'll stay till the 20th of June. But I'm not supposed to be on my feet or ride in cars; I have to live where there's an elevator, lie down a good deal, drink no wine. As you can imagine, this has turned our trip into a joke; it is harder on Bowden, really, who is condemned to semi-immobility without being pregnant. I'm not supposed to travel but to go to one place, by air, and stay there. All our Greek plans for the Peleponnesus and Olympia and Delphi had to be canceled; B. did not want to leave me alone in Athens. On the last day there, in what can only have been a burst of nationalism, the doctor said it would be all right to see the Acropolis, by daylight; I literally crawled over it and up the steps of the Parthenon. Rome is better; the Chiaromontes are here; and it is modern. So B. has been in Milan the last two days while the Chiaromontes have been chaperoning me. Paris will be better too. Our hotel, the Metropolitain, is near the Tuileries and the Louvre, and I think I can walk that far. After that, we go to London, to meet Reuel. If it were not for him, we would give up and come home. But in any case, our house has been rented,[2] and even if it weren't there would be the problem of the cooking and housework. I am probably better off in a hotel in Europe. And I'm hoping that the restrictions will be relaxed when I get past the third month, which will be about the 13th of June.

Excuse me for the tediousness of these details; there's not much else in my mind, though I'm writing in the mornings.

Write me if you have a moment (not that I deserve it). [. . .] I've thought about you a lot and talked about you a lot; I heard a report of you from Denver Lindley,[3] after he'd seen you in California. How was it? I'm dying to hear.

Much love to Heinrich. Please forgive the silence, which for the last six weeks has been due really to the fear of writing a letter just like this—dull and abstracted.

Are you going to Palenville? We get back to America late in August. Perhaps you'd like to come to us for a little while in September?

Much love to you,
Mary

P.S. Don't tell anyone this news yet. I don't want it to get back to Reuel indirectly and I'm waiting to tell him in person when he arrives in London. Incidentally, though this letter doesn't sound it, I am very pleased about having a baby; it's only the alarms and uncertainties of it that are wearing.

1. McCarthy was introduced to Ignacio Silone and Alberto Moravia, leading postwar Italian novelists, by Nicola Chiaromonte.
2. When he returned to the United States, Broadwater sold the Wellfleet house. With McCarthy's characterizations of local figures in A Charmed Life, she had stepped on too many toes to permit a safe return, and she never went back.
3. Lindley was Arendt's editor at Harcourt, Brace.

[Mary McCarthy miscarried in Paris, and her marriage to Bowden Broadwater came close to breaking up. Later that summer, she was introduced to Georges and Rosamond Bernier, who published the art journal l'Oeil in Lausanne. They invited her to write the first in a series of books they planned on the great cities of Europe: a portrait of Venice.]

5062 Campo San Lorenzo
Venezia
September 29, 1955

Dearest Hannah:

With the first autumnal wind whistling, I finally write. Everything changed today; the Grand Canal, roughened, turned a dark, brilliant blue; the little canal by the police station is a hard jewel-like green. The Piazza hours changed; now at four in the afternoon, it's full of people, walking and warming themselves in the sun.

Well, Dwight's visit was extraordinary. His first remark (I'm not exaggerating) was "Why don't they put outboard motors on the gondolas?" He really wanted to know and he repeated the question, thoughtfully, for several days. He also wondered, briefly, why they hadn't considered having cars here but was satisfied when I answered that there was no pavement for them to drive on. Like a child, he's content if you give him an answer that sounds final and practical. But he has no aesthetic feeling whatever and of course is unaware of it. In the six days he was here I don't think he once glanced at the Doge's Palace. He found a most wretched room, without running water, toilet up two flights of stairs, for seven hundred lira a night, bought himself two bottles of grappa and some cheap chianti and holed in. In the mornings, he came here to work and at once converted this apartment into a version of the town dump. His first action here was to break one of the signora's [Mary's landlady] more valuable pieces of bric-a-brac: a turquoise compote, quoted by the signor at five thousand lire. I just got the price yesterday and am torn as to whether to pay it myself and say nothing or take Dwight at his word and let him know the amount, which will probably give him a stroke. (My school-teacherish side tells me I should follow the second course, in the interests of his education.) Anyway, his visit was rather a strain; at the same time, I felt terribly sorry for him. He seemed so old and slack-muscled and tired, and he kept saying that he was too old, he guessed, to travel. I have the uneasy feeling that Europe may be too much for him, but perhaps what he's going through is only a first, paralyzing embarrassment before the unfamiliar. [. . .] And he has no pretenses, nothing to cover up with. And (which is the same thing) no protective mimicry; he doesn't notice what other people do and try to copy them, as one has to in a foreign language and country.

There was a whole overflow of people from the Congress [for Cultural Freedom] here: Nabokoff [sic] and Lasky and a man named Herbert Passem [sic] and Fleischman [sic] himself, who is homosexual, it seems, and is traveling with a young doctor.[1] Lasky is a strange person, appallingly vulgar but with curious convictions. He hates all of us, I think, and yet he has become in the last months very heatedly anti-anti-Communist; I suppose it is his practical side, which now looks on the Bert Wolfes and Hooks and Sperbers as absurd visionaries.[2]

They are all gone now, and I'm positively welcoming a little solitude, not that I'm getting too much of it, because the letters of introduction provided by the Silones and others have begun to take effect. I've met the head of the gondoliers cooperative, an old anti-fascist fighter who was jailed for four years under Mussolini and is now a leading civic figure and the head of an insurance company as well. He took me to a reception given by the Chinese Opera Company for the Venetian citizenry (the Opera was marvelously beautiful to look at, with exquisite pantomiming). It was an odd occasion; the Chinese, with one exception, spoke only Chinese, and their efforts to communicate with the Italians and vice versa were quite funny, I having to interpret since their interpreter spoke only a halting English, which I would turn into Italian—many smiles, toasts, clickings of glasses, exchanges of cigarettes. And it was odd to think that the people at my table, respectable plump ladies in French-style hats and lacy blouses, pillars of the community, had been in jail, some of them, under Mussolini. There were Communists present too, of course; I met only one—an ancient poet. In Venice, they are part of the community; with the veteran Social Democrats, they conduct a war of jests.

I've also met a count and a contessa and been to lunch in their palazzi. And Bernard Berenson, whom I'm to dine with again tomorrow night—a regular old Volpone of ninety summers, with a glistening gold smile, more like a puma, really, than a fox. As a case of sheer preservation, he's extraordinary; he keeps his prodigious memory and all his faculties and appetites. He was familiar with my work, greeted me with an apt and naughty quotation from the one about the pessary—imagine![3] I felt quite shocked.

And I've met at least seven new elderly English homosexuals, all "living quietly" here. And a dullish young Cambridge scholar who is working on the eighteenth century on a university grant [Francis Haskell]. And one night in the Piazza I saw our widower [Mr. Scialanga, who inspired McCarthy's 1948 story "The Cicerone"] in the company of a very good-looking young woman. In other words, ça va. Most of the people alluded to either have books or leads to offer on Venice. I've been on some nice walks and seen some beautiful out-of-the-way churches. And I chanced in on the synagogue (by Longhena) on Yom Kippur, which I watched from the women's gallery.

Write me about Rome. Or about Greece. I shall welcome a letter. I miss you here in Venice and generally. You were so *extremely kind and good*, here and in Milan; it broke the ice in my heart. Did you get the copies of your speech I sent?[4] I hope so. They don't seem to have manila envelopes in Italy. I'll have Denver [Lindley] send you my book [*A Charmed Life*] care of [Karl] Jaspers.[5] I hope nervously you'll like it. Oh, I did write a new jacket copy for them and they did use it. And it *was* Margaret Marshall who did the original one—isn't that spooky?[6] Bowden somehow elicited this fact from Philip [Rahv].

He [Bowden] hasn't got a job yet, but he has sold a few "ideas" to the New Yorker, which has been good for his morale. He still has a few prospects in the air. [. . .] One of the teaching jobs fell through and I presume the others have too, since I haven't heard. But he has a friend trying to find him something obscure on Life and another working on the Metropolitan Museum (which would be more congenial, I should think). And he says there is always Macy's. Whatever happens, I now am glad that I did go to Venice and let him be on his own; in his last letters he sounds much better, more alive. I'm only praying he doesn't have to relapse into Macy's.

Much love, dear Hannah. And just to please you, I'll write Philip.

Mary

1. Nicholas Nabokov, Vladimir Nabokov's cousin, was secretary-general of the Congress for Cultural Freedom in Paris. Melvin Lasky, a veteran of City College faction fights in the 1930s, was editor of *Der Monat* and, later, *Encounter*, both CCF publications. Herbert Passin was a Tokyo-based American anthropologist who ran the Congress's Japanese branch. Julius Fleischmann, a member of the Fleischmann's Yeast Company family, was the director of the Farfield Foundation, which was incorporated in 1952 to provide the CIA with its principal conduit for funding the Congress.

2. Bertram Wolfe, Sidney Hook, and Manes Sperber were typical of former Communists whom Arendt described in "The Ex-Communists" as Communists "turned upside down"; they had become "prominent on the strength of their past alone. Communism," she noted, "remained the chief issue in their lives." "The Ex-Communists" is reprinted in *Essays in Understanding: 1930–1954*, a collection of Arendt's essays edited by Jerome Kohn (1994).

3. Bernard Berenson, a collector and connoisseur of Renaissance art, quoted from "Dottie Makes an Honest Woman of Herself," the story of a Vassar graduate's visit to a clinic to get fitted for her first diaphragm, which appeared in the January–February 1954 *Partisan Review* and became Chapter Three of *The Group*.

4. Arendt had flown to Venice to be with McCarthy after the miscarriage in Paris and the temporary rift with Broadwater. From there the two women went to Milan to attend the Congress for Cultural Freedom conference on "The Future of Freedom," where Arendt delivered a talk entitled "The Rise and Development of Totalitarianism and Authoritarian Forms of Government in the Twentieth Century."

5. After her trip to Greece and Israel, Arendt went to Basel, Switzerland, in November to visit philosopher Karl Jaspers, a close friend and former teacher at Heidelberg.

6. Margaret Marshall, who had been a contender for Edmund Wilson's attention in 1937, was a *Nation* editor. She was coauthor with McCarthy of a series called "Our Critics, Right or Wrong" in 1935 (though McCarthy later maintained that she herself had written the lion's share). In 1955, McCarthy learned that Marshall was the author of the original, sneering, jacket copy for *A Charmed Life*.

presso Albonico
173 San Gregorio
Venice
[August 1956]

Dearest Hannah:

Forgive in advance what I know is going to be a boring, flaccid letter. It's a steaming scirocco day in Venice and my brain is sodden with the heat. Yes: Venice again. I could not resist it. We've taken an apartment (this time with no signora included) on the Grand Canal—four balconies, though admittedly very small ones. But large cool rooms and, to reassure you, not expensive or, let us be honest, not very. Less than a Cape Cod shack. We move in tomorrow and stay till mid-September, when Bowden flies home. I may stay a little longer, depending. Depending partly on you. *Are* you going to Pontigny? If so, I shall certainly meet you in Paris, assuming you still would like to do a little tour together. I think I shall go to Paris in any case, after leaving Venice; it's only the dates that are uncertain. Could you drop me a line fairly soon [. . .] so that I can begin to think about steamship passage home? (Incidentally, my passport runs out October 28, and the other night at a dinner party, I got into a furious fight with the American Consul here, who was drunk and throwing his weight around about Americanism, and he announced that he would refuse to renew my passport. This was just bluster; he couldn't go through with the threat, but it shows how some of our representatives feel free to act. He threatened one of the other guests too and insulted everyone present who disagreed with him. The issue was whether a passport was a privilege or a right.)

The above was my only political and indeed mental activity since I've been in Italy. I've seen a tremendous amount of art and architecture and feel as though I knew every provincial museum in Italy—an exaggerated claim. Turin and Paestum, Bergamo and Amalfi, Parma, Cremona, Verona, Mantua (again), Treviso, Bassano, Rimini and Urbino, Pisa and Lucca. We've done two tours hunting down obscure Palladian villas in the Veneto, and (I think) have viewed every last brick attributed to Bramante. And all the works of Alberti. What have you got to show for it?—as some American would say. I don't know. Perhaps nothing. Only a multiplied sense of recognition so that painters whom I'd never heard of six months or even three months ago now nod to me from the walls of galleries like old friends.[1] I've done no writing, except struggling with the New Yorker proofs of the Venice pieces:[2] an exhausting matter that kept us pinned in Milan three weeks while I wrote and mailed corrections and cabled. Did you see the pieces? Don't judge the book too much by them. The New Yorker, in cutting (they used only about a third), excised nearly everything except facts and figures. The editor, [William] Shawn, is really a curious person; he's a self-educated man and he assumes that everybody, like his own former untaught self, is eager to be crammed with information. A sentence larded with dates and proper names fills him with gluttonous delight—like a *boeuf à la mode.* He is utterly sincere in this pleasure, without commercial motives; the only commercial motive is his presumption that what he likes the public likes, an innocent presumption that calls to mind Mr. [Charles] Wilson's equally innocent statement ("What's good for General Motors is good for America"). Shawn would be genuinely shocked, I think, to learn that there were people who found dates and all that "boring." The only lesson I derive from this is that it is getting harder and harder for modern people, Americans, to imagine that there could be anyone different from themselves. And I must admit that I find this a difficulty myself, but at least to me Mr. Shawn is *conceivable.*

Of other news I have very little. Dwight is supposed to show up in Venice about the ninth of August. He will be disappointed to see that the gondolas have not been motorized, despite a New York Times story to that effect last autumn. Nancy [Macdonald] was here, with a pathetic cavalcade of divorced, alcoholic women, on her way to Greece. As you perhaps heard via Rose, I had a rather difficult time with Tillich on the way over.[3] Some time we must talk a little about him. I know you'll think it silly but he gave me a psychic shock that I was not altogether aware of at the time and that it took me ten days to get over; I was actually sick without anything organic's being the matter. I'm not so naive as to be surprised at a religious man's having what Dr. T. calls "pagan moments," but he takes it too much for granted in himself somehow, as though it were an effusion of godhead in him. I've never met a man with so much egoism and so little confidence in himself. He was going to Greece. " 'The oracle goes to Delphi,' " he quoted his students as saying. He was also under the impression that he brought bad weather with him, like Jonah. If I said, "It's stormy weather today," he'd answer, "I should call it rather 'Tillich-weather.' " And what about his wife? I didn't like her at all. Perhaps you do. So thumpingly pleased with herself, like a weathered stringy soubrette. Everything about both of them so ideologized. At the same time, I felt sorry for them, him especially, in a repelled sort of way.

There's an expedition to go to the lighthouse to swim, and I must stop. Much love to you and to Heinrich. I *hope* you're coming to Pontigny.

Mary

1. McCarthy was casting about for the city or cities that would be the subject of her next book after the one she produced for the Berniers, *Venice Observed* (1956).
2. Entitled "The Revel of the Earth," *The New Yorker* condensation appeared in two parts in July 1956.
3. Theologian Paul Tillich had tried to seduce McCarthy during the summer 1956 Atlantic crossing on the *Cristoforo Colombo*.

presso Albonico
173 San Gregorio
August 9, 1956

Dear Hannah:

Your letter was a telepathic answer to mine, evidently.[1] Yes, I should love to be in Paris October 1, and I shall keep in touch. What will your address be? I shall probably go to the Montalembert, if I can get a room there.

Thank you for what you say about the Venice piece. Yes, the New Yorker cut it severely. The two pieces, I think, are only about half or even a little less of the book as it will appear. This way it goes too fast, I agree; like an express train hurtling by the person who doesn't know Venice, I fear.

I wish I were doing something similar. But I can't seem to fasten on another entity that would hold together like Venice. Florence is a possibility, but one would have, again, to spend several months there. And I wonder whether modern Florence has much to do with Florentine history. Florentine history, so far as I can make out, stopped such a long time ago, while the city continued developing along normal modern lines. Just the opposite of Venice, which keeps reenacting its story in a sort of frozen form.

As for the smaller places—Parma, Bergamo, Padua, Mantua—I hoped to find something there but I did not. Of course, I didn't stay long enough, but nothing really tempted me to. Bologna perhaps. It's the only one that seems to have a mysterious life of its own that bears some relation, even if an inverse one, to its past. Red Bologna. We stayed there two nights recently, but the heat was frightful. It is really too hot to travel in Italy now—a fact I ought to have faced before. We went to Urbino too, but it is only a shell, though beautiful, like most of the old principates and duchies. Here as in Parma, for instance, the ruling princes went broke and sold all their treasures, or the Church took over and appropriated them. The Papacy, of course, as Berenson pointed out the other day, is the real story.

But who would dare tackle it? I don't mean for politic reasons, but just because the scale is so tremendous. One might touch on it through Bologna—a papal city. Bowden pointed out that the scale of the buildings—which I'd never noticed before, the proportions being so good—must have something to do with the Papal rule there. The arcades draw your eye onward, horizontally, but if you stop to look up, the buildings are staggering.

Do you have any ideas?

We've moved into our apartment, which is pleasant and cool, and we can stand like two Veronese people on separate balconies looking out on the Grand Canal. But there are too many people I know in Venice at this season: Americans, most of whom I wish I didn't know. Example—Johnnie Myers [a New York art dealer]. One feels one has not come to Venice to see such acquaintances, but it is unavoidable. Nancy Macdonald is back and I'm having her and the two boys, Mike and Nicky, to dinner tonight. I might as well be in New York. And Dwight and his family arrive Saturday. My curse is trying, unsuccessfully, to be nice. [. . .]

One bright spot, socially, is that Reuel is arriving from Paris some time today. He spent a lonely but good summer at the Sorbonne, going to lectures and the Comédie Française and rowing every afternoon by himself on the lake in the Bois. What troubled him was that he never met any French people.

Bowden is doing a lot of sightseeing. He's off on a Palladian tour today. I write in the mornings (a memoir of my Jewish grandmother)[2] and sightsee with him in the afternoons. Weather permitting. It's hot here too.

Much love to you, dear Hannah. I'm glad you're at work on your book [*The Human Condition*]. Berenson, by the way, whom I've become friends with, has a copy of *The Origins* [*of Totalitarianism*], which I doubt whether he's read but which made him curious about you. He asked a lot of questions.

Love to Heinrich too. Enjoy Palenville. And see you October 1.

Mary

1. This letter is lost.
2. The longest-lived of McCarthy's grandparents, Augusta Morgenstern Preston, died in February 1954. The memoir, "Ask Me No Questions," first published in *The New Yorker*, March 23, 1957, is the last chapter of *Memories of a Catholic Girlhood* (1957).

173 San Gregorio
Venice
September 19, 1956

Dear Hannah:

Very good. Suppose, if I don't meet you at Pan American in Amsterdam or leave a message there, you could leave a message for me at American Express, Amsterdam.[1] I'll inquire into the hotel situation and if it's necessary make a reservation. I won't force you into the luxury category either. Bowden can reassure you on this point.

By the time you get this I shall have left or be leaving Venice. I'll be several days on the road and then will put up at the Montalembert, Rue Montalembert, in Paris. If you should have to change plans, you can cable there, preferably before Friday, the 28th, since I've been asked to the country for the weekend, and if I go, won't be back till Sunday afternoon or evening.[2] I also have a vague notion of driving to Amsterdam, via Belgium, but Bowden disapproves of this idea—the driving in Amsterdam is said to be atrocious. But I just *might* do it anyway, depending on how the trip from here to Paris works out. (I was so shaken by my crossing with Dr. Tillich that when I drove the car off the dock into Naples, I almost instantly hit two people—not hard.)

Much love,
Mary

1. McCarthy and Arendt planned to tour art museums in Amsterdam.
2. It wasn't a weekend in the country that McCarthy was planning, but a secret rendezvous in London with an English book reviewer and former heavyweight boxer named John Davenport, whom she had met at the Hotel d'Inghilterra in Rome in May 1956.

Sunday morning, 7:30 a.m.
London [early October] 1956

Dearest Hannah:

I'm going to stay over till Tuesday. Could you, would you, mail the enclosed for me to Bowden? I'm afraid he will worry, not hearing from me, and obviously I can't send a letter from here. Also, would it be too much to ask you to call the Montalembert and tell them I'll be back Tuesday for sure? Again, I don't want them to know I'm in England.

Dear Hannah, it's been wonderful, more so than I could conceive, abstractly. The apartment is above a green square, and I stay here most of the day like a captive canary, high up, but we've ventured out a little and I've seen a new side of London, a side I love. Last night, we went to Hampstead and I waited in two pubs while he [John Davenport] visited his daughter, who'd just had her appendix out, in the hospital. . . . The whole family, except him, has been in the hospital, one after the other, since June; the youngest boy has just come out. It occurs to me that what is wrong with them may be the doctor, an idea I shall broach.

I told him I told you, and he sends you affectionate respects or respectful affection—I hope I have the mixture right. The respect is homage to an Intellectual Woman, and the affection is gratitude to you, on my account.

This has all gone very deep, on both sides. I no longer see a terminal point when I leave London. I told him you'd said, "This can go on for twenty years," and *he* said, agreeing with you, "She's a European."

Much love,
Mary

[The following year, McCarthy had committed herself to a narrative history of the Italian Renaissance, as exemplified by the sculptors, painters, and masterbuilders of quattrocento Florence. She had returned to Italy, by way of London—where she had hoped to resume relations with John Davenport, who had abruptly broken off communication the previous winter.]

Albergo della Signoria
Via dello Termo
Firenze, May 21, 1957

Dearest Hannah:

I meant to call you to say good-bye the day before I left, but that day proved too hectic, what with Harcourt Brace [McCarthy's publisher], photographers, an interviewer from Newsweek,[1] the return of my brother [Kevin McCarthy] from the Coast, etc. Anyway, I apologize and say good-bye and a very happy, fruitful summer for you and Heinrich at Palenville.

As for me, I had a bad blow in London, from which I seem to be still recovering. (I arrived here a week ago tomorrow with bronchial pneumonia, and this is my first day out of bed. Don't worry; I have an excellent, very cautious, young German-Swiss doctor.) But I had better tell you about the London experience, though I am most disinclined to do so by mail.

However, here goes. The morning after I got there, I called up the cousin, the lawyer in Belgravia, who said Yes, he would fix up a rendezvous that afternoon, at his flat; he would send John a telegram (the Davenport phone being shut off for lack of payment) and if the telegram failed to reach him he would send his housekeeper for him. He would give us a drink and then he himself would have to go out to some official dinner.

At quarter of six, I was ushered by the old housekeeper into a very elegant Belgravia flat; Mr. Hughes, a tall dark man in white tie and tails, stood up to greet me. There was no one else there. (Somehow I had foreseen this.) He had not been able to reach John, Mr. Hughes explained, though he had tried various means, but he would send his housekeeper now in a taxi to bring him back. We both looked at our watches; in thirty minutes, Mr. Hughes would have to leave for the official dinner: the Duke of Edinburgh was attending it so no one could be late.

While we waited for the housekeeper (named Evans) to return, we talked. He was a friend of Edmund's, he told me; we spoke of Reuel. Then we plucked our courage and moved closer to the subject of our meeting: John. How can I tell you? It began, more or less, with my saying something about his being John's cousin, and he said, "Cousin? Did he tell you that?" And he laughed, rather irritably. "I'm not his cousin. I'm no relation to him." I looked absolutely stunned, and he went on, in a hesitant way. "I think I'd better tell you that John is a pathological liar." Well, Hannah, that was how it started. His ancestry. All that was lies about him and his "gentle birth." Hughes says that his father was a drunk who was a writer of song lyrics and his mother was an actress who played chars, but he pretends, though no one believes him, to be related to everyone in Debrett. Then the drinking. It was much worse, said Hughes, than I could possibly imagine. He spent all his time in pubs (that was where he had looked for him) and most of it getting hopelessly, bestially drunk (Hughes' phrase). There was nothing much you could do for him, Mr. Hughes said; because of the lying, you never knew where you were with him. He also stole. Books and small objects. He, Hughes, indicated an old silver ash-tray that John had tried to hide under his coat. He stole books from the

Observer and sold them; all the reviewers in London knew it. And he bragged. He *had* talked about me, though not to Hughes; other people had told Hughes about it and said he ought to be stopped from talking so about a married woman. The fortunate thing, said Hughes, was that he was known to be such a liar that in this instance no one believed him.

In the midst of all this (I nearly fainting), the housekeeper came back, knocked on the door, and said something incoherent. The gist was that Mr. Davenport wouldn't be back that evening. I said: "She sounds upset. What's the matter?" Mr. Hughes said: "She's afraid of him, I think." It was true about the violence, and as for his wife's being mad, it was true that she had some sort of breakdown, but that in Hughes' opinion this was caused by trying to bring up her children under these fearful conditions. "But John goes around London telling people she's mad."

At some point, I drew a breath and said: "Perhaps I'd better not try to see him." Hughes nodded and said to think it over, that if I wanted to see him, he would still arrange it; he would call me the next day. We left in a taxi.

He called the next day and I said I had thought it over and had given up the idea of a meeting, for what was the point? We couldn't make love, thanks to the publicity he, John, had given the affair, and if we talked simply, I wouldn't be able to dissemble the knowledge I now had. This, it seemed to me, would be horrible for *him*, and he would probably edge out of it by lying or bad temper. It also struck me that *he* would probably rather not see *me*.

Who knows whether I was right or wrong? I repented the decision terribly before I left London; if I'd been able to leave at once, it would have been all right, perhaps, but I couldn't get transportation or accommodations for a whole week, so that I had to stay there, longing on the one hand to see him and terrified of a meeting on the other.

I don't know whether or not he knew I was there. Hughes feared he would be bound to hear of it, and it seems to me he must have, since I was even invited to a party given by the literary editor of the Observer. But if he did, he didn't try to reach me, which proves I don't know what. What troubled me most was my staying there and so publicly *not* seeing him, as if giving him the lie, which seems cruel.

The truth is, I still care about him, just as much as ever, though perhaps this feeling would not last if I saw him in actuality. But this caring, of course, is really hopeless now. Hughes says *he* is hopeless and I believe him. We (Hughes and I) had another meeting; he asked me to drinks and we talked again. This time he presented the more favorable side of John. As a lawyer, he said he felt it necessary, on our first meeting, to present, as it were, the case for the Crown. The second time he talked about his qualities in much the same way I've done, only he sighed over them as wasted: the love of books, generosity, loyalty, even a weird kind of integrity. Hughes says he started to write too late and lacks all discipline and habits of work, so that he keeps making these massive escapes into lies and drinking. Hughes says there's a strong self-destructive urge in him and that, whatever the superficial motive, good or bad, that made him break off our correspondence, the real thing must have been that he was rejecting the one thing that could have saved him.

Oh, Hannah, isn't it awful? I still would do anything for him, as I told Mr. Hughes, but what *can* I do? I asked Hughes to write me if anything drastic happened and that I'd be glad to give money, if he would do it for me and not say anything. But money doesn't seem adequately expressive of the tenderness (yes) I feel. Only seeing him would be expressive, but how *can* I see him, given the way he is? Hughes thought that before leaving London, I should write him a note asking him to please stop talking about me, but I couldn't see the point of this, for (a) it would not deter him, if love itself had not deterred him and (b) I would hate to have him know that I knew, that is, I would hate to think of him reading the letter that told him I knew he had betrayed me. Alas, alas.

I shall be looking for an apartment in Florence as soon as I'm allowed out—tomorrow. Do write. This hotel will forward; they've been wonderful to me during this week of sickness. Friday I go for the weekend to Berenson's. He is in a poor state, I hear, feebler, deafer, and one eye has had a haemhorrhage [sic] causing what they hope is only a temporary loss of sight. He lives only on gossip. What a rich feast I could give him, if I would, but I won't. Not even as a sort of blood transfusion.

Much, much love to you and Heinrich,
Mary

P.S. In case you see Bowden, he knows all the above, except about my feelings. Naturally, *he* is feeling vindicated and delighted that I did not see John. And loyalty to him (Bowden) under the circumstances was a motive that sustained me in not seeing John.

1. McCarthy's *Memories of a Catholic Girlhood* had just been published, to immediate critical acclaim.

June 7, 1957

Dearest Mary—

I trust Bowden wrote you how much I liked the Memories. Of all your books, I feel this is most as you are yourself—which is not a 'value-judgement'. Technically as well as artistically, the pieces are bound together by the comments in italics; there is a cheerfulness in the very relentlessness with which you separate factual truth from the distortions of memory. It is much more than mere absence of self-pity—most writers apparently being quite incapable of even mentioning their childhood without bursting into tears—, it is real gallantry and fairness from which the cheerfulness springs. I did not read the reviews and I don't know how it is selling—Denver [Lindley] very strangely not mentioning it to me and I being somewhat embarrassed and hence not mentioning it either.

Bowden was here last Sunday evening. I invited him and he, I think, was afraid the two of us would be alone for a whole evening (which I had not intended) and therefore asked [Niccolò] Tucci,[1] who however did not arrive. (When Bowden told me he had invited Tucci I almost heard him saying to himself: Hannah is too formidable for me to spend a whole evening with her. In which he is very wrong, but never mind.) We had a very nice evening; Heinrich was home and I had asked the [Norman] Podhoretzs [sic] (or what is his name, you know), who is one of these bright youngsters with bright hopes for a nice career. Bowden obviously is delighted about the outcome of the London affair—he made one little gesture which was quite telling. I did not react; he seemed to be in very good shape and I liked him.

I meant to write immediately when I got your letter, and then got wrapped up in reflections until I did no longer know *what* to write. Mary, dear, I am afraid you came into too close a contact with the English variety of the "lost generation"—which apart from being a cliché is a reality. They are always the best and the worst, but in such a way that every single one of them is both at the same time. The lying is *pseudologia phantastica* with the emphasis on the phantastic, and to lie about one's origin and to play the aristocrat in England is, it seems to me, as much satire on the English and amusement about their standards as it perhaps is also the attempt to lie yourself into something you are not. In a sense, they all appeared with a "Here you have somebody upon whom you cannot rely" (as Brecht once put it). Their charm is that they with all their lies are somehow more truthful than all the philistines who don't lie. I think what belongs to this charm is that their lies usually concern only facts—which will come out and show them to be liars no matter what they do. (Whereas if one lies about his "feelings," he is really safe; who can find out?) There is some supreme defiance in this, and what one falls for is among other things this defiance. You know I believe that one ought to trust one's senses, and I don't think, therefore, that you can have been wrong. Even the boasting about you must be seen in this light: since he was known to be a liar and knew this, he could really afford it—trusting that nobody would believe him to begin with. And you are completely free to say that he lied—I think without being really false to him. When an acknowledged liar speaks the truth, he does not want to be believed. But certainly, he did not want to be saved by you either. And this is the reason why I think you were right not to see him. The worst part of it is the bottle. But even apart from that: there are two things which could "save" him: either a woman, but then saved for what? Evidently for some form of respectability. Or: more than talents, namely almost genius, or a talent so compelling that it will overrule everything else. (This is of course the case of people like Brecht or Heidegger.) But if this Who they are is not matched by qualities and gifts, what can there remain to do? And then life becomes a very long and rather boring business; for the Who as such is nowhere recognized in our society, there is no place for it. Under such circumstances, to destroy oneself and become "self-destructive" can be a time-consuming and rather honorable job. More honorable and probably less boring than to save oneself. The only thing which is really not permissible is to drag other people into one's own amusements. So, you had to be frightened away; and he must have known that it would take rather drastic measures to achieve this. Certainly, there is a great deal of cruelty in all this; but then you can't expect somebody who loves you to treat you less cruelly than he would treat himself. The equality of love is always pretty awful.

Compassion (not pity) can be a great thing but love knows nothing of it.

Chicago was very nice and I had a very good time with the students, who liked me. The Vita Activa [Arendt's name for *The Human Condition*] is almost finished, the last pages still to be written, which I always hate and try not to do as long as I possibly can. Thus, I amuse myself with footnotes. I am a little overworked and need a vacation. Have been seeing people more than usual and enjoying it. Elizabeth Bishop came with her Brazilian friend who is an extraordinary woman whom you probably know.[2] If not, get to know her by all means. She is very amusing and full of well-told stories.

I gathered from Bowden that the pneumonia is over, and that you were with Berenson. Bowden did not know the new address, I write to the hotel, it will reach you somehow.

Write me and let me know how you are. I read the Alger Hiss book [*In the Court of Public Opinion*] but don't intend to write about it. It would involve me in disputes and controversy for the rest of my life. One thing is certain: he should be granted a new trial.[3] The forgery by typewriter, though rather difficult to imagine, is by no means impossible. But it could not be done without the help of the FBI: every historian will tell you that the history of secret services is such that this is a real possibility. I personally believe that by now half of the CP consists of FBI agents. That people like Chambers and Hede Massing and Elizabeth Bentley[4] can be brought to "remember" everything is obvious. The testimony by Chambers is even more suspicious and shot through with inconsistencies than I had realized. But Hiss is also even worse than I thought. Quite obsessed with the faults of copy-editing, the misplacing of commas etc. in the transcripts. He has the mind of a copy-editor, is incredibly stupid and also a liar, though different from the Chambers-variety. In brief, an Augean stable. I think of Clemenceau's l'Affaire d'un seul est l'affaire de tous [the problem of one is everybody's problem]; but I can't bring myself to do anything about it. (By the way, the Podhoretz kid, for a moment under the misapprehension that I wanted to do a piece on the book: "Oh, no, Commentary could never afford to take a controversial stand on the Hiss case."[5] Sic! This one sentence almost persuaded me to do something.)

Love—
Hannah

1. Niccolò Tucci (1908–), a Russian-Italian émigré, wrote criticism and fiction for *Partisan Review*, *politics*, and later *The New Yorker*.
2. The poet Elizabeth Bishop was McCarthy's classmate at Vassar. Her Brazilian lover, with whom she lived in Ouro Preto, Brazil, during the 1950s and 60s, was Lota de Macedo Soares.
3. Alger Hiss was convicted of perjury in 1950 for having denied to HUAC that while working for the State Department in the late 1930s he had given classified papers to a Communist Party member (Whittaker Chambers) for transmittal to the Soviet Union.
4. Hede Massing and Elizabeth Bentley were self-confessed Soviet spies.
5. Norman Podhoretz (1930–) was then an associate editor of *Commentary*.

[Mary McCarthy returned to Florence in May 1958 to finish *The Stones of Florence* (1959), much of which first appeared in *The New Yorker* in July 1956 under the title "The City of Stone."]

Piazza Salterelli, I
Firenze
June 14, 1958

Dearest Hannah:

What has happened to you and how did your lectures go? Someone here said they'd read in a newspaper about a lecture you'd given in Zurich, but that is all I know.[1]

I ought to have written sooner, but you know me and besides everything has been in a wobble of indecision until a few days ago, when I cabled Bowden to come here, *aux secours*. The photography hasn't been going well; everything I wanted photographed turns out to be unphotographable or so the camera-artist declares. And she herself [Evelyn Hofer] turns out to be a handful, a dark bird all a-flutter, fearful and obstinate, with as much temperament as twenty divas.[2] In her late thirties (I had thought younger), man-shy and man-crazy, having an unhappy love-affair [. . .] always in the back of her thoughts. An imperious will directed toward unachievable ends; the conditions she wants never exist, in photography or anything else. The light is wrong; the object to be taken is too high or too distant, or, if every other condition is satisfied, she has brought the wrong camera and will have to come back another day. She is the same in everything; if the perfect apartment is finally found for her, she laments that there isn't a good butcher nearby. She has the capacity for making everyone or at least me feel helplessly at fault, apologetic, as though one were the personal ruler of these arbitrary external conditions.

In the end, I wired Bowden to come and see what he could [do] with her, and he arrived yesterday. How they will make out, I don't know, but at least he can rent a car and drive her; one of her handicaps is that she can't drive. And neither can I; at least not in Italy.

So we shall stay here for the summer or anyway till the photographing is finished, which I hope may be in mid-July. Then we might go to France or Austria and Bavaria or Switzerland. How long will you stay in Zurich? I should love to come up for a few days to see you or have you come here. If you're leaving soon, I might be able to come while the photographing is going on, for a slight vacation. All this has been so distracting [. . .] that I still have my last chapter to write. But it shouldn't take more than two weeks. If there were a nice cool place in Switzerland, we might even come there after we're through in Florence. But how long *would* you be staying?

I've not heard from [William] Shawn about the New Yorker's reviewing your book [*The Human Condition*], and Bowden, before he left, had heard nothing from Dwight [then a *New Yorker* staff writer] on the subject. I shall write to Shawn this afternoon, sending him my penultimate chapter and asking what his decision about the *Vita Activa* is.[3] I learn from B[owden] that the Readers Subscription has taken it; that is excellent.

By the way, Italian is a language which exhibits quite a few peculiarities in respect to your distinctions. The regular word for work is *lavorare*; the noun is *lavore*. The word, *travagliare* (noun *travaglio*) is only used to mean grinding toil or doleur; it is not the regular word for labor in the sense of labor-union, etc.; this would be *lavore*. The usual word for worker is still different: *operaio*; a day-laborer is a *manovalo*. *Opera* can apply to the body of work of an artist; an individual work is a *lavoro*; "masterpiece" is *capolavoro*. A "hand" in the sense of a farm-hand is an "*operaio.*" The pains of childbirth are "*doglio.*" What all this means, I don't know. Either Italian discriminates more finely or has confused everything. It would seem to me, on the basis of my sparse Italian, that *opera* is the old word for labor; *operoso* means "laborious," also "active." But by a strange development, it also seems to be the highest word for "work" in the sense of a work of art. It *can* be used (contrary to what I say above) of an individual work of art provided that the artist is a genius and (usually) dead. That is, I could speak of an "*opera bellissima*" of Donatello, but of one of my own works or the work of a friend, I would have to say "*lavoro.*" Tell me what you make of all this. A craftsman, of

52

course, is an "*artigiano*." It would seem to me that all words for labor and work (except *travaglio*, rarely used) in Italian tend to approximate to craftsmanship, indiscriminately, and that *manovalo* is the only word that sees the worker as a pure laborer. To work the soil and to work (embroider) a piece of material are the same, and of course Italian farming looks like a work of art.

Please write soon. I loved the jewel-case; my few pieces of jewelry were always tossing about loosely before and in danger of being lost. Many thanks, dear Hannah. I miss you and long to see you. Don't forget to tell me how the lectures went.

Much love,
Mary

1. Arendt was embarked on another lecture tour in Europe, which included a nearly annual visit with Karl Jaspers in Basel.
2. Evelyn Hofer had been hired by Harcourt, Brace and Company to take photographs for *The Stones of Florence.*
3. *The Human Condition* was ultimately assigned to McCarthy, and her review appeared in *The New Yorker* on October 18, 1958.

Piazza de Salterelli, 1
Firenze
June 23, 1958

Dearest Hannah:

Forgive the delay in answering.[1] I've been trying to organize my plans and state of mind a little. Zurich this week, however, is plainly impossible. Chiefly because I still haven't finished my last chapter and there are too many details in it that would have to be checked on here in the course of writing for me to dare leave. Then there's the photographer. . . .

Last night, finally, she showed us the work she'd been doing in the five weeks she's been here. The result was exactly ten photographs that were usable (looking at it generously) and these not brilliant. After she left, Bowden and I didn't say a word—too dashed—but simply went to bed in silence. This morning we've hastily reviewed the situation and concluded that we'll have to find other photographs. [. . .]

She [Hofer] had already acknowledged that she couldn't photograph sculpture or painting; now we discover by the results that she can't cope with architecture.[2] The only thing she can do, with a certain little style, is landscape and genre. [. . .]

I've been so preoccupied and distressed by this sad little poltergeist that I haven't been able to think ahead. We still have no plans beyond the middle of July. [. . .]

If you come back to Zurich in early July, I *might* come then. But really I don't dare make a plan. Is there a hope that you might come here if you're free that week? I've met a young professor of the University of Florence [unidentified] who knows your work well and is eager to talk to you—partly to disagree and argue, partly to admire. We had a long talk about you on Saturday. One of his points of disagreement is that he thinks that totalitarianism ought not to be used as a substantive (this not from the point of view of belles-lettres), but only in the form of the adjective, *totalitarian*. I.e., he doesn't think there's enough agreement on what the word used substantively means and cited to back up his point an anthology of works on totalitarianism published by Carl Friedrich last year, where, according to him, all the contributors were talking about something different under the same name.

If you came, you might enjoy meeting him; he's bright and rather sassy. Has published a book on Democracy. [. . .]

Dear Hannah, please excuse the inexcusable delay. I'm not quite myself and don't know what to blame—the photographer, who is a veritable millstone, or something more impalpable. Poor old Berenson is now like some specimen preserved in a bottle and a fearful atmosphere proceeds from his house—of hate and fury—that leaves one feeling poisoned after having been there for an afternoon or an evening. Poisoned and sad and somehow unable to pity. Only to deplore and at the same time to feel yoked to what is happening there by a useless sense of loyalty. He has come out in boils, like Job, but he hasn't Job's patience. But what can one expect of a man of ninety-three?

Anyway, there is something *wrong* and dead somewhere in the immediate milieu, which may pass off, like the smell of a rat that has died in the walls; at least, I hope it will. It is *not* Florence itself, because it wasn't here last year.

Excuse all this, which is doubtless some form of superstition.

Best of luck with Munich [where Arendt was lecturing] and much, much love,

Mary

1. If McCarthy was answering a letter from Arendt, it has not been found.
2. This estimate was premature. Evelyn Hofer's cool black-and-white studies of Florentine art

and architecture, widely praised by reviewers of *The Stones of Florence*, convey a sense of inner form that perfectly illustrates McCarthy's appraisal of the Renaissance achievement. McCarthy herself later praised them.

[In the summer of 1959, with the research and writing of the Florence book completed, the Broadwaters rented a house in Pawlet, Vermont, where McCarthy picked up the broken thread of *The Group*.]

> Derby Hill
> Pawlet, Vermont
> June 28, 1959

Dearest Hannah:

Another vicious attack, as Philip Rahv used to say on opening his copy of the Hudson Review. Now it is *Commentary*. Do you realize— probably you do—that your attacker is the man of *The Groves of Academe,* the same one I saw in the school where I judged the literary contest?[1] This dual resurrection seems strange and creepy; he had dropped out of sight for so many years, ten, I should think. That review has the characteristic mark, a kind of glistening malignancy. And surface senselessness.

Do not think that man has any political convictions, right, left, or middle. In fact, he has no views of any sort, except always an end-in-view. Bowden thinks Sidney Hook may have put him up to this. I don't know; he used to know Sidney and probably at one time tried to get Sidney to sponsor or defend him. At Bard, he was a sort of Aristotelian, if I remember right; then he fastened on to A. J. Ayer and that school, to get a job in England.

Probably hatred of me had something to do with the review (Bowden felt he was attacking us both in the part on *précieuses ridicules*), and then Will Barrett is his wife's brother, and he used to hate Barrett.[2] Anyway, it all seems quite wicked; that review was certainly commissioned, the way you commission a murder from a gangster. There used to be some sort of ethic about not attacking people in print whom you had quarreled with personally—some liberal notion of the avoidance of even the *appearance* of bias in reviewing. (I don't mean Lincoln Reis had quarreled with you personally; I mean *Commentary*.)[3] But now no one seems to have any shame.

That whole issue of *Commentary* has a new and peculiar undertone, a sort of jacobinism. See the piece on Oliver Cromwell. Who is [the author] Shub? Where is that "leftist" note coming from? Is it a reflection of something in Israel? Or do I imagine it? Even the review of Harold [Rosenberg] had a kind of righteousness quite unlike the old *Commentary* cynicism.

It's nice here, though it has rained nearly every day since we arrived, sometimes fitfully, sometimes steadily. There's a perpetual low rumble of thunder that one takes for distant airplanes and swaths of soft gray mist lie over the hills. This mountain humidity is pleasant, though, and rather sensuous. I like the continuous sound of needle-like rain on the slate roof. We've planted a few flowers and herbs and lettuces, which the deer or woodchucks munch on and spit out, distastefully, and we've picked wild strawberries (again) in the meadows and seen some beautiful birds—yellow warblers, an oriole, an indigo bunting—brilliant blue. And there are toads in the cellar and snakes under the studio. We've been swimming, sometimes in the marble quarry and once in a waterfall, where the rocks are formed in basins of soft blue slate. There's something strange and folkish about this country; I feel this very strongly. An odd *underlying* feeling that one doesn't get anywhere else in New England.

Bowden had an awful blow. The book he was translating has been snatched, so to speak, out of his hands; [William] Jovanovich, cabling for rights, discovered that an English publisher had already commissioned another translation. So that was that. He went right on translating for a few days like a chicken that keeps on having reflexes when its head has been cut off. So far, no substitute has been thought of.

My own work has been going pretty well. I've finished a chapter [of *The Group*], written an article for Harper's Bazaar and started another chapter.[4] Last night, we saw our first human society in nearly three weeks: two domesticated pansies who have a little hand printing press and talk about wild flowers and cooking.

I must stop. We're going for a Sunday drive. Please come if you can and please write. I'm sending this to New York, not being sure of your Palenville address.

Much love and to Heinrich too,
Mary

1. This was Lincoln Reis, who taught at Bard when McCarthy did, and inspired the character Professor Mulcahy in *The Groves of Academe*. He reviewed *The Human Condition* in *Commentary*, June 1959.

2. William Barrett (1913–1994) was a philosophy professor at New York University and an editor of *Partisan Review*.

3. In 1957, *Commentary* had commissioned Arendt to write about recent civil rights legislation, and then, unhappy with her conclusions (she opposed the idea of making children and schools take the brunt of enforced integration) solicited a rebuttal from Sidney Hook. When, a year later, the article remained unpublished, Arendt angrily withdrew it. "Reflections on Little Rock" finally appeared in *Dissent*, Winter 1959.

4. With Arendt's recommendation, McCarthy had won a Guggenheim Foundation grant in 1959 to finish *The Group*. The article was "Brunelleschi's Dome," *Harper's Bazaar*, September 1959.

Palenville, N.Y.
July 27, 1959
Chestnut Lawn House

Mary—

I have not been aware that it was already a month. I was so delighted with your letter, meant to write quickly, somehow did not get around to it. You know how it is. Commentary—I had not the slightest notion of who the gentleman was (his name again escapes me), but I could see how glad Martin [Greenberg] must have been to get finally what he wanted.[1] There was, however, a tone of real hatred which surprised me. The reason now is clear. Obviously, the Greenberg Bros. [Clement too] identify us and preach the gospel. They could do much worse. [. . .]

We have been here for more than two weeks, quiet and beautiful as ever, my notion of paradise. Our dream house has been sold and we have to fasten our fantasies to some other place. I am working, about to finish the first hundred pages, finally in a shape which more or less suits me.[2] Heinrich is working for a new course in Bard and, as far as I can see, is very much looking forward to it. I often imagine you here and ask myself if you would think we are a bit nuts. But I don't really believe it. We have phonograph and records with us and, for the first time in 19 years, a set of chessmen. We play once in a while in the evening and tell each other how unspeakably lousy we have become. We also could play pool-shooting, but Heinrich is not yet in the right mood and I do not feel like practicing. We were, of course, too late for strawberries, but the raspberries are just right now and the blackberries are coming nicely.

I received an invitation for a twenty-minute talk from BBC. I was quite inclined to say yes and take this as a pretext to go to London in [the] fall. But they offer £30. —which seems to me outrageous even for Europe. What do you think? Which are their normal rates?? I get much more in Germany for similar programs. [. . .]

What do you think about this strange mutual [trade] Fair-business in Moscow and New York? I just made up my mind that I shall go to Berlin; I am curious to see how things look from there.[3] Also, it may be the last time. But in general, I am rather annoyed with this Europe trip. It interrupts everything and I shall have to spend some time with family from Israel—perhaps in Florence, mitigating circumstances. I hope I can see Chiaramonte [sic]. And I finally got around to reading Auden's review, and now I am even more embarrassed.[4] Somehow I am utterly unfit for the role of an author. It is a simple case of lack of suitable ideas.

Love, my dear, to both of you. And please write! I promise, I won't do it again [wait so long to write]!

Hannah

[. . .]

1. Arendt refers to Lincoln Reis's review of *The Human Condition*.
2. Arendt was expanding a series of lectures she had delivered at Princeton University in April 1955. The new version was published as *On Revolution* (1963).
3. Arendt did go to Berlin, where she occupied herself with "restitution business" (applying for one of the German government's payments to Nazi refugees). "I like being here, feel myself at home, even in the government offices," she wrote to Karl Jaspers on October 3, 1959. Berlin, she felt, had "grown back together again."
4. Arendt had a special feeling for poets, among them W. H. Auden, who wrote of *The Human Condition* that "it seems to answer precisely those questions which I have been putting to myself" ("Thinking What We Are Doing," *Encounter*, June 1959).

Derby Hill
Pawlet, Vermont
August 17, 1959

Dearest Hannah:

Now (as is more usual), I am the one who is remiss. I wanted to write back right away but truly I've been through a fearful ordeal (the worse for being indescribable) with New Yorker proofs [of "The City of Stone"] which have almost broken my nerve and darkened the summer. That magazine's special institution, the Checking Department, is to me a kind of third degree invented by some personal Prosecutor of mine to shatter the morale. I hate to be wrong about dates, facts, etc., for I trust to my memory the way one trusts to one's eyes. They found quite a few mistakes and, even more unsettling, things they insisted were mistakes and that I, separated from my books of reference, could only appeal to memory, poor fallible thing, to verify. The reference books in the nearest library (Manchester) are all out of date and themselves extremely inaccurate, I discovered, and yet I couldn't give up the quest for certainty. I found myself nearly going wild and unable to sleep over details like the placing of an accent. A normal person cooperates with the checkers or uses them as a convenience, but I cannot help competing with them. Then, aside from this obsessiveness of mine, the sheer physical labor and consumption of time is awful. In the last stages of each proof (in this case, three times repeated), there are daily telephone calls lasting up to an hour and forty minutes for three, four, or five days and sometimes three calls of this kind a day. Meanwhile, I was trying to work on my novel and rushing back and forth to the library in a futile manner. We also had a little unwanted company; my brother [Kevin], for instance, arrived with his maid and two children; one of Bowden's fellow-teachers[1] appeared with her husband for two separate stays, all in the middle of these proofs.

Well, enough of this; I hope to regain my or rather our tranquility, now that it's all over. Yes, those Fairs and the Nixon visit were a grotesque comedy, in a way like old-fashioned fairs with barkers and fakers and confidence men. The scene in the Model Kitchen[2] might have been invented by a modern Dostoevsky. I suppose it means a rapprochement, i.e., a decision that the Cold War, etc., has all been a "misunderstanding," and that we both palpably "want the same things" (e.g. plastics and Coca-Cola). And I fear that this is true. The discovery that the basic aims were the same could not have happened, I think, with Hitler. Such competing Fairs would have been unimaginable. I liked too (if "like" is the word) the floor's collapsing into dust in the American Exposition; one of the "experts" working on this was the man who, supposedly, fixed our house on Cape Cod, so that Bowden, as he said, was not at all surprised. . . .

Reuel has been to Jugoslavia, on a Lambretta he bought, and has just written me an interesting letter about it. His job in Paris collapsed after a month, rather like that floor, and he went off on the Lambretta, stopping in the high Savoy, to Venice and then, all alone, to Jugoslavia. He's now on his way to Florence, I think.

When are you going exactly? There's some talk, between Bowden and me, of my going abroad too, to work in peace, perhaps in

Venice, for a few months. Or we might rent a house in Newport up to Thanksgiving, and Bowden could come up weekends. But I shan't make up my mind for ten days or two weeks probably. This novel [*The Group*] worries me horribly; it's like a person that "can't live and can't die."

The BBC rates are $100 in New York, and I think the same in England, though perhaps they *are* a little less there; I can't quite remember. That, in my case, was for a thirteen-minute talk. Not twenty.

Now I shall tell you of my Temptation. Shawn, of the New Yorker, asked me, during one of those phone calls, whether I would do a profile of Jerusalem. Not the modern city; historical Jerusalem, from its foundation. It is an idea, he says, that he has had ten years, and has been waiting for inspiration to tell him who was the right person to do it. He imagines it is a two-year job. Bowden is very much against my even listening to this proposal, even though it is understood that I would not begin till this novel is finished. He says these years, the next ten, are the best years of a novelist's creative activity, and that it would be wicked to squander them on journalism, even very high-class journalism. He is right about "the best years"—at least for most novelists of the past, and he's thinking, I imagine, chiefly of George Eliot, who began writing fiction at about thirty-seven and reached her peak in her early fifties. And yet I *am* tempted, perhaps partly by the money, though I don't think this plays too big a part, and partly by a kind of glamour, a purple-gold glamour, that the name Jerusalem has for me. Also by the idea of learning something new, opening a new arcanum. Here is where your advice comes in. I know nothing, really, about Judaism, except the Christian Bible; Bowden says learning about Judaism, pre-Diaspora, would be, for me at any rate, a sterile occupation, quite different from learning or relearning about the Renaissance or studying philosophy, say. And of course Jerusalem wasn't a Jewish city for nearly two thousand years. The Crusader period appeals to me, and I know a little about that (through Venice, chiefly), but perhaps this appeal is only a sort of technicolor or historical novelist's vision that goes back to a child's interest in Richard Coeur de Lion and Saint Louis. Or perhaps I'm merely flattered, but the *kind* of thing one is flattered by tells something.

Probably Bowden is right, and I ought to agree with him even more strongly after what I've just been through. He says, too, that this project would be principally a library project, unlike Venice and Florence, where one entered physically into something still living. I hate judicious pondering about the Career, though as one grows older and there is less time left to pronounce the word that is in one (if it *is* there), one has, I suppose, to look to the ant instead of the grasshopper. But, oh dear, I still feel more like a grasshopper.

Anyway, tell me, if you will, what you think. But don't feel that I am shifting the burden of decision to you.

Please give my love to Heinrich; I hope your summer has continued good. Right now, we and all the trembling trees are waiting for the onslaught of one of the wild mountain storms that pass so quickly and sometimes forget to come.

Much, much love to you,
Mary

1. Broadwater was then teaching at St. Bernard's School in Manhattan.
2. At the U.S. pavilion at the Moscow trade fair, Vice-President Richard Nixon and Soviet Premier Nikita Khruschchev fell into a much-publicized "debate" over the relative merits of each other's consumer products and governmental systems.

Palenville
August 28, 1959

Dearest Mary,

I just finished reading the last (3rd) part of the Florence series in the New Yorker, but did not read the preceding ones and am quite unhappy about it. This *is* superb, and I loved the landscape description and the wonderfully precise and deft distinction between Spring and Fall. To me, the key to the riddle is in your "absolute equality and simultaneity between the dead and the living" and that "no standard could impose itself except the standard revealed in each work." I could not get hold of the earlier issues, heard about the appearance too late, no copies in Palenville, etc. I do not want to bother you with questions before I read the whole; but I think I shall even agree with your treatment of Michelangelo—you are much more careful than I expected, by the way. I want to take the articles with me when I go to Florence, and I hope the New Yorker will send me the two missing copies. The rigmarole they [the fact-checking department] put you through is terrible; this phony scientificality is no help and I think those who cooperate simply don't understand what it is all about. It is one of the many forms in which the would-be writers persecute the writer. And since this is nicely combined with job-holding and job-justification this kind of torture has become an institution.

Plans: We go home next week, Heinrich around Wednesday and I shall follow on Saturday. I need a few days for myself; we too had quite a bit of company, among others the son of Channan[1] [sic] (you may remember, Channan once picked me up at your place) who is a very nice and intelligent boy. Just graduated from Chicago—age 19, and will go back for graduate work. He is staying with us and beats Heinrich every night in Ping-Pong and me, a bit later, in chess. We take our revenge, correct his German and round out his education. It is rather fun and does not really interfere with work.

I probably shall leave on September 20, stay a couple of days or so in Paris and then proceed to Hamburg. What did you decide? Will you be in Italy in October? Could we meet? My plans got all a bit mixed up because an old acquaintance of mine, a woman from the Heidelberg days, wrote that she is dying of cancer. So, I have to go and see her. My probable schedule: Paris—Hamburg up to October 1st. Then 10 to 12 days Italy; then Basel for about 8–10 days. Then back to Germany, probably Munich, Frankfurt, Berlin and Cologne. And around November 1st back to New York via Brussels. I do not think that I shall have time to go to London under these circumstances.

Now your temptation: Bowden is right, Jerusalem will be an altogether different proposition, and probably much less rewarding for you than Florence or Venice. On the other hand, there is no book on Jerusalem and the market possibilities are certainly very high. Also, and more important, Jerusalem is the only city I know that gives you an idea what a city in antiquity was like. It has been frozen through religion, and though I would not know what exactly to *do* with this, I have always been impressed by the enormous quiet significance that is present in every stone. But leave the ant and grasshopper considerations out of the decision-making. You have plenty of time to become an ant if ever you want to be one, which I doubt. And anyhow, don't think of precedents, they are always wrong.

Love, Mary, and drop me a line, and many greetings to Bowden!
Hannah

1. This was the son of Chanan Klenbort, a Polish Jew whom Arendt met in Paris in the 1930s. He wrote Yiddish short stories under the name Ayalti.

[For six weeks in November and December, McCarthy, at the invitation of a Florentine friend, the Countess Anna Maria Cicogna, worked on *The Group* undisturbed in her villa in Libya.]

Villa Volpi, Tripoli
November 11, 1959

Dearest Hannah:

Forgive the silence, please. I arrived in Rome October 23, where I heard from Chiaromonte about his one-day visit to you in Florence and that you had already left for Switzerland which I knew or anticipated anyway. I didn't glean many details of your meeting with Nicola from him; maybe *you'll* tell me about it. In what cafes did you sit, for instance? I can see him in a certain one on the south side of Piazza della Repubblica or else at Gilli's on Piazza della Repubblica too. But I don't quite see you there. At Rivoire's on Piazza della Signoria? I wish I could have been with you in Florence. [. . .]

And what shall I tell you about "here"? Any fears of being corrupted were totally groundless. I am nearly bored to death except when working, which I've been doing up to ten hours a day. There's a succession of multi-course meals, dressing for dinner, undressing, a caged stroll in the garden. It's exactly like life on shipboard, including the fact that one eats too much at meal times, meals being the only red-letter events in days indistinguishable from one another. Life at Berenson's at I Tatti was a Roman orgy in comparison. Nothing happens to the very rich; that seems to [be] the definition of their state of being, which is close to burial alive. There are other guests in the house and no one has the slightest interest in me, including the hostess (or for that matter in each other); every now and then someone will pick up my hand in silence and contemplate a bracelet I am wearing, say. *"Bello."* Pause. *"Americano?"* Silence.

We *have* made a couple of expeditions to two excavated Roman cities: Leptis Magna and Sobrata. Leptis Magna is vast and extremely, brutally vulgar, except for a primitive nucleus that goes back to the time of Augustus; it is a complex of stadia and baths built by Septimius Severus. One of the choice items for the tourists is a show of latrines, like American outdoor privies, only more so and in solid marble with a sort of drain of running water along the front. A forum, which is actually very big, is utterly put in the shade by the sports fields, latrines, tepidariums, caldariums, Turkish baths, etc. They must occupy ten or twenty times the space given the forum and temples to the gods. In the sculptural and architectural motifs, there is already a strong African accent, with palm, palmetto, and papyrus patterns. A general gross [illegible] sense of *Aïda*. The old market and smallish forum of Augustus' time have a granite charm or pioneer innocence in comparison. Sobrata seemed to me better, but perhaps only because it's smaller and has some beautiful Christian mosaics of the time of Justinian. The informed archeological opinion here is to treat the Byzantines as barbarians because they tore down the temples and turned them into Christian basilicas, making pulpits out of friezes, etc. But I am rather on the Byzantines' side; their altars and pulpits and mosaics of the phoenix eternal and the Tree of Life and the Redemption do appear to be sanctified, touched at least with Grace and devotion. But I don't express these heretical views, partly owing to poor Italian.

The one thing you can say for these cities is that they do give an all-too-concrete idea of what life in a city of the Empire was like. Then there is a certain romantic beauty in the effect of ruined columns on the seashore, especially at sunset, when you see, as we did at Sobrata, a small owl on top of a column and a cat pacing the mosaics, and a great horned owl sailing across a deserted, crumbling amphitheatre. And behind you, in the desert, are shepherds with their camels and flocks, in violets, reds, and purples, the women veiled. I like the Biblical scenery, one *Adoration* after another. And I liked an oasis we visited, all laid out in rectangular gardens with date palms. And an eleventh-century mosque, made out of Roman pillars, with no decoration whatever, only a play of squares and Moorish arches.

The Arabs, except when they form a picture out of Italian painting, seem odious and unattractive. This is partly trachoma and other diseases and partly some psychic emanation. As you know, they're extremely superstitious. Every time I walk in the garden (which is worked by Arab women), some fat female in veils and drapery throws herself on the ground at the sight of me and begins to invoke Allah for protection. Anna Maria (the hostess) is an indulgent landlord and none of the Arabs seem to do any work at all; the supposed female laborers in the garden are all floating around saying *"Buona sera,"* and *"Bello"* and *"Carino"* when not prostrated in prayer or deprecation. The work of the house is done by Venetian servants. Anna Maria says the Arabs around here would be all right, given two generations of decent food and hygiene; that is, that they're not degenerate. But the better-fed ones, white collar workers, strike me as still worse-looking than the poor. I've been reading some eighteenth century letters from Tripoli, written by the sister of the British consul, which don't inspire confidence.

There's a bit about you in the current *New Statesman*, which I'll tuck into this letter. The writer, who appears to be their new art critic, seems intelligent though rather difficult to follow, especially when one suspects an irony.

Dear Hannah, do write me a word. I need mental stimulation. Please give my love to Heinrich, whom I wanted to call before I left. [. . .] Have you gone down to Princeton to hear [the critic George] Steiner? Not even out of curiosity? You know, probably, that I'm going to Poland and Jugoslavia, which will be a decided change.[1] I may embrace Communism.

[. . .] I expect to leave early in December. If I can only get two more chapters finished in that time! Tell me what you're doing and, among other things, how your situation with Harcourt, Brace has been resolved.[2]

> Much, much love to you,
> Mary

1. At Arthur Schlesinger's recommendation, McCarthy had been invited to join Saul Bellow on a speaking tour of Eastern Europe and the British Isles, under the State Department's "Experts and Specialists Program."
2. When her editor and friend Denver Lindley left Harcourt, Brace after differences with the company's new president, William Jovanovich, Arendt wanted to leave too.

Part Two

April 1960 – April 1963

[In December 1959, Bowden Broadwater and Reuel Wilson flew to Europe to join Mary McCarthy for a holiday tour of Vienna and Prague, after which they accompanied her to Poland on the first leg of the State Department trip. On December 29, they were met in Warsaw by the Public Affairs Officer at the U.S. Embassy, James Raymond West.

Before Reuel and Bowden returned to New York, in mid-January, West told McCarthy that he wanted to marry her. A hectic courtship followed, sandwiched between McCarthy's lecture appearances in Poland, Yugoslavia, and Great Britain, and West's official duties, along with his domestic duties as husband and father of three children. McCarthy flew to New York early in April to say good-bye to Bowden and pack her belongings. After a rendezvous with West in Vienna, she proceeded to Rome, which was to be her base until they managed to make a home for themselves—in Warsaw, McCarthy believed; in Paris, as it turned out.]

> Hotel d'Inghilterra
> Via Bocca di Leone 14
> Roma
> April 20, 1960

Dearest Hannah:

Here is the "Arrived safe" letter—a little late because I didn't get back from Vienna till last night. I expect to move to Carmen

[Angleton]'s apartment [. . .] today or tomorrow, providing the keys can be found; the butler, who keeps them, is in Milan. [. . .]

Vienna at Easter was alternately sultry and icy, with rain; we [she and James West] went Easter morning, under an umbrella, to hear a Schubert mass at the Hofburg Cappelle; every *bien pensant* Viennese was there in tweeds and mufflers; I was the only person in a light spring dress. Almost everything was either closed or sold out because of the long Easter holidays. We couldn't get seats to *The Magic Flute*, but managed to get into the Albertina (drawings) and the Kunsthistorisches Museum during the three hours they were open from Good Friday through Easter Monday. The Albertina drawings were marvelous, and there was a huge Rouault graphic show there, which was interesting as a study of progressive deterioration—a plentifully illustrated case history. The early Rouault drawings, very large, as large as paintings, were extraordinarily gifted facsimile copies of Italian Renaissance artists and of Degas; I should assume that he was insane, in an increasingly dull and repetitive way. Somehow, I thought of Lionel Trilling—a Rouault pietist—and began laughing. [. . .]

I want to tell you this much about Jim. It was a somber time (ours), in part, or chequered like the Vienna weather. He has been through a sort of hell in Warsaw (which he hadn't told me) with that woman [his wife] and the sight of the children. [. . .] Coming home at night for their bedtime, then going back to the Embassy to work till midnight or one; working in the same way weekends and having a sandwich and a whiskey and soda or a coffee for dinner, so as not to be at home with her. Or, when she was out, eating alone in the dining-room. Sleeping on the divan. Because she will not have the furniture moved around, so that the little girl could sleep in her room and he in the little girl's; it would cause talk among the Embassy servants, she says. In the mornings, he and the children tiptoe around in the dark, so as not to disturb mamma, who is sleeping. . . . When he got to Vienna, he suddenly discovered he was totally exhausted by this daily torture—all nerves; the second morning he abruptly wept for a minute or two. This doesn't mean a lessening of love; on the contrary, a hardening of determination. What he has been doing, in Warsaw, is confront, very grimly, the price, and the price is the children, whom he loves. He insists on seeing this clearly, without softening it. ("You will have them for the summer anyway," or "Maybe we can take all three of them, in time, or one at least"; these assurances, from me, don't palliate anything for him.) On the other hand, he *will* not live with her; the damage to the children, some of it, has already been done or was done at their birth. "I keep reminding myself," he says, sadly laughing, "that *I* asked that girl to marry me." While we were in Vienna, we drew up a sort of settlement plan, for her to live with the children in Washington, in his house, near her parents, and where the children have friends; the total cost was $9,670.00, including $1000 clothes allowance yearly for her. This will have to be reduced a bit; he can't really do more than about $8000, what with mortgage payments, life insurance, etc. still to be paid out of his salary, plus divorce costs, transportation back to the States, children's doctor bills, and so on. He says he won't take anything from me; "If I do this, I'm going to pay for it," he says. I shall be allowed to pay for my clothes and books and whatever I want and bank the rest for emergencies, he says. Or maybe I might be allowed to buy us a little car; he is going to give her their car and pay its transportation ($350) back. Perhaps she'll accept this proposition; it's far, far better than she would get in court, in a disputed case. And sooner or later there *will* be a divorce; that is clear. The question is only when. She may want to live in Paris instead, which would be all right—less good for the children, probably, but nearer him so that he could see them, and less expensive in some things, e.g. servant, schools. He's presenting her with the Washington proposal and figures (and the Paris alternative), the stipulation being a prompt divorce and immediate separation agreement. [. . .] If she doesn't accede, he'll withdraw the proposal (including the $1000 clothes allowance, $750 entertainment allowance, etc., for herself) and ask for a transfer, which would remove her from the scene. He's also insisting that she write to her parents, and, if not, he will write to them. He would like to see her get a job, at least part-time; she is a capable secretary and stenographer and there'll be a servant at home. He thinks it would be better for her; she's all right, he says, in an office. There's a parallel, he finds, between my spoiling Bowden and his spoiling her, except that Bowden has responded far less badly to it. . . . And he spoiled her from indifference.

Anyway, dear Hannah, I love him, more than before. He's the most wholly serious person I've ever known, anywhere; I don't mean lacking in gayety or human or wild high spirits. It is way beyond thinking about the pros and cons or having doubts; it's simply a fact. And I'm glad. But I'm alarmed, for him, for his nerves and stamina. [. . .] It's impossible for him to take leave more than every two or three weeks (there is too much work), but it's not the actual interval that's so bad, considered purely as time; it's what fills the interval there. That woman is a monstrous little horror; but I suppose there are many like her. Fortunately, she thinks I'm in America still; he went to Vienna, supposedly, just for a respite and to go to the dentist.

Perhaps you'd give me Gunther Anders'[1] address, which I might use if I go back to Vienna; Jim says he would like me to have someone I know there, in case something goes wrong—a plane doesn't fly or a sudden crisis.

I must stop. Forgive what must be a tedious letter for you. And thank you, for everything you did [in New York]. Jim wants me to thank you for him again too; he has been reading *The Human Condition* with delighted excitement and quoting from it—the last time, I think, on forgiveness . . .! Much love to Heinrich and thank him, too, for his benignity and kindness; I like to think of him smoking his pipe and judiciously considering . . . in German.

How is the translation going?[2]

Love and kisses to you,
Mary

1. Günther Anders, né Stern, was Hannah Arendt's first husband. They met in 1925 in a graduate seminar at Marburg University taught by Martin Heidegger.
2. Arendt was translating *The Human Condition* for the first German edition: *Vita activa oder von tatigen Leven* (1960).

[New York]
May 3, 1960

Dearest Mary:

I slowly get used to not having you around and still miss you. Your letter arrived just in time when I had started to think if I should start worrying. But had not yet. Today is a bad day for writing. Letter-writing-day—like housecleaning.

Sunday night, Bowden was here. Still very unhappy and sad, but better; less shattered although I think it only begins to dawn upon him what all this will mean for him and that parties won't be a way out. We had a very nice evening, I trying my best to cheer him up. He has plans—all centered, I am afraid, around leaving his job [at St. Bernard's]. The main problem is of course that he has no work and not the slightest idea what could interest him. He has a number of rather wild plans, the first condition of them all being to be able to get rid of the apartment. He wants to go to Italy, pretends to have job-possibilities in [the] art business in Florence (?); the truth is that he wants to bum around. And since this is somehow true to style, I was perhaps not convincing when I tried to dissuade him. Somehow, he is right in an odd way. Carmen apparently has not yet finished making up her mind about that other guy [unidentified]. I told him how charming she is, he agreed but without enthusiasm.

Then I had Harold [Rosenberg] for a Spaghetti dinner. His fault since he announced himself about half an hour before actual arrival. But it was very very nice. I never felt so comfortable with him before.[1] I am afraid I am almost at the end of my news, except that I accepted the offer from Wesleyan University[2] (you remember the visit of the President early in the morning) and I also agreed to give a graduate Seminar on Philosophy & Politics at Columbia this coming Fall term.

Vienna: if I don't write about it, it is not because I don't think of it. You know that I am frightened that you might get hurt and you know also that I am quite aware that this is nonsense. This weekend business must be quite nerve-racking. Is there any chance of spending a few weeks together during vacation? And how far have the divorce formalities materialized? Because of Bowden, you don't need to worry; he has not the slightest intention to make you miserable.

Guenther's address: Wien-Mauer (apparently a suburb) Oelzeltung 15. I shall write him today.

How is your work? Back to the novel? I am still translating [The Human Condition] and cursing God and the world, history and my own stubbornness. Except that nobody listens. Certainly not Heinrich [. . .]

Love and yours,
Hannah

1. McCarthy thought that Rosenberg and Arendt might have had an affair around this time.
2. This was an invitation to teach at Wesleyan's Advanced Study Center, where Arendt conducted seminars in the fall of 1961 and 1962.

Via Sansovino 6
Rome
May 9, 1960

Dearest Hannah:

I came back from Zurich last night and found your letter. [. . .] Jim and I spent four days in Zurich—a civic paradise, we thought. What a pity Lenin did not simply settle down there and become a burgher; there are so many inducements. Have you or Heinrich been there? We took an excursion on the lake in the sun; they go all the time, sometimes with concerts aboard; we rode in a cable car, dangling as in a ski lift across the lake; we walked in a waterside park and took trams, gay blue ones, and went to the museum, with wonderful modern pictures, and ate a lot, in excellent lively restaurants, with waitresses like hospitable spinsters serving food from long buffet tables, and drank wine from the Valais and bought handkerchiefs and books and presents for the children and kirsch in a beautiful bottle for me to take back to Italy. On every street corner, old men and women were selling bunches of lilies of the valley and Alpine roses and startling blue gentians and scented narcissus, and clocks with gilded figures were ringing the quarter-hours from the pale gray clock towers. The hotels are expensive but nearly everything else, *les plaisirs de la vie*, are either cheap or free, like the clean cool air. Miriam, whom I just talked to, says [Ignazio] Silone, who spent his years of exile there, talks of it in the same way.[1] It combines the virtues of the "old ways" with the modern; you should see the supermarkets and the department stores, and on the street, in the walls of buildings they have shining nickel automats dispensing fruit, drugs, chocolate, cheese, almost anything one would need on a Sunday when the shops are closed, or at night.

Do not worry about me. I *got* hurt, this time, and we both lay awake in a single bed while I wept slowly and steadily as we listened to the churches ring the quarter hours from three a.m. till six, and my chest hurt so it felt as though my heart were breaking. The occasion, weirdly, was Clem Greenberg; I'd engaged in over-exuberant reminiscence earlier and told about my affair with him,[2] together with a *description* of his appearance, slothful habits, and general character. This produced an angry and totally uncomprehending reaction: "How *could* you go to bed with a man like that?" Over and over, and all I could say was, "I don't know." I felt as if I

71

were being examined by some cruel magistrate who was going to be grilling me for the rest of my life and picking flaws in my story. Then, as I kept forlornly spilling tears, he grew aghast at what was happening and said, "My God, how are we going to stop this?" We both knew we could not go to sleep and leave it till tomorrow, as normal people would have done; we waited and listened to the clocks strike out the destruction of the next day. I'm familiar with mawkish repentances (Edmund [Wilson, McCarthy's second husband] was a great indulger in these), but there was nothing mawkish about this—just genuine horror and incredulous regret. And that of course made me feel worse—the image of his going back to Warsaw two days later and gnashing his teeth over what he had done. Nor did I feel altogether free of fault: why the hell *did* I sleep with Clem Greenberg and why bring him into the conversation, shortly after we'd been looking at some pictures of Jim's children, who, by the way, are *darling?* Anyway, we managed to terminate it, but the next day he was still wretched until mid-afternoon, when we rode on the cable car. But I felt it was better, since he has what he calls this "wicked strain" in his nature, to have had it shown me or shown both of us, for examination and perhaps, if we're fortunate, repair. (I don't imply there was any physical roughnesss, just harsh words and skepticism.) In the end, we were wildly happy again, and he did not *indulge* himself in remorse. I think this trait or habit can be cured; it is more a habit than a trait. He said I'd taught him a lesson, by scaring him, though that wasn't my intention. And behind it are the children and the strain of *willing* a new life, trying to bring it into being by main force. I love him even more than before; he has a kind of exquisite tenderness, toward *things* as well as persons, which I suppose is another way of being thin-skinned and quick to be affronted. I've never felt so comfortable, so at ease with any man, so much, I imagine, what I was when I was a young girl, alone inside my skin.

Margaret [West] is getting closer to accepting a divorce. It is now a question of when. Her present idea is to leave the youngest child with him, put the older boy in an English boarding school and the girl in a French boarding school, as a five-day boarder, while she lives in Paris and studies fashion-illustration! He is viewing these proposals with some suspicion, for he thinks that she wants to plant the little boy with him as an excuse to come back, meanwhile delaying on the divorce. [. . .] He has written a letter to her parents, suggesting his dissatisfaction, and is going to follow it this next week with a franker one; she refuses to write them. [. . .]

In June he has two weeks vacation and we're going probably to Normandy together; by that time, Margaret should have left for Paris herself. [. . .] Oh, these poor Iron Curtain country people! Watching them board the plane, they looked like another race of being, in their suits that look as if they were made of blue crumpled paper and their faces and bodies white and almost deformed by poor food. And he, with his very soldierly walk and silver-grey hair and well-cut American suit and solid body, looked like the West itself—no pun intended.

I must stop and cook myself some dinner. I've written you all this detail not to make you a confidante but so that you'll know, *if* you worry, what this is concretely. Tranquility has descended on me, even here in Rome, and the texture of life seems beautiful. But write. And do finish that translation. Where will you be in the summer? You talk about our seeing each other. But where?

> Much, much love,
> Mary

1. The Italian novelist Ignacio Silone (1900–1978), a leader of the Communist Party in his youth, spent his underground years in Zurich in the 1920s.
2. McCarthy had an affair with Clement Greenberg in the 1940s while she was married to Edmund Wilson.

> Via Sansovino 6
> Rome
> May 15, 1960

Dearest Hannah:

The next mail leaves in forty-five minutes, and I'm writing you this note for purely selfish reasons: because my heart is full of emotion and I want to talk. As if we were in your apartment. Bowden wrote me about his visit to you; in his version, the conversation seems to have been chiefly about Reuel. He has written three times in response to my last letter, and so I've purposely slowed down a little on answering, not to keep up a fevered correspondence with him, which would awaken all sorts of hopes. Indeed, they *are* awake. And it's so sad, because I grow fonder of him as he recedes a little into the distance and all the memories become good ones;

the thought of his suffering, moreover, makes me want to scream aloud. He writes that he is not sorry, in a way, that this happened because it made him realize what he wanted or loved, and that he never knew he wanted or loved anything before. But now he knows there is just one thing: me. I realize that there's an element of dramatization in this and even (perhaps?) of calculated play on my feelings. And yet I am so troubled for him. And this picture of a morally re-educated, redeemed, christened, so to speak, Bowden makes me smile as one would at a dear child.

Keep an eye on him, won't you? I've finally written to him this afternoon—a long letter but designed to keep hope at a minimum. Or so I delude myself.

Meanwhile, and as a strange soaring trumpet-music to this growing tenderness I feel for Bowden, my love for Jim is increasing till I am quite dizzy. I find myself changing or perhaps that is not the right word, coming to life in a new way, like somebody who has been partly paralyzed. And I've become conscious in myself of certain shrunken or withered character-traits that I never reckoned with before. Quite unpleasant they are too. You remember my telling you once that my marriage to Bowden was just two people playing house, like congenial children? Well, I slowly realize that all my love affairs and marriages have been little games like that—and snug, sheltered games. And that all this should happen with a U.S. government official seems utterly bizarre in a way.

Perhaps I too am sounding like the redeemed, christened Bowden, and these things are almost incommunicable, except to the two people concerned. So I shall stop and run for the mail and only end by sending you much, much love and winged thoughts.

Mary

[New York]
May 18, 1960

My dearest,

I had just sat down to write you when Esther [Arendt's maid] arrived bringing the mail and your winged letter. [. . .]

Your last letter and your letter today have done the trick, I guess. I can no longer worry. The story about the Clem-tragedy sounded very funny—how long some chickens take to come home to roost. No, I did not mean this kind of getting hurt—which is only another way of being alive. But, please don't fool yourself: nobody ever was cured of anything, trait or habit, by a mere woman, though this is precisely what all girls think they can do. Either you are willing to take him "as is" or you better leave well enough alone. What is going to happen to these poor children? To add to the shock of parental separation the shock of separating them from each other seems a bit unwise. But how can one judge without knowing any-thing[?] From what you write, it sounds as though Madame wishes to get rid of him as well as of the children and, I suppose, to have a "new start." Can't you simply take the children—which, after all, also will be cheaper when it comes to divorce proceedings[?] And probably will make her "happy."

Bowden: No. we did not talk about Reuel but chiefly about him-self. You are quite right about the "redeemed" Bowden. He never was so nice before, never. As though something had happened to wake him up. I told him rather bluntly he had lived so far in a kind of fairy-tale land, and he replied: are you sure I am fit to live in any other kind of land? Which of course is the precise truth of the mat-ter. His hopes—you are right, but for the moment I do not see how he could go on without them. I still have a little fond hope for him and Carmen; and from this viewpoint, it may not be so crazy for him to go to Italy for vacations. I also tried again, and very persistently, to talk him out of romantic job and no-job adventures. He said, already a bit softened, if he does not quit, he will at least know who he is (meaning without courage, etc.). I shall call him shortly again. By and large, I think this is a catastrophe for him, and it is still better than no catastrophe ever.

From here nothing specially new. I accepted the proposition of Wesleyan University with their Advanced Study Center, first for Fall 1961. Well paid, no duties except one seminar for honors' stu-dents, special housing near New York, etc. So, why not? I also shall teach a graduate seminar at Columbia this coming fall. We plan to be in Europe around January. Nothing definite yet. I still am translating and cursing, but almost finished. The thing begins to look all right in German.

What do you think about this too-beautiful-for words summit per-formance?[1] This huge clownerie which the Century of the Common Man offers us, except that the common men, at least in this coun-try, literally do not give a damn. —This somehow reminds me that

PR gave a cocktail party for Quasimodo[2] and I went for a short time. Quite nice, with May Rosenberg having her first book out and radiant with happiness and much more bearable.[3] And Harold towering above everybody, and little Podhoretz, already soooo "tired" like the proverbial Jewish waiter, and, of course Alfred [Kazin] whom Harold described to me as resembling in walk and posture an arrogant Camel—and I incapable to get that image out of my mind.

By the way: Do you know the work of [Nathalie] Sarraute? I am reading the Planetarium in French, very very amusing and witty, excellently done, great sense of sarcasm and humour. Don't believe anything about the anti-roman [anti-novel] talk or that this has no plot. It has a beauty of a plot—a young ambitieux who tried by hook and crook to get his old aunt's apartment.

Heinrich asked me not to forget to send you his love. And will you kindly remember me to the gentleman in question?

Love and yours,
Hannah

1. In May of 1960, President Eisenhower, Premier Khrushchev, Prime Minister Macmillan, and President De Gaulle met for a Summit Conference in Paris. Its nebulous goals were scuttled and it broke up when Khrushchev demanded postponement because a U.S. spy plane had penetrated Russian air space, and was shot down, on May 1.
2. Salvatore Quasimodo was an Italian poet, a Communist, who won the Nobel Prize for Literature in 1959.
3. The novel, by Mary J. Tabak, Rosenberg's wife, was about life in the Hamptons, and was called But Not for Love.

Via Sansovino 6
Rome
May 25, 1960

Dearest Hannah:

[. . .] Rome is getting hot, and I don't like living here. It's not only the present circumstances; I never have. I don't like the Romans, who are very brutalized people, including the intellectuals. [Alberto] Moravia took me to a literary party the other day, and it was like all the other Roman parties I've ever been to, but this time I was more detached and didn't suffer from a sense of indignity and maltreatment as I generally have. It's as though one were on a crowded street car, with everyone pushing and elbowing and no one to tell the stranger where to get off. If one is a stranger at these parties one is simply shoved aside. Nobody tries to start a conversation with you; there is no idea of conversation—only literary politics and personal concerns. People who are introduced to you turn away and leave you standing in the middle of a room or a terrace like a suitcase left in a station for a crowd to stumble over. The only person, at this party, who had the slightest sense of manners (i.e., who took my fur jacket, talked brightly about the theatre, told me who the other people were, and brought some up to be introduced) was a young man from Lombardy—not yet Romanized. And over it all hangs a heavy blanket of boredom, which chafes the more sensitive ones like Chiaromonte (he was present too) and Moravia. They—and most of the others—keep breaking off their conversations and going into the hall to make a telephone call, as though they were in a stand-up cafe. There's no sense of the social at all; it's a totally unfamiliar medium to them. Nothing between the family and the street. Chiaromonte says the Romans never ask anyone to their houses; the parlor is almost never used, except for funerals. Unlike the dear Florentines, they have no notion of hospitality. It's the same with the city itself; it simply sits there, indifferently. I have no inclination to sightsee; it's somehow not tempting. And you can't do it on foot; you take a taxi and go to a museum and that's that. On the other side of the coin is Roman corruption: drugs, homosexuality, murder. Every day the paper is full of suicides: servant girls, journalists, and the young sons of the aristocracy who presumably "had everything to live for." And a German sculptor has been arrested for having in his studio (which was used for assignations) photographs of over a thousand Roman adolescent boys taken in obscene poses, to show off their charms. A nice place.

This weekend, thank God, I'm going to meet Jim in Vienna; blessed be Decoration Day. His work has suddenly gotten very heavy [. . .] and I've tried to be "good," telling him not to come if it's going to be tough at the Embassy. But he brushes that kind of talk aside. Margaret has suddenly agreed to an "immediate" divorce but in September. For some reason I don't understand she is set on having her parents come to Poland in August. To show off her mondanity? But she says if he will let her parents come she will either go to Alabana in September or let him go to France and start divorce proceedings there—a matter of six months anyway. Meanwhile, he has written a lawyer in Washington to draw up a separation agreement, with alimony provisions, etc., for her to sign now. That will be the test.

About the children, Hannah, I too think it is very bad to send the two older ones to boarding school. And especially to separate boarding schools. But the mother in a case like this (and in almost any case) has the right to the custody of the children, and apparently it is "custody" to *her* mind to put them in schools. This is all her notion. Whether he could persuade her that it would not be a social defeat (this must be how she thinks) to leave the children with him now is a question. My guess is that he is proceeding with her on the principle of one-thing-at-a-time, and first the divorce. This week he told her about me—outright, though not, I assume, that I am in Europe. The effect seems to have been salutary, even though she turned all the colors and said, "I hope you don't want a divorce just to marry Mary."!! But I shall hear more about this over the weekend.

Hannah, I don't know what you meant about my getting hurt, unless (as I thought) that he had the power to hurt me, that is to use me badly, as they say. Well, he has and he could. It surprised him in Zurich that he could; I mean that he could let himself do it, as it were in cold blood.[1] It surprised me too. Our joint surprise was perhaps rather funny—naive. But it "taught" him something and me something. We've both been mulling this over by mail ever since—rather mulling over the implications. The problem is how to curb this tendency (which is really, with him, a form of self-laceration) without closing off certain areas. I.e., my natural tendency would be not to tell him things that I expected would bother him and his would be not to show that he was bothered, not to let me see his suspicions or jealousy. But that way you would soon land in a relation of complete falsity—manipulating the truth and each other. And the point of this love is its honesty; everything is offered, nothing is held back. It's total, like total war, and that power or drive comes from him. I have never known another man who had it and I've also become aware of how prudent (in spite of being romantic) I've always been myself, how many precautions I take against being wounded. So there is the dilemma. If we aren't careful, he *will* hurt me, for I'm particularly alive to a sense of injustice, of being wrongly suspected or accused, and if he hurts me I will start protecting myself by congealing [sic]. And yet we don't want to be "careful."

Despite your warning that nobody ever changes for a mere woman, I think we shall both change a little. What's the use of falling in love if you both remain inertly as-you-were? If he hopes for an inner change, a release from the monotony of certain habitual reactions, that's partly why he's in love, why he troubled, so to speak, to fall in love instead of just having an affair. And the hope is part of the man as much as the habitual reactions. If you take him "as is" you take the hope too.

He really hates my seeing other people, people he doesn't know, here in Rome; that is, he hates the idea of my having pleasure apart from him. Ideally, he would be running a one-woman seraglio. At first, I thought this was crazy, absurd; I could hardly even take it seriously. But I've come rather to agree with him, though not by dint of persuasion. I find I don't want to have "fun" here; the idea has become meaningless and unattractive. And if I wanted to (I suddenly realize) it *would* be a betrayal. Of course, he doesn't mean the Chiaromontes or, even, I guess, Silone, but he's a little dark about Moravia and his wife. And in a strange way he is right. That is, there is some suspect element in my relations with the Moravias— not sex, of course, but the fact that I don't really like them in the way I do the Chiaromontes and Silone, as part of one's eternal family, but see them for the sake of novelty and distraction. (Don't think he and I have been discussing this; I've figured it out for myself, noting certain little voice-changes on the telephone.) But I would be a millstone around the Chiaromontes' necks if I saw only them and Silone, so I shall continue to be a little false and see the Moravias, etc., occasionally.

Dear Hannah, enough of myself and Jim. [. . .] I'm glad you took the Wesleyan job. What is your Columbia seminar to be on? I've finished the piece for PR and started another but it's going with leaden foot.[2] I read one book of Sarraute, in English, and found it somehow pedantic. But I'll try the Planetarium. Meanwhile, I've been reading [Michel] Butor (*L'Emploi du Temps*) and [Alain] Robbe-Grillet (*Jalousie*); these "scientific" novels, at bottom, all reduce themselves to detective stories, with "clues." The summit performance, from here, seemed rather frightening; everyone felt close to war, at least to a "Korea."[3] Distance or lack of it does seem to play a part; Miriam and I both trembled when we read the first headlines. I shall probably hear something from Jim about the whole business this weekend—especially about the U-2 [spy plane]. You can't talk about anything like that in a letter owing to Polish censorship. Please give my love and kisses too to Heinrich. How is he? When do you go to Palenville? Or, no, you're not going this summer; can that be right?

Much, much love,
Mary

1. "It" was West's angry reaction to Mary's "over-exuberant reminiscence" of the affair with Clement Greenberg.
2. The first piece was "The Fact in Fiction," *Partisan Review*, May–June 1960; the second, "Characters in Fiction," *Partisan Review*, March–April 1961.
3. This refers to the showdown (which broke up the summit meeting) between Eisenhower and Khrushchev over the U.S.'s U-2 "spy flights" above Russian territory.

New York
June 20, 1960

My dearest Mary—

I am writing not to write a letter but to do everything required to receive one. I am quite unhappy that I missed Bowden [1] and I feel quite uncertain about his coming into your neighborhood. I was away from New York, an idiotic affair at Baltimore, honorary degree together with Margaret Mead, a monster, and Marianne Moore, an angel. Only one nice thing to report: we were talking about being taken to college next morning and being fetched separately, each one by her department. I said non-committally: nice of them to bother, or something to that effect. Whereupon Mead (one better call her only by her second name, not because she is a man, but because she certainly is not a woman) launched into a diatribe [about] how much all these people enjoy being with US—celebrities, etc. Before I could even get properly mad, Marianne Moore: "My, my, I can only hope we will be enjoyable." And that was that. Then two days sightseeing in Washington, chiefly galleries, quite nice and restful.

Otherwise: I finished the translation [of *The Human Condition*] before going to Baltimore and I do no longer curse God, the world and destiny. We had a lovely dinner party with Denver, Frances, Tim and Eric [sic] Heller, and Tim and Heinrich got along quite well. [2] And Denver gets nicer as he gets older and more bored with what he is doing. I tried (and still try) to get away from Harcourt, Brace. No results thus far. I had thought they would be relieved;

instead they doubled the advance.[3] I also thought that somehow I only have to say: I am not happy, and all agreements will vanish into thin air before my constitutional right to pursue happiness. Ivanovich [William Jovanovich] seems to think differently. Well, I suppose it finally will turn out all right. I can't get myself to take these things seriously—at least, so long as I have no manuscript in hand.

Much more serious is that I have not the slightest idea where you are and if this letter will reach you. Is the divorce business still on for September? Dear, please let me know. You know I worry and I also have somehow the firm conviction that as long as I keep worrying, things will straighten out. As though this is my way of keeping my fingers crossed.

I saw Harold [Rosenberg] and it was again very nice. Except that May [Rosenberg] published her masterpiece [*But Not for Love*] and sent it to me and it is simply lousy. And there I am, caught, because I must say something nice. And the book is not only devoid of talent, it is also rather nasty and unpleasant.

What I should have written you long ago is that one day Nataly [Nathalie Swan Rahv] called, asking (true!) if I remember her! Well, she invited me in style and we had a wonderful couple of hours together. She is Diana, unmarryable [*sic*], quite happy that this is over, pitying Philip—who apparently wants to be taken back—because he is so "domesticated," at the same time, "admiring" him; she forgot, unfortunately, in all those years to inform him of her admiration. I had the impression that she wanted above all to hear from you, and I informed her. She seems to be very eager to renew the old friendship. I stuttered something about her perhaps having been offended by the Oasis. Whereupon: "I? For heaven's sake, I never minded, Philip minded."[4] She is quite wrapped up in her job and happy in it. Of an incredible decency and trustworthiness in every word. Asking questions like—Why is it that intellectuals (meaning Philip) can be so stupid? I tried to clear that up—distinction between power of judgment (lacking) and brainpower like animals "reckoning with consequences." She got that all right. By the way, she drank like a fish, but without bad consequences. Very strange, but thoroughly nice.

I am half toying with the idea to get some magazine to send me to cover the Eichmann trial.[5] Am very tempted. He used to be one of the most intelligent of the lot. It could be interesting—apart from being horrible.

Summitry: Well, the net result is that the status of Berlin has remained unchanged. In the long run, this Japan business—which also was handled as though we are now governed by a bunch of feeble-minded kindergarten kids—is more serious.[6] And Cuba[7]— Here [in New York] is again a certain mood among intellectuals for Stevenson, and that precisely when Schlesinger et al. decided to switch for Kennedy. But nothing is likely to come of it. It looks like either Nixon or Kennedy. It is rather nauseating.

Much love and yours,

Hannah

1. Broadwater was on his way to Italy.
2. Denver Lindley, who had moved to Viking, and his wife, Frances, a senior editor at Harper's, art historian Frederick (Tim) Clapp, and literary critic Erich Heller were close friends whom Arendt often invited to dinner.
3. This was for a collection of Arendt's essays, which was published in 1961, by Viking, as *Between Past and Future*.
4. Both Nathalie and Philip Rahv are caricatured in McCarthy's *The Oasis*—Philip, more severely.
5. Adolf Eichmann, Chief of the Gestapo's Jewish Office during World War II, had just been captured in Buenos Aires and transported to Israel to stand trial for crimes against the Jewish people. Arendt subsequently wrote William Shawn to see if the *The New Yorker* was interested in sending her to Jerusalem. It was.
6. After left-dominated riots broke out in Japan protesting the ratification by Japan of a mutual security pact with the United States, the Japanese government withdrew its invitation to President Eisenhower for a state visit.
7. In May 1960, Cuba's new revolutionary government approached the United States to discuss their deteriorating relations. The U.S. refused and ordered Texaco and Esso not to process Soviet crude oil. Cuba then seized the refineries.

Hotel Bristol

Warsaw

June 29, 1960

Dearest Hannah:

Aren't you surprised by the above address? I arrived here, with Jim, from Vienna night before last and am going to stay two weeks. Madame is in Paris, supposedly seeing a lawyer and finding a place to live for the fall. My presence here is probably the height of recklessness, but he wanted me to come and so I came. And I am wildly, bemusedly happy.

This all came about because his vacation was deferred by the arrival of government inspectors and I went, instead, to the Cultural

Freedom sideshow in Berlin. There I heard that Danny Bell and William Phillips were going to Warsaw. Jim said, "Why don't you come with them?" Well, I couldn't get a visa that fast, so I went to Vienna instead where he met me and we waited and by a miracle the visa was granted in record time. Meanwhile, William had dropped out of the party. But Danny is here.

It would take a typewriter (Jim is going to borrow one for me tomorrow) to tell you about the Congress. One simply can't tell it in plain old-fashioned handwriting. The main event, from the point of view of sheer scandal, was a series of furious clashes between Mr. Shils[1] and William, on the subject of mass culture, naturally. I swear Shils is Dr. Pangloss reborn and without Dr. Pangloss's charm and innocence. I said so, in *almost* as many words, when I got into the fight myself. Another feature of the Congress was [Robert] Oppenheimer, who took me out to dinner and is, I discovered, completely and perhaps even dangerously mad. Paranoid megalomania and a sense of divine mission. It throws some light on the Fuchs case.[2] I asked him why he came to the Congress, which he was describing as "evil" and "sinful," and he said he had a message for the Chinese people which he wished to transmit from Berlin in his opening address. I said, "Maybe the Chinese people got the message but I missed it." Well, it seems it was contained in a sentence that said, in effect, that in a nuclear war no country would have enough living to bury their dead. I must put in that Jim doesn't think that was so crazy (i.e., he thinks maybe the Chinese government did get and decode the message), and Chiaromonte too doubts that Oppenheimer is mad and sees him, rather, as a man playing a role of which he's uncertain—an actor not quite sure of his part. However, I saw *much* more of him than Nicola did and Jim did not see him at all. O. turned to Nicholas Nabokoff [*sic*], for example, and said the Congress was being run "without love." After he had repeated this several times, I remarked that I thought the word 'love' should be reserved for the relation between the sexes. Miriam thinks I must be right about him.

Why are men so unwilling to concede a simple obvious fact like that? They fear we women are 'rushing to conclusions,' I guess. George Kennan was there and gave a very good and stirring closing address (which ought to have crushed Mr. Shils and all his Luciferian camp forever) but the rumor was that he was crazy too, though only partly crazy. Examples of nonsense talked: that Shakespeare, if he were living now, would be writing for television (Frank Stanton, CBS), that Madison Avenue was no different from the sale of indulgences in Luther's time, that the Soviet Union is a society that promotes individuality, as witness Pasternak (George Fischer). And Sidney Hook was very funny putting God to the test of logical empiricism and disposing of Him. Aside from these public idiocies, the Congress was fun. I enjoyed the gathering-in of old friends and new ones, which had a sort of millennial character, including the separation of the sheep from the goats. West Berlin seemed highly unreal to me, like some Coney Island transported into Eastern Germany and, in its unreality, precisely fitted for such Congresses. In which, I gather, it specializes.

Warsaw, on the contrary, seems real, pretty, and almost pastoral, shimmering in a deep summer green of thick vines, with pots of red and white geraniums lining the streets and the window boxes of houses, and a gold Bellotto light on the churches.

I've never been so happy or so totally, entirely in love, so that it doesn't appear to be an emotion you feel but an element you've been submerged in. A fixed element like time or space. Do *not* worry: all is well. I feel so comfortable, strangely, as if I belonged here; he comes at lunch-time and brings me whatever is interesting in the mail and the paper and the office gossip and the magazines that have come in; then at five-fifteen, again very domestically. Yesterday we drove out in the early evening to see the children, who are living in a summer hut with their nurse on a bluff by a broad river. A wonderful place, deep in peasant life, and wonderful children. He sat down on a stool outside the cook house, took a manicure scissors, and proceeded to cut the children's toenails and the hair around the youngest one's ears, very competent, concentrated and yet laughing. We brought them provisions from Warsaw and presents from Vienna, and everyone was gay and buoyant, including the driver and the nurse, a handsome young woman, who brought me a big pink rose and set out a dish of fresh cherries. He is sacrificing these children and he knows it (he thinks there's really very little chance of his having them, except for summers and vacations) and everyone, perhaps even the children, must know it, and yet everyone was, somehow, rejoicing, as if only good could come out of this occasion, which of course is not true. The children love him;

that was it, naturally, and were pleased to see him delighted and lining us up and taking our pictures. There's something I don't rationally understand in all this, perhaps because I can't see it in any traditional way, as a conflict between love and duty or something of the sort. There does not appear to *be* a conflict, that's the trouble, or rather the very idea of a conflict seems implausible, and the fact that the children will undoubtedly suffer does not appear as a fact. It was the same when we went back to his place for dinner; the cook was in a transport of smiles and she was humming in the kitchen—the first time, he said, he'd ever heard her do this. All this, of course, is a tribute to him and the reverse of a tribute to Madame. But (perhaps I'm being sentimental) it seems also more than that, and as felt by the children too—a recognition of something good.

To change the subject. Jim brought me the spring issue of *Daedalus* yesterday, with your piece on mass culture,[3] and this filled me with pleasure too and a recognition (of what I'd nearly thought and hadn't quite). I like particularly your treatment of "society" as the antecedent of mass society. What I've felt in everything previously written on the subject is the creation of a false antithesis or pseudo-alternative [between society and mass society], even if that "alternative" is located in the past. The only thing that bothers me in your later discussion is the perhaps summary dismissal of "entertainment," which avoids meeting, it seems to me, the whole problem of quality as seen not only in films, TV, comic books, etc., but in cars, furniture, architecture, design—the mass of *things* that people live with and that constitute their culture more than digests of classics or films "based on" *War & Peace* or *New Yorker* profiles and fiction. It could be shown that here too a genuine culture had been consumed and chopped up into something else (i.e., the modern idiom of art and architectural inspiration converted into a chair of "good design" or the "free forms" of automobiles and airports). But I think it needs analysis. I also would say, myself, that reproductions of works of art (Van Gogh) mass-produced and mass-hung do destroy them. By sheer multiplication—if you see what I mean. Multiplication destroys them as one-and-indivisible. Yet this does not seem to happen with music (records) and obviously not with books. Jim points out (we were talking about your piece) that a musical composition does not have durability (in the sense of a statue or painting) except through repetition; this is also true of a novel, though somewhat differently, since a text does not require performance. But if it needs repetition to achieve durability, then repetition cannot damage it. Something of the sort. Now I must stop. Please, dearest Hannah, write me and put the letter in an envelope addressed James R. West, American Embassy, Warsaw, Washington 25 D.C. [. . . or, if later] to James West, American Express, Paris, Please Hold.

Much, much love and kisses to you.
And to Heinrich.
Mary

1. Edward Shils, a sociologist, was a member of the Congress of Cultural Freedom's Executive Committee.
2. Klaus Fuchs, a German-Jewish émigré physicist, had been hired by Oppenheimer to work at Los Alamos. He confessed to British agents in 1950 that he had passed information about atomic research there and nuclear research in Britain to the Russians during and after the war.
3. Hannah Arendt, "Society and Culture," *Daedalus*, Spring 1960.

[New York]
July 25, 1960

Dearest Mary—

Your letter was such a joy and the description of the Berlin Congress wonderful despite its brevity. I quite agree about Oppenheimer; mad or not mad, certainly unbearable in attitude and mentality. If he actually believes the Chinese need his cryptogram to know what every scientific and non-scientific magazine can tell them, he must be insane. But it is unlikely that he believes what he says—or even knows what it means to believe what one says. By the way, what happened in Time magazine? You probably saw your picture with quote?[1] What *did* you say? My guess—that is the way Western literature appears to some people behind the Iron Curtain. I am glad I did not come to Berlin. You are quite right, West Berlin is unreal though not quite like Coney Island, but it is not unreal to me, and should not be. I would have been ashamed to be in Berlin in a crowd of celebrities. I half promised some one of the Brandt government to come and discuss actual political topics with students and younger members of the trade unions from East and West Berlin for a couple of weeks. I may do it this winter.

The culture piece: I think I agree with your criticism especially about mass production of works of art. "Multiplication destroys" if the thing itself does not need repetition in order to remain in the world at all. But the incessant repetition of some piece of music destroys it too. Hence, rarity to an extent is indispensable. But I think the real trouble with the piece is simpler and more fundamental. Culture and art obviously are not the same—which I somehow assume. My concepts are not clean. I finished this piece in the meantime, re-wrote the part you know and added another (larger) part about culture (the approach or mode of intercourse with art and the things of the world) and taste.[2] I now like it much better. And am very curious what you will say. Taste as a principle of "organization"—that is, taste decides not only the question of which things we like or how the world is to look and to sound, but also *who* in the world belongs together. (Excuse the ungrammatical English, I write in a hurry, and somehow without even that small amount of patience which I usually manage to have.) We recognize each other by what pleases and displeases.

We live here with the conventions which we watch dutifully on television. Result: Thanks God [*sic*] that Stevenson did not get the nomination; it would have been a catastrophe. Kennedy made a good speech, excellent delivery. The only one with ideas seems to be Rockefeller whom I shall watch this week. The whole thing is rather fun and television a blessing. Quite interesting the extraordinary role of the running commentators who have it in their power to break every attempt at cheap demagoguery. As a rule, the commentators are much more intelligent than the politicians.

Did you get my letter which I still wrote to Rome? We have a most delightful summer here, cool, no humidity at all, sunny. We probably shall go away a couple of weeks or so next month (mail will be forwarded).

Write me how things are going. Divorce proceedings included. Any chance of your coming to New York? I miss you very much. But you will have to come through NY at least to get your divorce. Where will you be after Paris? Try to keep me posted. How is the novel?

Much love and yours,

H

1. McCarthy was quoted as saying in Berlin: "Western literature is the mirror on the ceiling of the whorehouse" (*Time*, July 4, 1960).
2. The revised essay appears in *Between Past and Future* as "The Crisis in Culture."

[upstate New York]
August 28, 1960

Dearest Mary:

Just a line to tell you how absolutely delightful your article in PR is ["The Fact in Fiction"]. It was such a relief to read some sense on this matter instead of the more or less sophisticated nonsense to which we usually are treated. By the way, also the way you said what you had to say. Very carefully, precisely, often beautifully.

I write to Rome because I have no other address. I presume the Paris address is no longer good. Did you get my letter? I wrote once to Paris and before that once to Rome.

We have been away from NY for a few weeks, shall go home end of this week. Very nice here, in the mountains at a Swiss boarding house; people speak French or Swiss German, a huge estate with several natural swimming pools, quite isolated. I am not doing much, had to prepare a paper for the Pol[itical] Sc[ience] Ass[ocia-tion] and now that is finished I am reading and getting lazy with hiking, swimming and sun-bathing.

Heinrich sends many greetings; he too was delighted with the article.

With love and yours,
Hannah

Bocca di Magra (La Spezia)
August 30, 1960

Dearest Hannah:

Your letter reached me here, and I was very pleased (a) to get it and (b) with the contents. I am always honored to have a fan letter from you—starting with the first, on The Oasis. The sensation of being honored doesn't diminish with familiarity. And will you thank Heinrich for liking the piece too? The only other person who had read it (not counting William Phillips, who niggled rather) was Jim; he liked it but then he is not literary, besides being in love. [. . .]

This is a charming place, a little fishing hamlet on the border between Liguria and Tuscany, looking out to the marvelous Apuan Alps with their shining white marble quarries. I came because the Chiaromontes were here and because, when I got back from France and Germany three weeks ago, Rome was deserted and ominous with the impending Olympics. I intended to stay only till the 1st of

September, but it is so beautiful and tranquil and inspiring that I've decided to stay till the 15th of September. Miriam found me an apartment overlooking the water and the mountains, and I've begun to do quite a bit of writing, getting up very early, so as to have three or more hours of work before we all go in a boat at eleven or eleven-thirty to a rocky cove where we swim. There is an extremely nice French-Jewish intellectual family in the apartment below me, who feed me lunch in the garden every day [Mario and Angélique Lévi]. At night I eat at the hotel en pension. The chief occupations are reading, swimming, and chess. There are loads of delightful children, French and Italian, who take part in all the expeditions—boat-trips and mountain climbs—and in much of the conversation. I am feeling wonderful.

Jim's and my vacation was a disaster in everything but the emotional sense. For one thing, it rained all the time we were in France except for one morning and one afternoon, so that we went swimming once in three weeks. But worse than the weather was the car, which had just had a new motor installed in Poland, and which broke down part by part all the way across Czechoslovakia, Germany, Alsace, Vosges, Brittany, Normandy, Ile de France, and then back again. It was in 19 garages, with its own complaints plus language problems. On the way back, we were forced to spend days and nights in places like Freudenstadt and Schwabisch Hall—charming places, actually, but one could not put one's mind on them when a car was being pushed, towed, taken apart. I will not bore you with the history of it but it was a mechanical nightmare. Harder on him than on me, but even I began to identify the car's insides with my own, having seen it hoisted so many times onto a sort of operating-table while mechanics pulled, wrenched, and hammered at its various tubes and organs.

One could say, however, that we "got to know each other," he and I (the car too), for we spent, he counted, 47 days uninterruptedly together, starting from when I left Berlin for Vienna. And since a good part of that was spent, literally, in garages, it was a testing of love. Indeed, without love, it would have been totally impossible. Normally, one would have jettisoned the car, but in the circumstances that was impossible; it *had* to get back to Poland.

He's now in Warsaw, where his wife's parents have arrived, from Washington. Their appearance, though much dreaded by him [. . .]

has turned out to be for the good. They have more sense, at least, than their daughter and have told her to give in and leave, the jig is up. Naturally, they (or at least the mother) are making all sorts of extortionate demands as to alimony, etc., but at least this is on a plane of reality or what is commonly considered to be reality. They have engaged a lawyer for her in Washington; he has a lawyer in Paris. Letters and legal documents are crossing. She is leaving Poland definitely not later than October 15 and probably earlier; when she leaves, as things stand now, she will have given her agreement to an Alabama divorce. As soon as the terms are firmly settled, with both lawyers' concurrence. She will get the children; there's no help for that, at least for the moment. And the 8-year-old boy will be going to boarding-school in England. I don't approve of this; neither does he much (though the child wants to go). But he can't divorce her, allow her the custody of the children, and then turn around and tell her how that is to be managed. At least, I don't see how he can. I fear that he is signing away too much, both in terms of money and control, in his eagerness to be finished with her. But it's hard to discuss these things on the telephone. [. . .]

Carmen was here, a few days ago. She had spent the summer in Venice, as did Bowden, and as did also her ex-husband Ernest Hauser né whatever he was [Meyerwitz] from Konigsberg. I can't convince myself that there's any possibility of her marrying Bowden, especially since she reports such details about him as that he's started lying about his age. . . . This struck me particularly as out of keeping with any love between them. She reports that he left Venice about ten days ago in good spirits, on the surface, and below the surface at least somewhat reconciled to the fact that "Mary will never come back to me." He was living with one of the poets of the Beat Generation—Gregory Corso (not a homosexual) and was very active socially, very malicious. He and his whole set—all younger people, in their twenties, mostly—drank a great deal. She felt that he had acquired the confidence of having "established himself" socially, though not in high society. I had only one letter from him all summer and that an unpleasant one, which I did not answer. His name for Jim, which he has put into circulation, is the Old Pretender. I gather that he thinks of himself as the Young Pretender. I remarked to Carmen that there was less than six years' difference in their ages, and it was then that she described his new obsession with youth. . . . She also reported the following: a question directed to her one night, "Do you think Hannah or I is stronger?" Carmen replied that she thought Hannah might be stronger, whereupon Bowden answered, "I wonder," or "Wait and see." This exchange referred, though indirectly, to the divorce. Carmen's account of this—the divorce—was somewhat ambiguous and mystifying. On the one hand, she said that he'd told Peggy Guggenheim, on leaving, that of course he would give Mary the divorce. But if I said I thought so too, she assumed a warning tone—rather gypsy-like—though her actual words were moderately encouraging. I did not know what to make of this and decided to put it down to some curious psychological tic. She thinks he may have begun (or will soon begin) to sleep with casual women, and that he will try to keep this secret from me because it's inconsistent with his line of not giving a divorce because of his belief in monogamy. I said, "But that's very unprincipled." And she said, "But that's the way he is." I myself would not have thought Bowden so unscrupulous; nor do I. I believe he will give the divorce this fall.

I hope all the above has not bored you. Naturally I'm more interested than you are in Bowden's character. . . .

It looks as if I would come back to America, for the divorce, some time in October, probably toward the end. Whenever Jim is able to come. Then there's a two-months' waiting period before you can get married. So that would be around Christmas time. If Bowden is recalcitrant, I really don't know what I shall do. I cannot face the prospect at all and so do not. This life (though not here in Bocca di Magra) is terribly wearing and tearing, not to mention expensive. It is much worse, of course, for him in Poland, especially now with the wife and the parents and the children *and* her brother all there, plus 21 Negro doctors, 43 Lutheran ministers, a "People to People" delegation, and a journalists' group, all of whom fall in his province. [. . .]

No more, dear Hannah. If you feel like writing here, do, or else write to Rome after the 15th [. . .] Jim sends you his regards. He has a great admiration for you and always asks me sternly "Have you written to Hannah?" "Have you heard from Hannah?" As though, "Have you said your prayers?" Much love to you and to Heinrich. I miss you so.

Mary

[New York]
9/16/60

Dearest Mary:

Your letter reached me in the midst of the Am. Pol. Sc. Ass. meeting so no chance to reply to Spezia [Bocca di Magra]. I got envious, especially about the swimming in the rocky cove. Suddenly, I saw all this before me, simply the sheer beauty of it and this possibility to swing in, as it were, and keep swinging and being content; this kind of utter simplicity which, it seems, is almost impossible to achieve in America.

I saw Bowden and I know quite well what Carmen meant when she reported the conversation about me to you. Mary, for heaven's sake, don't think it will be a breeze to get the divorce from him. He is under the impression that he is being treated as a quantité négligeable and though he will finally give in (about this, there is no doubt in his or in my mind), he will do whatever is in his power to make you aware of his existence. Maybe, it would be wiser to answer his letters and to keep up some kind of relation. I am on very good terms with him and I must say that he makes it easy for me. This is the first thing in his life which really hit him, no doubt, and it has changed him in many respects. I do not believe Carmen's gossip and, as far as I know, Corso is a homosexual. Bowden did not talk to me about this at all, but if I had any suspicions in this direction, it certainly would not be "the casual women" line. And, of course, not Carmen either. The sad truth of the matter is that he loves you and that he has discovered this in a sense only après coup, after you left him. It is not likely that this is going to change in a hurry, no matter with whom he sleeps or does not sleep. It also has nothing to do with any principles, such as "belief in monogamy." Mary, I hope this won't be a shock for you; it really should not. And God knows I don't like this role of having to report what he tells me, etc. Only, I am afraid you may make mistakes unless you know what exactly you are up against. [. . .]

I saw Dwight before he left for England, very much better than before. Being away from Gloria [his wife] seemed to help quite a bit. I also read some of his film criticism, not bad at all. I also saw William [Phillips] who gave a party for Snow[1] and Philip [Rahv] with the newest acquisition of his, pretty horrible, the acquisition I mean. Quite ugly and rather slightly mad. I am trying to get back to work. I think I wrote that I decided to go to Viking after all; Jovanovitch [sic] still tries to prevent me, but he will give in. It is no matter of interest, only of power, and I guess I can persuade him to let me go. I gave Viking the Essays which I enlarged and partly rewrote [*Between Past and Future*]. Now I am back to Revolution [*On Revolution*] and hope I shall be able to finish by the end of the year. Then we go to Europe, Heinrich, as he keeps telling me, for two weeks, and I probably for a little longer. Otherwise, nothing special, everything quiet. We enjoy the apartment which to me looks more and more like a ship. [2]

> Much, much love and yours,
> Hannah

[. . .]

1. C. P. Snow (1905–1980), a British novelist, wrote a much discussed essay around this time about the gap between science and literature.
2. The Blüchers had recently moved from Morningside Heights to an apartment on Riverside Drive, on Manhattan's Upper West Side.

> Via Sansovino 6
> Rome
> October 2, 1960

Dearest Hannah:

This is going to be a hasty letter and written under the somewhat depressant influence of penicillin and sulfa, so if it sounds strange don't mind. Your letter came shortly after I got back from Bocca di Magra; Jim was here in Rome at a meeting of Public Affairs Officers, and I was just recovering from the flu, which I'd caught at Bocca, in the damps of the last evenings. Hence its news came to me as from a remote distance. The other day, though, Carmen, at lunch in her gloomy, Spanish-style villa, embellished with roses from her rejected suitors and huge oil paintings of wild goats, treated me to some rather shivery prophecies of what Bowden was going to do (or not do). After seeing her, I had a relapse (no connection) and have just got up again today. And meanwhile I've been talking to Reuel on the telephone; he has been in Warsaw, staying with Jim.

Reuel's advice (volunteered to Jim) is that I must take immediate action to get a divorce. That, if I don't, Bowden will become fixed in his ideas and attitudes toward me and it. He says Bowden knows very well that I shall never come back to him, but that if I don't show him that I mean business about the divorce and will get it in spite of him at any cost, he will keep us all in the present limbo forever. This doesn't sound very logical, but I know what Reuel means.

Actually, before I talked to Reuel, I had written Bowden, asking if he would give the divorce now because something had come up— a lecture at Columbia—that would make it very convenient for me to come to America at the end of October. Also, I have to leave this apartment then; Carmen's lease runs out in the middle of October, and she's planning to take a new place. So that if Bowden would agree to the divorce, I would come to America and, incidentally, give the lecture; otherwise not. I wrote this four or five days ago and asked for a prompt answer, so that I could let the Columbia people know.

It was after this that I saw Carmen. Her warnings were not to expect a favorable reply, that the figure of *two years* had been flourished in Bowden's conversation, that his dominating idea was revenge, on Jim primarily and incidentally on me. That he no longer loved me but wished someone to pay for his sufferings. That his attitude toward me was malicious. (This I can well believe from the single letter I had from him this summer; it was not I, by the way, Hannah, who stopped writing; it was he. For more than a month I did not even have an address for him.) She also told anecdotes of Bowden serving dinner to guests in New York and saying, as he invited them to table, "Sorry, the Mrs. has run off with the silver." This, perhaps unfairly, made me absolutely furious. [. . .]

In a week, at any rate, I should know what to expect from Bowden. Could I ask you to do one thing for me? Possibly I've become too mistrustful (see above) but the thought has occurred to me that he could say yes, come back, I'll agree to the divorce, and then back down on it after I'd arrived, either from instability or from a sheer spirit of perversity, in order to be able to laugh at me. It strikes me that he would be less likely to do this if someone else, someone he respected, knew that he had said yes, come. (That is, if he does say yes.) Could you talk to him, please, if only on the phone? Say that you had heard from me and wondered whether I was coming or not. Just so that he would be on record. I don't ask you to urge him, only to find out. If he says no, that is another matter. Then I shall take Reuel's advice and see lawyers to learn how one gets a divorce when the other party is unwilling. [. . .]

[. . .] I must do something, especially since Jim's divorce is really advancing. She is in Paris, finding an apartment and seeing lawyers, and is not coming back to Warsaw except to pack and leave, when the separation agreement has been signed. It will be a grim position if he is alone in Warsaw, having parted from his family, and I am in Nevada or somewhere for a year. [. . .]

My own opinion is that Bowden will say yes and live up to it, but no one seems to share this but Miriam Chiaromonte and she and I have not talked about it recently.

While Jim was in Rome, he met the Chiaromontes and fell for Nicola—yes, hard! This to me was an astounding surprise, for I'd worried, not at all about Carmen and Miriam, but about what the two men would find in common. And the liking seems to have been reciprocated; they talked to each other afterwards on the phone and murmurs passed of the "beginnings of a friendship." Nicola said to me, afterwards, "He is a very nice man." Which is praise. [. . .]

To say a final word about Bowden. I do not agree with you that he loves me. If he did, he would not have sat in Venice all summer making spiteful remarks about me and drinking cocktails and leading a bravura social life; he would have tried, I think, to see me, which would not have been hard. Or written me in a friendly way. At least to find out how I was. Certainly, he's been very much hurt, and his behavior is compatible with that. And he finds it less painful and more dignified, as a role, to say that he loves me than to say that he has been hurt. He has entered the love-competition and is playing a solo part in it—the man who loves alone, all alone on the stage. The fact is, I am not necessary to this performance; hence there was no reason to seek to see me. Jim was certain he would try to see me, and I was afraid he would and knew I would have to say yes, even if Jim did not like it. And I thought my heart would be wrung if I saw him in Rome, where we'd been together so many years ago. As it was, I was spared that and am grateful. But he did not spare me out of kindness.

Forgive this self-absorbed letter. I miss you and am hoping I can come home, not only for the divorce, but to see you. I was so pleased to have a letter from Nancy [Macdonald] saying you'd accepted to be Spanish Refugee Aid chairman. I think you'll enjoy it in a way; at least I did. [1]

Dear Hannah, give Heinrich my love. I am sorry to put you in the position of a go-between and if you don't want to call Bowden, don't do it. I shall not blame you. Do write me a line about the awful UN goings-on; one can hardly open the paper here without a premonitory shudder for what America is doing next. It is certainly the Triumph of the Little Man. [. . .] And Kruschev [*sic*].[2] It struck me the other day that he was not a human being but a figure in a serial comic-strip; that is what he looks like, an outline-drawing.

Much, much love to you,
Mary

1. Arendt succeeded McCarthy in 1961 as chairman of Spanish Refugee Aid, an organization founded by Nancy Macdonald to assist refugees of the Spanish Civil War living in France.
2. McCarthy probably refers to Khrushchev's vow, issued at the United Nations in September 1960, to "bury the West."

Via Sansovino 6
Rome
October 7, 1960

Dearest Hannah:

I fear I sounded very shaky over the phone. I *am* shaken. I don't know what you can do—nothing, I guess. The only thing, though, I think, that will affect him is the withdrawal of public approval (or what he feels is public approval) for his course of action.[1] In any case, I withdraw mine, that is, my non active *dis*approval, for up to now I've tried to take the line, even with myself, of understanding. If he still hoped for me to come back to him, I could still understand a little. But Reuel says, *underlined*, that Bowden now realizes fully that that will never happen.

I believe Jim will get his divorce and fairly soon. What disturbs me is not to have *any* idea whether, when he gets his divorce, we shall be able to marry or not. If not, the position will be intolerable. He will be in Poland, divorced, having sent his children away, and on a very reduced income because he will be paying a heavy alimony. And I will be where? I cannot live in Poland, undivorced and unmarried to him, because, aside from the diplomatic complications, I cannot get anything but a visitor's visa to Poland, that is, for a stay of three or four weeks. Nor will he be able to come out as he has been doing because he will not be able to afford it. [. . .]

You can't imagine, I think, how harrowing this uncertain situation is. Love apart, there is the impossibility of making plans ahead, the lack of a stable place to live, the prospect of being separated again from one's books and papers and living in hotels. All this, of course, is not sheerly dependent on Bowden; there is Margaret too. There are times when I feel inclined to tell him to throw up his job (he has proposed this) and that we will live together without being married. But this opens a new avenue of uncertainty, especially with the alimony and the child support; a man in his forties doesn't resettle in a new kind of job so easily.

I do not trust myself to write to Bowden yet, for I am too tremulous with anger, disappointment, and incredulity. Yes, incredulity, for I cannot see in what possible way he justifies this refusal to himself. Or for that matter to anyone else. In what way does his allowing me to be free depend on the date of Jim's freedom? This attempt to exercise control and to arbitrate in a godlike style seems to me completely shocking. Miriam says he must learn that he is not omnipotent, and I agree.

It strikes me (and I may as well say this) that he has somehow persuaded you that he is right. Or at least reasonable. Perhaps I am getting paranoid, to imagine this, but it is a suspicion that creeps over me. If he has, *how?* You take it as natural that he would not give a divorce until Jim has his, but I don't find this natural at all. One agrees or one does not agree to do a certain thing, but one does not, in any normal relation, tantalize the other person with the hint of a decision "later on," when other factors would be adjusted. Of course, even if he said to me directly that he would give me a divorce the day Jim was divorced, I would no longer trust it. His way of showing his sincerity ought to be very simple: by giving me the divorce now.

I would never go back to Bowden, Hannah, under any circumstances: if Jim were killed in an air crash and I no longer had any personal life left. And if he knows that, knows that it is inalterable, then why postpone? The date of Jim's divorce is irrelevant to what has happened to Bowden and me.

I begin to sound shrill. Like a lawyer. Forgive me. I must stop. Oh dear, I do wish I could have come home. I do miss you. Forgive the suspicions above but I thought it better to voice them.

Love, much love,
Mary

1. Broadwater had written McCarthy that he would not be ready to give her a divorce until West got his divorce.

[New York]
October 8, 1960

Dearest Mary:

I just talked to Bowden, did not tell him that I had called earlier nor that we had talked long distance.[1] [. . .] He read me your letter (I let him do it assuming that you won't mind) and told me his answer. My line was: If you give her the divorce *now*, you will still be friends, if not, you will embitter everything unnecessarily. The delay does not make sense, since you know it is only a delay. He said two things: a) he had figured he would give you the divorce at the latest one year after West has obtained his divorce, possibly earlier. b) He is kind of curious what you are going to do. I repeated: Give it now and be friends. He said: "Let us see what her reaction to my letter will be. I shall think it over then and call you and we may then have a consultation." I let it go at that point, it seemed to me unwise to appear as though I was pressing him.

My impression is as follows: If you start proceedings now against his wishes you will have to take into account that he will try to make things harder at every single step. It will take you at least a year, probably longer, and during this year, you won't be able to live where you please, which is rather important. You will not have gained time compared with his proposition to give you the divorce one year after the other divorce. You will only have made an enemy—something which he is not now. I suppose he will call me as soon as he receives your reply to his letter—assuming that you do reply. I shall try then again. I may be able to persuade him, although I am of course not at all sure of this. [. . .]

My dear, I think it perfectly beastly that you lose the apartment [Carmen's] and I can well imagine that this kind of life in limbo is kind of hell. Since—as I learned from your letter to Bowden—the ambassador has been informed, can't you take an apartment in Warsaw and let things take their course? That is not ideal, but probably much less nerve-wrecking [sic].

I am writing in a hurry, just the bare facts. [. . .] Nothing especially new from here. Oh, yes, I met Jovanovich and, to my amazement, rather liked him. He behaved like a gentleman and everything is all right. Also: We now plan to go to Europe around the 10th of January. For about 3 weeks, perhaps a bit longer. I decided that I wanted to attend the Eichman-Trial [sic] and wrote

98

to the New Yorker. (Just three lines, nothing elaborate.) Shawn called me and seemed to agree to let me go for them with the understanding that he does not have to print whatever I may produce, but that they would pay my expenses, or at least the greater part of it. This suits me fine. When I shall go, I do not know. The trial, originally set for March, has been postponed and they think it will last the better part of a year!! I don't yet know how I shall handle this, but I certainly shall not be in Israel the whole time. Hence, it now looks as though I shall be back in NY beginning February, go for one week to Vassar in March for an international Conference, then go for 2 months to Northwestern and fly to Israel in June for several weeks.

Love for you, and regards to Jim West, and please don't get frantic!

Yours,
Hannah

1. This letter, which followed McCarthy's transatlantic call, was written before Arendt received McCarthy's previous letter.

Grand Hotel
Warsaw
October 26, 1960

Dearest Hannah:

Please forgive me for not answering your letter sooner; I left Rome in a great flurry of putting things into storage shortly after getting it and have been in motion ever since. [. . .] Now I shall stay put, more or less, for the 30 days of my visa, except for going down to Cracow to visit Reuel.[1] [. . .]

Let me see where to begin. Well, first I think it's a wonderful and strange idea for you to go to the Eichmann trial for the New Yorker; I can't help grinning at the conjunction and wondering how it will come out. I like to think of you and the New Yorker grammar and checking department. . . . And if you and Heinrich, on your other trip, are in Europe in January and February, maybe we four will all meet. I should like to believe that I shall be married by that time.

I want to tell you, but you alone, that I am not going to accept the notion of waiting on Bowden's pleasure. I went to Paris and got legal advice, from an American lawyer, who turns out to be one of my readers and who is absolutely of my opinion on this point. So is Reuel—even more forcefully in direct conversation than he was on the phone to Rome. His conviction [is] that Bowden will never agree to a divorce and that if I want one I must take action. Even before I saw Reuel I had decided in my own mind that I was not going back to Rome and look for another apartment when my visa expires. Or going anywhere else except directly to get a divorce. The where of this is now being worked on by the lawyer.

I am more deeply in love with Jim than ever and vice versa, and it is simply too ridiculous for us to be the passive foils of other people under the circumstances. So that is that. Margaret has taken an apartment in Paris beginning December 1. She ought to leave here before that, with or without the children. Meanwhile Jim, whose patience has given out with the delays, has moved out of the apartment and is staying in this hotel, in a room across the hall. He has not told the Embassy that he has done it, which would be a form of asking their advice; he has just done it. So far it is not generally known, for Margaret has her own motives for keeping it quiet—her social standing. He stops in every day at home to see the children, but that's all. He has told her that entertainment must stop and he is about to get rid of one of the servants; she is now down to two and a sewing woman! At the same time, her parents are pressing her to hurry up with the divorce. I am sorry for her but not very. [. . .]

At the same time, as I think I told you, the new house the government is fixing over for him is almost ready, and the administrative officer told him that he'd better hurry up and pick out the furniture because if he didn't the government would. So we met in Copenhagen and chose furniture and have been struggling with budgets, measurements, samples of material, catalogues, prices. This business of the house and furniture rushing at us, unprepared, is quite funny, and so was my determined encounter with Danish modern, which ended—at least temporarily—in a personal victory. The house is going to be very pretty, and in a different vein from the other houses I've had. (Government policy doesn't allow you to buy antiques or any kind of old furniture; it has to be new.) I've had to pick out every item down to the last toilet-paper holder and soap dish; Jim had to go back to Warsaw after three days and left me in Copenhagen to finish the job. You can't imagine how difficult it is in Denmark to find chairs and sofas to sit down on that don't look like manifestoes and bathtubs and toilets that aren't colored and lighting fixtures that don't resemble sculpture. But it was fun.

To make the above clear, the government pays for all the furniture, except, oddly enough, waste baskets and ash trays and table linen (sheets and towels, yes), but you have to leave it behind you for the next person. Anything you want to keep you call "personal" and pay for yourself. I came back with some "personal" white glass candlesticks and a green glass lamp and some tangerine-colored material.

Anyway, the Polish contractor who is doing over the house was quite bewildered when I turned up with Jim and took measurements and examined everything; he had just recently been repainting Jim's apartment with Margaret in it. From this point of view the situation is a marvelous comedy of modern life. Including Scandinavian Modern.

Reuel was here over the weekend, and we spent a great deal of time together. He is unhappy about a painful love affair he left behind him in New York. He likes Jim *very* much, and it is mutual. This did a great deal for my spirits. He said he'd written Bowden straight out that he liked Jim, and I'm glad he did it, though Jim flinched for Bowden's sake. Jim had been very direct with him, as well as kind and concerned, and this directness and honesty went to Reuel's heart apparently. A student friend of Reuel's, a boy from Notre Dame, was with us part of the time, and there was a great deal of laughter and affection. Reuel remarked that it was a pity that Bowden had only seen Jim "at his worst," i.e., tight, tense, saturnine, and unhappy. He meant that this fact furnished Bowden with an argument which he could half or three-quarters believe.

Somehow, since leaving Rome, I've become confident that all will be well, and soon. Leaving was a kind of clarification, and I am feeling very happy and content. Your solution, of an apartment in Warsaw, would not work, Hannah. A) I couldn't get a visa, as a visitor, for longer than 30 days. B) I couldn't get an apartment, because of the housing shortage. C) There is always the Embassy. At the moment, my being here has passed unnoticed, except by the police and a few chance Poles; Margaret knows about it but apparently has said nothing. But that (its passing unnoticed) is because I'm staying at the hotel "nobody stays at" and I must say for good reason; it's new, ugly, uncomfortable, cramped, and rather spooky.

We've avoided the places foreigners go and are trying to hide without hiding. But that of course can't last forever. We're hoping it will last till I go to Cracow to see Reuel, just so as not to seem to be wantonly *provoking* a scandal. At the same time, we've decided that we will stay together no matter what. [. . .]

Now I must stop. I'm about to start trying to work on my novel again, though conditions in this room are very poor for that.

Much, much love to you. I hope I didn't offend you by what I said in my last letter about your seeming to condone Bowden's behavior, or whatever expression I used. I was really giving vent to a sense of mystification (sharply felt by Miriam Chiaromonte also) as to how people could accept Bowden's dicta as somehow "in order"— not shocking or surprising. As though there were some element in it known to you in New York and unknown to us in Italy. Nicola felt that if only someone talked to Bowden he could come to his senses and stop this performance. He could not believe that this would not be so. The only explanation Miriam and I could think of (I mean for the lack of indignation) was that from New York my life abroad—Rome, Vienna, France, Zurich, etc. —probably sounded very glamorous and enviable, while to us in Italy, close up, it seemed harried and difficult. Not to mention expensive. Or that Bowden was circulating some slanders about Jim that in the absence of any defense carried weight.

Well, enough of this. If you can clear up my mystification, please do. If the Chiaromontes had not felt as I did, I would almost have thought that I was the one who was crazy.

Love again and to Heinrich,
Mary

P.S. Do please write. [. . .] I seem to get letters chiefly from publishers. By the way, I'm not at all surprised you liked Jovanovich. It is funny, but one does.

1. Reuel Wilson was studying Polish and Russian in Cracow.

[New York]
November 11, 1960

Dear Mary,

I forwarded a letter to your Warsaw address a few days before I received your letter; it was sent to my address. And I do hope you received a letter from Bowden giving you the divorce. So, let us hope that that is that.

I am writing you today under the assumption that the divorce business is settled. I did not want to reply to your letters earlier. For you are right, of course, not that I "condone" Bowden—which to me does not make sense one way or another—but that there are things which I do not understand. As I see it, Bowden has not delayed, was not even in a position to delay, your marriage or anything you wanted to do by one week or by one day or even by one hour. This could happen only if he would refuse the divorce after Jim West had received his divorce. This was the reason why I never understood that you wanted to press this point. Obviously, he is not only not omnipotent but utterly powerless, and you know as well as I do that under such circumstances it is only natural for people to dream up some possibilities of power. Practically speaking, the only point that matters is that he agrees to give you the divorce as soon as you need it. Everything else is just talk. And if this talk consoles him at this moment, I see no harm in it.

Since I wanted to persuade him, I have seen quite a bit of him during the last few weeks. I could do this only my way and I am sadly aware of the fact that it was not the way you would have wanted me to do it. The alternative was to let things well enough alone, and this I did not dare to do because it seemed as though I had some influence. Hence, I talked to him without any threats or even implications of an 'or else'. I talked to him as a friend and I did not lie. For to me the fact is that you brought him into my life, that without you he never would have become—not a personal friend which, of course, he is not—but a friend of the house, so to speak. But once you placed him there, you cannot simply take him away from where he is now. As long as he does not do something really outrageous which he has not done so far and really turns against you which he has not done either, I am not going to sit in judgment. That his life is in ruins is quite obvious to anybody who is willing to have a look at him and his situation. I am quite convinced this was inevitable, and if he were to commit suicide which, I think, is not probable but not altogether impossible either, I would be the first to tell you that you are not to blame. But it is not exactly when one feels like adding insult to injury. I never believed that you would or could or should go back to him. But if I had been under any such delusion my conversations with him would have convinced me of the sheer impossibility. [. . .]

I do not know what Bowden finally wrote you, I did not want to ask or even [be] told. If he still insisted on the priority of the other divorce, I am reasonably sure that this plays no longer a great role in his thinking or rather dreaming; I believe you will have no difficulties if you start proceedings through your lawyer even now. You say you cannot trust him. Perhaps you are right, perhaps you are wrong, I have no idea. But it strikes me that you can forget so easily that you trusted him enough to be married to him for fifteen years. Or to put it another way: You write that it is just "too ridiculous" for the two of you (Jim West and you) to be "the passive foils of other people." If you want to look at the matter in these terms at all, then it seems to me rather obvious that you both are the victims of your own, self-chosen past. This may be inconvenient but it is not ridiculous, unless you wish to say that your whole past was not only a mistake, but a ridiculous one.

There is one more thing which I must tell you even though I suspect you know it already. Bowden told me some weeks ago that *Paris Review* had bought a story of his (for $500).[1] [. . .] I said: Congratulations, was glad he had something to hold on to, and forgot it promptly. Now however, he came and asked me to read the story. It was written some seven or eight years ago, and is about his marital situation with you in the background which actually is a foreground under the name 'd.w.'. You certainly know the story, and I do not know what you think of it. It occurred to me suddenly that Paris Review might have bought the story because of its news-gossip value and that the whole business may turn out rather annoying. But I do not know. —Mary, my Dear, I miss you! Much love and the best of luck. Yours, H.

1. Bowden Broadwater, "Ciao," *The Paris Review*, Winter 1961.

Grand Hotel
Warsaw
November 23, 1960

Dearest Hannah:

Yes, I got Bowden's letter, saying he would give a divorce when Margaret was free. And I feel greatly better for having it, even though at this moment the prospects of the other divorce have again receded. The point, for me, has been all along to want to *know* that when Jim got his divorce we could marry. Without this, his efforts would be not only painful but possibly fruitless.

This has been, in many ways, a terrible month—an agonizing seesaw—and I am, we both are, worn out by the strain and suspense. Letters back and forth to lawyers, the formulation of new drafts, always about the same thing (the custody and education of the children), delays in the mail, fearful domestic scenes and wrangling. Meanwhile, except for ten days in Cracow and southern Poland with Reuel, I've been living hidden in this hotel room, seeing no one but Jim, for lunch and dinner (except when official functions prevented), sometimes going out in the afternoon for a walk on streets where I'd not be likely to be noticed. It has given me a rather interesting view of the underside of Poland—my own anonymity corresponding to the anonymous character of the modern socialist state. Everything I saw before—everything personal and private— has been ruled out of my present life, with the result that I've been able to observe mass Poland in a pure state: the colorless crowds milling along the grey streets, the shops and restaurants all alike and all carrying the same products, the bookstores with the same books, in the hotel mass tourism (parties of Chinese, North Koreans, East Germans, Bulgarians, checking in and out under the supervision of their guides, eating in the hotel dining-room at long tables with their national flags in the middle, all badly dressed and nearly all carrying cameras and all low-voiced or silent). This on the outside, and *in* your hotel room, the listening device. Wow! The chief variety was provided by three visits to the Ministry of Internal Security to have my visa renewed.

Yet the business with Margaret (into which the Embassy has now entered) has been so depressing that we've come to look on my hideous room with flowered bedspreads and curtains decorated with Red stars and the listening device in the lighting fixture as a tenderly loved home and refuge. As though we were living a peculiar modern idyl: intense love in extreme conditions, to be transcribed by the Secret Police.

The current position is this. About ten days or two weeks ago, the Embassy took official notice, and Jim and Margaret were invited to "keep up appearances" until their affairs were settled, i.e., to appear at certain public functions together, to give a luncheon, etc.

He complied. She was delighted, since she's interested only in keeping up appearances. Nothing was said about me or my presence in Poland, fortunately, but this made us even more nervous about not being seen and about phone calls in the middle of the night and knocks on the door—the result, I think, of chaos and inefficiency rather than of a campaign of harassment, but still unsettling.

At this point, Jim decided he would have to take action. Margaret had come back from Paris with nothing done about a divorce; she'd found an apartment on which he'd paid the first month's rent for her, but she then announced she was not going to use it, that she might not leave Poland till February or later. February would then be April (because of the little girl's school); April would be June, and so on. So he made up his mind to go to the ambassador, and tell him the truth about his predicament. That Margaret would not leave Poland, and that he himself was ready to resign from the foreign service or ask for a transfer—whatever was necessary to detach her from himself. The ambassador listened, was sympathetic, and today called them both in and gave them an ultimatum. That Margaret would have to leave Poland by the end of December and take some action to show that she was really going to do so or that, failing that, he would have to ask for Jim's transfer by the end of this week. That he did not want to do this but would have no choice since the situation had become "an embarrassment to the Embassy." So she is to make up her mind before Friday. If she says, "All right, transfer him," that at least would move the problem out into the West, where he and I could *perhaps* be together without causing such a scandal and where he could perhaps set up a separate establishment even without a legal separation. But he would lose his hardship pay ($4000 a year extra for behind-the-Iron Curtain), which would make him poorer and less able to pay her the alimony and maintenance she has demanded; moreover, he thinks that in the end such an arrangement could not [be] tolerated anywhere by the Foreign Service and that if she's obdurate, he will have to resign. Which will leave him, of course, with no money except his income from a trust, about $4,500. Until he finds another job, and he's 46 years old and has spent most of his life in the military and foreign service. So there it stands. [. . .] He says that after his interview with the ambassador, offering to resign, he felt "small and light."

The story is a little more complicated than I've made it; she has talked a great deal, with her love of attention, to Poles and other people about him, to the point where her indiscretions have been in danger of getting him declared *persona non grata* by the Polish government or so her mother warned her. And some of her indiscretions have come back to the Embassy. [. . .]

Excuse me for running [on] about this, which must be boring to you. Maybe I'll destroy this letter rather than tire you with it. But my mind is stuck on this track except when I try to work, which I do every day, though at a dragging pace.

My visa has been renewed, but only till December 2. From the point of view of the scandal, I ought to have left long ago but I did not have the heart to. I shall probably go to Paris or else to Rome and will let you know which and where.

Thank you for your intervention with Bowden; I didn't know what had persuaded him to change, not having heard from you, and was inclined to think that perhaps Reuel's letters to him had had some influence. Reuel seems to be extremely attracted by Jim; I think he feels the lack of a virile and straightforward man in his family. Bowden is a child, and Edmund is an old woman. As for me, my love has become boundless or, rather, very definitely bounded and contained by these four walls.

> But much, much love to you
> and Heinrich,
> Mary

P.S. I kept this to mail in Paris. My address—till January 1 at least—will be 6 Rue Antoine Dubois, Paris 5 [the apartment Jim had just rented for his wife]. She *has* agreed to leave by the first of the year.

[New York]
Christmas 1960

Mary, darling—

the scarf is so breath-takingly beautiful that I don't even know how to tell you that you should not. Which nevertheless is the naked truth! Oh Mary, how I wish you were here and how tired I am of this letter writing. I somehow had the feeling during the last week or so that you would suddenly stand in the door. Then your gift arrived and I changed dresses to try it out. It is simply marvellous, almost too beautiful to become a use-object. But still it would have been better if you would have stood in the door.

I hope this letter reaches you in Paris. I saw Straus[1] the other day and he said you planned to be married by March 1. Does that mean that finally everything has worked out alright? And when will you come to have your divorce?

Because of the Eichmann trial I had to rearrange my plans.[2] I am going to Northwestern now, that is, for their winter quarter from January to beginning of March. If the trial is not postponed, I shall then have to leave immediately for Israel. All this was quite awkward. Heinrich and I had planned to go to Europe in January for a few weeks, only for personal reasons—see Jaspers and Heinrich's friend Robert Gilbert.[3] Plus one week in Rome. Heinrich's college starts only in February and I hate to leave him alone for the last weeks of his leave. At least, he promised to come and see me for his birthday, end of January.

This time of the year is hectic as usual. Even I have to give a dinner party—you can see how bad it is. For Auden and the Lowells[4] and Erich Heller. They probably all hate each other, I hope not, but if they do, I can't help it. I saw Lowell several times and we talked at great length. He somehow intrigues me and I think I like him. By the way, he really loves you, I don't think he pretended for my sake. His mental health seems to be perfect. Despite all this, I have worked rather well. But everything takes so much more time than one hopes it will. I am in the midst of the last section of the Revolution book and I hate to interrupt it again. But I think I shall finish it in Northwestern where I have only a seminar once a week and lectures twice a week. Since I leave so early, I had to give extra sessions here in Columbia which I did not mind because the class is so very good. We meet once a week and read Plato together and by now have become like old friends. Graduate Seminar in political theory.

I shall be in New York till January 8. My address in Evanston: Library Plaza Hotel. [. . .] Heller reserved a two-room apartment in walking distance from the University. Will you be able to come when and if you come to the country? And please write me where you will be after January 1.

Incidentally, I suppose Chiaramonte [sic] asked you too to sign this declaration in support of the 121.[5] Did you sign? I finally did—

though with misgivings. What decided me was the torture business which unfortunately was not mentioned in Chiaramonte and Silone's draft.

Love, dearest Mary, and all the wishes in the world. And greetings to West.

And yours,
Hannah

1. Roger Straus, Jr., a friend of both Arendt and McCarthy, founded the New York publishing house Farrar, Straus, later Farrar Straus Giroux.
2. One of the cancelled plans was the Vassar lecture. "To attend this trial is somehow, I feel, an obligation I owe my past," Arendt explained in her January 2, 1961, apology to the college (Elizabeth Young-Bruehl, Hannah Arendt: For Love of the World [1982], 329).
3. The writer and composer Robert Gilbert (1899–1978) had been a close friend of Blücher in Berlin in the 1920s.
4. W. H. (Wystan Hugh) Auden (1907–1973) was one of several poets for whom Arendt felt a special sympathy; the Lowells were poet Robert and his wife, Elizabeth Hardwick.
5. The 121 was a group of French writers and artists—among them, Sartre, Simone de Beauvoir, and Simone Signoret—who signed a controversial statement supporting FLN resistance in Algeria.

1 bis Rue Clément Marot
Paris 8,
January 17, 1961

Dearest Hannah:

I ought to have answered sooner your very nice letter, which made me jump with delight to get it. But my life here has been crossed with all sorts of tedious, time-consuming difficulties—the latest being an impossible surly maid whom Reuel (who was here for the holidays) finally inspired me to fire and who left, refusing to give up her back-door key and uttering various threats: that she would have the Law on me, that we weren't Americans but Poles, Russians, dirty spies, that she would come back to *surveiller* me. I moved out of my earlier place, which was in a pleasant *quartier*, near the Odéon, but which had every defect an apartment could possess, including being expensive and depressing. The present place is not bad, except for the maid who came with it and who had been preying on a feeble-minded rich English-Jewish girl—the real tenant. But life in Paris seems to be like that now; Left Bank or Right Bank, the French strike one as hysterical and chauvinistic; at the slightest criticism of an apple in the market, they start screaming at you about *la France,* "*vous êtes en France, vous savez.*" Reinhold Niebuhr's daughter,[1] who is here studying at the Sorbonne, told me that she was struck by a storekeeper in the Marché Buci because she touched a pear.

I'm pleased you liked the scarf; I quite liked it myself and hoped you would.

Yes, when will we see each other? Will you come here on your way to Israel? I have my present place till the first of March; after that, I don't know. Bowden has written me offering to go to Alabama himself and get the divorce if I would pay his flight for him. His letter was very disagreeable, not unlike the *femme de ménage*'s departure scene; he said he did not wish to hear from me further, except through my lawyer, that his feelings for me were contemptuous, etc., and he implied that I had somehow defrauded him of some money. I begin to wonder whether I've not unwittingly become the sort of person such accusations fit. My 'I'—I don't mean my ego but the self I thought I was familiar with—has become rather battered in the past few months, so that I hardly recognize it when it talks and suspect all its utterances as being specious or at least of coming from some undefined source. I think [it] must be partly the result of continual moving, usually from one uncongenial spot to another, and partly the result of love, which does seem to have the faculty of taking your identity away from you and not always in the way the poets mention. But I'm doing my best to steady myself, to work and resist nightmare fugues. I'm putting together a book of essays for Roger Straus [*On the Contrary*] and am just finishing writing up the last piece ["Characters in Fiction"]—the third of the lectures I gave in Europe last year.

One strange thing. Whenever I cry and afterwards reproach myself for weakness, I say to myself sharply, "You never would have been able to stand a concentration camp," as though this were the test one had to be ready to meet, even if one never met it. I wonder what the equivalent for this was in the past. Martyrdom for Christians up through the Middle Ages. But after that?

Perhaps it is always martyrdom, in one form or another, that one childishly feels one must ready one's soul for. Or maybe this is just my Catholic training.

Anyway, to get back to Alabama, I was relieved by Bowden's offer and accepted it. I wasn't eager to interrupt my work and come to America, especially when I knew you were going to be in Evanston [at Northwestern] and that therefore I probably wouldn't be able to see you. If Bowden goes by the end of this month and Margaret goes by the end of this month, Jim and I could be married the first of April. She was supposed to leave Poland for Washington and Alabama today, but instead (naturally) she got sick. However, she has her ticket for this Friday now, and Jim thinks she really will go. She has said good-bye to everyone and attended dozens of farewell parties. All of that seems decidedly weird, doesn't it[?] I mean having farewell parties, with little gifts, given for you when you're leaving to get a divorce. Or, rather, I suppose it's the rounds of farewell parties that make everything else seem weird and improper to her. [. . .]

He is the most true-hearted and complete and honest man I've ever known. So much so that I sometimes think I must be dreaming it. He has been living alone in that Polish hotel for months now, seeing nobody except the people at the office and his children, and in a strange way he is happy, though tense and tired from struggling with her for the divorce—happy and satisfied, reading, listening to music on his room-radio, making himself coffee with an electrical gadget in a cup, and thinking about the future. Rather like some trapper in the Maine woods long ago or a frontier boy, camping out. There's something very fresh and youthful in him—unspoiled. I told him I was glad Reuel was going back to Poland because I thought he (Jim) must be lonely. He replied that no, he was not lonely; he missed me, but he was not lonely. He is not tough, by the way; that was a mistake. Irritable occasionally, impatient with nonsense, occasionally ruthless, but not tough or hard. Reuel told me the people in Warsaw, the ordinary Poles, all love him.

Well, you've heard enough of Jim. You can meet him, I hope, if you come here on your way to Israel. He's always delighted when he hears I got a letter from you. Forgive me for the silence, and do write again. And excuse me for not reporting at least a few words on the [French] referendum. It's a subject that passionately doesn't interest me or didn't. I felt out of sympathy with those who were for it, those who were violently against it, and those who were in between. Like you, I signed the manifesto,[2] but only because of the general principles enunciated in it and which I thought were well expressed by Nicola and whoever wrote it with him; Rahv and Phillips changed the English version slightly. I *am* for the right of civil disobedience, and that, it seemed to me, was all the manifesto committed one to.

Much, much love,
Mary

[. . .]

1. Elisabeth Niebuhr (later, Elisabeth Sifton) conducted a much-quoted interview with Mc-Carthy on March 6, 1961. It was published in *The Paris Review*, Winter–Spring 1962.
2. "In Support of the French Intellectuals," *Partisan Review*, January–February 1961, was Rahv's and Phillips's slightly modified translation of Chiaromonte's statement supporting the 121 (see n. 5 to Arendt's letter of Christmas 1960).

1 bis Rue Clément Marot
Paris 8
March 11, 1961

Dearest Hannah:

I don't know where you are or when the Eichmann trial starts but hope to catch you before you start for Israel. I myself feel like a perpetual-motion machine, having got back yesterday from a week in Rome, where I went to collect my books, summer clothes, and odds and ends, to ship to Poland. Before Rome, I was in Paris two days, during which I gave a lecture; before that, five days in Copenhagen, where Jim and I were making a final list of furniture for the house, down to the last towel rack (he was left with one blanket and a set of candlesticks); before that, New York or, rather, Dobbs Ferry, where I was staying with my brother [Kevin]—very respectable.[1] I intended to call you in Evanston from Dobbs Ferry but never did because life was so hectic there. There were four telephones in the house and somebody was always talking on one of them, what with Kevin and Augusta's theatrical connections,[2] Jim calling from Poland, people calling me from New York, and the three children receiving calls from their playmates, not to mention the maid, who had her own string of telephoners from Harlem. I wanted to see Heinrich again but never did that either; there was too much social pressure from old friends and commuting back and forth and besides that I had to take time out while I was there to write what I fear was an incoherent piece on Camus for an English paper.[3] Incidentally, I do not see how people who commute stand it, unless they are regular office-workers who do it like automatons, which I suppose most of them are.

It's been a relief to get back to Europe. New York I found depressing and full of a kind of parrot-talk about politics, sex, Norman Mailer; the only people, not counting Heinrich, that didn't depress me were Rahv (who, everyone else says, has become a gloomy monster) and Cal [Robert] Lowell (who, I heard in Rome just now, has had another breakdown).

In Rome, I've been seeing the Chiaromontes every day and sometimes twice a day, taking walks and talking. Nicola has achieved serenity, like a smiling sage and commentator, but unfortunately this is the result of a disability. He has been having some heart trouble (angina or a coronary condition) and his brother, who is a doctor, has put him on a diet of vegetables, fruit, mild cheeses, little meat, very little alcohol, and allows him to smoke only three or four cigarettes a day. The effect of this natural regime has been to make him very peaceful and indeed simple and natural but it has deprived him (he says) of any inclination to intellectual work; the only intellectual activity, he says, he really enjoys is translating Greek, and he has a hard time even doing his weekly article for *Il Mondo*. This "writing block" he finds absurd and faintly alarming. I don't mean that he's suffered any loss of intellectual power in conversation; it seems to be rather a question of concentration. He says that without cigarettes he doesn't concentrate. And he doesn't at all like being prudent, like some petty bourgeois property-owner with a vested interest in his body. And he also likes to eat well. And to drink, from time to time. My own feeling is that this is going to pass; he doesn't look or seem to the slightest degree a sick man— rather very robust and sound as an oak. And his brother, like so many doctors, is rather a puritan. Though it's true that Nicola was smoking an awful lot last summer and that without it he does feel better. The pains he has (mostly after meals) sound like what I had four years ago, though less severe.[4] And there is nothing wrong with his heart, according to the cardiograph. It's "functional," his brother says.

I don't know why I tell you all these details about Nicola's health; he would certainly be cross with me if he knew. Rome, in general, was a curious change-back from Paris. The Italian intellectuals are so much more *intimate* with the Italian political and social scene than the French: they discuss, sarcastically, the Church, the Demo-Christians, censorship, criminal trials, the uglification of Rome, and exchange illustrative jokes and anecdotes—all this with a kind of exasperation that suggests a family situation. And yet they're completely without power or influence; they must be the most disenfranchised intellectuals in any Western country. There is nobody, even like Mendes-France, who can be said to "represent" them, and a figure like Sartre is unthinkable there. And it may be that it's just this powerlessness, as of a helpless son or son-in-law, that makes them sound so familial. At the same time, they're spectators, connoisseurs of the national idiocy. I cannot help loving the Italians and not loving the French.

The weather was beautiful in Rome, with a sharp golden light, like the light of October. It's beautiful, as a matter of fact, in Paris too, but in Rome even the weather seems to belong intimately to the Romans, while in Paris it is just a pleasant fact.

Jim and I are going to be married April 15—here in Paris. [. . .] By that time, you will surely be in Israel. The paper doesn't say just when the trial begins—only "next month." Heinrich said you would probably fly straight to Israel, but he wasn't sure. Is there any chance that you might come by way of Paris? I should so love to see you, for a few days or even a day in this Paris spring. Will you write me what your plans are exactly? I don't suppose you could come back from Israel via Warsaw? But who knows when the trial will end?

The Chiaromontes and I have been speculating, with smiles, on how you're going to adapt to the *New Yorker* manner or method. But our imaginations failed us. How *are* you going to? Perhaps you should have it ghost-written—"as told to" some *New Yorker* hack. This would be an innovation.

Dear Hannah, please write soon. Incidentally, an excuse for your coming to Warsaw would be that I might be able to help you with a little editorial advice on the *New Yorker* problem (assuming it will be a problem). I think I would be a better consultant than Dwight, because Dwight, I think, has too much accepted their formulae, instead of testing them to see where they could be beat or broken. As I told Heinrich, Dwight is very unhappy, suffering from a prodigious "writing block," tired and testy. He needs to get rid of that woman but, I suspect, doubts that he has the strength left to do so. [. . .] Even his voice sounds run-down, like an alarm-clock trailing off into silence.

[. . .] Jim, as always, sends you his greetings. Incidentally, he has always supported you on your Go-slow policy, even though he disagreed completely with it. But he said, "After all, this shows that she is your friend and cares what happens to you." And he applauded this. He is fond, also, of Nicola and *loved* Dwight when he met him. His opinion was that Dwight's writing block was simply due to Gloria. "It's clear that he doesn't want to produce for *her*."

Yes, I *must* stop. I'll send this to Riverside Drive.

Much, much love,
Mary

1. Before that, McCarthy had flown to Alabama to get her divorce; West had got his at the end of January. Broadwater's offer to file for divorce himself was rejected, in that it carried with it the charge of desertion.
2. Kevin McCarthy and his first wife, Augusta Dabney, are still busy acting today.
3. Mary McCarthy, "Exit a Conscience," *The Observer*, February 26, 1961.
4. In late 1956 or early 1957, at the age of forty-four, McCarthy had an angina attack which she later attributed to the "broken heart" she suffered at the end of the John Davenport affair.

Hotel Chambiges
8 Rue Chambiges
Paris 8
April 2, 1961

Dearest Hannah:

I'm worried at not having heard from you. Did you get my letter of about ten days or so ago? I now know the date of the Eichmann trial: April 12, it seems. From the woman (Mme. Chatelet) at Spanish Refugee Aid, I heard that you were planning to come via Paris. Meanwhile, I've moved (again!) to this hotel, which is quite pleasant and not too expensive for this arrondissement; it harbors chiefly French people.

We are definitely getting married April 15. Jim is coming from Poland 6 or 7 days in advance, and Reuel will be following him. I'm passing these days in relative solitude, reading, walking, shopping for household effects and for wedding finery—hat, shoes, etc.; I'm wearing an old dress. [. . .]

I suddenly realize that it was much longer than ten days ago that I wrote you because Nicola at that time had not had a heart attack. I remember I was worried about him while writing you. Well, it happened shortly afterwards—what's called a coronary in America. The first report was very frightening, but now he has been in bed three weeks and the doctors say he can get up in a week's time and resume a more or less normal life. They say the trouble isn't organic but "functional"—the result of nervous tension. This struck me to the heart myself; the first night I heard the news I couldn't sleep or, rather, kept waking up and remembering it. But now, like Nicola's other friends, I'm busy collecting cheerful precedents, starting with Eisenhower; the hardest thing for any of his friends to imagine for him is the life of a "cardiac patient." I got to know him much better than ever before this summer and fall and as a man he is wholly lovable. And his mind is full of justice; this is its leading trait. A black boy from Senegal who's a friend of his was teasing him while I was in Rome last by telling him that he was a "sage," like the African sages of his tribe, who were different, he said, from marabouts or holy men.

It's Easter today and the spring is lovely here—very leafy and light, like spring millinery. I read a nice thing in some art-review the other day: that the beauty of Paris was due, precisely, to the "plaster of Paris," the greys and whites of the walls being the "skin" of the Ile-de-France.

In politics everybody seems to have lost interest in the Algerian negotiations, which is a sign that they are, as it were, posthumous. It is acknowledged that the war is over and Algeria lost. [. . .]

Do write me a line and say whether you are coming.

Much love,
Mary

[New York]
April 5, 1961

Dearest Mary:

Your letter just arrived and I am snatching a few minutes to answer you. I postponed writing from day to day because my plans were in such an unfixed state—and then all hell broke loose with the child of my little Jewish friend (Channan [sic]) being 17 and here for vacations from college showing up with very serious symptoms which I just learned are Multiple Sclerosis. We now try to get the parents home, both of whom are in Israel and planning to go to Russia, waiting for their cable etc. Meanwhile, the child is here and my heart gets heavy and hot each time I see her.

Well, I leave here at the last possible minute, Saturday, and go straight to Tel-Aviv. I meant to come via Paris (I do technically still because I go Air France) in order to see you.

The cable just arrived—a weight of[f] my mind. I hated the idea to leave the child before her mother returns.

So back to my original plans. I could not make it because Heinrich has his Easter vacation and I did not want to leave him alone.

Mary, I am sorrier about this than I can possibly tell you at this moment. And also very sorry about Chiaramonte [sic]. But I would not worry too much; if he is careful he can live for many more years. But, of course, he will be a cardiac patient from now on. This is not the worst that can happen to people.

I shall write from Jerusalem. I am there on Sunday and I shall stay in the Hotel Moriyah, King George-street.

Mary, I would have loved it to be in Paris for the wedding, and for quite a while I toyed with the idea of getting later into Israel. But it does not make sense. I should be there for the beginning since I am going.

Let me have your address after April 15. What shall I say, what can one say?? Happiness—luck—great good fortune. Fortuna smiling. And warmest regards for Jim West (whom everybody loves, according to my reports).

Yours as ever,
Hannah

Hotel Krafft am Rhein
Basel
May 10, 1961

Mary—

Where are you? And can't I see you? I am back from Jerusalem, shall stay in Basel (with Jaspers) until Wednesday next week (May 17). Then Munich (Germany)—Hotel Biederstein, Biedersteinerstr. 21a—till mid-June. Then, probably, back to Jerusalem for about a week, and in Zurich on June 24th to meet Heinrich. For two weeks to Italy, back to Basel around July 10 and back to America at the end of July.

Can't you come to Munich?? [. . .]

Love
Hannah

[The day before their marriage, West's former wife had moved back into the Warsaw apartment, pleading a set of personal emergencies that made it impossible for her to leave for several more weeks. West and McCarthy learned of it only during their honeymoon trip through Switzerland. From the embassy point of view, the prospect of two Mrs. Wests in Poland, both traveling on diplomatic passports, was the last straw, and West was notified of his reassignment, effective August 1, 1961.

117

In May, McCarthy, forced to stay behind in Vienna, suffered a slipped disc. When she finally entered Poland, after Margaret West's departure, it was in a wheelchair, encased in a surgical collar.]

Dombrowskieyo 25
Warsaw
May 24, 1961

Dear Hannah:

Here is the promised letter [they had talked by phone] very badly written. My arm and hand (and neck) seem to be worse again, it comes and goes, quite arbitrarily. But Jim says I'm getting better, that he can observe it in my movements. And the pain, though acute, is not so *agonizing*, and more intermittent. However, I've had to resort to sedatives and pain-killers again. What most irritates me is the sense of how tiresome this is for the children. An adventure at first—a strange lady in a bandage—but soon merely a tedious presence in the bed. Or so I fear. They are here for a week more before going to Paris to their mother, and I should like to be better and have my neck uncorseted at least one day before then. Jim is wonderful—a Jovian shower of bouquets, magazines, alcohol rubs, fresh pillow-arrangements, glasses of iced ginger ale (the Polish doctor has even forbidden *coffee!*) and sheer love. But since we sleep in a double bed (I know your opinion of this, Hannah), he is getting rather worn himself, and pale, from my night-moans and tossings. [. . .]

Do you know, I always thought this slipped disc business was another modern medical racket—a wholly imaginary complaint? Every hypochondriac I know has been operated on for it. So I find it hard to believe this is real, just as, in a different way, I find it hard to believe I am in Warsaw. And married.

Much love to you, dearest Hannah,
Mary

Munchen, May 31, 1961
Pension Biederstein
Biedersteinerstr. 21a

Dearest Mary,

I was so relieved to see your handwriting and to have your letter! [. . .] Slipped disc—indeed so very unlike you, for I had the same notions in my head, of course. Don't you think it may be wiser to go to Zurich to this specialized bone hospital?? Perhaps this would save some time and pain. Annchen[1] told me marvellous things about it—all her friends from Belgium and Paris, etc. And Munich-Zurich is one hour by air!

I am half-way recovered from the Eichmann-torture which was not without a rather macabre humour. This pension is very nice and comfortable, a rather large room with a large desk, all furniture around 1800, really civilized. I went to Munich because of the very good libraries where my publisher had everything arranged so that I got the books delivered to my room. Time-saving devices. Munich is not bad and if the weather had not been so beastly, I would have enjoyed it. Today is a bit better. If I only knew when I have to go back to Jerusalem! The most probable date right now is the 10th, and perhaps even a bit later. On the 24th, I have to be back in Zurich, for Heinrich is due then. We shall go for about two weeks to Italy. On the 9th of July I have to be back in Germany for some nonsense which I accepted—trade unions, my curiosity was aroused—during the week after that (until about the 19th) we shall both be in Basel. And around the end of the month of July, we want to be back in New York.

Germany is rather tiresome and disgusting in many ways. The few days with the students in the Eiffel were rather nice and encouraging.[2] But then young people are always nice and encouraging and God knows what happens to them when they are no longer young. I am kind of impatient with everything and everybody here although less irritated than I was in Israel. The day with Günther (my former husand) was almost a disaster, but he does not know it, I behaved very well because I knew this of course beforehand. Only to see it in the flesh is again something else. He is completely disintegrated, lives only for his "fame" which is a kind of chateau d'Espagne, refuses to see anything real or to accept his own situation such as it really is. I have not seen him for more than 12 years and have not really talked to him for about 25 years. The funniest part of it was that he was exactly like his mother who also always lived in some sort of imaginary happiness.

Mary, my dear, if I only knew that you are better! I have it constantly in the back of my mind.

Much love to you and many greetings to Jim!

Yours,
Hannah

1. Anne Weil Mendelssohn had been Arendt's *beste Freundin* from their teenage years in Königsberg.
2. Arendt had met with former students of the German Scholarship Foundation in the Eiffel, a hilly region west of the Rhine and northwest of the Mosel.

[Paris]
July 24, 1961

WEST, AMERICAN EMBASSY, VARSOVIE

WORRIED WITHOUT NEWS FROM MARY AM PARIS HOTEL ROCHES-
TER 92 RUE BOETIE UNTIL SUNDAY THEN NEW YORK LOVE

[H]ANNAH[1]

1. The telegram, stamped "No Action," went undelivered. McCarthy and West were en route to Bocca di Magra, where they stayed until September 8. They then left for Washington, D.C. on obligatory home leave before the State Department assigned West to a new post.

Oct. 5, 1961
Middletown [Conn.] [. . .][1]

Mary my dear,

I am sorry that I did not see you any more. I felt too lousy for Sylvia [Marlowe, the harpsichordist]'s party. Where are you? And how was Washington? I hope these lines will reach you. Greetings to Jim!

Affectionately yours,
Hannah

1. Arendt was teaching an Advanced Studies seminar at Wesleyan University.

107 Water Street
Stonington, Connecticut
January 11, 1962

Dearest Hannah:

I'm returning this finally with some corrections.[1] I fear I've kept it too long to be of any use to you. But maybe it will be helpful in your proofs.

The essay is wonderful. After two careful readings, I would make only two criticisms. First, that you might add something—for clarification, really—on the early Slave Rebellions, Weavers' Revolts, etc. These were certainly manifestations of "unhappiness" and brought into the public eye the hitherto invisible masses. In the

Ciompi Revolt in Florence, the one I know most about, there was more too than a demand for bread; they wanted, and got for awhile, a political re-formation of the Republic. If it's not called a revolution, isn't this really because it was short-lived? A revolution, as we use the term, involves the notion of process. But in that case wasn't the Hungarian Revolution really a rebellion or a revolt? Also the 1905 Revolution? Both much shorter-lived and less efficacious than the Ciompi Revolt.

Second, the "Glorious Revolution." When I studied English History, this was in 1689—and therefore memorable because it was a hundred years before the French Revolution. It was, as you say, a restoration, but a restoration not of monarchy itself but of the "legitimate" Protestant monarchy—William and Mary—as opposed to the somewhat Popish James II, his wife, Mary of Modena, and his heir, the Old Pretender. I. e., it was a restoration of "constitutional" or limited monarchy as opposed to absolute monarchy on the French pattern. I have no books of reference here and may be a year off on the date; it might be 1688. But this is the way I learned the story.

Finally, a very minor point: would it be a good idea to define terror? In contradistinction to violence. We all know the thing you allude to, but a conceptual definition would be useful.

About the verbal changes I've made. The ones you may not understand have to do with whiches and thats. Which governs a non-restrictive clause; that a restrictive clause. Restrictive clauses are always set off by commas. The distinction between which and that hasn't always been made in English, and in the old days the shift from one to another was often determined by euphony—note your quotation from Lord Acton. But today the distinction is more rigorous. Exceptions are made when the "that" could be mistaken for the other kind of "that"—the demonstrative pronoun—or when two different kinds of "that" would come together or where there is parallelism with a "which" that happens to be restrictive in sense (with "in" or "to" or "on"). E.g., "the country which I love and in which I live." You could say "that" for the first "which," but it's optional. But if it were "the country which, God help me, I love and in which I live," which would be quite a bit preferable. [. . .] Normally, though, the test is whether the relative pronoun can be dropped altogether without violations of sense. If it can be dropped, either drop it in simple clauses ("the shrine I visited," not "the shrine which or that I visited") or use "that" ("the shrine that after many years I visited"). I'm doubtless boring you with all this, and if you don't want to worry about it, forget it. The only thing is that "that" used correctly sounds a little easier and therefore more English.

The other little corrections explain themselves, I think. "Usage," in general, applies only to use of words, except in such odd phrases as "hard usage," meaning not hard use but ill treatment. And one last point. Is your translation of Livy right? I'd think, very tentatively, that the "quibus" indicates that he means that a war is just to those for whom it is necessary, which gives a different shade of meaning. As for "les malheureux sont la puissance de la terre," words fail me, but I think you could do better. "The poor are the earth's might"? No. "The poor are the mighty on earth"? "The wretched are the mighty on earth"?

Dear Hannah, this is my first quiet day in a month. Jim has been called to Washington to prepare to go to Paris, and I'm alone in this big room.[2] If he's going to be in Washington any length of time, and if he can find an apartment for us to stay in, I'll go down and join him. Otherwise, I'll stay on here. But it's all so uncertain. We went to Washington last week—an impetuous decision; yet if we hadn't I truly believe nothing would have happened for weeks. The presumption in Washington now is that definitely he will go, but the decision rests with the Secretary General of the O.E.C.D. [Thorkild Christiansen], who is supposed to be a difficult type and who would have preferred someone with training in economics. I begin to understand that the Common Market is really capitalism's five-year-plan or something of the kind, and therefore feel more neutral than enthusiastic about it. It seems to get more and more difficult to *stay apart* from capitalism, and I don't think this is just a feature of having married a government official but rather of the whole polarization of current life.

Please write or call to say how you are and how Heinrich is. [. . .] With Jim gone, I don't know how I'll ever see you at Wesleyan, since I don't drive any more (or rather don't have a license) and there's not even a taxi nearer than Westerly. So it will have to be in New York on a weekend. But when? I've never been so disorganized in all my life, and I cannot even think it's my fault and set about rectifying it because every wise decision I've made or we've made recently has turned out to be unwise and vice versa. Jim has been wonderful and strangely at peace during this trying period; he keeps turning any place we perch into a love nest, as though to pacify my longing for stability, but this makes each transient place harder to leave. I.e., we keep moving in and buying plants, flowers, food, wine; now—the result of Christmas—we even have pictures and a phonograph and lots of books.[3] He's an intensely lovable man, the most so, by far, I've ever been close to, and he seems to be getting happier all the time, which is odd to see since when I first knew him he was indifferent to the whole idea of Happiness and cared only for something narrow and very personal and private called Experience. He likes you so very much, Hannah, and keeps telling me what a beautiful woman you are and what extraordinary eyes you have, which he says are not like most people's eyes but real windows. He was also very much taken with Heinrich and, if he were young, would like to study philosophy with him. Some of his likes and dislikes are totally surprising to me. For example, he adores [Niccolò] Tucci, whom I would have expected him to detest. And he likes "Bill" Phillips. Dwight he is rather fed up with, after an initial delight, and describes to me as a "Hoax"—quite a funny idea, which I fear may be partly true. I.e., that Dwight is a kind of self-made invention or impersonation masquerading as himself.

This letter is too long.

What I started to ask you during the grammatical section was what has happened to your Eichmann piece for the *New Yorker*? Everybody keeps asking *me* that.

Much, much love to you,
Mary

1. This was the manuscript of the concluding chapter of Arendt's *On Revolution*.
2. West was being briefed for a liaison position with the newly formed Organization for Economic Cooperation and Development in Paris. During the obligatory home leave, he and McCarthy had rented a house in Stonington, Connecticut.
3. Meanwhile, the furniture, books, china, and household effects shipped from New York, Rome, Copenhagen, and Paris to Warsaw, remained in storage in Poland, awaiting a new destination.

[While Arendt was teaching at Wesleyan in the fall of 1961, she was visited by a series of mishaps that set back the time when she could finally confront the mountain of source materials she had brought back from the Eichmann trial. In late October, her husband suffered an aneurysm in the brain; Arendt left Wesleyan to look after him in New York, and McCarthy went to Middletown to take over her Machiavelli seminar.

When Blücher's health stabilized in December, and Arendt completed the manuscript of *On Revolution*, she returned to the Eichmann material, once again to no avail. After fulfilling lecture commitments at the University of Chicago in January 1962, she came down with a cold and respiratory problems complicated by an allergic reaction to antibiotics. Not long after this, a taxi she was riding in was hit by a truck in Central Park, and she was disabled for nearly two months.

McCarthy visited Arendt in the hospital before returning to Paris with West, who had been named Director of Information for the OECD. On March 23, 1962, Charlotte Aron Beradt, a journalist and an old friend of Blücher's from Berlin, wrote this letter to McCarthy:

"The news is quite good: Hannah sitting, walking, reading already. Would even be allowed to leave the hospital on Monday. But talked into staying on until the weekend for precautions sake. The résumé: a list of very uncomfortable things; 9 broken ribs and a nearly broken wrist, left hand, discovered since you left, but nothing internal and serious.[1] Spirits high, collecting flowers (begging not even to throw away the wilted ones—yours are still fresh and beautiful by the way), letters, notes, telegrams like a child and fighting the mighty headnurse for fun.

"I am glad that I can give you that kind of report."]

1. Arendt had also suffered a concussion, multiple lacerations, and hemorrhages of both eyes, and, as it turned out, heart-muscle damage related to shock.

Hotel Chambiges
8 rue Chambiges
Paris 8
March 28, 1962

Dearest Hannah:

I didn't write from the boat; the trip (strangely) is too short— four and a half days. I was waiting to piece together a picture of the social scene for you and suddenly it was the last day and one had to be packing one's bags (of which naturally I had a great many) for landing. We traveled in great luxe, on the United States, which was surprisingly comfortable and attractive and nearly empty. The only notabilities were Dame Rebecca West (the one who is fascinated by treason) and the son of [mystery writer] Edgar Wallace with his American wife and 44 pieces of luggage. I learned an interesting fact about his father; he was a foundling who was brought up by professional criminals, a whole family of them who were very kind to him. Hence those improbable crime stories had a "real life" basis. Dame Rebecca is a good talker and cracked—paranoid, with ideas of reference; she imagines that various authors are alluding to her and all her relatives under disguises in their books. She gave me a picture of herself, her husband and her dog. Between her and Mr. Wallace there was much talk of Powers.[1] Mr. Wallace thought he should have been shot and Dame Rebecca was for life imprisonment.

We drove down from Le Havre, and France is so beautiful with its spotted cows and mistletoe and ivy and mosses. Spring is very late here—only signified by swallows.

Now I must find an apartment or a house. I should like to live in the country but don't know whether this will be possible.

Paris, as you can imagine, is in an ugly mood.[2] "Vous êtes chez vous en France, hein? [So you feel at home in France?]" in a nasty tone, from a bus(?) attendant when we'd parked by mistake in a wrong place. "Ça ne durera pas. [That won't last.]" Echoes of this all over, except in the crowded restaurants, where everyone seems in a good humor. Our friends are excited by the Monday massacre in Algiers.[3] "Now it is *their* turn," says the husband, meaning the Right. But the wife says no, she does not like police that shoot into an unarmed crowd, no matter who they are. The husband replies it is not the police but soldiers, and the wife says it is all the same thing. Etc.

It is nice to be back, just the same, with these domestic political arguments, in which the children join.

Jim's job is going to be hard at first, but fun, I think, in the end. Apparently he will have to revise everything that is being done, in information, by the O.E.C.D. What comes out now (according to Mario Lévi, an economist, Chiaromonte's friend) is a flood of publications that could not be understood by a professional economist—only by a statistician. He is going to have very good rank, just below that of minister, imagine, and $3300 a year for housing. [. . .]

Forgive this terrible handwriting—a bad pen. I know you are

better and that your swellings must have gone down. I stupidly left a package of dental supplies in your room; some time if someone is coming to France they might bring them if it isn't too much trouble. They are products you can't get here.

Much, much love to you, dearest Hannah. Get well. Don't overdo things. And please give a sign.

xxx, Mary

1. Gary Powers, the U-2 pilot who had been shot down over Russia, tried, and sentenced to ten years, had been exchanged by the U.S.S.R. for Rudolf Abel, a Soviet spy held by the U.S.
2. Repeated attempts to assassinate President De Gaulle made by rebel French army officers of the O.A.S., the Organisation Armée Sécrète, had convinced him to move quickly to end the war in Algeria and accept the inevitability of Algeria's independence. In Paris, the cease-fire precipitated a new outburst of nationalist sentiment for France d'Outre Mer.
3. This took place on March 19, 1962, when Algerian troops loyal to France fired on a demonstration of *pieds noirs* (French people living in Algeria) who were protesting a French army strike against an O.A.S. garrison. The previous week, immediately following the cease-fire, O.A.S. troops had gone on a rampage against Algerian civilians.

[New York]
April 4, 1962

Mary, my dear, how I miss you! You should not have come when you came, but now, if you were here, it would make such a difference! I came home from the hospital last Friday and everything goes very well. I have still two spots on my face which I can cover with powder, but I look almost normal except for the scar over one eye. My nine broken ribs make me still a bit uncomfortable, but I move around quite well. The head does not bother me at all; I don't think that I'll buy a whig [sic] until the hair is grown back, I rather wear scarves. Monday I went to the dentist who very kindly fixed me right away. Makes me feel much better.

But I am not yet supposed to work and don't feel like it. Slightly infuriating. Up to now I have been in very high spirits, simply happy to be alive at all. That began when I awoke in the car and became conscious of what had happened. I tried out my limbs, saw that I was not paralyzed and could see with both eyes; then tried out my memory—very carefully, decade by decade, poetry, Greek and German and English, then telephone numbers. Everything all right. The point was that for a fleeting moment I had the feeling that it was up to me to decide whether I wanted to live or to die. And though I did not think that death was terrible, I also thought that life was quite beautiful and that I['d] rather take it. When I came to the hospital and the young, very competent neurosurgeon, who then operated on me, declared: "It looks rather horrible but I think nothing serious happened," I was pretty sure that he was right. In the hospital, I came rather brutally face to face with our present-day world from which we usually are shielded. Medically, things were quite good; but the administration and the nurses plus their aides plus the food incredibly and outrageously bad. The whole thing run under the motto: We could not care less. The nurses, not tipped for services rendered, but bribed in order to perform at all. I did not do it. I finally tipped the few who had been all right. Result: They did not even take my temperature although there was, of course, a suspicion of pneumonia; it took me 24 hours to get some salt with which I was supposed to gargle, etc. The food so bad that I could not eat it; when I came home, I went straight to the ice box. And all this for $40 a day! [New York] Medical Center where Heinrich was was altogether different. My friends there very rightly wanted to take me; but during the first week, I was not supposed to be moved because of the brain concussion, and later it was obvious that I would be out of the hospital in a few days anyhow. My friend at [the] Medical Center, Nachmannsohn, rather famous in neurological circles for research, called immediately and came; they were quite impressed, and I am not so sure how the medical care would have been if they had not known that there was somebody from another institution to have an eye on the whole thing. This, too, quite disgustingly obvious.

And now, to conclude the incident—Dwight was very very nice; came to see me, brought things to read, sent a book, talked cheerfully. Such a good friend! He also wrote Chiaramonte [sic] who wrote a very nice letter. And I hope he wrote you. He [Dwight] was marvellous and without chi-chi.

Your letter sounds fine and I am so happy that everything worked out all right for Jim. Good luck for apartment-hunting. And thanks for the boat description which amused and entertained me. I hardly know Rebecca West but did not like her. Something profoundly hysterical about her. Dental supplies—I am afraid they are lost. I saw them when I packed, thought they belonged to the hospital . . . thought immediately: curious, they use here the same powder Mary uses, and left it there. Let me know what it was and I shall send it to you. I remember "Revelation" Tooth powder, but I do not remember the other things.

Love my dear and je t'embrasse
Hannah

8 Rue de la Chaise
Paris 7ième
May 4, 1962

Dearest Hannah:

Forgive me for this silence. I've been half sick ever since we got here—streptococcus throat, bronchitis, grippe—in bed one day, up the next, and for some reason very depressed and toneless. Perhaps this is a characteristic of the germ or perhaps it's change of life or still something else—I don't know. I've never felt depression as a physical thing before, like a heavy poison in one's veins, and have been dragging myself about, when up, attending social functions and looking for an apartment. I've not wanted to write you a dreary letter and have been more in a mood to hide myself, like a dirty bundle, in a hotel room, so that no one I love can see me; I don't mind about the others. But today, suddenly, I feel better and want to write.

We left our hotel three days ago and have moved into Inge Morath's apartment (the one who married Arthur Miller [and a well-known photographer]); it's not my ideal or even idea of an apartment, but the neighborhood is nice and one can have one's meals at home. Meanwhile, in a fevered haze, we've bought an apartment, which won't be ready, though, till the first of September. It's on Rue de Rennes, near the Gare Montparnasse—to be exact, near the St. Placide métro—on the top floor of a mid-Victorian building. Iron-work balcony on the front; behind a view of a convent and its large garden; lots of sun all day long—a gay apartment. Fireplaces, a large curving entrance hall with windows, living room, dining room, library, three bedrooms (one large), two maids' rooms above, heating, an old-fashioned bathroom, and a wonderful large oddly shaped kitchen, which however has not been touched for fifty years and will have to be scraped, refloored, etc. The price is a little over $31,000—thought by everyone including the architect we took to look it over to be a great bargain. The reason it is a bargain is that it's on the sixth floor, American style, and the elevator is broken. A new one will have to be installed, but this may take a year; the agreement of the other tenants is necessary, and one is holding out (the one on the second floor, naturally); pro-rated, the elevator will cost $2000 per tenant. I'm told that there's a law that says that if there has been an elevator in a building, it has to be replaced, so that sooner or later, if this is true, there will be one. The general on the fifth floor, who has just redone his apartment, is clamoring for justice, i.e., for the elevator. As you know, I don't mind stairs, but this could be a nuisance over a period for guests and also would make it hard to resell the apartment if you had to.

But, having viewed the real-estate situation in Paris, I decided that we would have to put up with one grave drawback in order to get anything nice; it was only a question of finding out, from looking, what that drawback would be. Prices are simply incredible, and most agents do not even list apartments for rent, because there aren't any—except for a few rackets. All this, as in New York, is the result of rent control, but it is worse than New York ever was because there has been, until now, hardly any new building. Most of the apartments I've seen to buy are lived in by very old people, who have decided to turn their homestead into capital and find some corner in Paris or in the suburbs to die in. This migration has something pathetic in it; as though a school of herring, bent on turning a profit, made for some Norwegian fjord to die rather than to breed. But one's sense of pathos is moderated by the avarice of these old householders, who haven't replaced a nail in fifty years and who now have the most millionaireish ideas of what their dark dens are worth; I saw one on the Rue de Seine, consisting of four almost lightless rooms and a kitchen, no bath, not even a toilet; the price was $40,000, as it stood, peeling, sagging, smelling, without heat, of course. The real estate agent said that some rich German would probably buy it and fix it up—for the address, which is considered chic now. A great many Germans, I hear, are buying on the Left Bank, as well, oddly enough, as in Ireland. [. . .]

Being in France makes one feel, even more than in America, that industrialization is really a cancer, spreading more rapidly than anyone could or can imagine, and absolutely inoperable. A terminal cancer, as they call it in medicine. Nor does it matter whether one is a progressive or a conservative in one's attitude toward it, whether one dreams of "planning" and garden cities or wants to retain "picturesque" slums and primitive farms. Both sides of this argument have been left far behind. America, I think, seems better in this context because it was always a "new" world. All along the Seine, as far as Normandy, where the white cliffs are, has been pimpled with cute weekend bungalows ("coquette," they call them in the ads) that are infinitely more hideous and unrestrained than anything in New England or New Jersey; Kevin's suburban Dobbs Ferry is the Vale of Tempe in comparison. It makes you want literally to cry.

Enough of this. I'm afraid this letter is dreary, after all. Please write and tell me how you are; I've heard news of you from William which is good and, I hope, true. You say something about a wig. I wonder whether in the end you'll need one. [. . .] You will see, as you say; your hair is so strong and, as it were, full of energy that you may well find some way of doing it to cover the scar. A series of curls that would come forward and roll under? Hairdressers do wonders with old people like Miss Brayton,[1] who has really lost most of her hair, but you would not think so after she's had it waved in New York. And this without any false hair added. When your hair grows out, you should go to a very good coiffeur—not just a little girl in a beauty parlor. But you know that yourself. I hope that it doesn't have to be a wig, but if it does you will, I suppose, get semi-used to it, as one does, but only semi, to false teeth. A painter here (Larry Rivers) has been doing a drawing of me, and he keeps saying he can't get the mouth right. I feel I *know* the reason but am too embarrassed to tell him it: that because of the bridge, my mouth, when closed, is no longer *my* mouth. How awful. I think I shall have to tell him, to put him out of his misery. Because he thinks it's some failure on *his* part—a loss of talent. A funny situation.

Please write soon. Have you been able to go back to Eichmann? Did you write some German poetry in the hospital? Lotte [Beradt]'s letter, incidentally, was somehow lost in the Embassy and reached me a month late. It filled in a gap or two when it came.

So much love to you, my dearest Hannah. How is Heinrich? Love to him. It will soon be time for you to go to the Catskills? Will you go? Please write frankly about how the repairs on you are progressing.

Love again and kisses,
Mary

[. . .]

1. Alice Brayton, whose topiary garden was a star attraction for summer visitors in Newport, was a neighbor of McCarthy's when she and Broadwater lived in Portsmouth, Rhode Island.

[New York]
May 20, 1962

Dearest Mary—

Good to hear from you; I am quite conscious of how much I miss you here. And Congratulations to the apartment. I know exactly where it is and it is nice to think back to Métro St. Placide with you somehow and unexpectedly alighting from a doorway. Depression—do you have a good doctor there? French physicians are either (seldom) the very very best or perfectly awful. I had the same thing about 3 years ago, clearly change of age, and did not go to a doctor because I hated to admit that I had a depression. Whereupon I lost it—after about 6 months. But I know that they have something or other to give you. And since you are nice and honest and not such a lying character as I am, you may be persuaded to try it. Do you work? I read an interview you gave to Paris Review and liked it; but you probably gave it years ago.[1] How is the novel [*The Group*] progressing? And Paris apartment prices—I know. Of course, it is all the result of rent control plus an incredible avarice, their national vice; and the rent control, don't forget, has been with them since 1914!

I am in the midst of Eichmann and rather desperate because I cannot make it as brief as I wanted to. I am swimming in an enormous amount of material, always trying to find the most telling quotation and shall have to write a second draft (something I ordinarily hate but it can't be helped because of too many documents). It probably will take all summer to really finish, but au fond I don't mind. On the contrary, [I] somehow enjoy the handling of facts and concrete things.

Accident—I am really perfectly fine. No whig [*sic*], I have no bald spot, must only wait until the hair has grown back because I was shaved on part of the head. I thought of a whig as a temporary solution, but it does not make sense. I wear a scarf turbanwise and in a few weeks the untouched part of my hair will have grown sufficiently to cover the growing part so that a veil will be all I need. The only thing that still bothers me are my eyes; one of the muscles in the inner part of the eye got hurt and I had a kind of double vision. It is much better now and it does not interfere with reading or writing (never did), but it is a slow process. I have several eye doctors because of my great lack of confidence in the whole profession, and they all assure me that it will be all right in a couple of months.

We just decided to go back to Palenville in the summer and retained already our bungalow. We shall leave at the end of June and stay until August. I have a great hunger right now for green and trees and water and swimming, so I look forward to it. I hope I can finish Eichmann in the first draft and then finish the manuscript there. I hardly see anybody except Tucci who amuses me. Harold was here and talked nonsense about art. (Once in a while, he reminds you of Clem Greenberg which, of course, is utterly unfair.) He was just back from Berkeley which was a success. God knows, his self-confidence did not need this extra lift.

Otherwise—nothing changed. Except of course for regular invitations of intellectuals into the White House. There is a nice story about Diana Trilling[2] buying herself the appropriate outfit, then becoming unsure and calling up the White House, describing her dress in detail, if it would do. But by this I do not want to imply that I think Kennedy is wrong in inviting these people. On the contrary, I think he is more or less right, the trouble is only that he will corrupt everybody without wanting to.

Mary, I am a bit worried about grippe and depression. Drop me a line, not just to reassure me. But let me know how you are and how things are.

> Much much love, and greetings to Jim.
> Yours,
> Hannah

1. This was Elisabeth Niebuhr's 1961 interview with McCarthy.
2. The critic Diana Trilling, with whom McCarthy sometimes sparred, was a frequent contributor to *Partisan Review*.

> 8 Rue de la Chaise
> Paris 7ième
> June 1, 1962

Dearest Hannah:

In the last two weeks I've been frightfully busy; otherwise I'd have answered sooner. My spirits have risen, I'm glad to say, and I've suddenly done some writing. Just reviews, one a long one of Vladimir Nabokov's new book [*Pale Fire*] that's coming out in this week's *New Republic* and a shorter one of Salinger [*Franny and Zooey*] for *The Observer*.[1] The last I did in two days and it is very viperish and mean and gave me no pleasure, except to get it out of the way, but I really fell in love with the Nabokov book and worked very hard on it, with pure joy. I'm very curious to know what you'll think of the book if you read it; to me it's one of the gems of this century, absolutely new, though there are flashes of *Lolita*, *Pnin*, and all his other books in it. Among other things, it is terribly funny, about the academic life, and terribly sad too. It seems to me to have more of America and of the "new" civilization in it than anything I've ever read, and it's the first book I know to turn this weird new civilization into a work of art, as though he'd engraved it all on the head of a pin, like the Lord's Prayer. It's a terrific puzzle or game and requires several players to work it out, which again seems fantastically appropriate to this age of groupiness. I ran around Paris, to the library, to friends who knew Russian, to friends who knew German, to friends who knew chess, and enlisted, miraculously, their interest, as though they caught fire from the book too, at secondhand. This contagiousness is one of its qualities. And it's all quite different from working on *Finnegans Wake*, say, because when you look up all the references there you're simply back with the text, but with the Nabokov book everything you're led to is beautiful in itself—rare birds and butterflies, the movements of the stars, curious chess situations, certain passages from Pope and Shakespeare, Plato, Aristotle, Goethe. . . . I'm far from having elucidated all of it and am dying to hear what other people will find that I've missed. So far, the few reviews I've seen have been absolutely stupid and missed just about everything—in a most predictable way, as though Nabokov, laughing, had written the reviewers' reviews. Well, enough of that.

Johnny Myers passed through Paris the other day and told me *he* had read the most beautiful book—a collection of Jaspers [*The Great Philosophers*] edited by you. What is this, and who brought it out? In a strange way, as he described it [it] sounded a little like *Pale Fire*— only in that it too called for the reader's collaboration.

Otherwise there's nothing specially new. Except a story about Aron[2] that is circulating. It seems he is a Don Juan with his girl students and has been inducing them to grant him their favors with all sorts of promises, which naturally he hasn't kept. But one of these girls has drawn up a bill of charges against him and has sent it, mimeographed, to the principal editors of Paris and to all the professors of the Sorbonne. One of his promises, textually quoted, is that if she will go to bed with him he will "take her on his arm to official dinners." Thwarted of this, she has taken her revenge. Some friends of mine say that this is the second mad girl he has been involved with; the first tried to commit suicide to embarrass him or rather staged a suicide. . . .

Jim is working too hard and we have to go to too many official parties. His difficulty is starting a new program with the same people as staff who "worked" on the old program—i.e., who have been happily vegetating for eight years while drawing salaries. He cannot fire anyone—the usual bureaucratic situation—only move them around and try to get some work out of them. This is not a popularity-winning process. Because of that I've been making a slight effort on the social side and feel I probably should make more. But the place we're living in is not equipped, really, for entertaining, except people one knows well or who are Bohemian.

For my part, I rather miss having a "circle" in Paris, i.e., a group of friends who all know each other, as I had in Rome or as we all have in New York. Here our friends seem to come in isolated pairs, as in the Ark. There is an American semi-Bohemian circle but of rather low quality, frankly: they're to be found usually at art-openings. The only French person I'd really like to meet is Nathalie Sarraute. But there must be others I don't know about. By the way, have you seen "L'Année dernière à Marienbad"?[3] We haven't yet, partly because it is hardly ever playing, which indicates that it must have been a financial failure in spite of all the publicity. And have you read Gunther [sic] Grass [The Tin Drum] and what do you think of him? My friend Anjo Lévi liked his book very much, in a French translation, and she is very critical. Ralph Mannheim [sic] is translating it into English and dashed me by saying that the French translation was no good. What Anjo said about the book made me think of Nymphenburg.[4] Oh, I do miss you, Hannah, and wish you were coming here soon.

They hanged Eichmann yesterday; my reaction was curious, rather shrugging, "Well, one more life—what difference does it make?" This cannot be the reaction the Israelis desired, yet short of rejoicing at his death, on the one hand, or being angry at it on the other, what else can the ordinary person feel? And just there is the problem. To execute a man and excite a reaction of indifference is to bring people too close to the way the Nazis felt about human life—"One more gone." My second thought was: "This will make it easier for De Gaulle to execute Jouhaud."[5] Perhaps this is a good thing; perhaps not. Anyway, how is your piece coming?

I must stop and start cooking a dinner. I am so glad, Hannah, that you're almost over the effects of the accident, and you *were* fortunate in misfortune. All my love to you and love to Heinrich and write fairly soon.

Mary

1. Mary McCarthy, "A Bolt from the Blue," *The New Republic*, June 4, 1962; Mary McCarthy, "J. D. Salinger's Closed Circuit," also appeared in *Harper's*, October 1962. Both are reprinted in *The Writing on the Wall* (1970).
2. French political commentator Raymond Aron (1905–1983) was professor of sociology in the Faculty of Letters of the Sorbonne from 1955 to 1968. He was an influential columnist for *Le Figaro* and after 1977 for *l'Express*.
3. This movie was directed by Alain Resnais and had a screenplay by Marguerite Duras. It enjoyed a brief celebrity in New York and Paris in 1962–63.
4. Possibly McCarthy refers to Nymphenburg porcelain, originating in eighteenth-century Bavaria and known for its rococo figures suggestive of the commedia dell'arte.
5. Edmond Jouhaud was one of four generals who broke away from the French army in 1961 to form the O.A.S. After waging a campaign of terror against the Gaullist regime in France and Algeria, he and O.A.S. general Raoul Salan were captured and sentenced to death.

[New York]
June 7, 1962

Dearest Mary—

I was just on the point of writing anyway when your letter arrived. I read the Macbeth piece[1] and immediately thereafter the Nabokov review in the New Republic. I fell greatly and enthusiastically in love with the Macbeth article, and Heinrich was even more enthusiastic than I—if possible. You are so entirely and absolutely right and said it all so beautifully! When did you write it and why did you not let me know? It was almost by accident that I saw it in Harper's. (How I miss you!) The Nabokov article—very very good, excellent as a matter of fact, very ingenious and puzzling—but I have not read the book. I am going to get it soon, but shall hardly have time to read it before Palenville. There is something in N. which I greatly dislike. As though he wanted to show you all the time how intelligent he is. And as though he thinks of himself in terms of "more intelligent than." There is something vulgar in his refinement, and I am a bit allergic against this kind of vulgarity because I know it so well, know so many people cursed with it. But perhaps this is no longer true here. Let me see. I know only one book of his which I truly admire, and that is the long essay on Gogol.

That is about all. It is evening now, and Tucci just left. He can be *insupportable* but today he was all right. He is greatly disturbed that you did not write him about his novel [*Before My Time*]. I liked the first part of it greatly—up to the scene at the tailor. After that, I thought it became heavy and repetitious but of course never told him so. The first part is good enough and really very amusing. What *do* you think??

I am still in Eichmann, have the portrait part almost finished—or so I hope. It is much longer than I thought, about 80 pages now. If I am lucky, it will not [be] over 160 pages. I am still glad I did it despite the staggering amount of sheer labor that has to go into it. My room looks like a battlefield with papers and the mimeographed sheets of the trial transcript strewn all over the place.

L'Année dernière à Marienbad—I saw it and thought it a bore. But have a look, it is interesting from a technical point. Sarraute: That should not be difficult. In case it is, let me know. Annchen [Anne Weil] knows her quite well and also another friend of mine, Nina Gourfinkel, also [a] Russian Jewess. Annchen comes to Paris rather regularly, I think. Perhaps Jim has met her in the Common Market business. Her official name: Mme Eric Weil from Brussels. If you have time and would like to see her, let me know. I think she would very much like to meet you—part sheer curiosity and part, perhaps, a bit of jealousy. But not enough to bother anybody!

I am glad they hanged Eichmann. Not that it mattered. But they would have made themselves utterly ridiculous, I feel, if they had not pushed the thing to its only logical conclusion. I know I am in a minority with this feeling. One reform rabbi came out for mercy and criticized the Israel execution as "unimaginative"! Isn't that marvellous? And also the other pleas that Israel should reach "divine heights" were greatly against my taste. The Prosecutor ([Gideon] Hausner) was received by Kennedy and told he had done "a very good job." Even if it were true, [which] God knows it isn't, it would be a scandalous way of putting it.

De Gaulle—I think the Salan business was and is a very real calamity.[2] The Jaspers thing: I'll have it sent to you, Harcourt Brace published it. No collection, but his "Great Philosophers" which I edited and [Ralph] Manheim translated. I am now doing the second volume. I like the book very much, perhaps best of Jaspers' later writings. It is quite original in that it is *not* a history of philosophy in the sense of a history of "ideas"[;] he takes them out of chronological order and it is as though you were entering a huge palace where somewhere, in some corner or other, you will find them all. They are all contemporaries and he talks with them and against them, sometimes even quite unjustly so, as though they were *there*. I know the Grass book but could never finish it. Certainly very difficult to translate. In my opinion, mostly second-hand, derivative, *outré*, but with some very good parts in it.

Poor Jim. I know very well how that is and how furious one gets if one can't fire anybody. But how do you two like Paris? I mean living in the city. When I was there last summer I thought again [it is] the only place entirely fit to live in. Because it is like a house [—] the whole city really is, with many many rooms; but you feel never exposed, you are always "housed," protected, an entirely different spatial feeling from all other big cities I know.

Love and yours,
Hannah

1. Mary McCarthy, "General Macbeth," *Harper's*, June 1962; reprinted in *The Writing on the Wall*.

2. In May 1962, a high military tribunal found "extenuating circumstances" in the case against Raoul Salan and commuted his death sentence to life imprisonment. Arendt presumably believed he should have been executed.

8 Rue de la Chaise
Paris 7ième
September 28, 1962

Dearest Hannah:

It has reached the point where I feel if I don't write you in the next five minutes I never will—I'll be too ashamed. I don't know exactly what has caused this silence. Lack of time to write a long letter, unwillingness to write a short one. Or you fell off my invalid list. Nicola says he observed that I wrote him as long as he was a classified invalid; after that, silence.

The summer went by very fast. I've been busy and sometimes harassed. We went to Bocca di Magra as usual in August; Jim came back the first of September and I stayed on alone for two weeks, to finish something I was writing in tranquility, for I'd not done as much work as I wanted with the three children there. I did finish it, and it was beautiful there in the early fall with only the Chiaromontes and my friends the Lévis and one or two others left. Now that I'm back there are lots of problems to cope with, which was why Jim encouraged me to stay away. The new apartment, which is still a *chantier* [work site] full of workmen, who keep telephoning me to come and decide where to put the sink or a washstand or choose a new tile or an electrical fixture or say how many shelves there should be in a bookcase. . . . The list is too long; I keep running back and forth there and roaming about Paris with staring eyes trying to find appliances, tiles, furniture, wallpaper. Meanwhile our maid has taken off for America, to be with her regular employer, the new Mrs. Arthur Miller, who is having a baby. So I have no help; Jim works the vacuum cleaner and takes the heavy laundry back and forth. But I'm washing, ironing, cooking, marketing and writing. I quite like it, we both like it; it's very real and affectionate. But it doesn't leave much time. I've not written to a friend—unless Reuel counts—for nearly three months. And I haven't done much reading.

The news. Nicola is much better but still leading a convalescent life. Late hours, alcohol, bathing (even for two minutes), parties immediately give him those angina pains, in the left arm; he has been on a low chlosterol [sic] diet and is much thinner. And naturally he chafes against all this and against the fact that he has to take a lot of sedatives and tranquilizers. It has slowed down his writing rate (it takes him two days to do an article that he used to do in half a day), but he's not sure that the writing isn't better. He is very nice, very angry with the world—I don't mean in his capacity as a cardiac patient.

Tucci turned up in Edinburgh, where I went to a Conference on the Novel in the middle of August—a fantastic affair; did you read anything about it?[1] Tucci there revealed a side of himself I'd never seen before—that of a *malade imaginaire*. He decided that he'd broken his arm carrying a pretty girl's suitcase on the train (the Scottish doctor said bursitis) and went around looking like an exiled prime minister, about the period of the Stresa Conference [1935], wearing a black suit, the arm in a sling made of an Hermes scarf, hand on his breast. When x-rays failed to reveal a fracture, he settled for a slipped disk. He made an awful spectacle of himself in one of the public sessions reading aloud an interminable attitudinizing letter from himself to the statesmen of the world re atomic warfare, was very angry with me because I failed to name him among the five chief American writers, and finally went off to visit some rich Scots he had picked up in Rome. I've just had a letter from him from Turin; he's staying in the villa of the Fiat people—the Agnellis. In short he was at his very worst; the appearance of his book seems to have endowed him with one quality he never had—literary vanity; the desire to cut a figure on a public stage. Up to now he's confined his acting to drawing-room performances. I'm very fed up with him but suppose I'll get over it if I don't see him for awhile.

Aside from him the Conference was bizarre enough. People jumping up to confess they were homosexuals or heterosexuals; a Registered Heroin Addict leading the young Scottish opposition to the literary tyranny of the Communist Hugh Macdiarmid (who had rejoined the party, after being out of it for years following the Hungarian Revolution); the Jugoslav group in schism and their ambassador threatening to pull the Belgrade Opera and Ballet out of the Festival because the non-official delegate had been allowed to speak before the official delegate; an English woman novelist describing her communications with her dead daughter; a Dutch homosexual, former male nurse, now a Catholic convert, seeking someone to baptise him; a bearded Sikh with hair down to his waist declaring on the platform that homosexuals were incapable of love, just as (he said) hermaphrodites were incapable of orgasm (Stephen Spender, in the chair, murmured that he should have thought they could have two). And all this before an audience of over two thousand people per day, mostly, I suppose, Scottish Presbyterians. The most striking fact was the number of lunatics both on the platform and in the public. One young woman novelist was released temporarily from a mental hospital in order to attend the Conference, and she was one of the milder cases. I confess I enjoyed it enormously. Do you know of an Austrian writer called Erich Fried? He and I made common cause in trying to establish a plane of sanity between the lunatics and philistines, though we were at odds ourselves on the validity of psychoanalysis[2] (his madness or my philistinism).

Enough of that. Nicholas Nabokov, on the telephone last night, told me that Cal Lowell was in a mental ward in Buenos Aires and that Marilyn Monroe committed suicide because she had been having an affair with Bobby Kennedy and the White House had intervened. This was the mysterious telephone call—from Kennedy's brother-in-law, the actor Peter Lawford. Our age begins to sound like some awful colossal movie about the late Roman Emperors and their Messalinas and Poppaeas. The Bobby Kennedy swimming pool being the bath with asses' milk.

Did you see the *Esquire* piece on me?[3] I imagine, if you did, that you were indignant at the freedom with which you were quoted; I was. To me the most astonishing thing was that the young man had assured me it wouldn't be a "personality piece," and perhaps he thought it wasn't. I.e., didn't know the difference. To assume a deliberate breach of faith is probably to flatter his powers of discrimination. The worst, I thought, was his looking up the court records of Edmund's and my separation suit and quoting, as if this were material I'd given him. Also quoting your aside about Philip Rahv and someone else's remark about my marriage to Bowden. The only fruit of this is that I have resolved never under any circumstances to give another interview, about myself or anyone else; I managed to keep this vow during the Edinburgh Conference. Whenever a journalist became pressing, I thought of Mr. Brower. I feel very apologetic about having got you into this and conclude I must be a poor judge of character. Jim was just disgusted with the whole thing but not particularly surprised; he had been against it from the beginning, on principle.

Have you read Gunther [sic] Grass's *The Tin Drum*? I've almost finished it and can't make up my mind what I think. I liked it very much at first, but it does become forced and tedious. The "epic sweep," I think, was a mistake—an error of vanity. But there are very good things all through. He has many of the virtues and faults of Tucci and of Nabokov too; it occurs to me that this grotesque posturing and arrogant acrobatics is a new genre—the genre of the displaced person.[4]

Well, I must stop. It's three days now since I began this. When are you coming abroad? I am thinking of coming to the U.S. in March and trying to weave the trip around some lecture engagements. Jim is fine; his job has lots of problems, but he's happy. The strain of the divorce-years has relaxed, and he's serene, even joyful. He has got used, too, to being with a new kind of person, without having to be on guard, like finding a new family. He was very content this year at Bocca di Magra, even during my week's absence in Edinburgh; he spent the month reading through the tragedies of Shakespeare. The children have learned French and were very content too, with the other children and with the grown-ups, whom they became attached to, especially the Lévis, Miriam and Nicola. In short all is well, and I am happy, besides being surprised at how well it is. The only difficulty is the organization of time.

Please overlook my silence and write soon. It alarms me how long it is since I've had news of you, even indirect. With much love to you and to Heinrich,

Mary

1. The conference was held during the annual Edinburgh Festival. McCarthy gave a much-publicized valedictory to the author of *Naked Lunch*, William Burroughs.
2. McCarthy disdained it.
3. Brock Brower's "Mary McCarthyism," *Esquire*, July 1962, appeared in tandem with profiles of Jacqueline Kennedy and Brenda Lee, and was the first major mass-media treatment of McCarthy's career.
4. McCarthy presented this thesis in her Edinburgh address.

Wesleyan University
Center for Advanced Studies
Middletown, Connecticut
October 30, 1962

Dearest Mary:

I know it is terrible to dictate a letter and not to write it but I don't know how long I would postpone answering yours otherwise. Please forgive me.

I was so happy with your letter. Everything sounds so good and you yourself sound in high spirits. I enjoyed the Edinburgh bit [handwritten insert illegible]. I think I read something about it. I knew that Tucci is a hypochondriac. He goes for a complete checkup twice a year to the hospital, each time in perfect health, but a broken arm is, of course, something new.

I was very sorry about Lowell. I hadn't heard from him but I was so little at home that I didn't find it strange. Will they be back in New York?

Esquire piece: The less said about it the better, I suppose. Jim, of course, was right and his principles are right, so let's forget the whole business.

The Tin Drum: I read it in German years ago and I think it is an artificial *tour de force*—as though [Grass] had read all of modern literature and had then decided to borrow and to do something of his own.

What do you say, since we are on literature, about the Nobel Prize going to Steinbeck? Rather surprising! Have you any idea who the alternatives were?

I just read in the papers about the De Gaulle outcome. Very surprising and perhaps encouraging, though what is going to happen if he actually should resign, I suppose God alone knows. From what I read in the paper, it is clear that he has a majority against him, since one has to count the abstentions.[1]

And Cuba, of course—but I am somehow in no mood to discuss that [the missile crisis] now. Let me know what your reaction is. I never believed that this thing could get really serious.

In conclusion, just my schedule. I shall come to Europe in February and stay until June which means that we will not see each other when you come to the States. Will you be in Paris in February? I may then stop over there. I would be on my way either to Cologne (some broadcasting which would pay for my trip) or to Basel where Jaspers has his 80th birthday. In March I shall meet Heinrich probably in Naples and we shall go for a long trip to Sicily, Greece, etc. I don't think I will be back in the States before July 1st. Heinrich has his sabbatical.

The Revolution book is finished and will appear in January. The Eichmann article has also become a book, and to everybody's surprise, has been accepted by *The New Yorker* almost in its entirety. They are starting the series of [five] articles end of January, which reminds me that Harold has now become their Art Critic and the first article appeared in the current issue. Just in case you should have missed it, I want to quote one sentence: "In our time, those who are content merely to paint pictures or to contemplate them are out of touch, either through choice or through ignorance, with the dynamics of creation in the arts; their norm is to be found in the canvases and picture gazers at the outdoor shows in Washington Square. Art, including its appreciation, has become an are[n]a of conflicting powers." Isn't this marvelous? God knows whatever possessed him.

Much, much love to you and Jim.
Yours, H

[. . .]

141 Rue de Rennes
Paris 6
April 12, 1963
[Postcard]

Dearest Hannah,

I came back that night [after they had talked by phone] and bought a thermometer. I had a temperature of 102; the next day it was 103. Stayed in bed in the Inghilterra 5 days. Then Francisco [Chiaromonte] (Nicola's doctor-brother) decided it was best to send me back to Paris to the hospital. So I'm in the American Hospital, Neuilly, and will be here for another week. It is hepatitis, probably viral. Am now feeling better; in Rome was awfully sick. Incidentally the trip back on the autostrada was *incomparably* beautiful—classic views and wild mountains. How are you and Heinrich? Love, Mary.

Athens, 4/21/63
[Postcard]

Dearest Mary—Just back from Crete, got card. *How perfectly Beastly!* How did you get it? It will take you some time to recover. Keep me posted how you are.

This here is perfect. We are staying in Athens at a sort of *pensione,* tout à fait chez nous, and make our trips. Very quiet. Crete was *great* landscape, but otherwise disappointing. *Very* little left of Minoan culture, and Knossos horribly restored.

Much, much love, my dear. Affectionate regards to Jim.

Hannah

Part Three

September 1963 – November 1966

[Mary McCarthy's bout with hepatitis, like the respiratory infections and "slipped disk," occurred after a period of intense work, when she had finally finished *The Group*. Exhausted, she had rewarded herself, as she often did at such times, with a trip, during which she collapsed.

The hardest of all her novels to write—it took eleven years—*The Group*, with a first printing in August 1963 of 70,000, and sales in hardbound and paperback of over five million copies, was by far her most successful. The story of how eight Vassar girls from the class of '33 come to terms, or don't, with the brave new world of New Deal America catapulted McCarthy into the limelight. It also threw her into a line of fire from fellow intellectuals in New York, led by Norman Mailer, the likes of which was exceeded only by the attacks hurled at Hannah Arendt after the publication of *Eichmann in Jerusalem: A Report on the Banality of Evil* in May 1963.

Arendt's report of the trial of Adolf Eichmann for his role in the "final solution of the Jewish question" first appeared as a series of articles in *The New Yorker* (February 16, 23 and March 2, 9, 16, 1963). After the book was published, she found herself at the center of a storm of controversy over issues she had only touched on in her text, which was based on the transcript of the trial and was not an inquiry into the massacre of European Jews.

Foremost among these issues was the conduct of the Jewish Councils, which had, in the early years of the war, complied with Nazi demands to inventory their congregations, thus facilitating their later

removal. Controversy over this compliance had, in fact, long sim-
mered beneath the surface of debate over the history of the "final
solution." *Eichmann in Jerusalem,* with its brief but searing testimonies of
cooperation, seemed to question the honor of Jewish leadership.

Such was not her intention, Arendt maintained, privately in letters
to McCarthy, publicly in occasional interviews or letters to the editor.
Her many critics, she insisted, had substituted an absurd "image" of
what she was saying for the more limited but unpalatable truths she
had to report.

With the Eichmann controversy, Arendt confronted the risks of
public life, from which she shrank with a horror unmixed with her
usual humor. Her gratitude to McCarthy for her unstinting support,
and her own sympathy for McCarthy's troubles with critics of *The
Group,* ran deep.]

New York
September 16, 1963

Dearest Mary:

I know how long this letter has been overdue. I liked the Group
very very much, it is quite different from your other books, at the
same time milder and sadder; it reads like a definite statement of
that period, but looked at from a very great distance. You have won
a perspective, or perhaps rather: you have arrived at a point so far
removed from your former life that everything now can fall into
place. You yourself are no longer directly involved. And this quality
makes the book more of a novel than any of your other books. I
don't need to repeat what everybody who knows anything says —
that it is beautifully written (the inner balance of the sentences is
extraordinary) and often hilariously funny. I also read with the
greatest delight the Italian story in the New Yorker.[1] That is one of
your very very best short stories.

Why did I not write earlier? Well, the truth of the matter is that
I did not "feel fine." Heinrich has not been well, he is much better
now, working as usual, etc., but I am still deeply worried and quite
unhappy that I have to go to Chicago. (But please, let this remain
entre nous.) We have been together for 28 years and life without
him would be unthinkable. Add to this the Eichmann-trouble which
I try to keep from him as much as I possibly can — and you will
understand that I am in no mood of writing. You probably know
that PR also turned against me in a rather vicious manner (Lionel
Abel who anyhow goes around town spreading slander about myself

as well as Heinrich),[2] and generally, one can say that the mob—intellectual or otherwise—has been successfully mobilized. I just heard that the Anti-Defamation League has sent out a circular letter to all rabbis to preach against me on New Year's Day.[3] Well, I suppose this would not disturb me unduly if everything else were all right. But worried as I am, I can no longer trust myself to keep my head and not to explode. What a risky business to tell the truth on a factual level without theoretical and scholarly embroidery.[4] This side of it, I admit, I do enjoy; it taught me a few lessons about truth and politics.

I am leaving New York next week. You can always reach me: Committee on Social Thought, University of Chicago. [. . .]

I suppose you are now back from Italy and I hope you had a very good time. I am glad to see you on the best-seller list, and also that you get so much money. That is the right thing for you, dear, enjoy it and be happy!

Give my love to Jim. I think we met, and understood each other in Paris, as we did not before.

Much love, yours,
Hannah

1. Mary McCarthy, "The Hounds of Summer," *The New Yorker*, September 14, 1963.
2. *Partisan Review* published "The Aesthetics of Evil: Hannah Arendt on Eichmann and the Jews" in its March–April 1963 issue. In it, Lionel Abel charged that Arendt had made Eichmann aesthetically palatable and the Jews aesthetically repugnant.
3. This was an A.D.L. memorandum to regional offices and national committees calling on B'nai B'rith to denounce Arendt's depiction of "Jewish participation in the Nazi holocaust."
4. The "truth on a factual level" probably refers to Arendt's account of the Jewish Councils' compliance with Nazi orders to register their members. Resistance wouldn't have prevented the extermination policy, she contended, but it might have made it harder to put into effect.

370 Riverside Drive
New York 25, N.Y.
20 September 1963

Dearest Mary:

Our letters crossed[1] and I am kind of sorry that I wrote you at a moment of depression. Heinrich is well again—enough. Today I can only repeat: your ears must be burning too, because of the many discussions about your book. Yesterday I had a long talk about it with Denver Lindley who likes the book enormously and so do many others. That the "boys"[2] have tried to turn against you seems to me only natural and I think it has more to do with "The Group" being a best-seller than with any political matters. By the way, I understand that they will not keep it up.

After receiving your letter, I did something which I wouldn't have done otherwise. I jotted down, for you and Nicola, a number of points against [Abel's review],[3] though I shall not answer for the reason I explain: This is a piece that is part of the political campaign, it is not criticism and it doesn't really concern my book. Like the [Michael] Musmanno review,[4] it is about a book which was never written. The attempt by the political campaign people is to create an "image" which eventually will cover the real book. I cannot do anything against it, not only for the reasons you mention, but because an individual is powerless by definition and the power of the image-makers is considerable—money, personnel, time, connections etc. My position is that I wrote a report and that I am not in politics, either Jewish or otherwise.

My reason for breaking with the P.R. people has nothing to do with the content of Abel's review, but with the choice of the reviewer. What is involved is a) that they knew that Abel had written a piece against me before [a negative review of *Between Past and Future*], hence was hostile to begin with and b) that they showed an extraordinary lack of the most elementary respect for myself and my work in choosing somebody like Abel as a reviewer. Dwight wrote them an excellent and very furious letter on the subject.

I may add that there are some points in the Report which indeed are in conflict with the book on totalitarianism, but God knows Abel didn't spot them. These points are as follows: *First:* I speak at length in the "Totalitarianism" about the "holes of oblivion." On page 212 of the Eichmann book I say "the holes of oblivion do not exist. Nothing human is that perfect, and there are simply too many people in the world to make oblivion possible. One man will always be left alive to tell the story." *Second:* If one reads the book carefully, one sees that Eichmann was much less influenced by ideology than I assumed in the book on totalitarianism. The impact of ideology upon the individual may have been overrated by me. Even in the totalitarianism book, in the chapter on ideology and terror, I mention the curious loss of ideological content that occurs among the elite of the movement. The movement itself becomes all important; the content of anti-semitism [sic] for instance gets lost in the extermination policy, for extermination would not have come to an end when no Jew was left to be killed. In other words, extermination per se is more important than anti-semitism or racism. *Third,* and perhaps most importantly, the very phrase: "Banality of Evil" stands in contrast to the phrase I used in the totalitarianism book, "radical evil." This is too difficult a subject to be dealt with here, but it is important.

You write that one hesitates to claim the right to define my ideas. As I see it, there are no "ideas" in this Report, there are only facts with a few conclusions, and these conclusions usually appear at the end of each chapter. The only exception to this is the Epilog, which is a discussion of the legal aspect of the case. In other words, my point would be that what the whole furor is about are *facts,* and neither theories nor ideas. The hostility against me is a hostility against someone who tells the truth on a factual level, and not against someone who has ideas which are in conflict with those commonly held.

I am leaving here on the 25th and my address is Quadrangle Club, University of Chicago. [. . .]

I am a little concerned about your health. Take care of yourself and let's see each other soon.

Love, much love

Hannah

This letter was dictated to a so-called bi-lingual secretary. His German *is* good. Forgive me.

1. McCarthy's letter is missing.
2. Arendt alludes to a larger circle of New York intellectuals than the *Partisan Review* editors, to whom the term "boys" commonly referred.
3. This four-page single-spaced thirteen-point rejoinder to Lionel Abel's *Partisan Review* article is on file with The Mary McCarthy Papers at Vassar College.
4. In his influential review of *Eichmann in Jerusalem* ("Man With an Unspoiled Conscience," *The New York Times Book Review,* May 19, 1963), Judge Michael Musmanno charged Arendt with defending the Gestapo and slandering the Jewish victims.

Bocca di Magra

September 24, 1963

Dearest Hannah:

Your letter just reached me. I understand why you don't feel like answering Abel and I'm very troubled for you about all this and anxious about Heinrich. You don't say in what way he hasn't been well, and I should like to know. The only thing that relieves me is that you felt you could go to Chicago [to teach].

I want to help you in some way and not simply by being an ear. What can be done about this Eichmann business, which is assuming the proportions of a pogrom? Whether you answer or not (and I still feel it would be best if you answered somewhere, even if not in PR), I am going to write something to the boys for publication.[1] But I'm condemned to silence till I get back to Paris, because none of us here has *Eichmann* or *The Origins [of Totalitarianism]*. Nicola has written a letter to Lionel or rather, in the course of a letter to him (they are friends from a long time ago, and I can only explain the continuation of the friendship by Nicola's loyalty or obstinacy), told him that he thought he was wrong in his attack on you. Very forcefully, according to Miriam.

Nicola feels that the issues raised by your book ought to be discussed. Not the debater's points "scored" by Lionel but the implications of your views about the role played by the Jewish Councils—that is, what is implied about organizations in modern society generally. He would also like to know why you think the Nazis failed in their anti-semitic [*sic*] program in Denmark, Bulgaria, and Italy—this apart from the presence or absence of Jewish Councils and from the sheer facts as you give them. Can a common factor be found to explain this? For if there is such a common factor, it ought to be cultivated and safeguarded by humanity for future emergencies. Or is there no such thing? Was it in some way random—here the personal courage of a king, there the natural easygoingness and humane realism of an old people (the Italians) etc.? And he would like to see you develop your basic notion of the ordinariness of Eichmann. What does this mean? If not the naive formulation that "there is a little Eichmann in all of us," then what? He thinks he agrees with what you are saying but he is not sure he has understood you. Of course, the idea of sustaining such a discussion in the atmosphere created by Lionel and thousands of preaching rabbis is somewhat farfetched perhaps. But perhaps just such a discussion, pursued in a thoughtful way, would be the necessary and in a way the only answer to what you call the mobilization of the mob. (For some reason I shrink from writing the word "mob" myself, possibly out of a kind of prudery or possibly because it sounds shrill, like a mob itself.) I am thinking of Socrates' *Apology*. [. . .]

Dear Hannah, I will see you in Chicago. I have to give a reading [of *The Group*] in New York at the Poetry Center on November 10, and that, so far, is the only certain date in my program. Since I'm going to Madrid October 8, for a six-day conference on the Novel, I will probably sail as late as possible and extend my American visit farther into November. I leave here for Paris the day after to-morrow.

Jim, who was here for a day, sends you his love. We've both been rather tried and beset this summer, partly by my health, which still keeps me tired and tense, and partly by the problem of his children, who have become very tense too (therefore trying even to robust nerves) and who are plainly showing the effects of a very bad environment. With their mother. The deterioration was noticed by everyone here. The question is what to do. You cannot change their mother, and though I've considered taking them all to live with us (assuming this would be possible either through a bribe to the mother or through legal action), I've concluded that it's not possible for me. It would mean in the first place finding a larger apartment, for with three children you would have to have at least a live-in nurse, if not a nurse and a cook, and I'm simply not equal to that at the moment. Not in Paris. In these last few days, I've thought of a compromise solution. To send the oldest (he's eleven) back to the boarding school in England, which he pines for and which represents his image of order and happiness, and to take a house (rent it) in the country outside Paris for weekend use.[2] Nothing fancy but a place where each child could have his own room and keep his things, including the one in boarding school. We could keep the car there too and go there most weekends and during Christmas and Easter vacations. Also perhaps for a month in the summer before coming here. It would mean real stability for them and being close in a solid way to their father, whom they love; they would also have the outdoors. Seeing them this way too, we could probably exercise an influence on them—their values at present are exclusively those of the PX and television and comic books and "How much did you pay for it?" I haven't yet told Jim this idea and I don't know what he'll think of it. But I suspect he'll be very happy, for the children are a thorn in his conscience. (Not that he talks about it.) I should like to see his soul more at rest. And I don't think it should be difficult to persuade his ex-wife, who could have them off her hands part of the time and economize on their *nourriture*, without losing face. [. . .]

I'm not deluding myself—after three summers with the children—that this won't involve a good deal of strain and effort. But if I don't take a hand in this situation, the moral strain will be worse than the physical and nervous. So we shall see.

Dear Hannah, write me soon again and keep me informed about Heinrich. My deepest love to you and tight embraces,

Mary

P.S. I'm pleased you liked the *New Yorker* story ["The Hounds of Summer"]. When I read the proofs I did not care for the end.

1. This became a twelve-page rebuttal of Abel's review, entitled "The Hue and Cry," *Partisan Review*, January–February, 1964.
2. Over the next five years, the Wests rented two successive "weekend" houses outside Paris.

The University of Chicago
Chicago 37, Illinois
Committee on Social Thought
October 3, 1963

Dearest Mary,

I hope you got my second letter in the meantime. As I said before, I am sorry for that first letter which I wrote you. Heinrich is all right again and I probably was over-anxious.

Let me answer your letter as briefly as possible. I am convinced that I should not answer individual critics. I probably shall finally make, not an answer, but a kind of evaluation of this whole strange business. This, I think, should be done after the furor has run its course and I think that next spring will be a good time. I also intend to write an essay about "Truth and Politics," which would be an implicit answer.[1] If you were here you would understand that this whole business, with few exceptions, has absolutely nothing to do with criticism or polemics in the normal sense of the word. It is a political campaign, led and guided in all particulars by interest groups and governmental agencies. It would be foolish for me, but not for others, to overlook this fact. The criticism is directed at an "image" and this image has been substituted for the book I wrote. To illustrate what I mean: something very similar happened in response to [Rolf] Hochhuth's play "The Representative" [*The Deputy*], which criticized Vatican policy during the war with respect to the

Jews. The play is not good, but the question Hochhuth raised is very legitimate: why did the Pope never protest publicly against the persecution and finally the mass murder of Jews? He knew of the details and this, as far as I know, nobody ever contested. In its attempt to discredit this question the *Osservatore Romano* wrote as follows: "If H's thesis is right then it was not Hitler, Eichmann, or the SS who were responsible for all the crimes but Pope Pius." (I translated from the German.) This of course was sheer nonsense and H never said anything of the sort, but it served an important purpose: an "image" was created to cover up the real issue. What the Vatican tried to do, though it did not entirely succeed, was to substitute an absurd position which could easily be knocked down, for the real issue. For there is of course no question that a public position by the Pope, with or without threat of excommunication, would have been a factor of the greatest magnitude, in Germany herself but especially in the countries under Nazi occupation.

Something very similar has happened in my case and I mentioned a number of phoney issues for which I am praised or blamed in my last letter. To repeat: the question of Jewish resistance substitutes for the real issue, namely, that individual members of the Jewish councils had the possibility not to participate. Or: "A Defense of Eichmann," which I supposedly wrote, is a substitution for the real issue: what kind of a man was the accused and to what extent can our legal system take care of these new criminals who are not ordinary criminals?

As to the points Nicola made: my book is a report and therefore leaves all questions of why things happened as they happened out of account. I describe the role of the Jewish councils. It was neither my intention nor my task to explain this whole business — either by reference to Jewish history or by reference to modern society in general. I, too, would like to know why countries so unlike each other as Denmark, Italy and Bulgaria saved their Jews. My "basic notion" of the ordinariness of Eichmann is much less a notion than a faithful description of a phenomenon. I am sure there can be drawn many conclusions from this phenomenon and the most general I drew is indicated: "banality of evil." I may sometime want to write about this, and then I would write about the nature of evil, but it would have been entirely wrong of me to do it within the framework of the report.

Incidentally, it seems the Rabbis would not comply with the circular letter addressed to them. And let me say that the word "mob" probably has a different significance for me. I use it as a term, so it doesn't sound "shrill" to me. [2]

I am worried about your health and even more worried about the problems of the children. You have such a tendency to overdo things. Be careful.

Let me know when you will be in the country. It would be marvelous if you could come to Chicago. How long will you stay in America? Much love.

Yours,
Hannah

I am so enjoying the luxury of having a secretery that I could not resist the temptation of dictating this letter too. Forgive me!

1. "Truth and Politics" was published in *The New Yorker*, February 25, 1967; it is reprinted in the 1968 edition of *Between Past and Future*.
2. In Weimar Germany, "mob" was a pejorative term applied to persons of influence, including intellectuals, who specialized in vilification campaigns against political or cultural dissidents, thus presumably aiding the rise of fascism.

Hotel Lucia
Madrid
Saturday [10/19/63]

Dearest Hannah,

I'm writing this in the middle of a writers' conference in Madrid. Literally in the middle—someone is talking in Spanish about "responsabilità sociale" and "Carlos Marx." It is very amusing and also sad and I will tell you about it later. In America. I'm sailing November 1 and will be in the U. S. till the end of November. I'll come to Chicago to see you, if you want, and I hope you do.

This whole Eichmann business is terrible. Now the English reviews. Jim has sent me here [R. H. S.] Crossman and [Hugh] Trevor-Roper. But he also told me on the phone that there was a very good one, in every sense, by [A.] Alvarez in the *New Statesman*.

Before I left Bocca di Magra I started an answer to Lionel Abel, wrote about four pages, and learned from Nicola that P. R. had gone to press. Instead, then, I wrote a letter to William and Philip (jointly) saying what I thought of their publishing Abel and in fact castigating them. It was very sharp but written as the counsel of a friend. I have not had a *word* in answer. Which is strange, even from a professional point of view, since I asked when the next number would go to press and said I wanted to write something about the subject. Of course one must reckon with their laziness.

I sent your documentation [the thirteen-point rejoinder to Abel] on to Nicola, who is here with Miriam. He has given it back to me and I am waiting now to see what will be the comment [. . .] of PR. As for myself, I don't want to answer with expertise but simply as a common reader—to whom, after all, the book was addressed. In what I started at B[occa] d. M[agra] I took up the question of "aesthetics."

Now the speaker has stopped [and so did the letter, which was sent with the next].

141 Rue de Rennes
Paris 6
October 24, 1963

Dearest Hannah:

I wrote the enclosed (which, I must say, seems hardly worth sending on) last week in Madrid. And never found time to mail it.

The writers' conference was curious. Surreptitiously backed by the Congress for Cultural Freedom and under the semi-protection of the French Cultural Institute, it was mainly peopled by Communists and their sympathizers. Some of the young ones were extremely nice—touching and provincial. For them modern literature was simply a battlefield between socialist realism and the *nouveau roman*. Lukács via Lucien Goldman[1] was their Aquinas, and their speeches were extremely scholastic. Only a few exceptions to this. Nearly everyone one talked to had been in prison, usually three times. The only foreign literature they knew was French, though some were aware of neo-realism in Italy.

For me it was an exhilarating respite. The mountain air and pure water of Madrid and the fact that no one had ever heard of me there. In Paris I am assaulted by clippings about *The Group*, many of them terribly hostile, and by requests for interviews and photos. Success seems to take so much of your time; you are devoured by it. And I confess I'm depressed by what seems to me the treachery of the New York Book Review [sic] people. I suppose you saw the

Mailer piece and the parody that preceded it.[2] I find it strange that people who are supposed to be my friends should solicit a review from an announced enemy[3] but even stranger that they should have kept pestering me to write for them while hiding from me the fact that the Mailer review was coming. As for the parody, they have never mentioned it to this day, perhaps hoping that I would not notice it. But if I'd agreed to do one of the many pieces they proposed, it would have appeared in the same number with the Mailer and constituted a sort of condonation. This leaves me bewildered and disoriented. I can't put myself in the place of Elizabeth Hardwick or even of Bob Silvers.[4] It parallels, as I foresaw, in a small way the Eichmann furore, but seems to lack even the hypocritical justification that Jewish piety there provided. It occurs to me that a desire to make a sensation has taken precedence in New York over everything else. The literary and intellectual world is turning into a series of Happenings, like the one at the Edinburgh Theatre Conference where a naked girl was introduced into the auditorium. The editors have become showmen and the reader is a spectator in a circus ring.

This is the only explanation I can find.

If I am upset, I can imagine what you must be. And combining being upset for you and upset for myself has made my head spin. In this revolving door one is caught without an exit, and in this multiple vision—like a Picasso image—there is no cheek left to turn. And to think about the whole spectacle impersonally only makes one, if anything, more depressed.

Anyway, much, much love to you and I shall see you in America, where we can enjoy guilt by association together. Love to Heinrich too and kisses. And love and sympathy from Jim.

Mary

1. Georg Lukács was an influential Marxist literary critic, one of whose interpreters was Lucien Goldman.

2. In "The Mary McCarthy Case," *The New York Review of Books*, October 17, 1963, Norman Mailer charged the author of *The Group* with having written a "lady-book," which did no more than match "the best novel the editors of the women's magazines ever conceived in *their* secret ambitions." Elizabeth Hardwick's unsigned parody, "The Gang," had appeared three weeks earlier.

3. At the 1962 Edinburgh Festival, Mailer had challenged McCarthy to a verbal duel on the BBC, and when she refused, McCarthy later reported, he had called her "the regent of American letters, but . . . a weak regent."

4. Robert A. Silvers was, and remains, coeditor of *The New York Review of Books*, which was founded during the *New York Times* strike in the summer of 1963.

Quadrangle Club
1155 West 57th
Chicago 37, Ill. . . .
[Fall 1963]

Dearest Mary—

This only to show you how you can reach me. And thanks for the letters. I read Mailer's review only a couple of days ago—it is so full of personal and stupid invectives (stupid means vulgar) that I can't understand how or why they printed it. I am afraid that Elisabeth [sic] had the brilliant idea to ask him—just as she had the brilliant idea to ask Abel to do the PR piece. I asked her and she said 'yes'—so no doubt about PR. But she probably would not have done either if there had not been fertile ground for precisely this kind of stab-in-the-back. And what surprises and shocks me most of all is the tremendous amount of hatred and hostility lying around and waiting only for a chance to break out. I wrote a few questioning words to Bob Silvers who is also after me for reviews—understandably since they treated me rather fairly.

How does your program look and when can you come here? Yes, fame is very tiresome and very tiring.

But let's postpone everything until we can talk.

Much much love
Yours,
Hannah

141 Rue de Rennes
Paris 6
December 28, 1963

Dearest Hannah:

One of my ambitions was to write to you before Christmas, but I didn't achieve it. I have thought about you so much and talked about you with Jim. And yet till today I haven't had time. The holidays. Presents for the children. A trip to London principally for Christmas shopping. Then flu. Jim had it last week; then I; then Jim again. He's still in bed, though he got up Christmas afternoon, because we'd invited forty or so people for an At Home, with a tree, presents, eggnog, ham, etc. Also one of my first acts on returning was to fire my maid, who'd done absolutely nothing during my absence but read the newspaper in front of the kitchen stove. So

156

I now only have a Swedish student part time, and it's not enough. Particularly with illness and trays.

The only thing I did manage to do was write an attack on Lionel Abel for PR.[1] Jim did not like it; he thought it was too long and too emotional. Probably he is right, but by the time he'd read it it was already mailed. Then—typically for PR—it went astray in the mails. They had not told me that their New York address was no longer valid. Cables from William. But apparently he got it, since I haven't heard from him again for some time. I hope the piece won't disappoint you too much. When I was planning to write you before Christmas I was going to send you the carbon. But now the magazine must be almost out, and besides it's Saturday afternoon and the post-office is closed, so that I couldn't get a heavy letter weighed for the right postage.

Have you written the piece for the *Herald Tribune?*[2] I must say, answering Lionel was for me a hard and depressing job. Not that his piece was "brilliant," as some people said, but because it was so fearfully crooked that it took all your strength just to straighten it out. Before you could find an argument to answer.

The main thing, though, I wanted to hear from you was how is Heinrich? Please write me a line as soon as you can. I have thought about him a great deal and with much love.

Yesterday I read your exchange with [Gerhard] Scholem in the new *Encounter.*[3] I thought your part was very good, but I didn't like his tone of infinite sad wisdom. I told [British publisher] George Weidenfeld, whom I saw for lunch the other day, that the net effect of all this controversy was to make me resolve never to set foot in the state of Israel. He was shocked.

There's not much news here. In London we saw some plays and pictures (two Goya shows), but here I've only been in the shops and at a few parties. But not very many of those, thank God, because of official mourning for Kennedy.[4] We have seen Milosz[5] several times, and he's convinced that the end of the world is at hand. I told him I agreed with him. Besides Milosz, the Lévis, Sonia Orwell, and a young Dutch writer; those are the only human contacts that are real for me here.

What have you decided about Chicago?[6] I wish I could talk to you.

On the nice side were Christmas presents from Jim. The complete Arden Shakespeare. The Nonesuch Bible. Verdi's *Requiem* and lots of Hayden [sic] and Mozart. And a warm raspberry colored house coat and long skirt. And a jewel, Russian, made of hyacinths and topaz. Christmas itself was rather fun, since most of the people who came were people we'd known a long time, like the Lévis and Janet Flanner and Peggy Guggenheim, who turned up from Venice. It was a rather sentimental party. People brought their mother or their small child or their new dog. Our children had Christmas here two days ahead of time and then went off to the mountains to ski with their mother. [. . .]

One strange thing that has happened is that I got a letter from Diana Trilling. It enclosed a clipping about the marriage of Lincoln Reis's daughter to the son of the head of Pan American. But I gathered that this was a pretext. The letter must be an olive branch. But why? She must mean that she is on my side about something. Can it be *Eichmann* or the *New York Review*? Or something else. I had a syrupy letter from Lizzie, saying that Cal was having trouble again but that she hoped he would not have to go to the hospital. I've been wanting to write him too but haven't. Now I shall do it.

De Gaulle's victory did not cheer my Christmas.[7] As you probably know, he's increasing the censorship on news, which already was stringent enough. Milosz's son was arrested during a student demonstration; actually he was simply passing by and stopped to see what was happening. For some reason, they released him, but all the other foreign students who were arrested were deported the next day.[8] I didn't see a word of this in the *Monde*, which did cover the demonstration. On television there was no mention of the demonstration—the principal event of that day.

Dear Hannah, a Happy New Year to you. I wish time would roll back and that we would be going to your New Year's Eve party and Tillich and Bertha [Gruner, Arendt's secretary] would get drunk.

My deepest love to you, and Jim sends his warmest affection to you both,

Mary

1. Mary McCarthy, "The Hue and Cry," *Partisan Review*, January–February, 1964.
2. This was probably Arendt's article on Rolf Hochhuth's *The Deputy*, published on February 23, 1964.
3. Arendt's exchange of letters with Gerhard (Gershom) Scholem, a friend from prewar Germany who taught the history of religion at Hebrew University, appeared in the January 1964 *Encounter*.
4. President John F. Kennedy had been assassinated on November 22, while McCarthy was visiting Arendt at the University of Chicago.

5. Writer Czeslaw Milosz, who was active in the Polish resistance to Nazi occupation in the 1940s, criticized Polish intellectuals for their accommodation to Communism in the 1950s. He had settled in the United States in 1961.

6. Arendt was expected to lecture at the University of Chicago again in the spring, but her husband's health made her uncertain about whether to go.

7. The President's victory in the November general elections gave the Gaullist party an additional sixty-four seats in the National Assembly; with conservative support, this gave it the majority De Gaulle needed to carry out his postwar plans to restore France to great-power status.

8. This incident was incorporated into McCarthy's next novel, *Birds of America*.

370 Riverside Drive
New York 25, N.Y.
January 13, 1964

Dearest Mary,

How glad I was to hear from you. I came back in the middle of December, when there were already sub-zero temperatures in Chicago. I promptly had the flu, too, which gave me a nice rest. Then Heinrich came home and was promptly dispatched to the doctor for a second checkup—he had a preliminary one during the Thanksgiving period—the result: absolutely nothing, everything completely normal, including circulation, encephalogram, etc. He also is less tired now and pretty much his old self.

I heard about your attack on Abel for PR, because William goes around complaining bitterly that you attacked the Jews and God knows what. He also feels that you are "unhappy." I suppose it will appear in due time and, need I say, I thank you.

I haven't yet written the piece for the Herald Tribune and am just about to finish the piece on Sarraute which became a little overlong, but I cannot help it.[1] I re-read all her novels and now feel, but didn't say, that only the two last comical ones are really successful.

Cal is in the hospital somewhere in Connecticut. I talked to Lizzie on the phone, because [British critic A.] Alvarez stayed with her. Lizzie was very optimistic, but, as far as I know, he is not yet back. I haven't seen many people, only Dwight and Auden. I am glad to be home, but I have nothing decided about Chicago. I shall be at Yale early next month. Things got rather complicated because I received in the meantime an invitation to Berkeley with financial arrangements so good that it is really hard to say no. Maybe one should try to make money as long as one can. And then again, maybe one shouldn't.

My *dear*, a happy New Year to you both and let's try to see as much of each other during it as we can.

Love,
Hannah

P.S. Needless to say I am delighted that "The Group" is still number one on the bestseller list. Incidentally, I've re-read it to compare it with Sarraute and it is really very very good! Was there any review worth reading? What I saw—pro or con—was rather idiotic.

1. Arendt reviewed Nathalie Sarraute's *The Golden Fruits* for *The New York Review of Books*, March 5, 1964.

[New York]
February 2, 1964

Dearest Mary:

I just finished reading PR, first of course your piece ["The Hue and Cry"] and then [William] Abrahams' review of The Group— the first I read that made sense. Your piece, I think, is splendid— or shall I join the chorus and say: Who am I to judge? The beginning quite funny and then of such a calm sharp and, as it ought to be, essentially simple intelligence that it was a great pleasure. I liked especially the paragraph about being *forced* to kill one's friend.[1] This kind of moral turpitude, for this is what it is, seems to me the almost general characteristic of all this kind of stuff. But it also shows how "innocent" people are when they condemn as "arrogance" every attempt at moral judgment. This, incidentally, showed a couple of years ago in the Van Doren case—the quiz kid who had cheated and when some one [sic] said (I think [Hans] Morganthau [sic]) that it is wrong to earn I don't know how many hundreds of thousands [of] dollars by cheating, especially wrong if you are a teacher and trusted by students, he received an avalanche of letters, denouncing him for "pharisaism" and "lack of Christian charity" because: Who could be expected to resist such a temptation? Answer: No one! Also: Of course, there is a trace of pity for Eichmann, at least of outrage when I read [Martin] Buber's statement that he feels "no common ground of humanity" with these people—a theologian! The point of the whole business was that we were supposed to look upon a human being (not upon the "Eichmann in us," God forbid), and to look upon him as human did not mean: There [but] for the grace of God . . . How you can report a trial, or for that matter ever become interested in it, without this is beyond me.

To the Abrahams piece: The difference is simply that he can *read* and hear. The trouble here is that the book looks so deceptively simple, and is actually the most complicated thing you ever did.

I am trying to write a short piece on the Hochhuth [controversy] for the Herald Tribune. Just received for it a pamphlet, issued by the National Catholic Welfare Conference, and written by whom? The Anti-Defamation League. As far as distortions go, it is perhaps even worse than what they did with the Eichmann. Incredible. For instance: One of the main points in this whole business is that individual priests and sometimes even bishops went much farther than the Pope who of course never did anything, remained full of sympathies for Germany up to the end and full of misgivings about Jews. The pamphlet presents everything as though these bishops acted upon orders from Rome; the opposite was true: Rome deserted them. (There are a number of Catholic publications which are quite candid and honest in this matter, surprisingly so, as a matter of fact.) But the nicest thing is the following: In the blurb matter from the publisher [. . .] it is announced that the American Jewish Committee will shortly make public a statement against Hochhuth—"after consultation with the Vatican." Gospel truth. If Montini [Pope Paul VI] promises to tell the world that not the Jews but all mankind killed Christ, then they will whitewash Pacelli [Pope Pius XII] for him. I am not so sure that even the first is so good for us (meaning us Jews), for the consequence is that neither Germans nor Ukrainians nor anybody else whom you could specify ever killed a Jew in a pogrom—but all mankind. This, I feel, is kind of uncomfortable. It is bad enough to be hated by this or that people—but by everybody? Thanks! Well—the whole thing is of course a joke, as was Montini's pilgrimage [to Germany], a Madison Avenue joke. And it is sad that this came immediately after Roncalli [Pope John XXIII]. Was he the last Christian?[2] [. . .]

The Kennedy assassination business is also quite sad and unsettling. Our confidence in the clan was perhaps misplaced, but it is too early to tell. How right you were when you wanted to found a Committee to Investigate [the Warren Commission]! I hope you saw the article in the New Republic. None of the points has been answered satisfactorily—the bullet hole in the windshield: it was made by the bullet that had hit him from behind; but no windshield apparently. Somebody said, they had the car immediately repaired—though this is hardly credible. The same thing with the time table: simple claims that the time table was all right, no proof whatsoever, not even the attempt at giving another reconstruction. And so on, and so forth. Disgusting.

By the way, read in Commentary the article about antecedents of the Hochhuth.[3] Quite good—though the clerical antisemitism [sic] in Germany is exaggerated, played a bigger role in France, and a number of things are over-looked. Still.

I am on my way to the Lowells and this I have to explain. Cal called for an evening with Spender. He [Lowell] is just back from the hospital and still, as he said, tired and shaky, I felt I should not say no and I hope you will understand. Things are probably bad enough as they are now between him and E[lizabeth]. I did not want to bring up a "problem," felt he could not handle it. Perhaps I was wrong, I don't know. I'll finish this when I come back.

Nothing special to report. E. like usually, perhaps less so because she was tired. Cal looks thin and not very happy. Spender—oh, well, you know. Your name was not mentioned. Only one thing of interest: Chiaramonte [sic], they said, claims Roncally [sic] had seen the Hochhuth play and said: You can't do anything against the truth. Would be nice if it is true.

Much much love and yours,
H.

1. McCarthy quotes Abel: " 'If a man holds a gun at the head of another and forces him to kill his friend, the man with the gun will be aesthetically less ugly than the one who out of fear of death has killed his friend and perhaps did not even save his own life.' Forces him to kill his friend?" McCarthy asks, and asserts: "Nobody by possession of a weapon can force a man to kill anybody; that is his own decision" ("The Hue and Cry," *The Writing on the Wall*, 68–69).
2. Arendt reviewed *Journal of a Soul* by Pope John XXIII in *The New York Review of Books*, June 17, 1965. In slightly expanded form the essay, "Angelo Giuseppe Roncalli: A Christian on St. Peter's Chair From 1958 to 1963," is reprinted in her *Men in Dark Times*.
3. Guenter Lewy, "Pius XII, the Jews, and the German Catholic Church," *Commentary*, February 1964.

141 rue de Rennes
Paris 6e
June 9, 1964

Dearest Hannah:

It's about time, indeed, I wrote you. Forgive my silence, which has no good excuse. Only extreme fatigue, after the U.S. trip, and accompanying mild depression. This has been made worse by the fact that I haven't really got back to work yet but am frittering away my time with odds and ends of literary and other professional chores, which, however, do have to get done. This week it is income tax; our deadline as foreign residents is June 15.

I told Jovanovich no on the Jerusalem book. Given the state of affairs described in the preceding paragraph, it would be crazy to take on something more. What I really want to do (or think I want to do) is start another book—a novel. And yet when, yesterday, I finally sat down to contemplate this, a horrible blank faced me, as when in the middle of a lecture you realize that you've forgotten the next point you want to make. It struck me that there was *nothing* I wanted to say. Or, more accurately, that I could not remember the person (me) who had been wanting to say something. That is in the form of a novel or even a story; I could think of articles I should rather like to write, but article-writing, in the circumstances, would be an evasion or distraction, like loud chatter to cover up a social silence.

Well, this terrifying moment or long minutes passed; otherwise, I should not be writing you about it. I did remember something slowly: an idea, though, not a concrete situation or episode that I was longing to tell about—which is how my other books and stories have always started. Except *The Group*. That must have been an idea too. Yes.

The present idea has to do with equality. I've long thought that this is the spectre that has been haunting the world since the eighteenth century. Or at least it has been haunting me all my life. Once this notion was introduced into the human mind, existence became unbearable, and yet once there it can never be banished. The only people who remain happy or content are those who haven't yet heard of it, for one reason or another—at either end of the social scale. The benighted squires (and there still are a few) who don't have a guilty conscience, and the benighted peasants (and there still are a few) who don't suffer from envy. Both these groups, as it were, don't question God's disposition of His favors, whether He smiles on them or frowns on them. But everyone else is only pretending if they claim to take inequality for granted. On *both sides*. "Why should I have this and not he?" or "Why should he have this and not I?" These questions, of course, are very old, as old as human history, but formerly they could be answered, even if the answer was that they were unanswerable, which is to invoke the mystery of Fate. But no one believes in Fate any more; this is the same as saying that nobody today "accepts his fate."

I suppose I've become more obsessed by these questions simply because of recent success—an increasing number of dresses in my closet, car, trips. Basking in the air of privilege. Which one can still enjoy if it's impermanent—a treat. But not as one's private air-conditioning. All this touches on what you say in your *Revolution* book about compassion.

At the same time, I have the sense, maybe subjective, that the worm of equality is not only eating away at the old social and economic foundations but at the very structure of consciousness, demolishing the "class distinctions" between the sane and the insane, the beautiful and the ugly, the good and the bad. To be concrete, I find that I feel guilty and awkward in the presence of a psychotic person, as though I ought to conceal my sanity in the interests of equality with him. The same with a stupid person; I am mortified in conversation with him, afraid of saying something that will disclose his stupidity to him. In fact, I am only happy in conversations with my equals or superiors, though of course my superiors may be feeling mortified for me. In short, you get a sort of round. Similarly, among young people, I hear, not to take drugs is a source of shame for the non-drug-taker, and this is not the same as wanting-to-do-what-the-others-are-doing, which has always been the case with young people.

Well, anyway, it has occurred to me to present this as a story whose hero would be a nineteen-year-old boy, a student abroad, from an old-fashioned "humanist" moderate left background; his father a professor in the U.S., probably a refugee—one of the Italian anti-fascists teaching, say, at Wellesley. The boy is three-quarters Americanized, comes from a large family of brothers and sisters, has been doing his junior year abroad at the Sorbonne and living in cheap hotels and furnished rooms, earning extra money by baby-sitting for Americans. He is a nice kid, very mature for his age intellectually (his family goes to Cape Cod for the summer, and he knows the Dupees, Dwight, Arthur Schlesinger, etc.), shy, scrupulous, very logical, and lonely but brave away from home. Models are the sons of Miloscz [*sic*], a bit of Vieri Tucci [Niccolò's son], a bit of Reuel, a bit of a boy called Carlo Tagliacozzo, a bit of a *Life* reporter called Jordan Bonfante, and a boy who was at the Sorbonne called Jonathan Aaron—the son of Daniel Aaron. A charming detail about Jonathan is that he had a plant in his room, which was on a dark court, and he used to take the plant for a walk to give it light. This rueful oddity is going to be characteristic of my young hero, whose name will be Peter Bonfante.[1] ("Bonfante" means "good soldier," though people think it means "good child.") The story opens with him in a cheap Roman hotel room during the Easter holiday; he is on his way, with a pack, to Jugoslavia. As the curtain rises, he is waiting, with his door ajar, to get into the common toilet—a daily ordeal for him in the kind of hotel he stays in. In the course of the book he is going to meet a lot of tourists and floating expatriates, young and middle-aged. I've often thought something should be done about modern tourism, and there's a relevance to the general theme, though I'm not sure yet what it is exactly. The book won't be a satire, at least not on the hero, though he has a vein of self-satire connected with his shyness.

Excuse me, Hannah, if I'm boring you with all this and tell me, please, that it won't come out like *The Catcher in the Rye!*

I won't make this letter much longer, since it's already too long. A couple of weeks ago Nathalie Sarraute asked me to lunch; we talked a great deal about you. She is smitten with you. We also talked about her mother and my Morganstern[2] grandmother; she says they were extraordinarily alike. Including the face-lifting scars.

Politics at the moment seem extremely discouraging, don't you think? Except for what is happening with the satellites, and it's too early yet—at least for me—to decipher that. Will they stop Goldwater in July? I don't think so. I must say, Eisenhower comes out even worse than I'd supposed—a mean, vicious, timorous old man. But the timorousness seems a part of the meanness. If they do stop Goldwater, will the Republican party split and the right wing join with the Wallaceites of the South? This seems logical, and yet, as people have pointed out, the American parties have not been ideological parties but coalitions of interests. Should the Republican party split, the moderates, surely, would be the losers from it. They would become a mere ineffective variant, like the British Liberal Party.

How did your lecture tour go?[3] And have you collected your honorary degrees? And what are you working on? Have you finished

165

the German *Eichmann*?[4] A queer book was sent me recently—a satirical novel about the Germans and a Jew by someone called Florence Helitzer. Harper's is going to publish it; the title is *Hans, Who Goes There?* It impressed me at first, as a curious mixture of Nabokov and Gunther [sic] Grass; the hero is a sort of Jewish Humbert Humbert recruited by the CIA to spy on a West German tycoon. There are some clever ideas in it, and yet I feel there's something wrong. Something I can't put my finger on. I haven't yet finished it, but I begin to suspect that it's a Zionist tract of some sort. If so, it is disingenuous, because the whole basis of a *Lolita* or a *Tin Drum* is a wild disengagement and sad mockery; the author cannot have a pious message. It might be worth your while to have a look at it.

I suppose you saw the piece about you in the TLS [*Times Literary Supplement*].[5] Sonia Orwell has promised me to find out who wrote it, but so far she hasn't delivered. It seemed to me a particularly nasty job and done by someone who was authentically stupid. They wanted me to answer it, but I didn't have the heart for it; I mean it was too discouraging. Hannah, let me tell you how I regret putting in Mozart and Handel.[6] Jim warned me, and my internal alert system warned me too. But just because of that I left it in. On the ground of refusing to suppress something—not to be like *them*, who would never tell the truth if the enemy could use it against them. And it was true that reading your *Eichmann* did have an exhilarating effect on me, which was close to that of those two particular pieces of music, both of which are concerned with redemption. Jim said I sounded too girlish in that passage, and I agreed, but I said to myself, "All right, I won't hide it." But neither he nor I ever thought that anybody would use it to show that I was exulting over the mass murder of the Jews. I don't even mind that; what I do mind is that they have used it to compromise *you*. That's why I should have shown more caution. Please forgive me, if you can.

We arrive in the U.S. July 1.[7] How I long to see you.

> Much, much love to you
> and to Heinrich,
> Mary

[. . .]

---

1. The young hero of *Birds of America*, who does take his plant for a walk, was finally named Peter Levi.
2. McCarthy anglicized her Jewish grandmother's maiden name, which appears as Morgenstern in public records.

3. Arendt's spring lecture tour had taken her from Yale to several campuses of the University of California.

4. *Eichmann in Jerusalem: Ein Bericht von der Banalität des Bösen* was published later in 1964 by Piper.

5. This was a review of *Eichmann in Jerusalem*, *The Times Literary Supplement*, April 30, 1964.

6. In "The Hue and Cry" McCarthy wrote: "To me, *Eichmann in Jerusalem*, despite all the horrors in it, was morally exhilarating. I freely confess that it gave me joy and I too heard a paean in it—not a hate-paean to totalitarianism but a paean of transcendence, heavenly music, like that of the final chorus of *Figaro* or the *Messiah*. . . . The reader 'rose above' the terrible material of the trial or was borne aloft to survey it with his intelligence."

7. The Wests returned to Stonington, Connecticut, for the obligatory home leave required every three years of U.S. Foreign Service officers.

370 Riverside Drive
New York 25, N.Y.
June 23, 1964

Dearest Mary:

This just to say that I count the days until you come. I showed your letter to Heinrich—by no means the rule—and he said spontaneously: how close she now is. Précisément. The letter to the Times [TLS] is very good; did they print it? They never asked me for a reply. Not that I mind, I would not have replied anyhow—too boring. I can hardly bring myself to read what comes out of the "mimeographing machine." And since we are with this subject: My [German] publisher asked me to use your PR essay and I told him I would ask your permission. [. . .] I just read the pamphlet by Helmut Heissenbüttel your [German] publisher brings out as propaganda material for The Group.[1] Well—it is neither good nor bad; it won't do any harm, is well-meaning, makes occasionally a good point (the best being that every scene in your novels has a play-character, as though it were acted on stage; quite true), construes flattering and complicated theories—and misses most of the points. It is as though these people have forgotten how it is to *laugh*. That things could be funny never occurs to them. Serious animals.

Let us talk about the equality business; most interesting. The chief vice of every egalitarian society is Envy—the great vice of free Greek society. And the great virtue of all aristocracies seems to me to be that people always know who they are and hence do not compare themselves with others. This constant comparing is really the quintessence of vulgarity. If you are not in this hideous habit you are immediately accused of arrogance—as though by not-comparing you have decided to be on top. An easily understandable misunderstanding. (As when William Ph. says of me: Who does she thinks she is? Aristotle?)

I also received the Helitzer book (Hans, Who Goes there?). I am afraid there is everything wrong with it. Innumerable details too— f.i. the Yellow Star was not introduced in 1938 but in 1941 or 42; no one could have obtained his degree of law in 1938 if he was a Jew; or belong to one of the fraternities; nobody ever says in German: Mein Herr, etc. I don't like Grass particularly, but compared to this lady he is a genius. The whole story completely implausible and stupid to boot. I read it because you mention it, but I can't finish.

Just one word about the Mozart business. I agree with Jim—not that it matters!—primarily because the comparison even of effects is too high. But I always loved the sentence because you were the only reader to understand what otherwise I have never admitted— namely that I wrote this book in a curious state of euphoria. And that ever since I did it, I feel—after twenty years [since the war]— light-hearted about the whole matter. Don't tell anybody; is it not proof positive that I have no "soul"?

I read German proofs and I promised Piper (my publisher) to come [to Munich] in September for publication date. I want to see Jaspers anyhow. Do you plan to come to the Book Fair? If you do, I may go to Frankfurt. Jovanovitch [sic] told me that they did not change the title of the book [The Group]. How stupid![2] Let us hope that the translation is all right.

Mary, as I said, I am counting days. Do you want us to come to the airport? [. . .]

Yours,
Hannah

1. This was an appreciative German review reprinted by Droemer.
2. Die Gruppe was ultimately changed to Die Clique.

141 rue de Rennes
Paris 6ème
December 22, 1964

Dearest Hannah:

Thank God for Christmas. Because it is making me sit down and write you this afternoon, in its honor. I've been wanting to write you all fall and kept postponing doing it till I'd have time to compose a "good" letter. Long and interesting. Now I've moderated my ambition. Just a letter.

I couldn't come to Frankfurt. And I didn't go to Bocca di Magra either; Nicola had left. This fall has been senselessly crowded, not so much with social life as with taxing and unimportant work. The kind of work a masochist takes on.

A) A documentary film on Paris for the BBC [title unknown]. I agreed to do it because at the moment we needed the money, and of course I've not yet been paid and now I no longer need the money either. It was amusing in a way; I'd never worked on a film before. We had a very good and imaginative camera crew—French; the only trouble was that most of my ideas proved to be impossible to photograph. For one thing (obvious, but I'd never thought of it), you can't photograph a negative statement. E.g., there are hardly any clocks in Paris. Also most of my ideas were of things that stand still, which means one thinks in photographs, not in moving pictures. The whole thing is essentially a little study of *bien pensant* France. It is still not finished; I have to see the rushes in January and write the ending. The actual filming is gruelling. This is one field where people work intensively and almost live together. A queer kind of democracy, pro tem.

B) The French translation of *The Group*. I spent seven weeks, working nearly five hours a day, including some Sundays, with another "team," in this case, the translator and a man from the publishing house. Both fairies. Rather sweet ones. The original translation was a comic disaster. The translator, known as "Coco" Gentien, the ex-doubles partner of Suzanne Lenglen, had given the second half of the book to his cousin, a business man known as "Fifi" Fenwick, to translate. The cousin completely rewrote the book or, rather, his half, upgrading the characters who were in the Social Register and downgrading the others. He presented me with a white cyclamen from his greenhouse and vanished from the scene.

C) A little report on a panel organized by the Communist Students at the Mutualité. Sartre and Simone against the *nouveau roman*. This has started a ten-day *cause célèbre*. The *Nouvel Observateur*, which had commissioned it, refused to print it without "softening"; they could not afford, they explained, to offend Sartre. It was then turned down with a rude note by the *Figaro Littéraire*. No one knows why, but it is thought that it was fear of Sartre again, unlikely as that seems. I finally gave it to [François] Bondy, who is printing it. The sad thing is that it's not even very good; I had to write it in less than a day. But now that it is an issue—one young writer resigned from the *Nouvel Observateur*, he claims because of this—it is going to be reprinted everywhere.[1] In Italy, England, Germany. *Die Zeit* just telephoned, but Bondy had already promised it to *Der Monat*. Since it has become a document, I can't even rewrite it.

D)   A translation of a very good piece Nicola wrote on Sartre and the Nobel Prize.[2]

E)   Two other BBC jobs.

Besides that I've gone to Hungary to a P.E.N. Congress and have been working on my new novel. But too sporadically.

We've also been to Bonn, Cologne, and Trier—and on an OECD trip for Jim. I loved Trier and the Cathedral in Metz, which we saw on the way back. And I liked a little double church we saw outside of Bonn.

My dissipated—in the sense of scattered—activities remind me slightly of Dwight, which I find ominous. I think I've been longing to get into a fight with someone—France or Sartre and Simone. It is the same thing. As De Gaulle said, *"Sartre est aussi la France."* I did restrain myself over the Warren Report. Just as well, considering those thirty volumes or whatever they are of appendices that one would have to read. I hope no one has thought of giving them to me, boxed, for Christmas. The Report, I thought, was unsatisfactory, and the more you thought about it, the more unsatisfactory it became. At his request, I wrote Dwight some of my impressions. I wonder what he will do with the Report; from his letters he sounded rather awed by it, as he was by the Ford Foundation.[3] It strikes me that the Kennedy assassination is going to be one of those litmus-paper issues or goat-and-sheep dividers, like the Moscow Trials and Pasternak and your *Eichmann*. Two of your adversaries tangled with each other in the English Sunday papers over the Warren Report; Trevor-Roper and John Sparrow, who seems clearly to have been the author of the *TLS* attack on you. I thought they were both awful, in different ways, on the Warren Report too. I have the clippings, in case you don't see them.

I wish I could talk to you. But when? Instead, this evening— i.e., in half an hour—I'm going to meet three Soviet Russians. This invitation I couldn't resist. And this letter has already been interrupted by a worker from the central heating firm; our heating stopped functioning altogether this morning, in the midst of a cold snap. He fixed the furnace and told me the chimney was out of order too. Then the lights blew in the ironing-room when the ironing-lady came and I was called on, unsuccessfully, to fix the fuses, and that is the way it goes here.

The good pieces of domestic news are two: we have a permanent live-in maid, our former Polish cook and children's nurse [Maria Dombrowska], and a new elevator, installed just in time for Christmas. In time, these two blessings will make a lot of difference.

Dear Hannah, Merry Christmas to you and Heinrich. I don't consider this a real letter, so don't dignify it with an answer. I shall write you another, when calm ensues after the holidays.

Meanwhile all my deepest love. I do miss you so.

Happy New Year,
Mary

1. Mary McCarthy, "Crushing a Butterfly," appeared in *Preuves, Tempo Presente, Der Monat,* and *Encounter* in the spring of 1965 and is reprinted in *The Writing on the Wall.*
2. Chiaromonte had debunked Sartre's celebrated repudiation of the 1964 Nobel Peace Prize in the Fall 1964 *Tempo Presente.*
3. Macdonald's report on the Ford Foundation was published in book form in 1956 as *The Ford Foundation: The Men and the Millions.*

370 Riverside Drive
New York 25, N.Y.
Christmas 1964

Dearest Mary—

Your letter arrived yesterday with the last mail until Monday and was the best possible Christmas present. I have been wanting to write, oh for ages, always trying to figure out how you are and what you are doing. Am very glad to learn a) that you did a film[,] b) that you have an elevator and c) a sleep-in maid—this in ascending order of importance. Also—kind of maliciously—I enjoyed your translating experiences: How much better off one is if one knows only one language! I spent more than a month rewriting the German 'Eichmann' (rewriting? writing, period) and am right now finishing the German translation of 'Revolution'. —I read about the Sartre & Beauvoir business in the New Yorker, very tamely written this time to my surprise. This is splendid that you caused a cause célèbre and

I am most eager to read it. Bondy can print it because he does not 'belong'. Also, I would like very much to read Nicola's piece on Sartre. I just finished reading [Sartre's] Les Mots—and was so disgusted that I was almost tempted to review this piece of highly complicated lying. It reminds me of what I heard recent scholarship has unearthed about Rousseau—he did *not* have five children at the orphanage for the simple reason that he was impotent, which I think is most likely. Sartre's case is precisely the same: You tell seemingly outrageous 'truths' with a great show of sincerity in order to hide the better what actually happened. I am wondering how he will explain or tell his sort of 'truth' with respect to the unpleasant fact that he did not participate in the resistance, in fact never lifted a finger. I am going to read les confessions of Simone—for their gossip value, but also because this kind of bad faith becomes rather fascinating. And nobody, nobody who pointed out the obvious. Or am I mistaken?

Warren report: Yes, Dwight will do exactly what he did with the Ford Foundation. As though an instinct for self-preservation watches over him like a non-guardian angel (a kind of opposite daimonion), ever since he switched from politics to 'mass culture'. I am very fond of him, did not yet see him since I came back from Chicago, but talked to him on the phone during the Thanksgiving weekend and told him at least to be aware that the Warren report distinguishes between: "there is no evidence" & there is "no *credible* evidence." But it won't help much, he is again "very impressed." I read only a resumé of Trevor-Roper's article according to which, if I remember rightly, he said: no one can understand why there exists no medical report from the original hospital and why the police interrogation of Oswald was not taken down in shorthand. If you can spare the clippings for a few days, I would like to see it. But it is not very important. Even here there are a few (very very few) people who say: This is at best the case for the prosecution. Which seems to be true enough. But nobody wants even to think of it—and this, I am afraid includes me.

I saw hardly anybody yet, just came back. Had a very good time in Chicago. For the first time in years (since 61) no worries about Heinrich's health. I worked quite a bit, lecture on Kant's Critique of Judgment, a seminar on the Critique of Pure Reason and another on Plato's Gorgias together with David Grene[1] of whom I am fond.

Saw little of Bellow, his father-in-law was dying. But I guess we are again good friends. Cal was here the other day, full of Miltown (or however that is spelled) and on the wagon again, which did not help much, quite obviously shortly before another breakdown, or rather in the midst of it: Hitler wrote "the greatest prose in our century," "why did Jesus die at the age of 32, and neither before nor after" and much more of the same. It was kind of heart-breaking. After he was gone, he called to apologize for "rudeness" and being "boisterous"—he was neither. But boasting with his ancestry and similar unimportant nonsense. He knows of course something is wrong. He has been invited he said to read a poem for the Inauguration and also to see Jacqueline Kennedy. Also: his play is being performed somewhere off Broadway. [2]

Mary, you see, *how* I miss you! When do I see you again? I won't come to Europe before [the] end of June, and then only for a short time. I had a very good time in Europe in [the] Fall, marvellous days with Jaspers, and an unexpectedly nice time in Germany— with I don't remember how many radio and television interviews. In my youth, I used to be rather lucky with German *goiim* (never, incidentally, with German Jews) and I was amused to see that some of my luck still holds.

Let's try to hear more of each other! Much much love et une bonne année! for both of you.

Yours,

Hannah

Give my regards to Nathalie Sarrautte [sic] in case you see her.

1. David Grene was a classics scholar at the University of Chicago.
2. The play was probably Lowell's adaptation of Melville's *Benito Cereno*, part of Lowell's *Old Glory* trilogy. It was performed at the American Place Theatre in 1964–65.

141 rue de Rennes

Paris 6ème

January 18, 1965

Dearest Hannah:

Here are the promised clippings. If more come to light, I'll send them on. My desk is in chaos, the result of a clean-up. With Christmas festivities, I tidied everything up, which means I hid everything.

At the moment I am rather browned off the Warren Report. I've discussed it so often and with so many people and am tired of making and hearing the same points. Nicola is here from Rome, and of course it was on the agenda of our first dinner together. He feels as most of us do that the Report is unsatisfactory but is at a loss for a counter-theory or, rather, at a loss to substantiate any counter-theory. Mario Lévi says it is not necessary to have a counter-theory to disbelieve in the case against Oswald. It isn't necessary technically but humanly it appears to be. Nicola agrees that the shadiest parts of the case are the Tippit killing and the attempt on General Walker.[1] It would be there one would have to go deeper if one was going to investigate. I'm left with the feeling that only a completely fresh investigation would yield anything; there are too many lacunae in the Warren Report for it to be a source for further work.

Where are you now? In New York, I assume, and working. But on what?

I've just finished the first section of my novel, which ought to make me cheerful. But I am sagging with doubts and apprehensions. The traditional novel, which this is, is so undermined that one feels as if one were working in a house marked for demolition.

We had a party yesterday for Nicola and Miriam. It was full of widows, like *Richard III*. Sonia Orwell, Francine Camus, and the widow of [French writer] Georges Bataille. For some reason all the guests depressed me greatly, except Nicola and Miriam and a Greek scholar, J. P. Vernant. *He* was on sure ground. Nathalie Sarraute was there, and she made a strangely unpleasant impression on me. She was talking about Nelson Algren and Simone de Beauvoir—the *Newsweek* piece,[2] and the malice in her sharp face was like a kind of voracious greed. She had a couple of little satellites with her—a sycophantic Cuban boy and a sycophantic German boy. The whole evening made me feel that a disappointed minority was assembled here. What used to be called the anti-Communist Left—that is, the minority of a minority. And the impression was of the second-rate or also-rans; perhaps France does that to slightly marginal people. Yet there was no one present, except Nathalie's two acolytes, whom I didn't like. Who wasn't in fact a friend. Perhaps it was just me.

Otherwise things have been rather pleasantly quiet. Work and a certain amount of theatre-going in the evenings. And a lot of music on the phonograph. We gave each other quantities of records for Christmas.

Jim has been having some new trouble with Margaret over the children. That is perhaps at the bottom of my *malaise*. She has become hysterically jealous of me, doesn't want the children to see me, refused to let Alison have a coat I gave her for Christmas. It is *terrible* for the children, except the smaller boy, who is not at all torn by what is going on, since he steadfastly loves his father and ignores everything but that main point. But for the other two, it's horrible. Apparently their mother feeds them with slanders about me, and since neither Jim or I ever say anything to them about these slanders (in fact until recently we were unaware of them), they are rather confused and mistrustful. Mistrustful of their own feelings too, because, I think, they like me. That is Jim's impression and Maria's and it was the impression of the Swedish *au pair* girl we had last summer. She told Jim, "The children look to Mrs. West to protect them." Yet we can't discuss any of this with the children without criticizing their mother, and I don't want to do that, since they live with her. [. . .]

Aside from this, Jim is fine, and in very good spirits. I am really fine too.

Dear Hannah, when *will* we see each other? I miss you so much. In Paris, I have no real friends; that is simply the fact. My friends like Sonia [Orwell] and Anjo Lévi have to be handled with so much tact or rather with so much suppressed impatience that you are never at ease with them. And vice versa, I suppose. Anyway, write as soon as you have time, and we will see each other in the summer. Meanwhile I will work and look at Gothic churches.[3]

It is such good news that Heinrich has been well. My love to him. And I'm distressed to hear that Cal is in poor shape again; it must be the most monotonous fate for him. That is the worst part.

All my love,
Mary

1. J. D. Tippit was a Dallas policeman allegedly shot by Lee Harvey Oswald shortly after the Kennedy assassination. The Warren Commission was criticized for not looking more closely into the circumstances surrounding Tippit's death. General Edwin Walker, a retired U.S. army officer and the leader of an ultraconservative group in Dallas, was shot at seventeen months before the President was killed—by Oswald, according to the Warren Commission.
2. "I Ain't Abelard," a review of Simone de Beauvoir's *The Force of Circumstance, Newsweek,* December 28, 1964.
3. McCarthy's tours of Gothic churches in France, England, and Germany seemed to offer a reprieve from more demanding projects, *Birds of America* and, later, *Hanoi.* The book she hoped to write about the Gothic led her to begin studying German in the mid-1960s. She never wrote the book, but her German-language studies continued until her death.

The Quadrangle Club
1155 East 57th
Chicago 37
April 2, 1965

Dearest Mary—

God knows why I did not write earlier. The winter months were pretty busy—lectures, trying to do several things which I probably am too stupid to do anyhow which is not going to prevent me from trying. Otherwise rather quiet and pleasant life, no parties, friends here and there. *I miss you.*

Now back in Chicago but only for this month. Some student unrest but less than I expected: Maybe I don't know enough. The very first day when I thought no one knew I was even here two students appeared about Vietnam—quite typically, I thought, our best and our worst together, but literally so, and the worst one clearly the leader. I wish I knew more about Berkeley, [1] the best report I saw was in The New Yorker; and a pretty good one in the NY Review of Books. I'll give two seminars, one on Spinoza, one on Rousseau, both in answer to students' request, both quite informally, nowhere announced. That this is still possible is one of the good things about this place. Less bureaucracy than anywhere else. The students are good, nothing to complain about.

I read Nicola's remarks about Sartre and really loved him for them. Read as [a] kind of sleeping pill for weeks in Beauvoir's La Force des Choses [*The Force of Circumstances* (1965)]. This is one of the funniest books I read in years. Incredible that no one has taken that apart. Much as I dislike Sartre, it seems he is punished for all his sins by this kind of a cross. Especially since her unwavering true love for him is the only mitigating circumstance in the "case against her," really quite touching. I think I can understand Sarraute's "malice"; to live somehow together with these characters in power and command must not be easy. It is easy to see the fun of it when one is not there.

Warren report—well, you saw Dwight's piece. [2] I am glad you kind of gave up about it. I still have the whole business in the back of my mind, but am convinced that there is absolutely nothing one could do about it. I agree that one needs no counter-theory to disbelieve in the case against Oswald. On the contrary, every counter-theory would make this disbelief suspect. As though one had an axe to grind instead of looking simply at the evidence or rather at the lack of it. We acquired a television set and use it very unfrequently for news and presidential announcements. The more I see of J[ohnson] the less do I like him. There is a good deal of sympathy in this country now for de Gaulle which I understand but do not share. When he dies France will be in a kind of similar mess as Germany is in now, perhaps not quite so grotesquely. Jaspers, who was quite seriously sick but is better now, gave a splendid lengthy interview on the extension of the statute of limitation for the *Spiegel*[3] (they had asked me because they did not believe that Jaspers would do it; I refused anyhow for obvious reasons).

Cal is back from the hospital, off to Egypt. I saw him briefly and he seemed quite well again. Before he went to the hospital, he called to tell that he had moved out again, taken an apartment with some girl and, as he then proudly proclaimed, furnished it. Then he went of course back where he belonged and never mentioned this episode again. It *is* strange. Meanwhile I saw Jarrell; I gave a lecture in North Carolina and he introduced me.[4] Now he is off to a mental hospital, Cal told me. He seemed quite sick when I saw him, chiefly depressed but with some streak of real insanity in it that frightened me; as though some altogether alien person was looking through him who still was He.

How is the novel coming? What are you doing? Do write me even if I behaved badly, not writing I mean. Tucci appears and disappears sporadically and can be very very trying for one's patience. I could get him a little money from the Rockefeller Foundation; that seemed to cheer him up a bit. He, too, very depressed and in the grip of what seems to me sheer graphomania. Oh yes, I saw Dwight of course, in good enough shape and health, ever so much better than a few years ago.

Mary, why don't you come? And how did things work out with the children, Jim's I mean? Tell Jim he should give you a little leave of absence. When you said before you left we won't see each other for a long time, I didn't realize how long a time it would be. Much too long. Well, we still intend to come beginning of July, or end of June. But not for very long. Where will you be then? Let us try to plan things properly.

By the way, you never sent me your piece on Sartre. Did it appear in Preuves? Do you ever see Lippman's [sic] columns about

Vietnam?[5] I thought them pretty good. But I must confess that I am less concerned than almost all people I know. Informed opinion here is quite unanimous against our policies—there is a consensus if that is what Johnson wants. The chief trouble seems to me still that no American statesman or politician is able to understand what a revolution is all about. There is a discrepancy between our talk and the facts of the case that is truly frightening.

Heinrich is back in Bard, in good shape. Give my love to Jim.

Much, much love, my dear—yours,
Hannah

1. Antiwar activists in Berkeley, California, had responded to the initiation of bombing raids against North Vietnam in February 1965 by stopping a troop train headed for the Oakland army base.
2. Dwight Macdonald, "A Critique of the Warren Report," Esquire, March 1965.
3. Karl Jaspers was interviewed by Rudolf Augstein for the March 10, 1963, Der Spiegel on the issue of extending the twenty-year statute of limitations governing the prosecution of former Nazis for war crimes. Jaspers took the German Ministry of Justice to task for opposing a five-year extension (later passed by the Bundestag). He also noted that German criminal courts had failed to try any judges or public prosecutors from the Nazi period, and that two of the more prominent ones, Hans Globke and Karl-Friedrich Vialon, held office in the Adenauer administration.
4. Poet Randall Jarrell was a friend of Arendt's from the 1950s. His satirical novel Pictures from an Institution contains a snapshot of Hannah and Heinrich Blücher and a takeoff of McCarthy.
5. Walter Lippmann's syndicated column appeared regularly in the Washington Post, among other papers.

141 rue de Rennes
Paris 6e
April 2, 1965

Dearest Hannah:

It worries me not to hear from you. Did you get my last letter—oh, months ago, with the Warren Report clippings? Nancy Macdonald writes that you are OK, so either a letter has been lost or you are busy.

I am in a state of doubt and dismay about Vietnam. This, I think, is true of a lot of Americans here, including official ones. News about the attitude in America itself is sparse. I read with slight relief the New York Times editorials and Walter Lippmann. But isn't there any movement of protest among private people—I don't mean nuclear disarmers? What can be done? So far as I know, nobody has offered a concrete proposal, except the Indians, who have suggested a two weeks' cease fire. A good idea, I think. We would have nothing to lose by it even if we undertook it unilaterally. It seems to me not enough to tell Johnson to stop bombing and gassing and burning. He ought to be told what to do instead. The argument, of course, is that if he doesn't stop the Viet Cong, Laos will be lost and Malaysia, and India will be threatened. Assuming this is true and that the spread of communism is a uniform disaster (the official line), it seems to me that there would be no point in repeating this horrible battle in Laos and Malaysia (although I'm utterly ignorant about Malaysia) but, rather, if we can get out of Vietnam to concentrate on protecting India, which at least wants to be protected and is a democratic state, despite all its minority and language problems. The British are concerned for India, which must be the real reason the Labor Party is still tagging along with Johnson, though he is making it increasingly difficult for them to do so.

Please write me, if you have a moment, what your views are. I find it very hard to think clearly on the subject. All alternatives are bad. If Johnson succeeds by these methods in forcing North Vietnam to negotiate, that is almost worse than if he fails, for then there will be no restraining him. On the other hand, if he fails (as of today he seems still to be doing), he is likely to go on escalating; if he bombs Hanoi, that is the end, as far as I am concerned. I would not find it acceptable to be an American any more.

The old Red-Dead jingle is coming true in a ghastly way. To me, there is no doubt that in Indochina it would be better for the vast majority to be Red. Such dilemmas, which have no meaning in countries like England, where they were posed, are perfectly real now in Vietnam. And of course there is the question of what color of red. If it is true that Hanoi is (or was) anti-Chinese and pro-Soviet, then the best solution for Asia might be a band of dissident Communist states to China's south, like the Eastern satellite countries here. God knows their life is not very good, but it is better than in the mother country and seems to be improving. [. . .]

To return to Vietnam, one of the errors, I think, is to act as if the main danger was escalation into nuclear war. This allows Johnson to feel virtuous as long as he doesn't drop atom bombs.

I feel anxious and hamstrung, because of Jim and his job. If it were not for that, I should like to write something or say something in public. As it is, I'm mulling over writing a letter to Stevenson or writing a letter to Johnson to be passed on by Dick Goodwin, one of his speechwriters. Jim is in favor of this, but it would have to be a very clear letter.

My impression is that everyone is waiting for someone else to speak up. We were at [U.S. Ambassador Charles] Bohlen's for dinner the other night and he seemed terribly harassed and uneasy, even puzzled. Puzzled, in fact, is the right word for the state of mind of the well-meaning kind of official. The more hopeful ones tell you that really negotiations are going on all the time and that this will soon blow over, etc. Jim himself is an absolute weathervane, though I'm not sure he realizes it. He thinks America has already done itself irreparable damage. On the other hand, having been a soldier, he has a kind of natural belligerency that cannot face the idea of a *retreat* from a position. In a half hour he will be on both sides of the same argument. And of course if it is a *French* person who criticizes. . . . ! But I have the feeling that his attitude is more or less everybody's and that if I could suggest some course of action to him that seemed to him to "make sense," it would appeal equally to most non-fanatical Americans. But you can't just say to him, "Get out of Vietnam."

I started to write you just a paragraph, dear Hannah. You see how I long to talk to you. When are you coming back here?

How is Heinrich and what does he think about all this?

Love to him and much,
much love to you,
Mary

The Quadrangle Club
[University of Chicago]
April 28, 1965

Dearest Mary:

I just debated with myself if I should go to one of Tillich's lectures or stay home and write you. You see how I decided—which means a letter to Tillich telling him that I have a cold. I trust this finds you back in Paris. Yes, what a curious coincidence of our letters crossing so to speak in the midst of the Atlantic.

This is my last day here and I am quite tired. We have in the Committee [on Social Thought] a kind of exodus from the philosophy dept. and absolutely no one to handle it except me. It was fun, but I am glad it is over. Also, partly, because the food here at the Club has become so bad that one can't eat it. And there is nowhere else to go. Tomorrow, I'll fly to Washington for a lecture and a discussion with Podhoretz and Dwight under Jewish auspices (Hillel). Then Sunday night back home. I saw Bellow once or twice; I have the impression that he avoids me and let it go at that. I think I told you that I'll be at Cornell (Visiting) next fall; it has its advantages, I can commute to New York. But next Spring, I'll be in Chicago again.

Viet Nam: I wish you had seen Morgenthau's article in the NY Times magazine on April 15th [1] and I enclose some columns of Lippmann's in case you did not see them. The Morgenthau article made a certain stir and received a furious reply from [syndicated columnist Joseph] Alsop (pompous ignorance—Hans was hurt, really). I am worried about the whole situation and I have no confidence in Johnson. He thinks in terms of prestige only, does not know how else to think. Is terribly ambitious and very impatient with disagreement of any kind. Also, quite primitive. His speech was a marvel of schizophrenia, the first part saying the exact opposite of what the second supposedly outlined. I am not convinced that he is in good faith. The academic community is almost unanimously against him, the people at large are quite apathetic despite all Gallup polls; nobody cares outside the Universities.

I suppose you saw the filthy attack on Shawn & the New Yorker in the Herald Tribune. [2] Since Whitney [Ellsworth, publisher of *The New York Review of Books*] had said he'd print letters etc., I wrote too. But they then selected only people with offices in the New Yorker—quite unfair, since I know that quite a number of outsiders wrote. This sort of thing gets worse and worse. I am glad I see no one any more except friends and, of course, "business" acquaintances.

Back to Viet Nam: I know very little about it, and agree with Lippmann and Morgenthau. The main point: This is a civil war situation and it is a lie that two nations, South and North Vietnam, are involved. What troubles me more than anything else is the sort of lying we have begun to practice. Morgenthau said the government's White Book [3] is simply a scandal. Also, we make all sensible and advantageous solutions (advantageous for us, and not merely for the poor people of Indonesia [sic]) impossible. If we only would let well enough alone, we would get there a variety of Socialist to Communist regimes with which we could live very well, some of which would be Russian-oriented and some more inclined to China.

I do not doubt that in the very long run, the whole of Asia will fall under Chinese influence but not necessarily under Chinese domination. If we should succeed in our folly to bring China and Russia together again—well, let's not finish this sentence. I read somewhere but forgot where and by whom, a neat little nightmare which seemed to me to sum up the whole situation: Suppose China declared war upon the United States tomorrow and declared unconditional surrender within the next hour or so, whereupon 5 to 6 million Chinese come marching across the border unarmed, with their hands over their heads to surrender. I suppose we would get out in a hurry. —However, one of our real problems is how to get out: we cannot simply let all people down and without protection who ever were on our side; they would simply be massacred. And this is not a question of Johnsonian prestige but of American honor. So the alternative: cease bombing and start negotiating.

Last by no means least, actually the reason why I write so quickly: we had to postpone our trip to Europe because of Jaspers, shall come end of July instead of June. *Where will you then be??* We could come via Paris, at least I could in case Heinrich wants to go directly to Switzerland; I could join him later in Zurich or Basel. For I suppose you will be in Italy during August. But perhaps we could meet in Switzerland? Anyhow, let me know. [. . .]

Dearest, do write soon! I miss you in countless ways and I resent writing. No reason for you not to write. Also, thanks for the delightful terracotta from the British Museum. It is sitting on my desk for consolation.

Love to both of you. Je t'embrasse.

Hannah

1. Hans Morgenthau, "We Are Deluding Ourselves in Vietnam," *The New York Times Magazine*, April 18, 1965.
2. Tom Wolfe, "Tiny Mummies: The True Story of the Ruler of 43rd St.'s Land of the Walking Dead," *The New York Herald Tribune Sunday Magazine*, April 11 and April 18, 1965.
3. Arendt refers to the State Department's 1965 White Paper entitled *Aggression from the North*.

141 rue de Rennes

Paris 6e

May 18, 1965

Dearest Hannah:

A hurried interim note to tell you that we will be here till August 1, when we go to Bocca di Magra. What a shame you can't come there; you would like it. Here means either this apartment or a little house in the country, near Rambouillet, where I hope to retire to get more work done than I am doing now. Far from the telephone. If you could come to Paris, it would be much easier for me than meeting elsewhere. Would you like me to get a hotel room for you? If you would have enough time, it would be marvelous if you could come to the country. You could meet the children, who will probably be with us; there is plenty of room. Nothing fancy but there is Nature all around. It is near Chartres too.

I've been reading about the teach-ins and about Morgenthau; tell me more. Obviously some new alignment is being formed or perhaps just explored. Bobbie [sic; Kennedy] would not attack U.S. policy if he were not confident of support. And I was struck by Schlesinger's role in the Washington teach-in; I would have expected him to take a straight official line. He is quite close to Bobbie. The removal of Tyler (whom I knew and rather liked) to Holland must be one of a number of moves on the other side: a Johnson purge of the State Department.[1] Whatever this means (if anything), the Bruces [Ambassador David Bruce and his wife, Evangeline] in London gave a huge party last week for [writer] Jimmy Baldwin. Not a routine U.S.I.A. party but their personal party. Cyril Connolly told me that Bruce is extremely impressed by Johnson, told him last fall that Johnson was "a force of Nature." I would have expected the Bruces to be Kennedy people. We didn't go to the party; now I rather wish I had. I was surprised that under the circumstances (Santo Domingo)[2] Jimmy Baldwin would let the ambassador give a large function in his honor; it was a vast supper, sit-down.

I am still in a state of great anxiety about the U.S. And there is nothing I can do, without (possibly) losing Jim his job, since Johnson appears to be a vindictive man. We have not discussed this, Jim and I; we've discussed the events but not our relation to them. I fear it may reach the point where I will be moved to ask him to resign.* But if it reaches that point, things will be so serious that my worries may seem unimportant—a wry consolation. Well, we'll talk about this when we're together. I have no thought of doing anything precipitate, and fortunately I'm not in the U.S., where I might feel goaded or stampeded. To say something or write something.

Now I must stop and rush this down to the mail box. More another day, when I have more time.

Much, much love,
Mary

*I say I *fear*; I'm aware of the egotism this would imply. Though he sometimes talks bitterly of resigning, but for different motives. He feels very estranged from the present U.S.I.A.

1. William R. Tyler had been appointed Assistant Secretary of State for European Affairs by John F. Kennedy in 1962.
2. U.S. marines had been sent by President Johnson to the Dominican Republic to put down a popular revolt against the U.S.-backed Belaguer regime.

141 rue de Rennes
Paris 6e
June 22, 1965

Dearest Hannah:

Forgive me for this awful delay in answering you.[1] I am gasping, literally, for breath. Jim's office social life (at its height in June), mine, attempted work, family, income tax (due June 15 for foreign residents; I do our return myself); incredible pressure from publishers and journalists demanding interviews; a conference for French and African students near Mont St. Michel where I gave a lecture; the hairdresser; fittings. And worst of all the May—June American landings in Paris. Everyone I've ever known, I think, has been here, including my brother Kevin, Carmen, Tucci and girl friend, Nancy Macdonald and son Nick, the Rahvs, Arthur Schlesinger's oldest son, Max Lerner, Johnny Meyers. Plus people you've never heard of—friends of my uncle, women I went to boarding school with. And others I'm forgetting. The telephone shrills like an air raid siren. This morning, for instance, a young Negro friend from Senegal who has just hit town (lunch); a Portuguese using an alias asking for help in publicizing the cause of the Portuguese writers (tea Thursday); my French translator (tea tomorrow); Carmen's ex-husband (dinner tonight); Lanvin telling me they have sent me the wrong dress and will I pack it up and return it to them. . . . Last night, among many other people, I saw Joe Frank[2] and his wife; he asked after you and wanted me to send you his best. He told me a little about [critic and poet R. P.] Blackmur's death.

Incidentally, I never told you that I met a young Dutch woman in Amsterdam named Renate Rosenthal (sic),[3] who has written admiringly about your Eichmann book. She sent me the piece, and eventually I'll send it on to you. If I stop to look for it now (my papers got all shoved away during the income tax torture), this letter will be even more delayed. It is in Dutch, but you can probably make it out. One thing she confessed to me that was interesting was that she had been extremely against your book before reading it and that afterwards she was unable to account for this to herself, since she is normally rather critical of received ideas, not pro-Zionist, and had independent knowledge of Jewish cooperation with the Nazis in Holland. In fact, several people there said that many things that happened in Holland were much worse than anything described in your book. However, they did not specify. Some time you might like to meet the Rosenthal girl. Also Harry Mulisch. [4]

I'll not write about Viet Nam, etc., for lack of time. The fact that I signed the Lowell telegram [5] has elicited a number of letters and telephone calls of congratulation from French friends and even from people (French) that I don't know.

Now about August. It would be infinitely better for me if you could come to Bocca di Magra. We will have the children for the month only this summer—at least as it now appears—and I don't think it would look good to them if I disappeared immediately on arrival. Their mother tries to tell them that I don't like them, and I hesitate to do something that might lend support to this propaganda. It isn't that I'm *necessary;* we have someone to take care of them there, as well as Jim, but the family ambience is important. Anyway, I wouldn't urge you if I weren't convinced that you would like Bocca di Magra. The Chiaromontes will be there and the Lévis, and the atmosphere is ideal for peaceful conversation. *There are only two parties a summer!* They are children's birthdays and occur in September. The swimming is normally very nice. People read a good deal, play chess, swim, and sometimes argue in the evenings. And are in bed, usually, by eleven or eleven-thirty. We have room to put you up, but if you prefer, you can be in a *pension.* The place is small.

The problem is to get there from Zurich. I shall have to put my mind on this. There is surely a Zurich-Milan plane, and at the very worst we could meet you in Milan. Pisa has an airport, but I think most of the flights to Pisa come from London and Paris. If a Zurich-Florence connection were possible, that would be splendid. But I rather doubt that there is such a connection. Bocca di Magra, in case you don't know, is just south of Lerici. La Spezia is the nearest express train stop, but a train would take too long. Besides, I don't see how a train from Zurich would possibly get to Genoa, which is the point of juncture. Or even to Turin. In Italy, train travel from north to south is easy, but from west to east or vice versa is very difficult. Even by car it is hard because of the Apennines, unless you go up the Arno valley. I will stop by Swissair to find out if there are any flights that could get you to Florence or Pisa. If not, the best thing will be for us to drive to Milan. [. . .]

I'm going to England for four days next Monday, to see and review the new John Osborne play [*A Patriot for Me*]. But Jim will be here, in case a letter from you comes.

How is Cal? Naturally, it worries me that all the political excitement may go to his head. . . .

I've begun to see a few more French people. Nathalie S[arraute] and I have become much more easy with each other. Through her, I've met a young woman writer called Monique Wittig, who has written an odd book called *L'Opoponax*,[6] which I liked very much. But more of them when we see each other.

Dear Hannah, that will be *nice!*

Much love,
Mary

1. Arendt's letter or card is missing.
2. Joseph Frank was a professor of comparative literature at Princeton University.
3. The "(sic)" after Renate Rosenthal, whose surname was actually Rubinstein, was inserted by McCarthy.
4. Harry Mulisch is a Dutch novelist whom McCarthy befriended at the Edinburgh Festival in 1962.
5. Robert Lowell publicly declined his invitation to the White House Festival of the Arts in June 1965, to protest the Vietnam war. The next day, a telegram of support, signed by a number of prominent intellectuals, including McCarthy, appeared on the front page of *The New York Times*.
6. McCarthy's review of Monique Wittig's *L'Opoponax*, *New Statesman*, July 1966, is reprinted in *The Writing on the Wall*.

[Palenville, N.Y.]
June 26, 1965
[Postcard]

Dearest Mary:

[. . .] Of course, I can come to Bocca di Magra. Could you let me have your telephone number? Jaspers is rather sick, I am very worried, and I would like first to call him the moment I arrive in

Zurich and then call you to agree about dates. It will be in the first half of August, anyhow. If I remember rightly, one can fly to Florence via Milano; but it does not matter, I can also come by train (overnight): I love good trains and I know there is a direct train from Zurich to Pisa or to Florence, I think to Pisa. Don't bother, I can manage. [. . .]

Love to both of you from us both—
Hannah

141 rue de Rennes
Paris 6e
July 21, 1965

Dearest Hannah:

Trying to answer some old correspondence, I discover that I neglected to pass on to you a request from the Renate Rubinstein whose review of *Eichmann* I sent you.

She is an adviser for a Dutch publisher called Moussault, who want to publish a Dutch translation of *Eichmann*. They were told by Viking that you were difficult about giving rights. Their agent is in touch with Piper, who says it is all right for them to use the German translation; because of the new introduction, they prefer the German version. Since her letter was written late in May, perhaps you know about this already and have decided one way or the other.

I've just written her, though, that I would ask you. I told her that if you were "difficult about rights," it was probably because you were concerned about the translation, especially with a book like the Eichmann. She herself is German-born, and I feel sure she would be very strict about supervising the accuracy of the translation, especially since she is your sympathizer. But she is that way naturally; she wrote in to a Dutch newspaper to correct a misquotation from me in an interview. Something about Sartre and the Nobel Prize. [. . .]

[. . .] I know nothing about Moussault, but if she is their adviser, they must be one of the most serious. You never make any money out of Dutch editions because most educated people there read English. But it is a nice country.

Now that Bastille Day is past, there's a slight lull here. Nearly everyone who lives in Paris is gone, but visitors keep coming. The latest are some Hungarians, oh, dear. I long to leave for Bocca di

Magra. You will be amazed to learn that we just turned down a glorious villa in the hills there on the grounds that it was *too expensive!* So that we will be back with our old landlord, Tommarchi, whose phone I gave you. He had been acting rather tricky about the agreement we thought we had with him. When you come, we will be humbly installed as usual. The children have already gone (a change in plans), and Jim is working very hard at the office; he has a Ministerial Meeting this week, which is exhausting—among others, [Daniel] Bell is coming from America.

Our only official friend here, Tom Finletter, ambassador to NATO, has just resigned, which is sad. He is one of the last of the Roosevelt people, a very straight, forthright man. He did not have any reserves about giving (at least to us) his views about Viet Nam. He said that he had been thinking that some new political alignment might be coming in America—like what happened with the Whigs before the Civil War. But we could not decide, discussing it lightly, which of the present parties would be the right-wing one.

Did I write you about being threatened with lawsuits by about forty homosexual actors in London? Me and the *Observer.*[1] It seems to have blown over. Too long to tell about in a letter.

You must have read about the two drunk Marines who set out to bomb Hanoi. What is going to happen? I have nightmares about atomic bombs—there, not here. Last week I told Jim that if we bombed Hanoi he would either have to leave the U.S. [Foreign] Service or get a divorce. Perhaps this is hysterical on my part, though at the time he rather agreed that if we did bomb Hanoi he should resign. I keep wondering whether there isn't some preventive action that could be taken to deter Johnson from such a step. Stevenson's death seems like something in one of Shakespeare's chronicle plays—another victim of the usurper king. The photograph taken of him the day he died was horrifying; he had aged at least twenty years since I saw him winter before last. It ought to have been clear to everyone that he was an old, dying man. I can understand that he stayed at the U.N. for high motives, out of some sterile and limited notion of duty. He must have argued that he was exercising some restraint on Washington and that his successor would be worse. The latter part is probably true. But the spectacle of his humiliation and impotence was a political evil in itself.[2]

I didn't mean to write all this when I began. I do miss you so much; that is what this babble is saying.

> See you soon and
> much love to you both.
> Mary

1. McCarthy's review of *A Patriot for Me*, "Verdict on Osborne," *The Observer*, July 4, 1965, provoked this suit.
2. Adlai Stevenson had been appointed U.S. Ambassador to the United Nations by John F. Kennedy, and in the early 1960s played an activist role in resolving international tensions. By 1964–65 his role as a mediator in East-West conflicts had been frequently derided by President Johnson. He died on July 14, 1965 in London.

> Cornell Residential Club
> One Country Club Road
> Ithaca, New York 14850
> October 20, 1965

Dearest Mary,

God knows why I never wrote. I meant to write all the time. The few days in Italy [Bocca di Magra] were marvellous, and the farther they are away the brighter they shine. Basel—Jaspers sometimes better, but in the constant ups and downs no certain trend. Absolutely himself though, but tired, easily exhausted and almost constantly in pain. I was a couple of days in Zurich but otherwise stayed there until we had to leave. Heinrich came for about 2 weeks. My family from Israel came for a few days, then Annchen [Anne Weil], then friends from Cologne. I read the proofs[1] and saw people on and off, but was mainly with Jaspers. Always thinking it could be the last time, and though I doubt it, it was the first time that I thought along these lines constantly. And was at the same time more at home there than ever. As though the approach of death makes everything even easier; what considerations could possibly count?

The best new thing was a pupil of Jaspers, a Swiss from Bern, married, with four children, beautiful wife, he plus children constantly in and out of the house.[2] I never saw anything like this before. He is shortly before his PhD and writes a dissertation on Kant's political philosophy that is entirely original in approach and content. Also very well written. For Jaspers a really God-sent [*sic*], in my opinion the first real disciple J. ever had. Also: I was overjoyed talking with him [the Swiss student] about the *Group*. Both had read it, and I first thought: they can't understand this, they are very simple people, not at all sophisticated, only intelligent, and without any typically modern experiences. (Both former grammar school teachers.) Well, I couldn't have been more mistaken and I hardly have met anybody who understood so well. (Speaks for the German translation, incidentally.) She said, when we were talking about the pessary business: the whole book is so "clean" (sauber), which of course is precisely the point. Annchen too, it turned out, is a great admirer of you. So, somehow you were present there all the time.

Then Holland and Renate Rubinstein and a mob of Dutch intellectuals [. . .] Quite nice and interesting and sympathique. Heinrich and I liked Holland very much, even more than when we were there [before]. There is a solidity in their prosperity which is so very pleasant, quite old-fashioned in their way of life though not at all in their thinking. A country without hysterics. Very anti-German, by the way, more so than any other country I can think of, even England. They refused to speak German although it turned out that everybody knew and understood and spoke German better than English. And then back home via Rotterdam on the SS Rotterdam, a very nice ship with abominable food. And on to Cornell where I am now for 2 1/2 days per week, commuting back and forth [to New York] by air. It is all right, better than being away from home altogether. Teaching is nice, though I wished I had more time for myself. Well, it can't be helped. I got myself into something absurd—Macmillan had asked me years ago for my dissertation on Augustine. I needed the money (not really, but could use it) and said yes. The translation[3] arrived two years ago and now I ran out of excuses and have to go over it. It is kind of a traumatic experience. I am re-writing the whole darned business, trying not to do anything new, but only to explain in English (and not in Latin) what I thought when I was twenty. It is probably not worth it and I should simply return the money—but by now I am strangely fascinated in this rencontre. I had not read the thing for nearly forty years.

Dearest, what happened with the homosexuals? Annchen [to] whom I told the story is willing to start the collection.[4] So of course am I. I read Bondy's piece on Beauvoir and like it very much. Does he print it in Preuves?[5] I was again struck [by] how intelligent Bondy is. If I only could trust him! I heard little from Chicago;

190

Bellow, I am told, is much attracted by Washington now, planned to write a book on Humphrey of all people, had to drop it for political reasons (God knows what reasons) and wants now to write a book on Bob Kennedy.

Did you see in the papers that Randall Jarrell committed suicide? A very very sad story. Breaks my heart. I saw him last winter when I lectured at his college in Greensborough [sic] and he introduced me. Talked with him for hours. I knew how sick he was. [6]

You probably saw the entirely unprovoked attack on you by Kazin in his new book [*Starting Out in the Thirties*]. It made me mad but probably does not bother you. The cheapness of the whole thing is so revolting. These people get worse as they get older, and in this case it is just a matter of envy. Envy *is* a monster.

I heard from Dwight and from Cal but haven't yet seen either. Tonight, while I am writing this, Soerensen [sic][7] lectured on the campus. I decided not to go, too many people and somehow I am quite disgusted by his performance as well as by the performance of Schlesinger [not described]. [. . .]

Write me a line! Just how everything is! Give my love to Jim and also remember me to the children. And excuse this letter which is a no-letter.

je t'embrasse, yours,
Hannah

New York, Saturday. I forgot to mail this letter in Ithaca, dragged it back to NY, and now read that Tillich is dead. Wretchedly, all I can feel is the fear, the certainty that others will die too. All the obituaries mention Jaspers and Heidegger—as though to rub it in.

Yours sadly,
H.

1. These may have been proofs of Jaspers's *The Future of Germany* (1967), to which Arendt contributed the preface.
2. This was Hans Saner (1934–), who was Jaspers's assistant until his death in 1969.
3. E. B. Ashton's 1963 translation of Arendt's 1929 dissertation, *Der Liebesbegriff bei Augustin* (The Concept of Love in Augustine), was never revised to her satisfaction, and remains unpublished.
4. Annchen's "collection" was a jesting reference to the defense fund McCarthy might need if a threatened lawsuit by some forty homosexual actors in London was filed.
5. François Bondy reviewed *La Force des Choses* for *Preuves* later in the year.
6. A memoir Arendt wrote for *Randall Jarrell, 1914–1965* (1967) is reprinted in her *Men in Dark Times*.
7. Theodore Sorensen had been Special Counsel and speechwriter for President Kennedy.

[No letters remain from the ten-month period from October 1965 to August 1966. Perhaps there were few, or none at all. McCarthy was absorbed with *Birds of America* and with the intricate complications of family life with the West children. Arendt, who was busier teaching and lecturing than ever before, was newly caught up in the political affairs of her students, who were organizing against the Vietnam war.]

[Palenville, N.Y.]
August 24, 66
[Postcard]

Dear Mary, dear Jim:

Thanks for the card from Venice. This only to let you [know] I think I'll be in Basel Sept. 15 [. . .] hopefully at the Euler Hotel, Bahnhofsplatz. I'll stay in Basel appr. 3 weeks. When do you come back from Bocca di Magra? Can't you come via Basel? We are still in Palenville but shall be back in New York next week—Aug. 31. Heinrich who will not come to Europe sends his love. Everything fine.

Love,
Hannah

presso Tommarchi
Bocca di Magra (La Spezia)
September 8, 1966

Dearest Hannah:

This is being written in haste, with the hope of catching you before you leave for Basel. I like very much the idea of coming back from Bocca di Magra via Basel but don't know yet just when I'll be leaving. It depends on the weather partly. Jim goes back Saturday (the 10th); the children leave the next day. I should like to linger for another ten days or so and do some writing, if only it doesn't start raining. If it does, I shall have to leave. September is too cold here, without heat, unless the sun is out.

Another problem is that, no matter when I leave, I shall have a lot of baggage. Books, writing materials, typewriter, as well as summer clothes, bathing suits, towels, etc. Maybe it would be best to go home first, then fly to see you in Basel.

A final complication is that there is, as of today, a serious crisis about the children's future. A telegram from their mother this morning announces that she "must leave Paris" and that they are either to be put in English boarding-schools or shipped direct from Italy to Washington. Jim is beside himself, and I'm quite shaken too. Margaret has been involved for some time with a [. . .] New York-based business man of Polish origin [. . .] described by one of the children as looking like a gangster. In any case, it looks as if she were [. . .] going to marry him. [. . .] The children know nothing of any of this and are tranquilly preparing to return to their Paris school for the fall term.

We shall have to tell them, within the next twenty-four hours, but we're deferring it till we have some notion of a solution. The idea of their going to America to live with this man as a semi-parent seems utterly inacceptable. English boarding-schools might be a compromise, though hard on Jonny, the young one; at least we could see them quite often and have them over vacations and also they like England and have friends there. But Jim is very dubious of Margaret's power to get them into schools at this late date. And of her good faith. He wonders whether this is a lure to get him to hand the children over.

Anyway, he's busy telephoning his lawyer in Paris for advice and practical help, and we're both entertaining fantasies of kidnapping, hiding out, etc. My own feeling is that in the long run the children will decide what is to happen to them. Danny is already fourteen. If they want to remain with their mother, they will, and if they don't, they won't. Nobody can keep children of that age by force, especially when there is another interested parent in the offing. But the problem may be that they won't know *what* they want. Except the little one, who has never desired anything else than to be with his father.

It's particularly painful, this bolt from the blue, because they have been marvelous this summer, opening like flowers. A point noticed by all here, not just by us.

My own summer has not been so marvelous. My brother [Kevin] came to visit, with his two little girls, stayed for nearly a month, and was a terrible strain for me. He has been transformed by his divorce [from Augusta Dabney McCarthy] into a weird, false being, an actor in every sense, so that it's impossible to be with him without transports of embarrassment and horrified pity. Then the weather has been ghastly and various other people have descended on us, so that I've got almost no work done and no vacation either.

What I glean from this is that virtue is its own punishment. In short I'm in a state of fatigue and mild depression and not prepared to face fall in Paris unless I get a little solitude, reading, work, and rest first. Jim too is rather tired and driven. We've both, I think, without being aware of it, been living in a state of apprehension, since in mid-July we had an intimation of the blow in store for the children or at least for us on their behalf.

Please forgive this harassed and egotistic letter. I am so glad you and Heinrich are fine. Nicola and Miriam are well; he is to give the Gauss lectures in Princeton starting in October. But everyone here has been under a slight cloud, a reflection of the almost daily clouds in the sky: hardly any Punta Bianca [beach] this year.

You can reach me here unless you hear to the contrary. And I shall try to reach you at the Hotel Euler. [. . .] It will be wonderful to see you in Basel and I shall manage it somehow. Come what may.

Much love,
Mary

[Basel]
9/19/66
[Postcard]

Dearest Mary:

Just in case—Jaspers' telephone number (0601) 23 81 21. The number in parenthesis is for Basel. I am soooo looking forward— Room in Euler is reserved.

Love
Hannah

141 rue de Rennes
Paris 6ème
October 11, 1966

Dearest Hannah:

Thank you for all the pleasures of my stay with you. *And* for the bracelet. I think it must be a charmed bracelet because I am feeling in much better spirits. An additional reason for this may be the absence of Maria on vacation. As you know, I like doing cooking and marketing and the more refined side of housework, such as polishing silver and furniture. It's pleasant to do these things again, that is, to exercise arts or crafts which reward one with a sense of order and purely private accomplishment. Jim is in better spirits too, though he's been having a harassing time with his Enemy in the office. However, as the Enemy remarked of him, sotto voce: "He's a fighter."

Nicola has been here, and the Congress [for Cultural Freedom] did get the Ford Foundation grant. The C.I.A. accusation has been totally bypassed; no one mentions it here. [1] And what would it serve Nicola and Silone, for instance, to insist on knowing the truth? If they were told, now, in confidence, that the C.I.A. had been subsidizing them a number of years ago, what could they do with this knowledge? The only thing is that in England, the *Sunday Telegraph* has repeated the gossip about *Encounter* in a series they're running about the C.I.A. It's thought that if they can't get a retraction from the *Telegraph*, they will have to sue. Not to sue (in England, where the libel laws are so strict) would be to acknowledge that the gossip is true. But to sue might land them in a worse fix. That is, if the *Telegraph* could produce evidence. . . ? But the Congress boys here (I mean the bureaucrats) act as if *Encounter* were a distant cousin. Concerned, curious, dryly sympathetic. "Yes, Mel [Lasky, *Encounter's* editor] seems to be having a bit of trouble there." It is quite funny.

In any case, a new overall board is being instituted by the Ford people. Headed by Raymond Aron. None of the editors of the magazines will be allowed to serve on the board—a rule (I think) that must be directed against Lasky. On the board, among other Americans, will be Saul Bellow. A strange choice. I hear that Saul is in poor shape again, attacking what he calls the American Establishment, meaning his critics. He gave a [. . .] lecture in London and the audience was asked to stay in its seats for ten minutes (or five?) after the lecture was over, so that no one would approach him for his autograph on his way to his getaway car. He also told the chief editor at Jonathan Cape that I, like him, was very "unhappy" with Weidenfeld. A complete invention. There was a Round Table here yesterday on *Herzog*, which is just coming out, and Saul is not going to be any happier if it is printed (as is planned) in the *Nouvel Observateur*. There were two violent attacks on the book, and François Bondy and I were its chief defenders. In between, there was a great deal of fence-sitting. "Oui, c'est un bon roman. Mais pas un *grand roman*." And one female idiot, who gently preened herself during the discussion, as though she had the inside track (had Saul slept with her?), did speak up for it, comparing Herzog (yes) to the queens of Racine.

Do you know that extracts from *Eichmann* are appearing in the *Nouvel Observateur*? With an extremely mealy-mouthed and cowardly preface, written, one of my friends thinks, by Jean Daniel.[2] Whoever wrote it cites Raymond Aron and me as endorsers of the book. When I read that preface, I reached for my typewriter. But then I calmed myself. There will be plenty of time, I reckoned, to get into that controversy. Meanwhile, I decided to wait and see. My friend (Eileen Geist; did you ever meet her?), who's close to the publishers of the *Nouvel Observateur*, though not to Jean Daniel, thinks the book will get a quite different reaction from French Jewry than it got in the United States. The French Jews, she said, are not so *Jewish*. She's a strong admirer of the book herself, which may be indicative, since she's taken on a decided French coloration after thirteen years here. She and her husband, though they're friends with all the New York gang (including Saul, a bosom friend), never budged from their position of support.

By the way, Sylvia Marlowe [the harpsichordist], who came to dinner the other night, told me that she was "crazy" about your Rosa Luxemburg piece.[3] She thought it was "Hannah's most personal work." Her idea was that you "identified" with Rosa Luxemburg, seeing her quarrel with the German Socialists as *your* quarrel with the organized Jews. "Such passion," etc. I told her that I did not see this at all, in fact became rather annoyed at her insistence. It was as if this identification theory were a big keyhole through which she could look into your hidden emotions. She's a gruesome *voyeur*, that woman. But perhaps *I* am wrong.

The news about the book (I mean Mrs. Grumbach's) is not good at the moment.[4] Jim and Janet Flanner, between them, worked me up to a pitch of alarm, which proves in the event to be justified. I've not had a syllable in reply to the long letter I wrote her. Nor from her publisher. Meanwhile they (Coward McCann) sent the galleys to Edmund [Wilson], who naturally is very angry, though he was calmed down somewhat toward me when he learned that I had not authorized these revelations. He's hoping to stop the publication of those sections of the book that deal with our marriage. Urged by Jim and Janet, I called Jovanovich, who sounded quite pessimistic about the result of any legal action and even more pessimistic about the workings of grace in the hearts of the author and her publisher. I have sent him copies of all the correspondence between her and me; my memory of this was correct. She did assure me that she would quote "only the most innocuous stuff" from the tapes. She asked and got permission to use two items about Edmund, both perfectly harmless (one she didn't use in the end), and she asked permission to use a third item identified only by initials. I wrote back: "I don't understand. Who is P. W.?" She replied that it must have been a mistake for "E. W." I now suddenly realize that "P. W. was Payne Whitney—the story of my incarceration there. So that in fact I never gave permission for that nor refused it in so many words, though of course I did by implication since she was aware that she needed to ask.

[. . .] I am not libeled, so far as I can see, in the book. And he [Jovanovich] thinks that invasion of privacy may not apply with a public figure. A spoken and written agreement has been violated, but it was not, of course, a contract. [. . .] Meanwhile, he has got in touch with Edmund, who has sent him his set of galleys. They may be able to work out something in concert. For surely *Edmund* has been libeled. I'm also, for the time being, refusing permission to quote from any of my books, which is a small weapon but a weapon. It would be cheaper for them to remove the offensive passages than to reset all the quotations, which would have to be paraphrased. Unfortunately, as is clear from his advertising in the *Publishers Weekly*, the publisher hopes to make money from this book as a sort of *Confidential*-style document. The author's original letter says that she wants to stay "far from hearsay, gossip, and the usual bilious tittle-tattle of friends and former friends." !! And her reason for seeking an interview was to straighten out certain bibliographical problems. Or so she said. In writing.

I can hardly believe that I've been the victim of a confidence-artist. In fact, I don't believe it. One of her problems, I think, is that she doesn't seem to have kept copies of her letters to me, so that she doesn't know what she said and what she didn't. In effect, this allowed her to think that I "wouldn't mind" whatever she wrote.

Dear Hannah, I must stop and go out to get some supplies for dinner. I loved being with you and we must plan to be together again quite soon. Maybe I shall have to come to the U.S. about the above. Keep well, keep Heinrich well, write soon.

> And many more thanks,
> Mary

[. . .]

1. In April 1966, *The New York Times* published the results of a seven-month investigation that substantiated rumors of CIA ties to the Congress for Cultural Freedom and its many conferences and magazines, including *Encounter* and Chiaromonte's and Silone's *Tempo Presente*. In October 1966, the Ford Foundation agreed to fund CCF programs and magazines, but neither *Preuves* nor *Tempo Presente* survived the further disclosures of CIA funding that made headlines the following year.
2. Jean Daniel, then editor of *Le Nouvel Observateur*, had turned down McCarthy's 1964 report of the literary debate at the Mutualité, with its acerbic portraits of Sartre and de Beauvoir.
3. Hannah Arendt, "A Heroine of the Revolution," *The New York Review of Books*, October 6, 1966. It is a review of J. P. Nettl's *Rosa Luxemburg*, and is reprinted in *Men in Dark Times*.
4. Doris Grumbach's book about Mary McCarthy, *The Company She Kept*, was published, with a few cuts and disclaimers from McCarthy, in 1967.

> 141 rue de Rennes
> Paris 6e
> November 21, 1966

Dearest Hannah:

Just a rapid note. We'd missed that number of the *Observateur* [with the *Eichmann* excerpts]; I think it must have come out when we were in England. I got someone to send it to me the other day and flew into a passion. Wanted to write a letter at once. Jim deterred me, saying write to Hannah first; she may not want you to continue this controversy. Well, time has passed; I've been very busy this last week. But I should *still* like to do something, though it's probably too late to have anything printed in the correspondence column. I could write to Jean Daniel personally, though, or see him. Or write something elsewhere. Make Bondy, if I can, print a comment by me in *Preuves* on the *Observateur*'s conduct in the whole affair. Which to me is worse, in a way, than anything that happened in America, because so typically unprincipled. A sales promotion stunt, coated over with "anti-fascist" piety.

I asked someone I know, who's in touch with the *Observateur* people though at odds with them, *why* they printed that headline "*Est Elle Nazie?*"—a question that was not raised even by their own indignant correspondents. And he said "*Pour vendre des exemplaires. C'est tout*" [To sell copies, that's all]. Another friend, Georges Bernier, remarked that it was typical *France-Dimanche* journalism. You know, every Sunday there are headlines—like "*Philip trompe-t-il Elizabeth?*"; when you read the article, you find that *tromper* refers to some harmless activity like playing the horses without telling his consort and that the answer in any case is No. According to Georges, the whole supposedly left-wing staff of the *Observateur* moonlights on *France-Dimanche*. . . .

But I've heard no expression of indignation on the subject, except my own. Well, yes, Anjo Lévi did say it was *"abominable"* though without any great passion, as though it were only to be expected. [. . .]

Anyway, please write and tell me yes or no. I don't mean whether you ask me to do something but whether you consent to my doing something. If you do, I may get in touch with Raymond Aron for advice.

I'm glad of your [telephone] account of Reuel. You're probably right about the long flight from linguistics. And *thank you* for seeing them.¹ [. . .]

By the way, what *do* the newly released x-rays of Kennedy reveal? We can't make out from here. If the wound in the back was where the Warren Commission says it was—i.e. high—this would damage many of the conclusions of the Epstein book.² And I read somewhere that Epstein is now convinced that the Report was right.

The idea of Mark Lane as the investigating counsel for the Russell Sartre Commission is somehow both funny and sinister.³ I feel he is a figure that we will hear more of on the political scene, now that he is launched.

Otherwise no particular news here. My book seems to be going somewhat better. Paris has been full of English friends for the last week, because of a Francis Bacon show that opened at the Maeght Gallery. Also English art critics come to see the Picasso exhibitions. Any cultural center now looks like the Métro during the rush hour—tremendous lines, even in the rain, people pushing and shoving. The Vermeer has been like that for two months, and now it is the Picasso. And Saturday we went to see the Bonington show at the Jacquemart André, which you would have expected to find deserted. But you could hardly see the pictures for the throng, including a guided tour of Parisians. I don't know what all this means. Certainly it has nothing to do with art-appreciation. Because you *cannot* appreciate anything under those conditions. The only exception is a Polish painter I know called [Joseph] Czapski whom we saw at the Vermeer show; he is an old man, six and a half feet tall, and he was moving contentedly through the crowd like an ostrich, taking pictorial notes in a sketchbook. This art stampede has been building up in Paris for about two years; the first real queues, though, going part way around the Concorde, were last year—to see the Guillaume Walter collection at the Orangerie.

Jim has stopped smoking. The result is a physical shambles: insomnia, upset stomach, hoarseness, sore throat. It is now more than two weeks, and he's still not back to normal. Inspired by his example, I've cut down to ten cigarettes a day, which I broke yesterday for the first time, when I had to take part in a panel discussion. In general, it's not too hard to keep, and I don't notice any physical effects—either bad or good.

Dear Hannah, I do miss you tremendously. I am really homesick for you.

Much love,
Mary

[. . .]

P.P.S. [. . .] Glad you are made up with Harold [Rosenberg]. Give him my love when you next see him.

M.

1. Arendt had visited Reuel Wilson, who had recently married and was teaching in Chicago.
2. Edward Jay Epstein, *Inquest: The Warren Commission and the Establishment of Truth* (1966).
3. The Bertrand Russell War Crimes Commission, led by Sartre and Beauvoir, met in Stockholm and Copenhagen in 1967 to review evidence of American war crimes in Vietnam. Mark Lane, whose *Rush to Judgment* charged the Warren Commission with a conspiracy to withhold the truth about the assassination, does not appear in published reports of the Russell proceedings.

Part Four

February 1967 – November 1970

[At home, Hannah Arendt remained relatively aloof from the deepening crisis in Vietnam, although she was impressed by the nationwide mobilization of students against the war. In mass demonstrations and teach-ins—in the conquest of "public space" by private citizens incensed by government policy—she thought she saw a reaffirmation of the *vita activa*.

Mary McCarthy's horror of the war increased apace, as did her frustration with the limited means of protest available to a diplomat's wife in Paris. In March 1966, when *The New York Review of Books* asked her to go to South Vietnam, she had declined, on the grounds that it might cost her husband his job. When nine months later she was asked again, there were 400,000 U.S. troops in Vietnam, and opposition to the war had spread within the diplomatic community itself. She accepted. One year later she went to Hanoi.]

141 rue de Rennes
Paris
February 1, 1967

Dearest Hannah:

I am leaving tomorrow morning at eleven for [South] Vietnam; it's now eleven-thirty at night. But I couldn't go without writing you to say good-bye and that I hope you approve of the trip. I had to do *something*.

All this last week I've been wanting to write you a long letter, but there have been too many petty administrative things to do, such as visas and currency and making my will (you will get two little pieces of jewelry that I think suit you) and dictating masses of less personal correspondence. And suddenly it's nearly midnight—*la veille.*

I shall be staying at the Hotel Royal, Saigon, for roughly three weeks, starting February 3. If I can get a visa for Hanoi, I shall go there before coming back.

How are you, my dearest Hannah? And Heinrich? It was so wonderful to be with you in New York. Especially that last night.

I am taking the bracelet for protection against all sorts of demons, including that of stupidity.

Much, much love,
Mary

P.S. Jim *approves* and sends love too.
P.P.S. In Vietnam, I shall be "Mary McCarthy."[1]

1. McCarthy, who was "Mrs. James West" on her diplomatic passport, had been issued a nondiplomatic passport for travel to both South and North Vietnam.

NEW YORK NY
[February 10, 1967]

MARY MCCARTHY HOTEL ROYAL SAIGON
ALL MY WISHES ALL MY LOVE TAKE CARE OF YOURSELF PLEASE

HANNAH

[In the summer of 1967, with the prospect of another home leave upon them, Mary and Jim West bought a house in Castine, Maine. For McCarthy, who was becoming more outspoken in her opposition to the war in Vietnam, and thus more closely aligned with the antiwar movement in the United States, it was time to come home, to reestablish her roots. Not far from Elizabeth Hardwick and Robert Lowell (who first told them about the property on Main Street), the big captain's house, with its back pasture and extensive gardens, supplanted Bocca di Magra as the Wests' summer residence.

For Hannah Arendt, on the other hand, the escalation of the war and her fear of domestic repression, together with the breakdown of social services in New York, came close to convincing her and Heinrich Blücher to flee the United States for Switzerland. "Times are lousy and we should be closer to each other," she wrote Mary in February 1968, pining for the relative tranquility of Europe.]

Main Street
Castine, Maine
September 12, 1967

Dearest Hannah:

It was so good to hear your voice. *Please come.* There are several flights a day to Bangor on Northeast Airlines. Bill Jovanovich took one that got him in shortly after eleven in the morning; most people seem to favor one that gets in at 5:25 p.m. We'll meet you at the airport and be home well in time for dinner.

Our house is full of workmen, but that won't disturb you. The bedrooms are peaceful (they aren't being redone), and there's also a whole separate apartment—studio, two bedrooms, bath, kitchen—over the garage, where you can be by yourself if you want and even work a little. It's an excellent place to work.

The only other visit we have scheduled is from Reuel and Marcia [Reuel's wife] on the 20th. I don't know yet how long they'll stay—rather briefly, I think. Did I tell you they're expecting a baby in January? Between ourselves, relations with them have been very strained, to say the least, during the last month. Both Jim and I are very much distressed and worried about what this portends. His relation with me is turning into that of an extremely hostile parasite. It's impossible to find out anything from him about the progress of his work; he appears to have passed one set of orals but either deferred another or failed it—his statements on the subject are highly guarded and elliptical. I'll be glad to have your advice and good judgment about what is to be done. It's clear that the coming baby means increased support from me—with increased resentment on their part. Classic. His recent outbreaks of hatefulness may have something to do with her pregnancy. It's all directed on me; they are both beaming fondly on Edmund, who ceased his contributions several years ago.

I am so pleased to hear that Heinrich has been so well this summer. Did you hear that I'm going to Hanoi? In October, probably, unless something goes wrong with the plans. It's a group of three or perhaps four chosen by the people around *Liberation*.[1] Jim isn't looking forward to this eagerly, but he agrees that it's necessary for me to go, if allowed to by Hanoi. Of course if American bombing increases (and a radio story this morning suggests it is), then Hanoi may withdraw its promise of visas; I gather it's a matter of pride with them to be able to give security to visitors. I won't hear more till toward the end of the month.

Let me know when your plans are settled. We will have our maid, Maria, with us till the 18th, when she goes to Expo 67 [in Montreal] and on visits. If you come before then, she will bring you your breakfast on a tray—one of her pleasures. If you come after that, you can help with the dishes if you insist.[2] But we're living very simply owing to the presence of the workmen, and, as I said, there is *no social life* whatever. That ended with the departure of the Lowells.

He is taking some new drug, a kind of salt [lithium carbonate], that is supposed to guarantee that he'll never have another manic seizure. But what it has disclosed, by keeping him "normal," is how mad he is all the time, even when on his good behavior. It is as we said last December. And this, we hear from Lizzie, is the view of the new doctor, who is more a physiologist than a psychiatrist: "The salts," he told her, "will prevent manic outbreaks, but they can't change the fact that he is crazy." He's very tense and, when he's drinking, quite grandiose; he oughtn't to drink and has stopped for the moment, but I don't think he can keep it up. It's as though the drug were depriving him of his annual spree and he compensates for the deprivation rather cunningly by using the license given to drunkards. My opinion is that it would be better to let him be crazy once a year, be locked up, then emerge penitent, etc., than to have him subdued by this drug in a sort of private zoo—his home— with Lizzie as the keeper. But she prefers it that way. So long as he doesn't drink, she says.

I must stop and do a little work.

Much, much love and to Heinrich,
Mary

[. . .]

1. *Liberation* was a pacifist magazine published in New York. McCarthy's traveling companion in March 1968, when she finally got her visa, was the China scholar Franz Schurmann.
2. Blücher's poor health kept Arendt from going to Castine that first year.

Main Street
Castine, Maine
September 19, 1967

Dearest Hannah:

I'm returning the [Walter] Benjamin manuscript, marked.[1] That is, in the first section I've put *inside* brackets and indicated with x in the margin the parts I think should be saved. In one case—Goethe's Ur-Phänomene[2]—I didn't have the temerity to try to free it from the surrounding tissue, for it would mean writing a new sentence or two. But, as I've indicated, that too, I think, ought to stay in.

The purpose of my suggestions is to retain a continuous narrative and yet avoid an arena of controversy—with Adorno—that would be obscure in any case to the ordinary American reader.[3] Obviously what's left would have to be smoothed out and perhaps slightly expanded. I've corrected a mistake in English: "ignore." In English that means to deliberately not know, e.g., "When I came into the room, she ignored me." It's the source of countless mistranslations from the French and vice versa.

I haven't touched the second and third parts, which I like very much. Your remarks about quotations summon up Eliot's "These fragments I've shor'd up against my ruin"—an epigraph to *The Wasteland* [sic] and itself a quotation. But I think it's better not to make the allusion yourself but to allow the reader to make it on his own. . . .

Do I need to warn you that what you say about German Jews and Jewishness, even though backed up by the sacred authority of Kafka, will probably cause another storm?

Strangely—and this of course isn't the first time—certain passages in your essay set bells ringing in my mind, because I've been touching the same themes in what I've been doing this summer. You'll see if you ever see my book, which keeps dragging on. . . .

I can't write more because—perhaps by sympathetic vibrations with Jovanovich—I've developed an acute pain in my arm. My left; his right. It came on yesterday afternoon, and I imagine it must have started from holding the line on the sailboat; or else from constantly ducking my head there. We went to see the doctor this morning, and he diagnosed a "tendonitis" and gave me a very large injection of cortisone into the most painful area. He says it will get worse in the next twenty-four hours and then clear up within the week. He had exactly the same thing this summer. He prescribed some demerol, which so far I've dispensed with. But it hurts to type.

Thank you for calling last night.

Much love from us both and love and sympathy to Heinrich,

Mary

1. Arendt's essay on the German critic Walter Benjamin (1892–1940) was published by *The New Yorker*, October 19, 1968, and reprinted in *Men in Dark Times*.

2. An *Urphänomen* is an archetypal phenomenon; in Goethe's view, an object one comes upon in the world of appearances wherein word and thing, idea and experience, coincide.

3. Arendt's distaste for Marxist sociologist Theodor Adorno, a leading member of the Frankfurt School, began in Frankfurt in the early 1930s when Adorno blocked her first husband Günther Stern's dissertation proposal. In 1933, he was ridiculed by the Frankfurt student newspaper for attempting to appease local Nazi intellectuals in a review. The "real infamy," Arendt wrote to Jaspers many years later, was that he had hidden behind his mother's Italian family name, Adorno, instead of his Jewish father's name, Wiesengrund.

141 rue de Rennes
Paris, France
December 19, 1967

Dear Hannah:

This is a fine time to be thanking you for those beautiful yellow roses. But at least soon enough to wish you and Heinrich Merry Christmas and Happy New Year. Are you going to have your party this year?

I don't know what has happened to me this fall that I've not found time to write. Nothing very positive. I've done a bit of work but not as much as I should have. I've reorganized my library and finished reorganizing my files. We've had unusually little social life. And I've been ill, more or less, off and on, for the last month. A very unspectacular intestinal flu, followed by a very bad cold, followed by bronchitis. It's a bug that's been all over Paris, and everyone has the same complaint: of not being able to throw it off, dragging about aching as if with fever after the fever has long gone. My secretary [Mary Brady] has caught it (though not the intestinal part), Maria has caught it, and now Jim has it. In my case, it's now reduced to a cough, and a little energy is coming back.

And you? How did the capsule course work out at Chicago? Are you involved in any of our friends' Resistance activity? A letter from Cal that came this morning doesn't mention any of that. But I read that Susan Sontag was arrested [in an antiwar demonstration]. And what about her? When I last watched her with you at the Lowells', it was clear that she was going to seek to conquer you. Or that she had fallen in love with you—the same thing. Anyway, did she?

The gloomy world situation, from here, seems to have infected everything. Like an actual contagion. People are falling ill, having heart attacks, being x-rayed for suspected cancer. Sonia [Orwell], when last seen a few days ago, was making her will. She is going to have a hysterectomy—not for any grave reason but because she's been having backaches and other female troubles. On a serious plane, there is Bill [Jovanovich]. I talked to Martha [his wife] last week and this morning had a more reassuring cable from her. But I am frightened for him, even if he recovers. It was not possible to learn from Martha what exactly the doctors think. She spoke of a cardiac arrest, but I don't understand whether or not they've finally determined what's causing all this. When I last saw him, in [Columbia] Presbyterian [Hospital], they had diagnosed "total exhaustion" rather than anything specifically organic. The firm [Harcourt, Brace & World] incidentally, must be very much shaken by the seriousness of his condition. George Weidenfeld, whom I saw in London, talked as though a take-over by ATT or some other electronics concern would be imminent if Bill couldn't resume control fairly soon. He must worry about these things.

Nicola, who was in Paris recently, had a much more serious illness than I knew last spring. I don't know whether he knows it himself. Outwardly he seems quite well except for a strange suppressed excitement that makes one quite nervous, especially if one has just been told by Miriam not to let him overtire himself, not drink too much or overeat, and to be sure and see that he has his nap, etc. Her solicitude, which includes a great deal of whispering (so that he won't hear), obliges one to look on him as an undependable child or as a prematurely senile old man who can't be trusted either. The result is that he begins to behave like that. Anjo Lévi reports that she came home one afternoon to find him with her children (he is excited by youth) holding a large glass of whiskey in one hand and a cup of coffee in the other. Both highly frowned-on items. Despite her sympathy for Miriam, Anjo feels—and I agree— that he should be left to decide for himself whether he wants to live or die. As it is, he is submitting to *Miriam's* decision.

Hanoi. The last word, now six weeks old, was "early in January." But I've grown to doubt whether the trip isn't a mirage. The bombing is, of course, much worse, which explains this.

141 rue de Rennes
Paris
January 26, 1968

Darling Hannah:

The enclosed pre-Christmas letter [above], started over a month ago, never got finished. The holidays overtook it. And now I have something else to thank you for—the marvelous flowers which came, via Max Schling [a New York florist], last week and which are still very beautifully throning in the dining-room. You and Max Schling have discovered a Parisian florist—in the 16th [arrondissement]—with exquisite taste.

I have a present for you too. Something Greek, which I found in Sicily, where we went over New Year's. The problem is how to get it to you. I'm afraid to commit it to the mails; though its antiquity should clear it through customs, it might get broken. The best thing is to wait and give it to some New York-bound friend to deliver.

Since I wrote the enclosed, I'm in much better spirits. Health too. We spent twelve days in Sicily—a bit all over—and it was extremely tranquillizing. We missed the earthquakes luckily. Have you ever been? I think not. It does not strike one as at all Italian, except the bit around Taormina, which resembles Capri, both physically and morally. Nor is it quite like Greece either. Perhaps more like North Africa, though without any immemorial desert. A continuous backdrop of mountains and typical mountain weather, storms alternating with brilliant sunshine. Very fertile and verdant, which makes the black poverty more surprising. One great oasis, except in certain stony stretches. The oranges and lemons were on the trees while we were there and the prickly pears and wild iris was blooming near the roadside and around the temples. Yet it isn't sweet landscape but rather harsh or severe. And it does seem mythic, like parts of Greece. You're seldom out of view of the sea, because of the great heights and long perspectives, and most of the temples and all the theatres we saw looked out onto the sea, even if from far away. It's a land of rainbows—water magic; I'd forgotten about rainbows, which seem to be associated with being a child. We saw an extraordinary, almost unbelievable one, as we were crossing through the mountain passes of the interior one stormy day—a huge colored belt across the sky, and you could see both ends of the arc, which hardly ever happens and made it seem like a vision and not just some little floating phantasm.

We liked Palermo and Syracuse best, among the cities, and the temple of Segesta best. Agrigento has been all-but-ruined by cheap housing developments in the medieval town above and hideous bourgeois villas in the middle distance. Selinunte is rather good, especially its post-Armageddon scenes of broken giant pillars. In Taormina, outside the Greek theatre, we saw an amusing sign:

"Please don't write on the plants"—cacti. There's a splendid baroque sculptor in Palermo—Paolo Serpotta—with a strange imagination that made me think of the dwarf, Cuvillies the Younger, in Munich, though there's no resemblance visually; visually, he has something of Watteau. I should like to see much more of his work, but Sicily is too crammed with sights. The Italian Touring Club guide we had said the visitor might get a *superficial* notion of Sicily if he stayed three months.

In London we stayed with Sonia, who was in bed, recovering from her hysterectomy and simply pouring down the white wine, like somebody drinking from a faucet. I persuaded her to go on the wagon till Easter, and she sounds somewhat chastened and mistily "good." Natasha Spender remarked that she had seemed to think that having her female organs out was going to cure her automatically of drinking, as though *that* would be cut out of her too. In disappointment, she took to the bottle. I had hoped myself that it would calm her, since she is literally *hyster*ical, and perhaps it will now that she has promised to give herself a chance to recover. [. . .]

Harold Rosenberg was here, with May, and I found him in poor condition—boastful and noisy and with very little to say, really. No ideas to spin. I think somehow his nose has been put out of joint by the Vietnamese war. He would like to find some independent and hard-headed position to take, but all the positions have been taken and there is no reserved seat for him. If it weren't for the hold of his past, he would like to be a hawk, I think; maybe that is partly physical—he's certainly no dove but one of the predators. A lazy one. Anyway, he seems to take the war *and* the opposition to it as a sort of personal affront. Jim felt this too. Harold, backed by May, spoke lovingly of you, and in fact those were the only pleasant parts of the conversation. Maybe he was simply drunk. He had had a long cocktail date before he came here. Or maybe it was the Baudelaire seminar he'd been attending; those French critics can make an outsider feel so non-existent or invisible that he needs a microscope to find himself.

Reuel and Marcia have had the baby—a boy, whom they've named Jay Hilary. I think Jay is after her brother. This sounds like a proclamation of her dominance; I was taken aback, having expected somehow that since this child is the last male Wilson he would be named probably after Reuel's father. Or after someone in Edmund's family, just as Reuel himself was. In my view, Marcia overreaches herself; it would have been better to flatter Reuel, besides being the usual thing: the woman, generally, doesn't carry the names; they come down the male line, even in undistinguished families. Oh well. The baby has the Wilson coloring; his hair, Marcia writes, is the color of Reuel's beard—reddish.

Here I've gone back to work on my novel, though lamely for the moment. Hanoi has now been postponed indefinitely. I guess I'm relieved.

Where are you? I can't place you with the certainty I'd like. Have you started at the New School?[1] Or is that for the spring term? What do you think about coming to Castine during the summer? We'll surely be there in August and perhaps part of September. If I thought you'd be there, I'd come earlier—in July.

Nor have I seen any publications of yours, which makes me feel you're preparing a bomb. You must have seen my controversy with Diana [Trilling], and you may not applaud my part in it.[2] That woman is such a fool; if she didn't occupy her absurd place in the New York establishment, they would have thrown her letter in the wastebasket. More on my side is coming—she answered, and Danny Bell wrote in, supporting her—but after that I promise to stop. Jim is disgusted if he comes home and finds me typing out some screed on Diana instead of working on my novel. His view is that one shouldn't deign to answer; he says she's an example of brain drain without geographical displacement. But for me she has become an occasion for articles—like occasional poems.

He is well and sends you both much love. The Sicilian interlude did him a great deal of good; he was tired after devaluation, Britain and the Common Market, etc., which made a great deal of work at the OECD. On me, looking at works of art in museums and churches again made a strange impression—after my immersion in politics. As though they had lost their affect or faded in vigor. After a while, this passed off and it was never true for the temples. But while it lasted it made me feel that it was such a long time ago that you and I were together, "discovering" Venice [in 1955], as though that excitement belonged to a protected and almost childish past, as though that past of ours itself were an historical curio. Jim, by the way, took a lot of pictures, very good ones, which we'll show you some time, maybe in Castine. He was very much elated by

Segesta and by Frederick of Swabia's castle in Syracuse, which somewhat resembles Castel del Monte in Apulia—he has a crush on Frederick.

I must stop. I miss you very much. More than ever recently.

Much love and to Heinrich,
Mary

P.S. Tell Heinrich that we've been seeing some Greek friends, whom he met with Lotte [Beradt]. The [Vassilis] Vassilikoses. They are now in exile in Paris; at least in the sense that he can't go back—he was outside of Greece on a trip when the coup happened. Roger Straus is bringing out one of his books,[3] and I'm helping him go over the translation, which is pretty bad. As a writer, he is rather a primitive, but we both like him and the girl.

1. Arendt's appointment as University Professor at the Graduate Faculty of the New School for Social Research in New York began in February 1968.
2. The McCarthy-Trilling dispute, "On Withdrawing from Vietnam: An Exchange," first appeared in The New York Review of Books in the wake of McCarthy's reports from South Vietnam. It is reprinted in the collection of McCarthy's wartime writing, The Seventeenth Degree (1974).
3. This was the novel Z; the French edition came out in 1967.

[New York]
February 9, 1968

Dearest Mary,

Each time I receive a letter from you I realize how much I miss you. Times are lousy and we should be closer to each other. I guess I have been depressed all winter. The daily news are [sic] like being daily hit over the head. And I have the impression that Johnson is not just "bad" or stupid but kind of insane. Frightening—a few days ago the remark, spontaneous and quite his own, if people tell him he cannot take care of domestic problems and of Asia plus Africa plus Latin America, he feels as though he were told he could not take care of Lucy and, at the same time, of Lynda Bird (or whatever the names of his precious daughters are). The Times featured this as the Quotation of [the] Day but hardly anybody mentions this sort of thing, and perhaps it is unimportant in view of whoever it is who is now in charge of this country.

But let me report. Heinrich had a relapse after you left[1] but has been well for months. Chicago was nice and seems to work. The students all mentioned with great enthusiasm and warmth your book on Vietnam; never before was your name so much mentioned.[2] Constantly. I have not taken part in resistance activities. I suppose you saw Dwight's letter—not paying taxes—in the NY Review. In December there was a panel discussion about violence in the Theater of Ideas—with Cal, [Conor] Cruise O'Brien, [Noam] Chomsky and me, with [Robert] Silver[s] as mediator. None of us was really good. The "activists" are in a mood of violence, and so, of course, [are] the Black Power people. Meanwhile, more crime in the streets, open defiance of laws by the Unions, and everywhere some inarticulate fear of mob rule. Then, you know, travel restrictions which perhaps will not pass Congress, and the only one, as far as I know, to see in these an open threat to freedom of movement—we shall have authorized and unauthorized travel, as we have already with the present restrictions, only more so—was Milton Friedman, a well-known "reactionary" of Chicago, the same man who proposed the negative income tax. The only consolation—public opinion is more anti-Johnson than ever before and, perhaps, our defeats in Vietnam. Although I am also quite worried when I contemplate the various possible consequences. For the first time, I meet middle-aged, native-born Americans (colleagues, quite respectable) who think of emigration.

Bill J. is very much better, right now on his way to Florida and then probably back in the office. I have not seen him or spoken to him. We exchanged a few notes and he sent me beautiful roses. I am very fond of him. And, anyhow, convinced that Harcourt, Brace could not go on without him. Cal was fine up to now; I saw him and Lizzy a few days ago and, for the first time, had a less good impression of him. But I may be mistaken. Dwight is in a lamentable state; the old story, writing block etc. Something should be done to finance him for one year of non-writing. I did the introduction to Politics[3] but couldn't yet show it to him because he left town hurriedly, completely exhausted.

I started teaching at the New School this week. Some rather bright students but the whole atmosphere very different from Chicago. Harold: I guess you are right; I am on good terms with both of them. Just read his article on the Paris conference in the New Yorker, pretty bad.[4]

Bill J. Heart arrest means what it says. He had a coronary. If the heart arrest had happened anywhere outside the intensive care room of the hospital he would be dead. The former diagnosis was, of course, wrong.

And now Sicily: Yes, it is neither Greece nor Italy. We were there after a long stay in Greece which probably was the wrong way to go about it. (After Greece I can only see Paestum. Everything else is a subtle disappointment.) We loved Syracuse, stayed in a Hotel quite near the castle. Did you see the Castello Ursino in Catania? And the small theatre Palazzolo near Syracuse?

I read your answer to Diana Trilling and liked it, but generally incline to share Jim's opinion. It is a waste of time and brains. I haven't yet seen the sequence. Yes, and Sonia Orwell. I liked her when she was here and I usually don't like hysterical women. (Which reminds me that Elizabeth Lowell's voice has suddenly changed, about a quint I would say. And I was really ashamed of myself to see how much difference this made in all my reactions. I still think—about meeting people—trust your senses, but I begin to suspect that I often overdid it.) Give her (Sonia) my regards.

And Reoul [sic] and you having become a grandmother—about which I write last because it was foremost in my mind. Also, because I did not keep my promise and see them when I was in Chicago. It was impossible, the students had come to fetch me at the airport, had scheduled seminars even for Sunday, and constant meetings, parties, colleagues, etc. for the rest of the time. I could not. What you write is sad, as though he had turned his back to everything and everybody of his own past. Have you any idea how he is doing at the university?

I am not preparing a bomb by any means. Unless you would call preparations for writing about Thinking-Judging-Willing (a kind of part II to the Human Condition) preparing a bomb. On the contrary. I have a feeling of futility in everything I do. Compared to what is at stake everything looks frivolous. I know this feeling disappears once I let myself fall into that gap between past and future which is the proper temporal *locus* of thought. Which I can't do while I am teaching and have to be all *there*.

We have not yet any plans for the summer. I suppose I'll have to go to Basel immediately after the academic term (May) if not earlier. Will you be in Paris at that time? I'll also go and see Heidegger. But all that is not yet final. And certainly [I'll try to] come to Castine when you are there.

Give my regards to Vassili Vassilikos. He is a nice boy but not much more. But now in exile— Incidentally, a Frenchman (Sephardic Jew) by the name of Roger Errera will perhaps call you. He works at the Conseil d'Etat and writes for Critique and other journals. He taught here at the Woodrow Wilson School in Princeton. He wants very much to know you. But do as you please—nothing very important.

Love to both of you—*yours*

Hannah

1. McCarthy had visited New York in the fall of 1967.
2. McCarthy's *New York Review of Books* series on South Vietnam was published by Harcourt, Brace & World in 1967 as *Vietnam*.
3. Arendt's introduction to a collection from the magazine, "He's All Dwight: Dwight Macdonald's *Politics*," was published by *The New York Review of Books*, August 1, 1968.
4. The only article by Harold Rosenberg in *The New Yorker* around this time was a review of *Constructionism*, by George Rickey, January 27, 1968.

141 rue de Rennes

Paris

March 7, 1968

Dearest Hannah:

I am going to Hanoi. Leaving next Tuesday. Please don't tell anyone until I'm gone. I've written to Jovanovich but to nobody else yet—not even Silvers. But I'll drop him a line—and the Lowells— before I go. Two nights first in Cambodia and then the I.C.C. plane.[1] After that two weeks in the North.

Jim will probably be going to Tokyo shortly after I leave, for the OECD, and if everything goes right, we will arrange to meet in Bangkok or Rangoon or New Delhi. It seems a good solution that this Japanese trip has come up for him; better than staying in the apartment and being harrowed.

He approves of my going. Or thinks fatalistically that it is in my character to want to take action. We've agreed that if the bombing gets much worse while I'm in Phnom Penh, I just won't go on. In that event, the trip might be canceled anyway, though, and I'd be spared the agony of decision.

This has knocked most other thoughts out of my mind, but I've been going on with my novel. And doing things like getting shots and remaking my will. I've made Jim and Lizzie Hardwick co-executors. She would be excellent at handling publications problems. In case, for some reason, she can't serve, I've put you down to replace her. I hope you don't mind. It's a chore as I know from Edmund's serving as Scott Fitzgerald's executor, but that was only literary, and this might imply other decisions, e.g., what to sell for death duties, etc.

I've left you two pieces of jewelry that I think would look well on you. All that part of will-making is rather fun.

Enclosed is a ridiculous letter from Jean Daniel. He wants me to write for them, and I said I couldn't. "Why?" "Because of 'Hannah Arendt: Est Elle Nazie?' " He then began saying "Vous avez parfaitement raison. C'était honteux" [You're perfectly right. It was shameful], etc. Wondered how he could make amends. I said that was his problem. The result is this letter. I think I will answer and tell him that if he is serious about doing penance he can find occasion to allude to you, editorially, in some other context and attach words of praise and, if possible, regret. It seems unlikely that he will do that particular trip to Canossa, though. From another source, I've heard that it was not in fact Daniel who composed that headline—for the sheer purpose of selling copies—but the publisher. Daniel opposed it, I gather. But then he ought to have resigned. To say that here is of course ludicrous. No French intellectual would ever resign on a point of principle unless to associate himself with another clique.

We heard from Charlotte Berard [sic] that you and Heinrich were thinking of emigrating and had asked her to look over possible places in Switzerland. Hannah, I hope you aren't serious about that. [. . .] I feel very strongly that you would be *wrong* to take such a step. At least as long as it's still possible to fight in the United States, teach young people, encourage others. My own feeling is just the opposite: that it is a moment not to leave but to *come back.* That was one of the motives behind Castine.

Enzensberger's letter is causing a great stir here.[2] It was reprinted in the *Observateur* to the sound of applause. The fact is, far from being in Cuba, he is in California giving lectures, where he has been for a month, apparently. From there he goes on to lecture in Australia, then to Tahiti and other pagan paradises, then back to West Berlin. His wife is staying with Nathalie Sarraute, which is how I know all this. Nathalie thinks it is a rather dishonest comedy. But don't repeat that. She gathers that what happened is that

Masha, the young wife, got bored in Wesleyan; "Magnus" too. He makes a valid point about the emptiness of the "freedom to criticize"—a mere American luxury, like consumer products. I've often thought this myself, i.e., that actual repression might remove some of the unreality and lead to a new kind of opposition, touching other circles in the U.S. But I'm not sure, and in any case we can't *ask* Johnson to take away our freedom of speech. Moreover, repression wouldn't limit itself to putting all of us in jail; it would be the signal for repressing the North Vietnamese or the Chinese with atomic war.

Enough of this. Don't worry about my health. They have very good medical services in the North. The bombs are something else. I am not such a fool as not to quail at the thought of them. It is a gamble or a défi.

The hotel I'll be staying at is the old Metropole. But I can't recall its new Vietnamese name.[3] In Phnom Penh, I'll be at the Royal. And you can reach Jim here until he leaves. He is so fond of you. Me too. Till Castine.

Much love,
Mary

1. Under the 1954 Geneva agreements following the French Indochina War, International Control Commission (ICC) planes were the only aircraft authorized to travel between Vientiane, Laos; Hanoi, North Vietnam; and Saigon, South Vietnam.
2. The young German writer Hans Magnus Enzensberger had put forth a theory concerning "the industrialization of the mind," in which the cherished rituals of dissent in liberal democracies are seen as providing a harmless outlet for frustrations that might otherwise upset the status quo.
3. The new name was Thong Nhat (Reunification) Hotel.

New York
5/28/68

Dearest Mary:

This is a hurried note to fix dates—or approximate ones—if possible. I just booked our return (by ship) from Rotterdam on September 7. We shall leave by air around August 3rd—take or give a couple of days. And go directly to Zurich. However, I'll not go to Basel before August 10 or 12th, so the best time for me would be beginning of August. When you are in Bocca di Magra. Could you come to Zurich—you liked it—or should we meet in Italy? Or even in Bocca di Magra if you can get a hotel reservation for me there, and if it is not too complicated to reach, and—are you sure you want me there?[1] Could you let me know soon? I'll stay here for another ten days or so and then go to Palenville until the end of July. [. . .]

Teach-ins etc.: [Hans] Morgenthau has advanced to national figure or something of the sort. But seriously, he has been very good on the issue: I was not in Washington but heard he had been excellent. You are quite right about the new alignment: Johnson wanted the consensus, and by God he has it, but against him. I wished you could hear news reporting on television (NBC or CBS, no matter): today interviews with reporters of the great newspapers who unanimously declare that the government does not tell them the truth, misleads them, etc. They sounded as though they were up in arms. [. . .] In all intellectual circles it requires a certain amount of courage to be for the government. And those who are for the administration sound very apologetic indeed. [Lewis] Mumford, President of the Academy [of Arts and Letters], gave a violent speech against Johnson at the annual ceremony which created a minor scandal. I sat beside Truman Capote who was outraged—misuse of his position, no one ever talked politics here, etc.—and so were a few other elderly gentlemen. But the majority was for Mumford. Lippmann, who has been most consistently against Johnson, received the golden medal and Schlesinger—glib and rather foolishly pompous—introduced him. The audience gave Lippmann a standing ovation—for political reasons entirely. By the way, Capote *very* unpleasant, vain and vulgar.

I don't think that you should do anything; I don't do anything either, except when I am on campus. I signed one of the many protests and that is that. I don't intend to make a profession of it. But what J[ohnson] wants is quite clear—Pax Americana, the very thing [John] Kennedy denounced. Hence, how could Bobby [Kennedy] be for him?

I miss you dreadfully especially here in NY. Give my love to Jim. Heinrich is fine and sends his love.

De tout coeur à toi.
Hannah

1. Arendt seems to have forgotten that McCarthy now spent August in Castine, not Bocca di Magra.

[New York]
June 13, 1968

My dearest Mary:

I wanted to write yesterday just after reading the third instalment of the Hanoi book.[1] I rarely saw Heinrich so enthusiastic; I love it enormously. This still and beautiful pastoral of yours has the effect of showing the whole monstrosity of our enterprises in a harsher light than any denunciation or description of horror could. It is beautifully written, one of the very finest, most marvellous things you have ever done.[2]

Had I written yesterday I would have gone on with this. But today I can't. Heinrich who had a series of light heart attacks during the last 4 weeks or so had one considerably worse this night. It isn't a coronary but no one can tell if it will not develop into one. We are trying to get him into the hospital, which up to now we both refused to do; it would not have altered things in the slightest. The doctor thinks the next two weeks may be crucial and if nothing happens until then the whole thing might still blow over. Not altogether, of course.

You see, my plans for the summer are no plans. I just wrote that I cancelled my trip to Europe which actually I did about two weeks ago but did not announce.

I miss you. There are many things—also political things—which I wished we could talk about. Tell Jim how grateful I am for his little notes from time to time. Things, of course, look pretty bleak. Do you happen to know Dani Cohn-Benditt [sic]? He happens to be the son of very close friends of ours and I wish I knew a way of contacting him. I know him, though not well. He was in this country and in Palenville about 4 years ago. An awfully nice kid incidentally. If he stays on in London I suppose one can write via BBC. I just want him to know that the old Paris friends—chiefly Channan [Chanan Klenbort] and we—are very willing to help if he needs it (money).[3]

Much much love
Hannah

1. *Hanoi*, a compilation of McCarthy's reports from North Vietnam, which originally appeared in *The New York Review of Books*, was published by Harcourt, Brace & World in 1968.
2. Arendt was less pleased, McCarthy suggested later, with other chapters in *Hanoi* in which she expressed her admiration for the courage of North Vietnam's leaders, and took herself

and her generation to task for overindulging, in times of crisis, in the pleasure of intellectual detachment.

3. Daniel Cohn-Bendit, or Danny the Red, as the press referred to this leader of the May 1968 revolts in France, was the son of German Jewish refugees whom Arendt and Blücher had known in Paris in the late 1930s. In addition to offering Cohn-Bendit money, Hannah wanted him to know, as she wrote him on June 27, 1968, that "your parents [. . .] would be very pleased with you if they were alive now."

141 rue de Rennes
Paris 6ème
June 18, 1968

Dearest Hannah:

We were away—in London—when your letter came. I shall try to call you this afternoon but meanwhile write anyway. There's no use talking about Heinrich's heart condition until I know more. I am so anxious for you but hope that it may be unnecessary. It's so many years now that you've had these awful scares for him. I remember so well the time at Wesleyan when we were in Stonington. And then last fall in Castine. And in between. He is frail but has great resilience; I am counting on that. Has he been taking care of himself? Can you make him when he comes out of the hospital?

Thank you for what you say about the third Hanoi piece. Strangely, it was the one I worked hardest on and felt most uncertain of. I have the sense that I'm losing touch with my own writing, that is can't rely, with these articles, on my usual separate judging, critical self. But it may be partly the circumstances. It was weird, writing about North Vietnam during all the turmoil and passionate excitement here.[1] Hanoi seemed so far away—several centuries. Then there were the physical difficulties: the third piece I had to send over *Newsweek*'s teletype, which meant I reread it all in capital letters like a telegram.

I found the events here shaking. Hanoi was shaking too but this more so because closer to home both figuratively and literally. All one's habits, possessions, way of life, set ideas were called into question, above all one's critical detachment. I had not recognized how detached I was—see above. The performance of the Parisian literary people was simply ludicrous, in my view, and disgusting. I mean people like Marguerite Duras sitting on revolutionary committees. And the *Tel Quel* group issuing manifestoes to the effect that all literature henceforth must be Marxist-Leninist.[2] The story of the occupation of the Hotel de Massa is a gem. Molière. I'll tell you about it when we see each other. In fact there was a great deal of *tartufferie* [e. g., pious hypocrisy] in all the peripheral behavior. But this was not so with the students, at least the ones I knew already or met during the "revolution." One doesn't know whether to put that word in quotes or not, and there possibly is the tragedy. And there has been a tragedy for the young people, maybe for France, with buffoonish interludes. Most of our friends' children were in the fighting, including a thirteen-year-old. None hurt, luckily, or arrested. At least not yet, as they say in Hanoi.

The Odéon was marvelous.[3] Now that is over, and obviously it couldn't have lasted. Already in the last days, they say, it was turning into a tourist spectacle, though not as much, in my opinion, as angry students thought. Though it became the "thing to do" to go to the Odéon after dinner or on Sunday afternoon, many people who went were very much affected. The group that held the Odéon seemed to be more anarchistic, in the libertarian sense, than the dominant groups in the Sorbonne. The *liberté de la parole* [freedom to speak] was respected to a fantastic degree, and there were people of all ages and from all walks of life discussing issues: young workers, businessmen, an army colonel, school teachers, a cafe waiter, pretty young housewives. Many of them would have been afraid—and justly—to put their noses in the Sorbonne, where those who disagreed were shouted down and even (so I hear) ejected. What was extraordinary at the Odéon was the ability of the young people to keep order, without even a shadow of force, and while allowing total freedom. The audience quickly learned to discipline itself. At the Sorbonne, which was more authoritarian, authority kept breaking down; people smoked for instance, while implored not to by the *service d'ordre*; they pushed and shouted. That was true anyway of the huge mass meeting when Sartre spoke (not very well)—a very inflammatory situation, no air[;] they couldn't get a window open because people wouldn't move away from it, [and] there was a rush from the audience onto the stage. It was a miracle nobody was hurt that night.

One's friends showed new sides of themselves during those weeks. The foreigners tended to huddle together and practice mutual aid. Stephen Spender was very good throughout; I saw a great deal of him. I think he was expiating the CIA. For him, amusingly, the moral problem turned on his house in Provence—a ruin they bought and have been slowly fixing up with the revenue, drearily earned, of his American lectures; he decided, in the first days, that he did not "own" that house and that if the revolution took it, OK. Whenever he would be talking to some especially *enragé* student, he would say to him, mentally, "Yes, yes, you can have my house!" He took money around to a group of American draft-resisters, whom he found in total isolation in a room in one of the Facultés and virtually, he thought, starving; he got other people to go visit them. Vassilikos was good and sweet, very unhappy about his mail; as an exile, dependent on news, he suffered most from the postal strike. Bondy was good. And two young Dutch writers. Most of the foreigners I was seeing were more gloomy and skeptical about the outcome than the French, who, as Vassilis said, took their desires for the reality (that was one of the slogans). Jim was in Japan during most of the crisis, so I was perched here alone.

I didn't meet Cohn-Bendit, though Stephen and I tried to. But the Sorbonne was terribly disorganized, especially their Press Bureau. One of my friends in London knew him too; his mother was a friend of *her* mother's. As you've probably read, he flew from London to Frankfurt. If he tries to get back into France again, I'm afraid the police will get him this time. The reaction is sinister, to say the least. They're arresting and deporting all sorts of young foreigners— on mere suspicion. Yesterday (I heard) the police were tear-gassing tourists near the Odéon. Just like that. Though things are more or less functioning again, nobody is happy, I think. Unless the extreme Right. I haven't yet been out on the street since we came back but I hear fire engines and ambulances going past. My own impression is that de Gaulle has made a mistake in his rapid veer to the Right; he will scare the middle voter whom he was *hoping* to scare with his anti-Communist rhetoric. Everybody appears to realize that there will be an economic crisis, and nobody is offering any solution for that. The tourist season is over before it began—empty hotels, and all bookings for the Riviera canceled. Or so the radio says. It's a devastated country. I don't see myself how it can make a fresh start *without* a revolution. But what kind? Jim shares this pessimism, if pessimism is the right word for foreboding combined with lack of sympathy for the ends sought by *all* the regular political parties: stability, that is, a return to the *status quo ante*.

And what's going to happen in *our* country? If it's a choice between Humphrey and Nixon,[4] I agree with the French student slogan: "ELECTIONS: TRAHISON." We shall be coming to Castine in mid-July. This makes me happy because I shall see you.

Now I must stop. [. . .] But there's so much more I'd like to say to you. And hear from you.

> All my love, dearest Hannah,
> and my anxious love to Heinrich—from Jim too;
> embrace him for us,
> Mary

1. The French student revolts, which began on the Nanterre campus of the University of Paris and then engulfed the Sorbonne, triggered university closings and strikes by sympathetic factory workers and civil servants throughout the country. The 1968 revolt was in full swing when McCarthy returned from Hanoi.
2. *Tel Quel*, a French literary magazine, was an early mouthpiece for deconstructionist theory.
3. The Odéon, a government-supported theatre in the Latin Quarter that was taken over by students, was the center of a nonstop public debate about confrontation with traditional authority.
4. Lyndon Johnson had announced in March that he would not seek reelection; Senator Robert F. Kennedy had been assassinated in June after his victory in the California primary; and Senator Eugene F. McCarthy's so-called Children's Crusade had not been a major player in the Democratic convention. By the end of the summer, the choice was between Democrat Hubert Humphrey and Republican Richard Nixon.

[New York]
July 5, 1968

Dearest Mary: I didn't write out of sheer superstition. And now it seems no longer worthwhile writing. In about a [month] or so you should be here. Hence, just bare facts.

Heinrich as though wanting to perform according to your judgment has shown what the doctors, rather helplessly, call "a basically splendid constitution." He went to the hospital with an "impending coronary" and promptly got so much better that they dismissed him after 8 days. No attacks any more, not even shortness of breath. Completely normal electrocardiogram, blood pressure, etc. Without medication except for a saltless diet. Also, complete disappearance of all other minor symptoms. He had a last check-up on Wednesday and was kind of dismissed. On Monday we go to Palenville—there is a good heart specialist in the neighborhood, just across the river. But I am no longer worried. I think the whole business that started last fall is over.

There is so much to talk about that I don't even start. I heard indirectly that Dwight is about to write a new Constitution! I suppose I should call him but have no time. Will you stay in New York before going to Maine? Call me when you come. [. . .]

I can always come to New York and perhaps also to Castine. Heinrich would come too, but he does not want to move. Prepares a lecture course for fall in Bard where they start right after Labor Day. I am very tired and want to work in peace. If I go to Europe at all then certainly not before fall. I first want to be sure that H. is really all right again.

This is all for today. I am sooo looking forward to seeing you again. [. . .]

Je t'embrasse. De tout coeur
Hannah

[Paris]
Oct. 22, 1968
[Postcard]

Dearest Hannah:

Surely you know Autun [site of a twelfth-century cathedral]? We went back there last weekend. One of those sleeping kings (see reverse) looks slightly like [former French President] Léon Blum. I'm reading my Solzhenitsyn: the first parts are wonderful and terrible, the part about Stalin, which I've just finished, is less good, dropping into a coarse burlesque that seems typical of Soviet writers.[1] You saw it in [Andrey] Sinyavsky. . . . I *love* you for taking me to the airport and wish you were here this minute. So much to talk about. Nixon is getting more ominous, isn't he? Best to Heinrich & kisses,
Mary

1. This probably refers to *The Gulag Archipelago*.

141 rue de Rennes
Paris
December 16, 1968

Dearest Hannah:

I've been slow in writing you because I wanted to talk to you about your book [*Men in Dark Times*], which in turn I've been slow in reading. Parts of it I've found very difficult—more than any other work of yours I know—and my circumstances haven't been suited to rigorous reading. First, like so many other people, I've been having a recurrent grippe complicated by tracheitis; the effect is like whooping cough, and the course of treatment involves a lot of sedatives. Then I went for a ten-day lecture tour in Italy—the only bright period of the fall, partly because of beautiful weather and partly because I left my various injections and inhalations and drops, etc., at home, with the result that I felt more like myself. But the tour was much too hectic to allow any quiet reading: Turin, Genoa, Milan, Rome, Bari, Rome.

Now I'm feeling somewhat better and have finished your book. The essays I like best are those you've written in English: Brecht, Rosa Luxemburg, Jarrell, Isak Dinesen, [Waldemar] Gurian.[1] I was especially touched by the memory of Gurian you brought back to me; that is a masterpiece of evocation in which the man, the human being, is the key that opens himself to the reader. This is true too of Jarrell, as you show him: a figure out of Grimm. Surprisingly, the Walter Benjamin, though you were worried, I recall, about the translation, came through to me on the whole quite directly too, which I cannot say, really, of the essays on Jaspers, and above all of that on Brecht. There are wonderful thoughts in the Lessing speech but sometimes they have to be sensed, rather than clearly perceived, through a fog of approximative translation, e.g., "humanity," "humaneness," "humanitarianism," which are occasionally treated as synonymous and occasionally not. Your habit of making linguistic distinctions is not well served by your translators, whose language, far from achieving precision, creates a blur. For me, this occurs once in the Benjamin piece: "the consistence of truth." I don't know what this means—consistency in the sense of firmness, thickness, density or in the logical sense of agreement or connection, absence of contradiction? I think it means the first (with an implication of the second), but then the word should be "consistency," which is the normal word anyway for either meaning. In a recipe, you say "Stir until the mixture is of the right consistency." Or the "inconsistency of his argument," meaning it doesn't hold together. Such a key term ought to be pinned down for the reader. Maybe by expansion, the best way in English, which is so impoverished in its philosophical vocabulary. When you write yourself in English, you're conscious of the problem and find a means of making your distinctions visible and palpable, but your translators often don't bother.

As for the substance, I am struck, astonished, by the *folkishness* of these portraits. In a way you have written a series of fairy tales of the Northern forests (sometimes a forest of language). There's a gnomic quality in most of them (in both senses of the word) and something of the woodcut. It's most evident of course in the Walter Benjamin, with the little hunchback and "Mr. Bungle sends his regards," but also in the Brecht, in Gurian, in Isak Dinesen, Jarrell, even here and there in the Lessing, though not at all in the Rosa Luxemburg—unless it is in the strange glimpse of her lover. I see why you were to draw Angelo Roncalli [Pope John XXIII], the Bergamask wise-simple peasant, into this family or medieval guild of persons; to me, he doesn't belong, and I can't say why—this, to me, is the least successful of the essays, maybe because you aren't close enough to the churchman in him—stone and marble vs. wood. I suppose the funny animistic magic of these likenesses comes partly from the terror you surround them with, "the dark times," which makes their lone enterprises heroic, hand-carved, home-made destinies. You turn their lives into runic tales, with formulas like rhymes carpentering them together: Rumpelstiltskin. Of course you are coaxing them to tell you (and us) their secret name. This book is very maternal, Hannah—*mütterlich*, if that is a word. You've made me think a lot about the Germans and how you/they are different from us. It's the only work of yours I would call "German," and this may have something to do with the role friendship plays in it, workmanly friendship, of apprentices starting out with their bundle on a pole and doing a piece of the road together. All this gave me much pleasure, as well as surprise.

My reaction may owe something to our revisiting Basel and my pondering a good deal over Konrad Witz,[2] whom I love more and more, and then being plunged into a totally other element: Italian painting and architecture and Italian light. I wonder how it is that the figure Synagoga with her blindfold doesn't appear in the South, as the opposite of Ecclesia. We have seen her in Trier, Metz, Strasbourg, and Basel, but never in Italy. Maybe she is Rhenish. It might be fun to be an art historian if you did not have to be [art critic] Meyer Schapiro.

But to think of being an art historian is to dream oneself at the opposite pole of current events. I fear that you and Heinrich will not even find haven in *Switzerland*. Italy was shaking while I was there; Hochhuth, who followed me on my lecture circuit, seems to have gone through a real nightmare of *contestazione* in Rome and to have lost his head completely—I am trying to find out more about this. I avoided *contestazione* by a certain amount of feminine strategy, of which an honest, dogged man like H[ochhuth] would be incapable. I only got a little, from the right, in Genoa, and nobody nowadays minds being attacked from the right or even the center; for one thing the audience will defend you. In Genoa, when a maniacal woman began making speeches about our duties in Vietnam and how I stood for the worst elements in American writing (*"I droghati, i perversi"* [drug addicts, perverts]), a solid man in his early thirties got up and shouted at her: *"Ho pagato 500 lire per sentire la Signora McCarthy non per sentire LEI"* [I paid 500 lira to listen to Signora McCarthy, not to *you*]! At which point the house collapsed in laughter—the Genoese are proverbially stingy—and peace was restored. But wherever you go, there is an insurrectional atmosphere; you begin to feel you are not safe near a bank, near the American Embassy, on the Faubourg St. Honoré. The other night we went to a party given by *Time* on a *bateau mouche* [a sightseeing boat on the Seine], and the thought actually struck me (I did not mention it to Jim) that we might be blown up. I should hate to give up the ghost with a lot of *Time* executives.

I cannot imagine what will happen next, especially in the U.S., after the Nixon inauguration. And with Biafra starving and general misery one is ashamed to go on with one's Christmas shopping and other preparations and yet one cannot simply stay in the house with shutters closed and wait till it's all over, like the Flood. One has to *behave* as if something resembling the present world will continue. At least I do. But if one really wanted law and order and police protection at all costs, one would defect behind the Iron Curtain, probably. Providing one was not Jewish and was wholly non-political. Perhaps my antennae are all out of order, but I do not sense the approach of fascism or any right-wing repression of a serious kind. What I sense is universal civil war and destruction of the technological fabric (except maybe in the East). If there was going to be repression, you would expect to find it here, and I personally see no real signs. It's true there are a lot of police trucks and Black Marias in circulation, but they can't keep the universities open or even the lycées. Nor can the government keep prices down or people from buying gold. The only restraint being shown is that the Parisians are doing very little Christmas shopping this year; the stores last Saturday were almost empty. It's the opposite of what's happening in England, where people are said to be buying frantically against inflation and another round of devaluation. But why the French aren't hoarding, on the same principle, is a mystery to me. Unless they think *nothing* will be worth anything tomorrow— not TV or washing-machines or jewelry or fur coats. Maybe they have already sent all their money out of the country. . . . The emptiness of the stores was most noticeable in the luxury streets.

The *Monde* is moving closer to the center; i.e., it's taking a more middle-aged line, though still way to the left of the *New York Times*. In fact, so far as I can see, there are no politics here, no clear positions, except that of the Communists (law and order) and of the extreme left student groups, who are both violent and afraid of their own shadow. For instance, the students of Nanterre, out on strike, or in on strike, were carrying placards *"Nous sommes tous complices avec Andrée Destouet!"* (the girl who was caught having thrown a charge of *plastique* at the Banque de Lyon) while at the same time issuing a statement *against* the use of violence at this stage of events and claiming that the police were bombing the banks *themselves!* If she is innocent, then they are not *"complices,"* obviously. There seems to be a good deal of hysterical double talk in the universities: one manifesto said that the police, through *provocateurs*, were trying to make drug addicts of the student militants.

Mentally I sometimes say a sad farewell to Castine; if Black Power or Tom Hayden doesn't take it, the fascists will take *me*. Yet we shall go ahead and have Christmas and eggnog, etc., and presents for everyone. I wonder what has happened to Senator [Eugene] McCarthy, who has been transformed back, I assume, into just another politician.

My dearest love to you, Hannah, and Jim's too. And to Heinrich. We shall think of you at Christmas and again and still at New Year's. If anybody is going to the U.S. that we know we shall try to send you presents.

Embraces,
Mary

P.S. How is it with Jaspers?[3]

1. Waldemar Gurian (1902–1954) was a German Socialist who emigrated to the United States in 1937 and taught political science at Notre Dame.
2. Konrad Witz (1400–1445), a late Gothic painter, was one of the first European artists to incorporate realistic landscapes into religious paintings.
3. Jaspers, who was eighty-six and ailing, died on February 26, 1969.

[New York]
December 21, 1968

Dearest Mary,

Your letter came just when I was trying to figure out what to say as discussant about a paper on Collective Responsibility next week in Washington, Philosophical Society, without losing my temper and becoming outrageously impolite. The irrelevances of academe are beyond belief and expectation. I was just on the point of becoming depressed and your letter got me out of it immediately. I was especially delighted about the coincidence of moods—but about that later. [. . .]

[Meanwhile] your lecture tour. What were you lecturing about? Vietnam? (I just received a pamphlet "Hanoi" by Susan Sontag; haven't read it. The whole thing seems too obvious.) Hochhuth: I won't take that too seriously. The new play [Soldiers] is really quite bad and he himself, though quite "honest and dogged," unfortunately not very intelligent. Let alone gifted. But otherwise I agree—there is no safety anywhere, and though I don't believe in either the fascist or the communist danger, I also think that Law and Order is the last thing we can expect. I don't even believe in civil war in the old sense of the word, but I have also the impression that the whole "technological fabric" is coming apart. It will be kind of chaos and the larger the country the worse. The currency crisis is quite menacing. The French, incidentally, are probably not spending because they have indeed sent all the money out of the country and are out of cash. De Gaulle has now been opposed, it seems to me, by the same people, haute finance including middle-class, who brought the Blum government down in the thirties by speculating against the franc and sending their money to Latin America (this time, it seems, to Germany) as soon as they could lay hands on something. The whole thing probably a reaction not to the student riots but to de Gaulle's grandiose ideas about worker participation in the factories. Anyhow, the financial trouble in America without such complications is also quite real; and the truth of the matter seems to be that both Russia and America are bleeding their countries white with their insane armaments policy. What we are heading for is a kind of state bankruptcy for the nuclear powers.

And meanwhile, at least here, crime in the streets. Which is not so surprising if one remembers that every criminal, from bank robber to pocketbook snatcher, has about ten chances to one never to be bothered. The truth of the matter is that the police is [sic] absolutely incompetent and probably also unwilling to do anything about crime in the streets. One estimates that about 50% of assault, mugging, etc. are never reported even. That the police is all the more willing and enthusiastic to beat up demonstrators who, after all, are sitting ducks and generally quite harmless (comparatively speaking) seems only natural. No work connected with that and little danger. The high-brow sociological talk about "roots and causes" [of street crime] seems to me nothing more than a red herring.

The students, to come back to the technology business, are perhaps the modern machine smashers, except that they don't even know where the machines are located let alone how to smash them. But if I look at the steadily decreasing efficiency of all parts of the system—schools, police, mail, transportation, currency, garbage, etc. etc.—I sometimes feel as though the students dance only a ritual dance to the shattering music of machines that smash, as it were, themselves.

Add to this our specialty—the Negro question. I am pretty convinced that the new trend of Black Power and anti-integration, which comes as such a rude shock to our liberals, is a direct consequence of the integration that preceeded [sic] it. Everything went about all right so long as integration was what was called tokenism and actually was integration of the relatively small percentage of Negroes who could be integrated without seriously threatening the normal standards of admission. The general civil-rights enthusiasm led to integrating larger numbers of Negroes who were not qualified and who understood much quicker, of course, than the others, full of good will, that they were in an intolerable competitive situation. Today the situation is quite clear: Negroes demand their own curriculum without the exacting standards of white society and, at the same time, they demand admission in accordance to their percentage in the population at large, regardless of standards. In other words they actually want to take over and adjust standards to their own level. This is a much greater threat to our institutions of higher learning than the student riots. By the way, to identify crime in the streets with Negro hatred of whitey is ridiculous; nowhere is crime in the streets worse than in Harlem, which is even less policed than the rest of the city; the majority of victims are Negroes. Streets that are not safe for white people are even less safe for blacks.

The trouble with the New Left and the old liberals is the old one—complete unwillingness to face facts, abstract talk, often snobbish and nearly always blind to anybody else's interest, as f. i. in Elizabeth Hardwick's article about the Wallace-man.[1] The hypocrisy is indeed monumental. Integrated housing is of course quite possible and absolutely painless on a certain level of income and education, and it is a fait accompli in New York precisely in the expensive apartment buildings. No trouble whatsoever. The trouble begins with the lower income groups, and this trouble is very real. In other words, those who preach integration etc. are those who are neither likely nor willing to pay the price. And then look down their educated noses upon their poor benighted fellow citizens, full of "prejudices."

Does all this add up to "the Flood"? Perhaps, probably. And I agree it is kind of silly to wait for it or to do something about it. Haven in Switzerland has more to do with age and the wish to live less exposed than it is possible here. Also, to have more comfort than is possible in big cities. You see, we still dream of it and even thought of going to Locarno now for a few weeks and look things over. Now with Hong Kong [flu], I don't know. But perhaps we can swing it a bit later. End of January I have to be back here for the Spring term. I'd rather have time for myself and for writing—a kind of second volume of the Human Condition—but I must admit that the only joys one now has are students. Chicago was most rewarding. I did the Nuremberg Trials together with a young professor from the Law School, students also evenly divided between ours (Committee on Social Thought) and law students. We had six long sessions and it went very well. Also, I have done a good deal of lecturing with good discussions. Needless to say, no trouble anywhere. On the contrary. I think it is very different here from France, Germany or Italy, and have been confirmed in this by colleagues from Europe who are rather surprised how reasonable students still are here—except in particular cases. Did you read the Cox report about Columbia?[2] And the report on the Chicago riots during the Convention? And the excellent article on the legislature versus the Supreme Court in the New Yorker by a certain Richard Harris? So you see—plenty of reasons to stay here and plenty of reasons not to. Also, Heinrich was very pleased with his class at Bard.

One more word on the campuses: The crisis of the university is very real regardless of the student riots which only brought it out into the open. The question is: what are these institutions there for? Service to Society with the Social Sciences, an abominable discipline from every point of view, educating "social engineers"; or "search for truth" and knowledge? The students have been taught Service for Society, and their only disagreement with the powers-that-be is that they want a "new Society" while the latter wish to train them for the status quo. The only man I know of who faces the question squarely is the new president in Chicago, Edward Levi, who is firmly committed to "search for truth," rather old-fashionedly and without understanding how difficult this enterprise has become because of the crisis in nearly all disciplines. Still . . . And he has said privately that in an emergency, caused by the students, he would be willing to suspend teaching altogether, cut the salaries of the faculty, and go on with "research" alone! Interesting, isn't it. It may foreshadow a development in which we would have teaching institutions of various qualities, i.e. professional schools like vocational schools, on one side, and pure academies, the famous "community of scholars," with very few students, la creme de la creme, on the other.

I am very very happy about your comments on Men in Dark Times; and the reason I did not write first about it is that the other things were so uppermost in my mind, or rather became uppermost because of your remark about the "technological fabric." First, the technicalities. I know about the translations, still it is mostly my fault—it is so tedious to correct them, you get so tempted to re-write the whole damned business, and that is precisely what you want to avoid. The only one I rewrote, or very nearly did, was the Benjamin essay. I am sorry for the Lessing essay and the Jaspers Laudatio. The Broch essay is anyhow the weakest, though the most complicated, in the book—I originally wrote it with great mental reservations, felt obliged to do it because no one could write the introduction to his "philosophical" essays,[3] which he, however, thought to be the most important part of his work, wrongly I think. Hence, why did I include it—frankly out of regard for Bouchi [Broch's wife, Annemarie]. But: Consistence versus consistency is my fault. I meant "Stir until the mixture is of the right consistency" and used "Consistence" because consistency is usually used in the sense of logical consistency. And succeeded in convincing the copy editor as well as Mr. Shawn, probably because neither ever read a cook book. Benjamin uses "Konsistenz" which has only one meaning in German. The Jaspers piece I could not rewrite under the circumstances; otherwise I might. I myself think that the Gurian piece is the best; and I was so glad you mentioned it. About Roncalli we might have an argument; I think it was precisely the churchman in him whom he discarded as Pope—and the consequences, as we now know, have been pretty serious. You cannot be a Christian and preserve the hierarchy, even if, as in Roncalli's case, you have no heretical thoughts whatsoever. Without *nulla salus extra ecclesia* [no salvation outside the Church], which he repudiated on excellent theological authority, the hierarchy can't be maintained. Poor Paul [Pope Paul VI, successor to Pope John]—who in addition to everything else is a political idiot; he could have left the Pill very well alone.[4]—I don't quite know why you think this book is "German," but you certainly are right about the fairy tale quality of the portraits, to the extent that they are portraits, although I was not aware of it. I do think about people in these terms. What I thought I was doing was rather "silhouettes." And of course friendship in the sense of "doing a piece of the road together"—as distinguished from intimacy. *Thanks!*

All this, much too long of course, a demonstration of how much I miss you. What are you working on? Did you write the piece on Orwell? I received the four volumes—awfully nice of Sonia—but have not yet looked into them, except cursorily.

A Happy New Year from house to house—
much love, yours,
Hannah

[. . .]

P.S. Just one more thought about the technological self-destruction of society: the constant strikes. Take f.i. the present dock strike.

232

Loading and unloading machinery have been automated. That would mean either unemployment or featherbedding. Since everybody is deadly afraid of the former, we get the latter. The unions have the power to enforce it. The workers, far from smashing machinery, demand automation—rightly, loading and unloading is a backbreaking job. And they demand to receive guaranteed wages no matter how many or how few hours they are actually working. The automated machinery is very expensive; wages rise instead of decreasing. I suspect that we have already a huge unemployed and unemployable proletariat—living off society instead of society living by exploiting it. I am convinced that this is by no means restricted to welfare recipients. And the more we improve our machines and the less the workers actually work, the greater are their demands, for the simple reason that they know best that they are no longer needed and feel they need more and more guarantees against their shrinking power. All the strikes in the last ten years or so were connected with automation. Full employment is no longer an economic factor but a condition enforced by political power. How long will the economy be able to stand this? Quite apart from the otherwise very important demoralization of the whole population in matters of work, reliability, workmanship, etc.

1. Elizabeth Hardwick, "Mr. America," review of *Wallace*, by Marshall Frady, *The New York Review of Books*, November 7, 1968. Arendt's reference echoes Stuart Alsop's October 31, 1968, column in *Newsweek*, "The Wallace Man."
2. Harvard law professor Archibald Cox led an inquiry into the grievances behind the student takeover of buildings on the Columbia University campus in April 1968. The report recommended, among other things, greater student participation in university decision-making.
3. The essay on Hermann Broch was written in German to introduce a two-volume collection of his work, *Gesammelte Werke* (1955). "Hermann Broch: 1886–1951" is reprinted in *Men in Dark Times*.
4. Arendt refers to Pope Paul VI's proclamation forbidding Catholic women to use the birth-control pill.

141 rue de Rennes
Paris 6ème
March 19, 1969

Dearest Hannah:

Here is your violence piece back with corrections.[1] Some, I fear, are barely legible. It would be better if I could see your original essay—preferably in typescript with wide margins and triple spacing. Best, of course, would be to go over the whole thing together, but that is a dream. Have you decided what publisher to give it to?

Jovanovich has written me that he's very eager to publish it. If you do give it to him, why not ask to have a typescript made in the office that one could work on? For that matter, Viking could have it typed equally well.

I've heard a great deal of praise of the piece. Incidentally, there was a nice review of *Men in Dark Times* in the New Republic of January 19; the tone of admiration and friendly respect pleased me—a corrective to "the family."[2] I stupidly threw it away, but probably you will have seen it.

There's not much new here, except spring. We're thinking of going to Germany for the Easter holiday, driving from Stuttgart (to get the car fixed) to Heidelberg, then north to Bremen and crossing into Dutch Friesland. I shall think of you in Heidelberg, and it should be fun to get an idea of Hanseatic Germany. Germany, thanks to Hitler, is very much *terra incognita*, making one feel like an explorer. This is an odd contrast with the nineteenth century and struck me reading the life of George Eliot.

Excuse this short letter, my dear. I must get back to work this morning. Much love to you and to Heinrich.

Mary

P.S. Thank you for the books about Columbia, which just arrived. In return, I'll send you, when I've finished it, *La Prise de l'Odéon*, which contains a partial transcript of the oratory there.

1. McCarthy was correcting published copy of "Reflections on Violence," probably from *The New York Review of Books*, February 27, 1969.
2. "The family" was the term Norman Podhoretz used to refer to New York's Jewish intellectuals in his memoir *Making It* (1967).

[New York]
May 19, 1969

Dearest Mary,

I should have written long ago and thanked you. And also thanked you for your willingness to become my "editor." It's a scandal that I didn't write earlier, and the scandal is compounded by the fact that I dictate this letter. I'm simply buried in student business— papers, dissertations, dissertation proposals, student and faculty meetings, and all that on top of regular duties.

This only to let you know that we will be in Switzerland on May 28 at Casa Barbaté. [. . .] When do I see you? I'm going to call you up, but if you are not in Paris, please drop me a line. One more request. You know that I am going to publish the "Reflections on Violence" as a book with Bill [Jovanovich]. I'd very much like to dedicate it to you. Is that O.K.?

Bill was very enthusiastic about the last chapter of your novel [*Birds of America*]. How far are you, near the finish? All good wishes to both of you, and much love.

Yours,
Hannah

P.S. Here goes everything from bad to worse. It looks like the end of the Republic, though not necessarily of the country. If you can, try to get the memo that James Forman read to the churches.[1] It is a fantastic document and has been published by nobody. Instead, the churches offered him two million dollars, and he gracefully refused. Everybody seems to believe that if everybody keeps quiet and does as though nothing has happened, everything will blow away. I fear it won't. If Jim can't get you the memo, I can have it xeroxed here.

1. James Forman's "Manifesto to the White Christian Churches and the Jewish Synagogues" charged U.S. religious groups with institutional racism and demanded reparations for the black community. The document was published by *The New York Review of Books*, July 10, 1969. Forman was a former Executive Secretary of the Student Non-Violent Coordinating Committee. Arendt's reaction to the "Manifesto" was mixed. "Hannah might have thought it quite an imaginative way to get money and might have laughed," suggests her literary executor, Lotte Kohler. At the time, however, she noted the fear the document provoked among the "authorities" and wondered whether the "Negro community" might become trapped by its own rhetoric if, given "a little appeasement money, [they] will be be forced to execute a program which they themselves perhaps never believed in?" (*On Violence*, 1969).

141 rue de Rennes
Paris
May 22, 1969

Darling Hannah:

I was just thinking about you, indeed talking about you, when Maria came in with your letter. Bill, as you may know, is bringing out a book of my essays [*The Writing on the Wall*] and I was just about to sit down to write *you* a letter asking if you would mind my including the Eichmann piece. If you have any misgivings at all, please tell me and I shall have him strike it from the list. I hesitated myself, partly on purely technical grounds (it is not strictly speaking literary and all the others are) and partly out of a slight reluctance to stir up all that dirt again. Bill was in favor of including it, and reading over the collection, I decided he was right. It let some air, the fresh air of controversy, into the book. At one point, however, Jim said, maybe Hannah wouldn't like the subject reopened. And maybe you wouldn't. [. . .]

In the pasted-up manuscript I've just sent off, I left the Eichmann text as it was, except for a few minute revisions for the sake of greater clarity. It seemed to me unethical to revise what is a piece of history and I refer the reader in a footnote to the replies of [Lionel] Abel and [Marie] Syrkin. (Of course I revised the other, "literary," essays considerably.) Anyway, tell me if you have doubts; you *know* I won't be offended. . . . If it's OK, don't bother to write; you will be busy with your departure.[1]

Please dedicate "Violence" to me; I'm honored, delighted, moved, that you want to.

There's a bare chance I may go to London May 30 but only for two days. Jim will be in Japan; he leaves tomorrow for about two weeks' absence. I've been asked by some of the Peace people in London to come over for a reception they're giving for [Noam] Chomsky. I'm somewhat curious to meet him but not very. In any case, we'll talk on the telephone as soon as we can after you arrive. I leave for the U.S. June 27, but that gives us nearly a month in which to see each other [in Europe].

I've been missing you painfully during these last weeks. From here too, it looks as if it may be the end of the Republic, and I'm desolate and also puzzled. What can one do? Both sides fill me with antipathy, which shifts as if in a balance depending on which side I'm reading. In fact *all* utterances on the subject of student violence, black power, etc., fill me with nausea. The "moderates" are almost the worst. I was reading this in *Time* today from the parent of some "militant": "There is a proper way to express dissent: through the spoken and written word." That man no doubt supposes he is being *thoughtful*. On the part of older people there is a sudden enormous production of clichés, which is how you know that what's being said is false. And what is strange—and that I've not yet arrived at understanding—is that in this situation truths of political philosophy turned overnight into clichés too, e.g., the ends-means "law." Which perhaps means that they are *irrelevant*. As for the language of the young, it resembles incantation. But the incantation may work, as incantations probably did quite often in the days of "superstition."

236

I should like to see the Farmer [Forman] memo and if you have time to get [it] xeroxed I'll be grateful. Maybe HB could do it for you.

My own feeling has been that if Nixon doesn't extricate himself from the war with great rapidity, he will bring the whole structure down on his head, and the only satisfaction is to think that he will perish with it—at least politically. And so far as I can read the signs, he has no real intention of ending the war, though he may have believed he did back in January. Someone who saw the North Vietnamese recently at a congress in Stockholm reported that they were quiet, noncommittal, and sad—a great contrast to how they were a year ago. Obviously they would like the war to end too, but according to my source their attitude now is one of resigned fatalistic acceptance of an indefinite postponement of *any* resolution. Of course that was only his impression.

In any case, it may be too late to hope to calm the U.S. by ending the war, even if Nixon were able to bring himself to the point. It has gone beyond the point of removing the original irritant and sitting back to wait for a cure.

By the way, did you see the newspaper photograph of a demonstrator looking very unconcerned walking straight at the police bayonets in Berkeley? What a horror, I mean the shooting and the bayonets, but he looked eerily like Nicholas Macdonald.

The only non-nauseous contribution to this whole subject that I know is your "Reflections on Violence." Write more. I am having an odd reaction on a personal scale: to go and order a lot of dresses made, as though they would be my last. The reverse of a hope chest. And I have visions of Castine burning, just as soon as we get it fixed up.

Did you see Nicola's piece in *Dissent*?[2] Though he said many things that I agreed with I had a great feeling of disappointment, almost disillusionment. As if he had mistaken what the subject was. So little was to the point. It may be that he's been deeply scarred or crippled, poor man, by the CIA experience and that whatever he writes or thinks is in some way a *justification* of it, over and over.[3]

I must stop and pack my suitcase. Tomorrow morning I leave for the Dordogne to spend the Pentecost weekend with the Dupees, who've briefly rented a house there. I don't know most of these churches and abbeys, and it ought to be fun.

Speaking of Pentecost, wasn't it funny about the desanctifying of the old saints? All my childhood favorites were cut off with one blow. People in authority must be mad these days. Obviously the next to go will have to be the Virgin Mary. And then Jesus?

Let us share our thoughts soon, though I'd rather listen to yours. Much love, and to Heinrich, and keep well.

Mary

And thank you once more—the dedication!

1. It was presumably "OK," for "The Hue and Cry" did appear in *The Writing on the Wall*.
2. Nicola Chiaromonte, "On Modern Tyranny: A Critique of Western Intellectuals," *Dissent*, Mar./Apr. 1969.
3. Chiaromonte and Ignazio Silone co-edited *Tempo Presente*, one of the Congress for Cultural Freedom magazines whose CIA funding was exposed in 1967.

Tegna, [Switzerland]
June 3, 69

Dearest Mary—

(an impossible typewriter, jumps) in case you want to take the train [from Paris to Locarno]: There are two good possibilities. Night train with wagon-lits [. . .] Day-train [schedules included for both]. Bellinzona is only a few kms from Locarno. Domodossola about 120 kms. The night train has the obvious advantage to give us more time. There are plenty of planes: [schedules included]. It is easy to pick you up however you decide. Come soon! It is so beautiful and so calm here that one forgets the whole world. Strange—

Much much love. Give my love to Jim.

Yours,
Hannah

141 rue de Rennes
Paris
June 14, 1969

Dearest Hannah:

I'm hurrying to send you back *Critique*, which does put the Heidegger case very honestly—or so it seems to me.[1]

Stephen Spender's address is 15 Loudon Road, London N.W. 8. I hope you haven't already sent him your fan letter to 10 Loudon Road. Nothing could be more tragic than a lost fan letter at our time of life. Though actually, even if you sent it to 10, I suppose it will reach him. He must be quite well known to the postman after all these years.

Thank you and Heinrich both for those wonderful days [in Tegna]. Already I miss talking to you *so* much. Argument last night after dinner with a professor and his wife [. . .] about students, the New Left, etc. Very much the same conversation as at Tegna at lunch. Again the difference struck me as being one of philistinism or its absence. But I am puzzled as to why just that should be the earmark of the anti-student breed, since philistinism, after all, refers to insensitivity about *artistic* matters. So is the New Left an aesthetic?

We heard from Stephen, whom we saw two nights ago, rather disturbing things about what sounds like a virtual crusade against Silvers and the *New York Review*. S[pender] was cornered by the Trillings and the Podhoretzes and accused of "objectively" aiding the enemy by writing for the *New York Review*—on no matter what subject. They also attacked Isaiah Berlin, who was present, on the same grounds. Apparently one is supposed to boycott Silvers. I couldn't learn exactly from Stephen what evil cause they claimed he was promoting by writing for the NYR. "What is Silvers supposed to stand for that's so terrible?" Well, withdrawal from Vietnam, it seemed, but beyond that it was all very vague.

My cold got slightly worse on my return and I found Jim somewhat under the weather too. It seems there's a widespread bug here. Today we're feeling more normal. If we're up to it, we're going tonight to a party given by the Resisters here for their benefactors. . . .

I saw Vassilis [Vassilikos], depressed and mystified by the Panagoulis affair.[2] There are some strange angles. According to the Athens press, Panagoulis was caught *in his own apartment*. If true, this is very odd, unless he went there on the Purloined Letter principle. But his prison was near an airport, near two airports, in fact. V. doesn't understand why he would have gone to Athens, which is far from the prison; he had hoped he would have made his getaway by plane immediately. It sounds as if he had been completely alone— no organization working with him to help hide him and get him out.

This is an exception in my correspondence—a short letter. Low vitality. When I see Bill in New York, I shall write again. Meanwhile the only other news is that George Weidenfeld has been knighted by the queen (telephoned this morning to say so) and that [critic] Leslie Fiedler is in Biafra! Jim agrees with you that I shouldn't try to do the lunar landing.

                                        Much, much love to you both from us,
                                        Mary

<hr>

1. This journal cannot be found. *Critique: Studies in Modern Fiction*, an American revue, contains no references to Heidegger in 1969.
2. Efstathios Panaghoulis, who had been imprisoned and tortured by the Greek military dictatorship in May 1969, was apparently a friend of Vassilikos. McCarthy's letter suggests that he had escaped and was recaptured at home.

                                        Main Street
                                        Castine, Maine
                                        July 7, 1969

Dearest Hannah:

This can only be a note, because I've had a slight recurrence of that slipped cervical disk, affecting, as before, the right arm and fingers.

I saw Bill for dinner. He looked badly but was in very good spirits. He's resentful of the drugs he has to take, whose purpose is to damp down his energy. That is the problem; he doesn't seem to have that loss of vitality that's characteristic of cardiac patients; he "overdoes" and has warning symptoms, is ordered to rest, then feels freshened for work, starts over, etc. His mind is extraordinarily active. We had a very good talk; he was extremely candid about himself, his sons, his business . . . I do *love* him.

I don't think he's over-expanding in a manic way. The textbook business, not only his, is in deep trouble because of the school and university crisis, which he's not optimistic about. The company he just bought is a cushion—too long to explain with the painful neck and arm, but it makes sense.[1] I expect to see him again; I may go down to New York for a few days before Jim comes.

Here beautiful weather and an exquisitely beautiful house (I think)—Dutch interior light effects that make me hold my breath with pleasure. Very serene. But everybody is at sixes and sevens because the painters put things away in weird places. It is like an Easter-egg hunt. I have managed to find the TV set, one of the boys' Navajo rugs, Jim's linen suit, a strayed chair, the pictures, but there's still a missing bed leg—such an odd item to lose.

Fred Dupee's wife [Andy] drove me up and she's been helping

me, because I'm not supposed to lift things or raise my arms to range articles on high shelves. She left this morning.

Don't worry, by the way. The doctor here thinks it may be a very light recurrence (brought on by a nearly bad fall), and it seems to have reached a stationary point; it's certainly not getting any worse.

My fondest love to you, my dear, and to Heinrich. I do hope you can come up on your return. Our garden is now full of wild strawberries, which we transplanted last year from the fields. The peas are growing, and I'm already picking lettuces. When you come, if you come, it will be jelly-making time.

xxx
Mary

1. This was Academic Press, which is still part of Harcourt Brace & Company.

Tegna
August 8, 1969

Dearest Mary,

I would and should have written much earlier, but immediately after your letter I got the Review of Books with your Sarraute piece,[1] and then there was so much to write that I gave up. I read it with great enthusiasm, not just because of the quality of the piece itself but rather because there is so much in it that is very very close to things I have been thinking about in recent years. The whole question of inner life, its turmoil, multiplication, the splitting-into-two (consciousness), the curious fact that I am One only in company,* the importance or non-importance these data have for the thinking process, the "silent dialogue between me and myself," etc. I am now rereading [Sarraute's] Entre la Vie et la Mort—thanks that you brought me another copy—I am sure I did not get it when I first started and stopped. I thought she suddenly takes the social comedy seriously. The most important sentence for me and my special purposes in your essay is: "inside . . . no differences exist; all are alike." And this is literally true, not merely metaphorically; only what *appears* outwardly is distinct, different, even unique. In one word, our emotions are all the same, the difference is in what and how we make them appear. To put it differently, nature has hidden

* [Marginal note:] "Tantôt, je pense, tantôt je suis" [At times, I think, at times I am], says Valéry.

241

all that is merely functional and has left it shapeless. What is outward and appears is f. i. strictly symmetrical, colored, etc., the inner organs of all living things are nothing to look at, as though they were haphazardly thrown together.

Ad [concerning the] alter ego: The silent dialogue of thought goes on between me and myself, but not between two selves. In thought, you are self-less—without age, without psychological attributes, not at all as you "really" *are*. This two-in-one can be perverted, and then two selves talk with each other, each claiming to be the "true" self, crisis of identity and all that nonsense, including the infinite regress inherent in it.* It is true of course that something always and constantly goes on within myself; this "something" is in relation to the outward world, it is something "inward" looking "outward." Where else could it look? If it begins to look inward** it stumbles at once into the infinite regress, not one self but multiplication. The "projection of [one's] own ego into the world" is either an actual project—I will do, I shall say this or that, etc.—or it is a projection of the world into the own ego [*sic*]. The Cartesian *cogito me cogitare* [I think myself thinking] as the only reality. Not *cogito mundum* [I think the world] or whatever else, but *cogito me cogitare*, *cogito me cogitare cogitare* [I think myself thinking, I think myself thinking the thinking], etc; with the result that now the world is subject to the same endless kaleidoscopic change, infected as it were by the inner turmoil of the self, its *shapelessness*. In this inner turmoil, all identities dissolve, nothing any more to hold on to. Identity depends on manifestation, and manifestation is first of all outside. The "primitive function" of the word, the 'Ouch!' or 'Pow!' as distinguished from an inarticulate crying out, is already manifestation before it can become "sign or indicator." Speech is outward manifestation of something inside; but it is a mistake to believe that this presentation is a mere reflex representing a kind of carbon copy of what went on inside. Speech, gestures, expressions of face—they all make manifest something hidden, and it is this manifestation that *changes* the shapeless, chaotic inside in such a way that it becomes fit for appearance, for being seen or heard. By the same token, it pins us down, commits us, etc.

One could say (with Aristotle) everything that is appears, but the

---

*[Marginal note:] —many also claiming to be the "true" Ego.
**[Marginal note:] se replier sur soi-même [to retire into one's shell].

point here is that everything alive, every living organism seems to have an "urge" to appear; modern biology, especially A. Portmann[2] and his school, has shown to what an extent the functional explanation of natural data—self-preservation and survival of the species—fails to account for the very richness of the phenomena. Portmann defines life as "the appearance of an 'inside' in an 'outside'," and here too that what actually appears is of course not at all the same as what "is" inside the insides we can see when we dissect. As I see it, the difference between man and animal would not only lie in manifestation, by which I now mean the deliberate choice of what I want to appear, but in speech insofar as it is not only communication for certain purposes—the "language" of the bees, their dance, or the sounds of birds are quite adequate for the purpose of mere information—but that words by definition survive and transcend the life-conditioned purposes, at least so long as the species lasts, words become part of the world.

If one looks at the "inner life" from this viewpoint, the inner uprush is like the inevitable noise of our functional appar[a]tus, which Broch called *Seelenlärm*, soul-noise. It is what makes us tick. It is no less indecent, unfit to appear, than our digestive apparatus, or else our inner organs which also are hidden from visibility by the skin. Thus, "the action in NS [Nathalie Sarraute] emerges from the murk that conceals it with a degree of visibility that is almost *immodest*" [McCarthy]. If the murk itself appears it turns out that we are all "alike," and it appears only when we are sick.

This was written somewhat hastily and impatiently—just to let you know how, and how much, I was impressed by your piece. I hope my impatience does not make it incomprehensible. If so—tant pis. One other thing: "The force of repetition kills eternal truths" [McCarthy]. I think this is true, but it is very strange and rather disturbing.

I hope your slipped disk is all right again, and you are still breathless with pleasure in your home. And thanks for the news about Bill. Let us hope. —I have finished the Violence-Essay and will have it retyped when I am back in New York. We had a spectacularly marvelous summer, many guests also, but not bad. A week ago we had the children of my Israeli family, and the daughter, an old love of mine, is now a completely grown-up and very lovely and likeable young woman, open, honest, quite intelligent. It was a real joy. We shall leave here in about a week, first for Zurich—with Basel and Freiburg thrown in, and fly home on the 23rd. I shall call you and we then shall see when and where we'll meet. We probably shall stay in NY, no Palenville this year, Heinrich does not want it; I'll air-condition the apartment. I'll have to do the Heidegger-thing[3] for the Bavarian Rundfunk [radio], and God only knows how long that will take me. Here, everybody still talks about your appearance (apparition rather). [. . .] Heinrich is fine, thinks, talks of you and greets you with great affection.

How is Jim? How are the Lowells? Well, how is everybody? Did you know that Saul Bellow and Harold Rosenberg want to start a new magazine together? Strange, isn't it?

My dear, be well, take care and much much love to both of you.

Yours,

Hannah

It was wonderful to have you here, we will try to see you as soon as possible.   your Heinrich

1. Mary McCarthy, "Hanging by a Thread," *The New York Review of Books*, July 31, 1969, was a review of Nathalie Sarraute's *Between Life and Death*. It is reprinted in *The Writing on the Wall*.
2. Adolf Portmann (1897–1982) was a Swiss zoologist whose *Animals as Social Beings* (U.S. edition, 1958) may have inspired this reference.
3. After a friendly reunion with Heidegger in Freiburg in the summer of 1967, Arendt had agreed to contribute to his eightieth-birthday festschrift. Her piece was "Martin Heidegger at 80"; it was first published in the German magazine *Merkur* in 1969, then in *The New York Review of Books*, October 21, 1971.

141 rue de Rennes

Paris

September 23, 1969

Dearest Hannah:

Here is the manuscript [of "Reflections on Violence"], I hope not defaced by my corrections. You'll find some questions in the margins. On the question of De Gaulle's journey to Baden-Baden:[1] it took place by day. Apparently he was back in Colombey-les-deux-Eglises by five in the afternoon. At six he was walking in his woods there. When exactly he left is not clear to me, but at eleven that morning he telephoned [Prime Minister Georges] Pompidou, whether from the airport at Issy-les-Moulineaux or from the Elysée, I don't know. He referred later to "my six hours in a helicopter," which implies he left at eleven a.m. At four in the afternoon Pompidou talked to Massu in Baden-Baden, who said everything was OK; at that point the general must have been on his way home. My information is from [Jean Raymond] Tournoux, *le mois de mai du Général*. Tournoux, by the way, denies that he [De Gaulle] went to make a deal with Massu. The release of Salan and Jouhaud had been agreed on in principle earlier, he says—some time around Easter. His view is that De Gaulle wanted to establish a capital-in-exile for himself, in case Paris should be occupied by the rebels; he was afraid of a march on the Elysée. That capital might be in Lorraine (very solidly Gaullist), Alsace, or even outside France. Tournoux thinks the support of the army was never in any doubt. But all that of course is speculation. There are two other books on [the] May [revolts] and the General, which I haven't read but which differ with Tournoux and with each other on a number of points. But the time-table seems to be a matter of record.

You'll find a question [on the manuscript] about the People's Park. [2] I don't have the relevant number of the NYR here or I'd look it up myself. But I recall reading somewhere that the occupants of the park were hippies from the local population, having few if any university connections. The students embraced them as a cause.

Already I miss you enormously; I feel homesick for our days and evenings of dialogue. [3] My head is still fuzzy from jet travel, but Paris is pleasant and Jim had the apartment all polished and furbished and full of flowers. He had put up all the glass curtains and draperies and washed a good deal of the woodwork. In return I am cooking nice meals for him.

Nathalie came by for tea yesterday and stayed more than six hours, in a tremendous emotional state. She was back from Israel and full of passionate partisanship for the Israelis, which she has expressed in a very polemical letter to the *Nouvel Observateur*. She gave it to me to read, which was disheartening. I told her I was afraid it would not convince anybody, being much too justificatory in tone. I half-wish I had advised her, in so many words, not to publish it, for her own sake, but I couldn't bring myself to do it and perhaps it was really up to her to draw that conclusion. What she says in conversation about her trip is a little different—mainly reservations about the Israeli way of life and the kibbutzes, which she was half in love with and half repelled by. Or maybe I should say a quarter repelled by.

Her angle of vision on Israel is unusual, in that she kept comparing it with the Soviet Union, which she knows quite well, and naturally Israel comes out ahead in that contest. She was impressed by the *voluntary* communism of the kibbutzes, though acknowledging, somewhat later in the conversation, that this amounts to rule by your neighbors, which can have quite unpleasant features, particularly when it's the neighbors who decide whether you merit a trip outside the country or should be allowed to devote yourself to painting or writing. . . . I said I thought it might be preferable to be ruled by the state, which at least would leave you the psychic freedom of disagreement. But in general she takes the familiar view that any improvements will have to wait on the coming of peace— which of course becomes an alibi for everything. I've never seen her so excited, so unlike herself (though she took my criticism very well, indeed admirably); she's obsessed by the *survival* of Israel, as though it were a beloved person in danger. I myself don't see how, short of a miracle, Israel can survive in the long run *qua* Israel, i.e., as an artificial willed circumstance. Though if the Soviet Union deports its Jews there, that at least will be a demographic boost. . . . But of course as long as anti-semitism [sic] is virulent in the East the reason for an Israel *qua* Israel becomes more evident, even imperative, as a reception-point, a homeland, making a vicious circle. I mean, if there were no anti-semitism, there would be no pressing need for Israel, but Israel, in turn, placed where it is in history and geography, excites anti-semitism or, at the very minimum, offers a pretext for it. I do not see any way out of this. If the Israelis make concessions to the Palestinians (which they ought to do anyway), then they are or will be in danger of losing their national identity, of becoming once again a minority which could anticipate persecution. Yet along this road, it seems to me, is the only place where a miracle might occur. . . .

Now I must stop and eat some frugal lunch and take your ms. to the post office.

I thank you so much for going to the airport with me and for everything, dear Hannah.

All my love, and to Heinrich,
Mary

1. In May 1968, President de Gaulle met secretly with General Jacques Massu in Baden-Baden to ascertain whether he had the army's support in handling France's deepening internal

crisis. Massu apparently reassured him that he did on condition that he grant a general amnesty for all military officers, including Generals Raoul Salan and Edmond Jouhaud, who had been sentenced for crimes committed during Algeria's fight for independence.

2. People's Park was the site of a turf war between young radicals and the police in Berkeley, California, in 1967.

3. McCarthy had visited Arendt in New York on her return to Paris from Castine.

[New York]
October 17, 1969

Dearest Mary—

God knows why I write only today. I wrote you countless letters—thanking you, missing you so much, thinking of you with a new closeness and tenderness. The trouble is that in order to write you must stop thinking; also, thinking can be done so comfortably, writing is so troublesome. Forgive me. But think that in the morning we have your divine jelly, the best I ever ate, for breakfast, and in the evening we drink your wine. And in between, I read (or did anyhow) the mss. you corrected for me. How are you supposed to write to somebody who is always around?

Today is different. The Moratorium [1] was a splendid thing, and I am cheerfully happy. One feels once more the hopes one had during the McCarthy campaign. But this is better because it bypassed the whole party system altogether and rested solely on the constitutional right of the people to assemble and petition. Hence, one is tempted to conclude, the Constitution is still alive and the party system, though of course not dead, has become a nuisance. Also: the complete freedom within the organization—you could do as you please—demonstrate in the street or on campus, in church or in Wall Street. No ideologies, no *weltanschauungen*. But clearly: potestas in populo [power resides in the people]. I don't know what the results will be; I very much hope that the November demonstrations will come off. [2] Also: the whole business organized by the new generation who now perhaps will really come into their own, lose the "extremists" with their hollow rhetoric, and perhaps rediscover the republic, the public thing.

We almost missed being in New York. We wanted to spend a few weeks in the country, tempted by beautiful fall weather. We went not to Palenville (great mistake) but to Minnewaska in order to be a bit more comfortable and have better food. Well—the rooms were worse and the food miserable. The large park very nice for walking and hiking; even Heinrich took long hikes enjoying it. Still the whole thing somehow artificial, including the horse-drawn carriages. Hence, we left in a hurry and arrived [home] just in time for the Moratorium.

When I came home I found a very strange letter: Dwight's lawyer sent me a copy of his Last Will with me as co-executor, not literary executor—there is none. I haven't yet done anything about it, have not called him or the lawyer because I am so astonished, don't know what to do. [. . .]

Bill: Was here, still quite melancholy, somehow changed psychologically. I thought he looked well enough but Heinrich, who had not seen him for quite a while, thought differently. He now looks strangely young and lovable, lovely. Cal: we had a surprisingly good talk for a few hours; he showed me new poems. I thought he is fine but somehow exhausted; also afraid of *not* writing poetry. "If I don't write I am a blank."

The Heidegger business: Did not hear from him—perhaps he is too worn out from the birthday trouble, perhaps he is offended. God knows. Otherwise, I heard rather enthusiastic reactions but few; inconclusive. The printed version appeared only now. I wish you would read it.[3]

You went back to your novel [after *Writing on the Wall*]; the New Yorker piece from the essay book ["One Touch of Nature"] has not yet appeared. I am doing the German version of Violence, rather reluctantly and angrily, because I want to do the Thinking business.[4]

Met somebody remarkably nice and intelligent, both. Joan Stambaugh, originally a Vassar girl (class 53), now professor for philosophy at Hunter. I know her through Heidegger and knew her very good translations of some of his work.[5] [. . .]

A few remarks [about] the [Violence] mss.: I changed the de Gaulle thing—many thanks. Also corrected the People's Park business in Berkeley. It was a mixed affair. The "Near is my shirt, but nearer is my skin" is taken from the Oxford Dictionary—seems to be British, I could not find it in Webster, but I let it stand.

Nathalie's reaction to Israel: quite understandable. I still remember my first reaction to the kibbutzim very well. I thought: a new aristocracy. I knew even then, of course, as she probably does too, that one could not live there. "Rule by your neighbors," that is of course what it finally amounts to. Still, if one honestly believes in equality, Israel is very impressive. However, the main point is of course the survival business. And this is two-fold: one very potent factor is the survival passion which has possessed this people since antiquity and has actually made it survive. The whole legislation of Esra [sic] and Nehemia[6] has no other goal, and God knows it succeeded. The second factor is of course Israel itself and the fear that there may be another holocaust. The argument: you need Israel in case another catastrophe happens in the Diaspora or/and because antisemitism [sic] is eternal etc., is specious. The Jews actually are as afraid of complete assimilation as they are of extermination. Ben Gurion, probably the most intelligent one of the older generation, once said something to the effect that he hopes his sons will die in Israel, but that he has little hope that this will be true for his grandsons. If you then ask: Why then do you try this nearly hopeless business? The answer, that is the really Jewish answer, is: A second catastrophe (after the destruction of the Temple in 70 a.d.) will do for the coming centuries or perhaps millenia what the first did in the past. The memory will keep the people together; the people will survive. That is au fond all that matters. Jews think: Empires, governments, nations come and go; the Jewish people remains. There is something grand and something ignoble in this passion; I think I don't share it. But even I know that any real catastrophe in Israel would affect me more deeply than almost anything else. Nathalie's partisanship is naive and childish, she talks like any unreflected [sic] Jew. But it is quite characteristic that she has reflected upon herself almost excessively and still it never occurred to her to examine herself qua Jewess.

> Give my love to Jim,
> Heinrich sends his to both of you.
> much much love, yours
> Hannah

1. The October 15 Moratorium demonstrations began with a massive door-to-door campaign by students to mobilize public opinion for withdrawal from Vietnam.
2. This was the National Mobilization to End the War, a larger coalition whose demonstrations took place in Washington on the weekend of November 4–5.
3. Arendt refers to her "Martin Heidegger at 80."
4. The "Thinking business" was the first of the three-part investigation of Thinking, Willing, and Judging that Arendt planned as a sequel to The Human Condition. In the fall of 1971 she published an early reflection: "Thinking and Moral Considerations: A Lecture," in Social Research.

5. Joan Stambaugh, a professor of philosophy at Hunter College, translated Heidegger's *Identity and Difference, On Time and Being,* and *The End of Philosophy.*
6. Nehemia, a Babylonian Jew appointed governor of Judah in 444 B.C., directed the rebuilding of the walls of Jerusalem and the reform of religious observances, which were then enforced by Ezra, a priest and scribe who came from Babylon around 400 B.C. Central to the "legislation" was tithing, observance of the Sabbath, and prohibition of intermarriage with "foreign" women.

141 rue de Rennes
Paris 6ème
October 20, 1969

Darling Hannah:

Your splendid letter came this morning. I was just about to write to say that—yes!—I am coming to New York this week. For the usual tiresome reason: dentistry. My Dr. Bonwit, in September, expressed dissatisfaction with the work he'd done and volunteered to do it over free—a big job. I decided to let it go till spring. Meanwhile, though, I've had what I suppose is a small abscess (now better), and Jim, always an actionist, declared that I should go to New York while he went to Japan. So . . . I am not very eager to do this, on account of the work-interruption, but anticipation of seeing you is suddenly quickening my pulse. The dentistry will take about two weeks.

I arrive Air France Friday the 24th at eight p.m. It is too much to hope that you will be free that evening, on such short notice. But if not then, maybe Saturday? Sunday night I am going to read at the Poetry Center. I arranged this hastily, to earn at least part of my way and make it tax deductible, and am still undecided as to what to read. A chapter from my new novel? Or, in the mood of the moratorium, something from *Hanoi.* Perhaps you'll counsel me when we see each other.

I don't yet know where I'll be staying. I've written to Bill's secretary, asking her to try to get me a room at the San Carlos, which is convenient to the dentist. But it's hard to get in there. She will probably end by putting me in the Barclay.

Dwight, I learn from the morning mail, is going to introduce me at the YMHA [the Poetry Center]. We'll talk about his will. I mean you and I. I've heard something about this document from Nicola, who was asked to witness an earlier version, in great secrecy, so that Gloria would not know he was leaving something to his children. That seems to be the problem.

Poor Hannah, you can't be *everybody's* executor. I am just redoing my own will and find that I made you and Jim co-executors. When we last spoke of this, I was under the vague impression that I had made you a substitute. To explain one point—the formula, literary executor, seems to be no longer current in legal circles. The co-executor (i.e., the second named, the first being usually a lawyer or man of business or, as in my case, the husband) of the estate of a literary person is expected to advise on or administer the part of the estate comprising author's rights in past and future publications.

If you shrink from doing this in my case, please tell me and I'll ask someone else. I've already asked Bob Silvers to serve as a substitute, in case for some reason either you or Jim couldn't act. If he accepts, he will be replacing Jovanovich. In an earlier will, I'd made Lizzie a co-executor with Jim (I think). [. . .] Fred Dupee would be very capable and professional, I think, but as one of the two executors, not in the back-up position. For the back-up position, you're supposed to name someone younger than yourself.

Why am I writing all this when we are going to see each other so soon? Perhaps because it's dull but still has to be dealt with and better to have it on paper.

Enclosed is Nathalie in the kibbutzim [photo or manuscript]. Oy, oy! Woe is me. I *wish* she wouldn't.

LOVE,
Mary

141 rue de Rennes
Paris
January 25, 1970

Dearest Hannah:

Bill says you wonder why I haven't written. I wonder too. I think it must be that you are dear to me, which precludes my writing a less-than-good letter. And things are so saddening—I mean in the world—that I scarcely want to think or communicate about them. E.g., Biafra[1] but especially the heart-stopping headlines Israel is making.[2] I can't discuss Israel any more with Nathalie. She is completely fanatical on the subject, which is understandable in view of the atmosphere here, at least on the Left, where El Fatah[3] has suddenly become far more popular than the poor Vietnamese. The only person I can talk to about Israel is my friend, Anjo Lévi, who, like me, is sympathetic to *an* Israel and very pessimistic. Her husband, Mario, takes the conventional Left position, more or less, and they fight about it constantly, so much so that their son, who is some variety of Maoist, instead of taking the extreme view that would be normal for him, has been forced into the role of peacemaker.

For Nathalie, a pessimistic attitude is practically a war crime. You might as well be for El Fatah. Ben Gurion is "senile," and so on.

The news from Russia and Czechoslovakia gets worse all the time. It worries me slightly to think of Cal going to Russia under the present circumstances. I don't mean the morality of the trip but the effect on his mental balance. He could find himself in a madhouse, though I suppose the Embassy would get him out.

As for Vietnam, the only hope is that Nixon may get tripped in his own policy. And I think this is a real possibility. Yet I don't see the end of it. If the Thieu-Ky government falls,[4] under the burden of Vietnamization, what does Nixon do then? Had he allowed this to happen early in his administration, before he'd committed himself and the country so firmly to those people, then there mightn't have been a problem—at least in terms of face-saving. I'm not wholly convinced by the people who say that Nixon intends to stay in Vietnam forever, etc. I think he may not know *what* he's doing or wants to do and is also probably acting on mistaken information about Thieu-Ky's capabilities. This is a more optimistic view than the other, except that a man [who] doesn't know what he's doing may become dangerous when he finds out in fact what he *is* doing.

Aside from this, I'm working on my novel [*Birds of America*], with some crazy hope still of finishing it by the end of March. The most I can say is that it's physically possible. I feel stirrings of life in it, but that's usually toward the end of a day's work, and the morning brings pessimism in the form of dissatisfaction, so that I start undoing the web I thought I was spinning. The truth is, I have no idea how I'm going to end it, and this is what I have to learn—the only way I know being intimacy with the novel, which for me comes with this endless rewriting.

I have greatly changed the end of the chapter you heard [at the Poetry Center] (though you of course didn't hear the end). It is coming out in *Playboy*, thanks to the placement efforts of Harcourt Brace. At least some money.

One thing about myself as a fiction-writer I've observed just now (it should have been plain all along) is that I think of chapters in a novel as composed like short stories, i.e., tracing a sort of circle. Which is very un-novelistic. In real novels, for instance Dickens, a chapter doesn't come to rest at the end; on the contrary, it leaves you with unfinished business—in suspence [sic].

Dear Hannah, I am going to stop now. My intention in this less-than-good letter is just to make you a sign.

Jim is in Japan again. I suspect he'll be sending you postcards. I expect him back about the 4th of February. Then he goes again early in March. These absences of his are rather useful, so far as the novel goes. If I can only restrict my social life to a minimum. When he first leaves, all is silence here, but then gradually the phone begins talking.

Will you be coming to Switzerland in February? If so, alas, I *shan't* be able to join you, assuming the novel is still alive. . . In April, assuming it's finished, I go to Japan for about three weeks. So unless you come through Paris—or to Paris—it looks as if we won't see each other till early May. That thought, which I have just faced, is depressing.

Much, much love to you, my dear, and to Heinrich, and please make a sign too.

Mary

1. Biafra, a secessionist Nigerian state, had surrendered to Nigerian government troops on January 12, ending its two-and-a-half-year struggle for self-determination.
2. In January 1970, Israel was in the midst of the War of Attrition. Its air attacks on Egypt intensified, and on January 22 its forces attacked the island of Shadwan in the straits between the Gulf of Suez and the Red Sea. Two days later they withdrew, taking Egyptian military equipment and prisoners with them.
3. El Fatah, an Arabic acronym in reverse for the Popular Front for the Liberation of Palestine, was the leading faction within the Palestine Liberation Organization, then based in Jordan.
4. General Nguyen Van Thieu was president and General Nguyen Cao Ky was vice-president of South Vietnam.

[New York]
February 4, 1970

Dearest Mary—

The Nature-essay (New Yorker) is absolutely splendid.[1] Such a joy to read. I didn't clip it because I suppose it will be in the Essay-Book. I wanted to discuss a couple of things, but they slipped my mind. I am going to re-read it anyhow. I always meant to write, but after you left I had to write my Chicago lectures in a hurry and was completely absorbed. Then Chicago for two weeks and then great laziness—reading Plotinus and Schelling and this and that. Also people. Talked yesterday with Bob Silvers who just returned from Israel. He too is very impressed, reported rather interestingly about some opposition within the government [re] the excruciating stupidity of Golda Meir; he saw everybody who was anything thanks to Isaiah Berlin.[2] This Israeli program to invite the intellectuals pays handsomely. Silvers said how much he was tempted to found a bilingual magazine in Israel for the small but intelligent opposition in the country. Nothing he said was in any way outrageous or fanatic. And still— Also: Saw Jovanovich before he left for Florida. He appeared with a huge & impossible flower-arrangement—very touching. He looked better but the urinary business is still with him. His heart condition seems ever so much better. He bought again quite a few new businesses;[3] I have the impression that he is no longer much interested in books. And I also am a bit afraid that he over-expands to a dangerous degree. There is something hectic in the whole empire business. Nothing we can do about (or rather against) it, I suppose; but the decline in the actual working of the publishing house is noticeable. I just received jacket copy for the English edition of the Violence book (Penguin) and was reminded of the incredibly stupid and wrong copy I had received from Harcourt Brace. This, on the contrary, was very good; obviously, somebody read the book before writing it. In Harcourt Brace I am sure that no one read the book, except Bill. Also, the design was poor etc.

Israel once more: I too am quite pessimistic—for many reasons but also because of the stubborn rigidity of the Israelis. Ben Gurion, incidentally, is very worried and has absolute[ly] no influence. Here nothing new—things go from bad to worse but very slowly and gradually, almost imperceptibly.

When does your chapter come out in Playboy? I never see it. We shall go to Switzerland in the middle of March. I accepted a couple of lectures in Colorado (money). I then have to prepare the law lecture but can probably come to Paris for a few days. End of April I go back to New York for about a week, then back to Tegna. Finish your novel, don't get depressed—one always does at the end of a book—and don't bother to write: I shall call you when we are in Tegna.

Give my love to Jim. Heinrich sends his love.

Je t'embrasse—Hannah

1. Mary McCarthy, "One Touch of Nature," *The New Yorker*, January 31, 1969; it is reprinted in *The Writing on the Wall*.
2. British historian Isaiah Berlin cultivated a wide circle of like-minded intellectuals throughout the West and, during these years, in Israel.
3. These were the History Book Club, *The Instructor* (a magazine), and the Psychological Corporation.

[New York]
March 3, 1970
[Postcard]

Dearest Mary:

I suppose you got my letter. But I have to cancel: Heinrich came down with a phlebitis—not too bad, he is already partly up but still— We shall not be able to go to Europe before beginning of May. Too bad. When and where do we meet?

How is the novel going?

Yours and love,
Hannah

141 rue de Rennes
Paris 6ème
March 5, 1970

Dearest Hannah:

This, I hope, will catch you before you leave for Switzerland. I just want to thank you for the beautiful, beautiful roses, which lit up my study as for some festal mass. And they lasted nearly a week. As I wrote you once before, you have a very good florist contact.

I haven't written sooner because of the horrible novel, which is now drowning in verbiage as though it had a stone tied around its neck. Jim is back in Japan, and this gives me the whole day and evening to work. Too much time perhaps on an uninterrupted daily basis, on the same principle that the smaller your staff is, the more you get done. I am very pessimistic about the outcome. Indeed just about hopeless.

To turn to something cheerful, I heard from somebody at Harcourt that Bill was back from Florida looking absolutely marvelous. I haven't heard from him directly.

When is *Violence* coming out? I must tell you that I had the opposite experience from yours. The English jacket copy was much worse than HB's and their design was awful. I made them redo it. I am speaking of Weidenfeld, but Penguin committed some dastardly

255

act on *Hanoi,* which for some reason has vanished from my shelves, so I can't give you the details. . . . It seems to be sheer chance, unless someone like Bill intervenes personally, that a book today is produced in a reasonably literate way.

I long to hear from you in Tegna. Jim's plans have changed slightly; he'll be back in mid-March, and we'll leave for Japan together about April 8.

Much love. To Heinrich too.

Mary

Paris
May 30, 1970
[Postcard]

Dearest Hannah:

I will arrive at Domodossola at 17:17 the afternoon of the 11th. Plan to leave on the 15th at about the same time. Look forward *greatly* to four days together.

Love
Mary

[New York]
June 4, 70
[Postcard]

Dearest Mary, I got your card only today, was a few days in Bonn. The 11th at 17:17 Italian time and 16:17 Swiss time is perfect. I'll be in Domodossola to pick you up, and we'll come "home" either by car or by train. [. . .]

So much to talk about. We both are looking forward,

Love
Hannah

141 rue de Rennes
Paris
June 26, 1970

Dearest Hannah:

I ought to have written sooner to thank you both for those lovely days, but here things are in a hectic state, mainly owing to the June social season at the OECD, to a flurry of departures (goodbye drinks, dinners, cups of tea) and arrivals of Americans starting their vacation in various Left Bank hotels. Then I made another trip to England—Manchester, this time—for the BBC.

There's a piece of news I must tell you right away. Cal has a new girl and has broken completely with Lizzie. He called from Oxford to tell me, and then I saw him and the girl in London on my way back from Manchester. Spent the evening with them. As it happens, I know the girl well, born Lady Caroline Dufferin (of the Guinness family), married first to Lucien Freud, the painter, then to a musical character in New York called Israel Citkowitz. Three children by Citkowitz [. . .] Bob [Silvers] has been in love with her for years and for years she has refused to marry him. A beautiful, odd girl, somewhat like a blonde Carmen, somewhat schizoid, history of psychiatric treatment, mysterious, childlike, innocent, candid—I have always liked her since she said to me during the McCarthy period, she aged about nineteen then and a lady-in-waiting to Princess Margaret: "Tell me, is America *completely* fascist now?" In fact she isn't stupid but what you might call self-educated, like so many daughters of the very rich that become Bohemian. A waif.

As for Cal, he doesn't seem to me to be manic, though naturally somewhat excited. I at once asked him the question and he replied: "No. And other people don't think so either." That, I found, was so. He is still taking his pills. And he spoke with horror of his old mania, like somebody who has been through a terrible searing fire. Apparently Lizzie doesn't think he's manic either. If one has known him so long, one is alert to the signs. There was one ominous one, I must admit, during the evening we spent together: he mentioned *Hitler*. In a guarded but somewhat commendatory way. I said: "Cal, if I hear the word 'Hitler' again, that finishes it." He then subsided. But aside from that, he was rational and quite determined on his course. They aren't talking of marriage but just of living together. He plans to spend the summer at her house in Kent.

He broke the news to Lizzie by telephone. She apparently suspected something since she hadn't heard from him for a long time. The affair has been going on about two months. What Lizzie's reaction has been is not exactly clear. I gather that she realizes that this isn't just another girl; there've been many in recent years, as Cal has been hinting in his poems. My doubts aren't so much about Cal's seriousness as about Caroline's ability to bear the weight of his personality, which can be crushing, overbearing, and so on. I wouldn't have the strength to live with him twenty-four hours. But he seems to feel in Caroline or in a life with Caroline some source of potential change, renewal. Of course people in love always feel that, and once in a while it happens. He seems quite ready to turn his back on everything, all his old myths, including the Maine one. He's renounced, with slight sadness, any thought of returning some day to Castine. "Lizzie can sell the house," he said. It did not occur to him that Lizzie might want to keep the house. . . . As though, without him in it, it could have no further interest for her. Of course he may be right about that.

To me, his finding another wife could be a blessing for Lizzie. For both of them. But maybe this is like my saying, in a much criticized sentence, that it was probably a blessing for Orwell that he died. Still, seeing her as I've done so exhausted, beaten, and unhappy, one couldn't have much hope for a miraculous improvement of the marriage. At least she has the *New York Review*. That interests her (or did) a lot more than coping with Cal, who I think more than anything else has *bored* her the last few years, to the point of excruciation, though he cannot have guessed this. And maybe she not either.

Well, the summer will probably show. If Cal is advancing into mania by some new route, that will finally become evident. I hope he isn't. For then what? Another trip to the sanatorium and then back to Lizzie? And what if Lizzie won't have him this time?

I am beginning to ramble on about this. I wish we could talk. Fortunately there is no action called for, on the part of friends. One can only watch and listen. Lizzie may think friends should interfere, to stop him, or he may think friends should interfere to reconcile Lizzie to the inevitable, but neither of these in practice would be feasible. As for Harriet [Lowell], for once the child, of all the parties, seems to be the least vulnerable to damage—the damage there has already been done. And she's fourteen years old and probably stronger than both her parents, certainly than poor Lizzie.

As you can imagine, there's a lot of talk about this in London. And Cal's schoolboy friend, the ever-loyal Blair Clark, promptly turned up in Paris to mull it over with me. But so far there seems to be no side-taking, though I heard—a weird detail—that Lizzie had stopped talking to Bob Silvers because he had introduced them to each other. Bob is said to be "prostrated."

I wonder what Heinrich will say to all this.

While I was with you in Tegna, Jim got a rather bad blow. A letter from his older boy, Danny, announcing that he would not come to Castine this summer but would work in a hotel in Montreux as a desk boy. The hand of the mother is in this, certainly, though it's true that Danny was already eager to have a summer job, and in Castine, since he doesn't drive a car, Jim had only been able to find him a promise of outdoor work, cutting lawns, etc. It was a falling-domino situation. Next we heard, as we expected, that Jonny, the younger, would rather not come either all by himself or only for a couple of weeks. This is very hard on Jim, who is depressed and would be still more so except for the long loving letter the younger boy wrote, trying to explain and excuse his older brother to his father.

On top of all this came the word of Cal's defection, which shook me. Me more than Jim, as it turned out. As far as he was concerned, the loss of the Lowells left the temple standing undisturbed but *I* saw Cal as a wild Samson leaving us to the rubble and the Philistines, of whom Castine contains quite a few.

Tegna seems remote and very eden-like in the circumstances. Are you both well? [. . .]

We go to Castine probably about the 15th. Our address is just Main Street. We count on you and Heinrich to come. How is the Thinking book coming on? I haven't been able (or barely) to get back yet to work. But I shall feel better when I do.

Thank you again, my dear, for everything, and all my love,

Mary

P.S. Oh, I forgot, I asked Anjo Lévi about *un café crème*. You are right; it is what you order in a cafe. But what comes is a *café au lait*, in a small cup. So we are both right. I said what is the difference between a *café crème* and a *café au lait*, and she said the second is what you have for breakfast at home and the other is what you have in a cafe. But both are made with milk. They don't put *crème fraîche* in coffee because it curdles slightly.

Tegna
June 30, 1970

Dearest Mary—

so good to get a talking letter from you! I talk back, leave everything else—all the unfinished correspondence duties. I am just back

259

from Munich where I talked at the Academy of Fine Arts. Nice and friendly and unimportant. Then one day in the Museums with my niece and her husband, not so good. Also theatre: Horvarth's [sic] Last Judgment.[1] You may not know him, very gifted Austrian (?) dramatist who died young in the late thirties, was killed by a tree on the Champs-Elysées. Very good, but the theatre half empty. Also my first trip with Jim's pencil [a gift]—I don't know how I ever could live and travel without it.

Cal: No, I don't think either that he is manic. The Hitler-thing is bad precisely because it never was just sickness. When he was sick, he lost control. And he has resented the NY Review clique for a long time. He was bored with New York, Harvard, and the rest of it. The whole English enterprise was already in the mood of escapade. This may or may not be for keeps, but I doubt that he will ever go back to Lizzie. Only if he gets sick again—unlikely. Heinrich's reaction—he wishes him good luck and is interested only in whether or not he will write good poems. I am afraid you will miss him in Castine, Jim will too, despite everything. And especially after the refusal of the two boys to come. It will change things in Castine. I am less optimistic for Lizzie than you are. To be sure, it could turn out quite well for her, but she will think of it in terms of prestige. I hardly know the child. I am sure I shall miss his occasional visits in New York. Also I have the feeling that Auden will also not come back. The winter looks rather bleak—lots of trouble at the New School. Good for work, I suppose.

There is one very good church in Como,[2] not the cathedral but San Carpoforo. I was busy with proofs,[3] no time for work. I shall start tomorrow, just re-read what I had written before—about appearance as the natural realm from which thinking withdraws. I rather like it and [wish] only I could stay and work under these paradisiadical [sic] conditions but with my books for many more months—no teaching, no demands, no household. And, please, a little boredom—boredom is so healthy in small doses. Right now, whenever I am tired and a bit bored I read or rather re-read (after many decades) Hamsun.[4] Not great but very entertaining. July will be pretty much without guests. Lotte Beradt will come for a month or so (she will stay longer than we do) and at the end of the month Glenn Gray[5] and finally my Israel family. At the moment we are the only guests and today we are even the only people in the house.

Also, I just read an interesting article on Calhoun[6] and begin to think how to change and enlarge the Civil Disobedience thing. By the way, great trouble with Rostow.[7] Bill called from NY to tell me that we shall need a lawyer—which means a lawyer against the Bar Association! Bill again incredibly nice, friendly (from friendship), reliable, generous, and thanks God [sic] so intelligent! [. . .]

The café crème: I think they put fraîche crème [whipping cream] into it, not milk and of course not crème fraîche [a thick sweet cream].

We shall probably leave here on the 8th of August and leave for NY on the 9th from Zurich.

Dearest, much, much love to both of you.

Hannah
and from me too
Heinrich

1. Odön von Horvath (1901–1938) was a Hungarian-born playwright and novelist who lived in Germany.
2. After Mary left Tegna, the Blüchers took a trip into the mountains and to lakes Lugano and Como.
3. These were probably *New Yorker* proofs for "Civil Disobedience," which appeared on September 12, 1970.
4. Knut Hamsun (1859–1952), a Norwegian novelist, poet, and playwright, won the Nobel Prize for Literature in 1920.
5. Arendt became friends with the philosopher J. Glenn Gray at Wesleyan University in 1961 and later encouraged him to undertake a U.S. edition of Heidegger's untranslated work.
6. John C. Calhoun, proslavery statesman and advocate of states' rights, served in Congress and as U.S. secretary of war and of state; he was vice-president of the U.S. under Andrew Jackson.
7. "Civil Disobedience" was to be reprinted in an anthology edited by Eugene V. Rostow, *Is Law Dead?* The "great trouble" concerned the editorial note introducing Arendt's essay, which was subsequently revised to Jovanovich's satisfaction.

[New York]
October 3, 1970
[Postcard]

Mary— the telephone is a nice institution!

The Kant-portraits:[1] The only collection of engravings, drawings, busts, etc. I could find here (not the book itself) is: Karl Heinz Clasen, *Kantbildnisse*, Königsberg, 1924. A very nice one which I did not know is the frontpiece in Reichl's *Philosophischer Almanach auf das Jahr 1924*, Darmstadt, 1924. This is from about 1755—when he was 31 years old. All the others were taken when he was old, and are rather conventional. This one is different. No source was given.

All the best and
much love to both of you
Hannah

1. McCarthy had asked for a likeness of Kant to guide her in writing the final scene in *Birds of America*, in which Kant appears at the foot of Peter Levi's bed, wearing a powdered wig with a gray bow, to tell him "Nature is dead."

[New York]
October 7, 1970

Dear Mary,

Just a note, dictated, about this Kant business. I finally found where I'd seen an especially nice painting (by Becker, around 1768, when Kant was about 44 years old). You'll find it in Hans Saner, *Karl Jaspers* [. . .] p. 152. He did not tell in the book where he found it. I propose you write to him directly, in French preferably. [. . .] The book, by the way, is excellent.

In haste—
yours
Hannah

141 rue de Rennes
Paris
October 14, 1970

Dearest Hannah:

Thanks for all your trouble about the Kant likenesses. I have been given one here by Jean-François Revel, [1] which shows him with powdered hair or a perruque with a bow in back; he is in profile and looks to be in his thirties, except for some wrinkles (indicating reflection?) over his left eye. There was no source given on the print: just "*Kant, Philosophe allemand.*" I wonder if it could be the same as one of your references. I am going to write to Hans Saner in Basel and some day, if my morale is good, I shall try to follow up your other references in the Bibliothèque Nationale.

Meanwhile I've reread your piece ["Civil Disobedience"] and read the Reich essay. [2] It seems to me you've considerably improved your piece since I saw it, though this may be a pure illusion arising from the difference between reading something in print and the same thing in manuscript. The printed text always appears more "finished." Hence perhaps I have the impression that it's better pulled together than it was in Tegna, where my chief criticism was that it seemed to fly off in a half-dozen directions. But even on rereading, though I withdraw most of that criticism, it's not the piece of yours I like best. I have tried to think out the reasons but alas don't have the time to put them at length in a letter. A real discussion will have to wait till we see each other. But I would say that, number one, the tone is somehow too imperative for the matter, which after all has to do with freedom, which maybe one can't be too legislative about. You appear to be laying down the law, and this may go back to the fact that the original speech was addressed to lawyers. Second, I am not convinced, finally, by your distinction between conscientious objection and civil disobedience. I *understand* the distinction but am not persuaded that it is so cut-and-dried as you make it sound. To me, civil disobedience remains a matter of conscience and the inner light, whether it's practiced by one person or a group. What stands out in draft-resistance or tax refusal (or abolitionist activity) is not the collective but the separate individual souls who are saying no. I think this is clear from the fact that nobody could seriously speak of violations of the Prohibition amendment as being instances of civil disobedience (whether one is thinking of bootleggers or private drinkers and speakeasy customers); the reason is that nobody broke the law in that case as *a matter of conscience.* There was massive lawbreaking by ordinarily law-abiding citizens, but it belonged in an entirely different category from tearing up your draft card, singly or in a group, or harbouring a fugitive slave. I see that the whole question of conscience, when religious sanctions are no longer operative, makes civil disobedience a very difficult nut for the law to crack, i.e. as you say, why should *my* conscience be respected rather than my neighbor's? If we all have the right and/or the duty to break the law whenever conscience urges, then how can there be any law? I can't answer that—certainly not in this letter even try to—and yet I feel that your solution or answer is evasive. Maybe this question simply will not yield to rational analysis and can't be disciplined into doing so. Finally (and perhaps all my three objections are related), when you talk about "we," who do you mean? Society presumably, but sometimes, it would appear, the lawmakers, or society-as-its-own-lawmaker. In the context, I find this "we" disturbing; as far as I'm concerned, if there's a "We" in the civil-disobedience vis-à-vis the law equation, the "we" is the law-breakers. That is, I identify myself with them and their conscience, whether they are Dwight or Dr. Spock or whoever, and not with the lawmakers or society-as-a-whole which is attempting (in the meeting you attended) to find some way of coping with them, a place to fit them in the American legal fabric. If there *were* a place to fit them, whether you consider it as belonging to a doctrine of a concurrent minority or history of voluntary association, then their activities would have no purpose, since their real purpose is to run counter to society, to collide with the law. In fact, it seems to me that the government by recognizing the right of religious dissent—above all, in the case of pacifists—deprived that dissent of its force and validity. Nor is it, I think, just a puritan scruple that makes me feel that one must suffer for one's beliefs, put down a real stake, in order to validate them. If I suffer for my beliefs by going to jail or into exile, then my suffering becomes a pain not just to me but to society as a whole. And there is its efficacy—in creating a scandal. Dr. Spock behind bars would be a scandal, which is why, in my opinion, the government, through its judiciary system, didn't put him there.

Perhaps I'm not making myself clear, but it strikes me that you have seized the problem by the wrong end, and your "we" sums this up. (And the fact that the "we," which is normal for the discourse of political philosophy, should sound—at least in my ears—so dubious in this context probably shows how touchy the subject is.) Of course none of these hasty comments of mine do justice to the complexity of your argument, not to mention the brilliance of so many of your *aperçus*. I'm only trying to put my finger on what it is that leaves me dissatisfied with this article—a feeling different from disagreement.

About the Reich article, I respond very negatively to that kind of rhetorical hysteria. It is like [Noam] Chomsky at his worst, worse than Chomsky at his worst. Whether Reich is hating or smarmily loving, he is unctuous in an unpleasant priestly way. I hate prophets. A lot of what he says in his doomsday way is nonsense, e.g., "Power to make one publication available to airline passengers but not another"—as though that were terribly sinister. He doesn't stop to reflect that the only way to curb that power would be to make *all* publications available. The man seems to have no historical sense; he seems to believe that every evil he finds around him is new. Or invented by Roosevelt and his counselors. Of course he's right in much of what he says about the New Deal, and quite a few of his other remarks, here and there, are true. But as Janet Flanner said, apropos of this article, it would be hard to write such a *long* article and not say *something* true. The only point I found at all interesting was the inherent contradiction between the willing worker and the willing consumer. So far as I know, he is the first to look at the two sides of this coin in conjunction. And doing so explains quite a bit. But the whole thing is almost pathetically academic, esp. his love affair with the young. I think I notice the influence of Norman Brown, whose treacly ideas are flowing around like slow-moving molasses.[3]

And what did you think?

I must stop because I'm going to Rome in a couple of hours. To take another look at the Sistine Chapel for my next-to-last chapter. Back next week.

We saw Bill here twice. I finally understand why he has heart attacks. The last night he was in Paris (he had to leave his hotel at the very latest at eight-thirty in the morning), he stayed talking here with some friends till two a.m. I had to beg him to go home. The first time I begged—at a quarter of one—it did no good. Considering this pace, he looked quite well and claimed not to be tired. But somehow I felt deeply sorry for him. Almost anguished.

Please write when you have a minute. I miss you.

Much love and to Heinrich too,
Mary

1. In 1970, political commentator Jean-François Revel published *Without Marx or Jesus: The New American Revolution Has Begun*, with an Afterword by McCarthy.
2. This was a long excerpt from Charles A. Reich's *The Greening of America* (1970) published in *The New Yorker* on September 26, 1970.
3. Norman O. Brown's popular book at the time was *Life Against Death*.

Nov 1 or 2, 1970[1]

HEINRICH DIED SATURDAY OF A HEART ATTACK

HANNAH

1. Date is in McCarthy's handwriting.

Part Five
November 1970 – April 1973

["How am I to live now?" friends remember Hannah Arendt asking when they assembled at her apartment the night after Heinrich Blücher's death. Friendship provided part of the answer, as the sudden ingathering of fellow émigrés, American friends, and colleagues—including Mary McCarthy, who flew in from Paris the next day—made clear; friendship, work, and travel.

But the depth of Arendt's sorrow is suggested by the fact that her first impulse was to give her non-Jewish husband a Jewish funeral service, with kaddish. It was what she remembered of her father's death in 1913. The memorial service at Riverside Chapel on November 4, 1970, pleased her, nonetheless, as did a later ceremony at Bard College ("Very good, very right"). Both were simple occasions, permitting the Blüchers' many friends to share their memories of Heinrich with each other.]

141 rue de Rennes
Paris
November 12, 1970

Dearest Hannah:

It was good to hear your voice last night. I think about you, and we both talk of you—and of Heinrich—whenever we're together, which in the last two days has been frequently since the Armistice Day holiday was followed by a day of national mourning for De

Gaulle and offices were closed. I don't know what the domestic reaction to De Gaulle's death was—certainly not a universal shock, though, despite that pretense in the press.

We went to the Panther movie the other night—a sort of profile of Cleaver in Algeria plus documentary material.[1] The censorship here hasn't let it be shown publicly, and if I were the Panthers, I'd endorse that censorship. Cleaver appeared childish and somewhat insane (or drugged). One scene shows him buying a knife in the Algerian bazaar—much caressing of the blade, etc., while he tells you on the sound track that he's going to use it on Mayor Alioto of San Francisco. . . . If this movie were shown in the U.S. those Panthers in New York would not stand a *chance* of a fair trial.[2] There was also much boastful talk on the part of Cleaver and other "heroes" about guns and bombs to be used on the pigs. The whole thing had the character of a night-club performance that was failing to go over with the diners. Hence a certain pathos.

Important people were there, e.g. [French publisher] Claude Gallimard. God knows what they thought. Applause was spotty. My main response was infinite weariness and a feeling that the Panthers, hopped up on their own rhetoric, were in for some awful clash with reality.

Otherwise I've simply been working. Writing about Peter and the *clochards* [tramps], concerning whom I'm very ignorant, but then so is he. Jim says why do I have to bring them in, but they've been there (in the novel) in a state of latency from the beginning and must finally show their faces.

There is still a lot of student violence—mostly at Nanterre, but some at Censier and all over. At Censier, the Maoist bands attacked the Trotskyites and a group of Communist youth, and one young Trotskyite is in serious condition in the hospital. Professors have also been mauled again. You could say that all this is interesting, and I must admit that it's the only news category I turn to with eagerness in the *Monde*. It is a sort of serial story, in episodes.

My dear, I hope the Bard ceremony will not be too harrowing for you. It's hardly a question of reopening a wound, so maybe it will be of some solace. Heinrich anyway would have been pleased by some aspects of it. And amused. Jim is looking forward to the photos.

And by the way he was struck, even startled, by yours of Castine.

"Why, she takes a good photo," he said. "Excellent composition." Evidently he didn't expect this of you.

All my love, my dearest, and take care of yourself just a little.

Mary

[. . .]

1. This film was made by French-American director William Klein. Eldridge Cleaver ran the Black Panther Party's International Section in Algiers until he was expelled from the party in 1971 for his advocacy of terrorism and his denigration of Panther service programs in the United States.
2. On April 2, 1969, twenty-one members of the Black Panther Party's New York chapter were charged with conspiracy to blow up police stations, department stores, and the Bronx Botanical Gardens. Two years later the "conspiracy" was traced to an undercover policeman named Gene Roberts, and the "Panther 21" were released.

[New York]
Saturday [11/14/70]
[Postcard]

Dearest Mary: The Kant quote: In German "Die schönen Dinge zeigen an, dass der Mensch in die Welt passe und selbst seine Anschauung der Dinge mit den Gesetzen seiner Anschauung stimme." (Akademie Ausgabe, vol. XVI, 1820a) Rough translation: "The beautiful things in the world (meaning natural things) indicate that man is made for and fits into the world and that his perception of things agrees with the laws of his perception."

It was good to hear your voices. I keep thinking of you.

Hannah

[Paris]
11/18/70
[Postcard]

Dearest Hannah:

Thank you for Kant. Very little time here for a letter. Maria is on vacation, in Portugal, and the replacement she found has fled, after a crisis with the vacuum-cleaner. At night, in bed, I am reading the Albert Speer book [*Inside the Third Reich*]. Extremely curious as to what you make of it. In fact have been holding imaginary conversations with you about it.

All my love, Mary

Dearest Mary:

I almost called just to ask you and Jim what you think about the Vietnam-bombings.[1] But thought I wanted to write anyhow. Your cards and letters—so dear and then also so immensely sensible, just the day-to-day continuity of life and friendship.

The Bard ceremony: Very decent, especially Shafer[2] who read from the Apology, Socrates's words about death, concluding with the great last sentence—we must go now, I to die, you to live. Which is better is known to the god alone. Such decency, and rightness. And from a clergyman. The cemetery is a piece of woods with markers here and there not even real graves. Very good, very right.

After that, the very next day, back to school. I was very frightened; gave a very good seminar and, on Thursday, the lecture course all right. Am not at all sure if I should not be ashamed of myself. The truth is that I am completely exhausted if you understand by that no superlative of tiredness. I am not tired, or not much tired, just exhausted. I function all right but know that the slightest mishap could throw me off balance. I don't think I told you that for ten long years I had been constantly afraid that just such a sudden death would happen. This fear frequently bordered on real panic. Where the fear was and the panic there is now sheer emptiness. Sometimes I think without this heaviness inside me I can no longer walk. And it is true, I feel like floating. If I think even a couple of months ahead I get dizzy.

I am now sitting in Heinrich's room and using his typewriter. Gives me something to hold on to. The weird thing is that at no moment am I actually out of control. Perhaps this is a process of petrification, perhaps not. Don't know.

Auden came—looking so much like a clochard that the doorman came with him, fearful that he might be God knows what. The evening was strange to say the least. (The following just for you, please remember): Said he came back to New York only because of me, that I was of great importance for him, that he loved me very much, etc. I tried to quiet him down and succeeded quite well. In my opinion: Oxford where he hoped to go for good has turned him down (I suppose) and he is desperate to find some other bearable place. I see the necessity but I know also that I can't do it, in other words, have to turn him down. I have a hunch that this happened to him once too often, namely being turned down, and I am almost besides [sic] myself when I think of the whole matter. But I can't change that; it would simply be suicide—worse than suicide as a matter of fact. I have got to call him up—his poem in The New Yorker,[3] tomorrow at the latest. I don't know what to do. When he left he was completely drunk, staggering into the elevator. I did not go with him. I hate, am afraid of pity, always have been, and I think I never knew anybody who aroused my pity to this extent.

Mountains of mail, among them students' letters—some very good, very touching. In Bard, [William] Lansing, the chairman of the philosophy department who had always been his [Heinrich's] enemy. Sobbing, out of control, how terrible the last semesters had been without Heinrich. He is the hunter there and the "love" of firearms or bow and arrows had been the bridge between them. So I gave him Heinrich's rifle.

Thanks for the description of the Panther-movie. Of course that is the way it is—insane, hopped up on drugs and rhetoric. The students here are very quiet but I don't know how it will look tomorrow after the news [of the Vietnam bombings]. Can't get myself to look at television. Whatever, I don't think I shall have difficulties. Both militants and conservatives are extremely considerate with me, almost tenderly so.

I am glad with the news about the novel. Good that the clochards get in. Paris is not Paris without them. Do they still have the sign outside the commissariats de Police saying somehow—Messieurs les clochards sont invités de passer la nuit au commissariat pendant le grand froid [Gentlemen of the streets are invited to spend the night at the police station during cold spells]? And I am of course terribly proud of Jim's praise of my photos. Still, he is of course right with his original suspicion.

I wrote today to Annchen, telling her to come around Christmas time. Dwight first called, then wrote a very good, very perceptive letter.[4] I'll send you a copy one of these days. Dear, dear Dwight. I shall see him this coming week. Just now, Alfred Kazin called, asking to come. In the mountains of letters: from my whole past, layer upon layer, none conventional, with sympathy or old friendship still alive. Strange. I told you, I think, that Heidegger wrote—

immediately upon receiving the news from Glenn Gray. Including a very beautiful poem.

Bill will pass by next Wednesday. Helen Wolff calls regularly, sends flowers, is very touching. [. . .]

De tout coeur—
Hannah

1. With the Paris peace talks between the United States and North Vietnam stalemated for the second year, President Nixon launched new bombing raids against Hanoi and Haiphong.
2. Frederick (Fritz) Shafer was Professor of Philosophy and Religion at Bard.
3. W. H. Auden, "The Aliens," *The New Yorker*, November 21, 1970.
4. Arendt sent Dwight Macdonald's letter three weeks later.

141 rue de Rennes
Paris 6ème
December 1, 1970

Darling Hannah:

Yesterday about 8 p.m. I finished my novel. In the ultimate version your Kant quotation is in. I thought of a way. And I've found a marvel for the dedication page. Wait and see. Of course today I had to make little corrections and then collate those with the carbon and two photostats, but the manuscript of the chapter has winged off to New York, after a classic dispute with the postoffice, where a grumpy employee told me I couldn't send a manila envelope with a metal clasp (I do it all the time). So I demanded to see the *chef* and said what am I supposed to do, the metal clasp is *interdit* and scotch tape is *interdit* and as you can see for yourself the glue on the flap isn't sticking—it never does? He said I could use scotch tape under the circumstances and explained the circumstances when I couldn't, e.g., for a registered letter (God knows why). Then he actually went and found some scotch tape and applied it himself, all of which I consider a Victory.

The rest of the day I've been doing my checkbook, cleaning up my desk, having a fitting for two dresses, so it's only, at six in the evening, that I sit down to write to you.

Thank you for your wonderful letter. Yes, I knew for ten years that you were afraid of that sudden death, knew and, being more or less Anglo-Saxon, didn't speak of my knowledge to you, only to Jim. It occurred to me, flying over, that you had lived with that death for so long that the actuality must be in some way a relaxation of tension for you. Or not perhaps that exactly but a sort of purging, leaving you empty, doubly empty, even, to have lost your fear and Heinrich together. Yet the absence of the familiar fear must be in some degree a relief—a poisoned one. I do not know how you will manage this. I can't guess. You must feel as if you were living with somebody you hardly knew—yourself without anxiety.

But I don't understand why you feel that maybe you should be ashamed of giving a good seminar. Even if that's partly a wry joke. Do you mean ashamed *socially*, that you ought to be visibly "broken"[?] I can't think you mean that. Or do you mean the fact that the teaching, if it can go off so well under the circumstances, has no true interest for you and is just a function, like eating and elimination, which go along pretty much by themselves[?]

About Auden, we knew something of this already. Stephen Spender was here and announced that he was feeling like a matchmaker, wouldn't Wystan make a good husband for Hannah? I said coldly "Are you mad?" But putting this together with your letter, I think Auden must have confided—one can hardly say "hopes" but perhaps longings—in him, and Stephen was feeling me out to know what your response might be. At the time I thought S. was simply being frivolous and callous, but probably he spoke with Auden's interests really at heart. He is fond of him. Anyway, of course you had to turn him down. It *would* be worse than suicide. I wonder if you will get more ill-timed proposals, surfacing from long-concealed and agitated depths. It wouldn't surprise me if you did. Anyway, of course I shall say nothing to Spender when I see him again. It's typical of a homosexual—I mean Spender—to have been married for twenty years and know so little about marriage that he could venture such a thought.

I've never seen the invitation to *clochards* you speak of posted on the *commissariats*. I don't think that exists any more. But Jim, who vaguely recalls such a thing, thinks that it was a typical French police dodge, masked in ceremony, for doing nothing about those wretched beings. In other words, if somebody says to a gendarme, "What is that poor creature doing, in this cold, sleeping on the street?" the gendarme replies that it's the *clochard's* fault, he has been formally invited to sleep in the police station. But maybe there's a kinder explanation. In fact in London you can always sleep in a police station; two little French girls I knew did when they lost the key to the place they were staying. But they said the police weren't very friendly and made them leave too early in the morning.

What did you think of Kazin's Bellow review?[1] It started out surprisingly well, I thought, and then lost steam. He didn't have the courage to confront Bellow's current politics and in fact left the meeching impression that he rather agreed with them. Bellow's fault was just being unkind about *people* or, as Alfred would surely say, "human beings," the warmer formula. K. was best on Jewishness.

And I'm eager to hear your view of the Speer book. Did you get my postcard about that?

We go to London Thursday and I shall see Cal. I'll write you about that. Did I tell you that he wrote me that he is planning to go back to "Lizzie and Harriet"? I wonder if she knows this and if she does what reception he will get. I feel very sorry for Cal and troubled about him, and yet this final piece of arrogance makes me almost angry. Women's Lib.

Dearest Hannah, when you get around to it, send me a copy of Dwight's letter.[2] [. . .] I am glad about the Bard graveyard. I hoped it would be like that. And Shafer.

Let's call each other again soon. We shall be in London probably till the 7th or 8th. I may try to talk to you from there, but we're staying with friends and I rather hate to have intimate conversations on other people's telephones, even if they can't hear. You'd never think that, though, from some of the Jim calls to and from Riverside Drive!

Not a word from Bill about the illustration for the jacket [of *Birds of America*]. He must be angry or hurt. But you would have done the same in my place, I know, if you'd seen that "wistful" little Establishment lad in blue jeans (aged about twelve!) they were all so pleased by at Harcourt. Here I may have made the opposite error. We sent to Holland for a strange young Dutch artist, a wild frightened creature, a bird and animal lover. He has produced a beautiful drawing, after two terrified days in a hotel down the street. In some ways it's an uncanny portrait of Peter Levi. But Harcourt will think it too sad, too "pessimistic," I fear—not a real American kid. To tell the truth (but don't tell Bill) the boy the artist has conceived doesn't look very American, especially in his clothes, but rather like a

Wandering Jew. We can perhaps get him to change the clothes a little—at least the shoes, which aren't an American style.[3]

Jim has come home, and I must stop.

All my love, as always,

Mary

1. Alfred Kazin reviewed Saul Bellow's Mr. Sammler's Planet in The New York Review of Books, December 3, 1970.

2. Dwight Macdonald's letter, Nov. 18, 1970: "Dearest Hannah— Will appear then at 270 R. D. Friday the 27th at 8 PM, and we'll talk. About Heinrich and other things. . . . . . Meanwhile let me try to put down in random fashion as they come to me—and as he'd have liked—why I had a special feeling about him. . . . Well he was to begin with a true, hopeless anarchist both in mind and in temperament—always ready to respond to a stimulus (or an argument, bad or good) in a reckless, wholehearted way that was never so reckless or emotional—except in form, at times, but O ye Pharisees & Scribes & precisionists—as to miss the main target, The Point—and his aim was all the more admired by me bec. he didn't seem to draw a bead at all, like those Zen archers, but just let fly 'at random'—rationally—but not at all randomly in terms of his experience up to that moment, w. was brought to bear, without his conscious thought perhaps (or perhaps not unimportant) wholly on the subject— his arrow hit the center most times, as I saw it. . . . Often unexpectedly—you couldn't predict Heinrich's reactions, esp. his moral ones—another thing I loved about him—and even when you thought him wrong-headed, 'difficult', even perverse (though in my memories of him, he was usually all those things for the conventional idées réçue[s] liberals but not for me, I began with a prejudice in his favor) even when you couldn't swallow his contrarieties, they forced you to think bec. they were his and not others'. . . . . . His low-keyed grumblings and flashing-eyed shoutings (how desperately precise his enunciation was when he felt himself driven into an argumentative corner from which he saw an existential exit denied him by the Rules of the Game!) were a humanistic obligato to many arguments I've been present at, and taken part in, conducted on a plane that was intellectually higher, or rather more rule-respecting, than Heinrich's, but—when you came to think about it later—lower in terms of imagination, and common sense, than his. Also I liked one quality, among others, he shared with you: the ability to commit himself to a position, passionately, and damn the horses—or the expense! Of course they were always positions I thought were both decent and reasonable but what can I or you or he do about that, dearest Hannah? . . . . . . See you next week, love, Dwight."

3. The drawing by the Dutch artist, Peter Vos, was used on the jacket.

141 rue de Rennes
Paris
December 11, 1970

Dearest Hannah:

This will be a stupid note. I have an awful cold, and my brain is stunned by some anti-histaminic product recommended by the pharmacist. But I must thank you for the *wonderful* flowers, which are still glowing in splendor on the mantel-piece. And additional thanks for sending on Dwight's letter. May I keep it? He seizes very well some essential qualities of Heinrich's, catching them almost on the wing, and I feel grateful to him for that, especially the Zen archers and "low-keyed grumblings and flashing-eyed shoutings," which bring Heinrich back into the room with me. If he has to include a certain amount of self-flattery, that must be accepted as Dwight, not the old Dwight but the sadly vain one of recent years who's unable to admire without locating himself somewhere close to the center of admiration. Of course he was always vain but in former days more simply so.

Five days, nearly, in London, very social. I saw a lot of fashion-mad people, including the current Women's Lib idol, an absurd Australian giantess [Germaine Greer] who made remarks like "We must make them understand that fucking is a *political* act." And here's a marvelous one, quoted from Sonia [Orwell] by Stephen Spender: "Auschwitz, oh, dear *no!* That person was never in Auschwitz. Only in some very *minor* death camp." The ultimate in English snobbery. Amid these silly zombies, Cal seemed calm and rational. God knows what he is up to, though. He made so many contradictory statements about his intentions that it was like a true-or-false test: "I am/ I am not/ returning to Lizzie and Harriet." Underscore correct answer. And seeing him with Caroline and hearing them talk together about Lizzie made me feel that whatever he hopes or imagines he *cannot* go back. During one of his momentary absences, I managed to ask Caroline in a whisper what was going on. She: "I don't know. I'm floating." Reading some of his poems to her (new), especially one where they are both looking in a mirror, I thought that what binds them is madness. The first time he has been able to share it.

But you'll be seeing him shortly. He does seem determined to go to New York for Christmas, staying with Blair Clark and visiting L. and H. The only problem there is that the Home Office has his passport and he has lost the slip of paper they gave him that was meant to serve as a travel document. . . .

When does Annchen arrive? Jim and I are going to Rome for eight days on Christmas night. While we were in England, he went down to the Isle of Wight and saw the two boys. This passed off well. Danny was friendly and fairly open with him. But the mystery remains as to what is supposed to be the matter with him. I don't mean its technical name, even, but such a simple concrete fact as what are or were his symptoms. . . . He talked about an "identity problem," but that guff obviously comes from the psychiatrist. No boy of his age says "I must go to the doctor because I don't know who I am and he can help me find out." Jim didn't manage to see the doctor, who was in bed with the flu. But anyway he's in more cheerful spirits about Danny, now that he's seen him.

Nothing much new here. Yesterday a big demonstration for the Basque defendants.[1] But as a cab-driver said to me, that will accomplish nothing. A few economic reprisals might help a little. If the Left would stop going to Spain for its vacations . . . But I doubt that they will. They haven't even stopped going to Greece.

I had lunch with Nathalie, who is off to lecture in Canada. Returning by way of New York in early February. She wants to see you and wondered whether she would be an intrusion on your private grief. I said no, you'd welcome a talk with her. She's all keyed-up about an onslaught she's planning to make, during her lectures, on the *Tel Quel* group.[2]

I have to name books I liked during the year for the *Observer*. I want to include "On Violence" but was it published in England? It doesn't matter, actually; I'll name it anyway.

All my love, dear Hannah,
Mary

1. Fifteen Spanish Basque nationalists had received harsh sentences in Spain for separatist activities, precipitating the demonstrations in Paris.
2. McCarthy shared Sarraute's dislike for the intransigent literary politics of *Tel Quel*.

[New York]
February 5, 1971

Dearest Mary—

Annchen left day before yesterday for an extended Greyhound tour to the West Coast; she will be back in a month and then leave for Nice. I did not write, was somehow squeezed in between her and Lotte [Beradt], quite irritable but not monstrous, and I am now rather relieved. At the end, it got somewhat better, as though I woke her up by my outbursts of impatience. She has lost all contact with the world, is usually quite happy but half-asleep; Lotte, on the contrary, full of dramatics. And I, caught in the middle, trying to concentrate on something. It is not worth discussing at any length.

I read the Winter Visitors[1] with the greatest delight, talked about it with Bill, hoped he would report to you. This nature novel, old fashioned at first glance, strikes me as the most "relevant" piece of fiction one could possibly read, hitting this whole technological question of the time at its most human and most neglected point. Among your own books, it is the least "social" or society-minded one, and in tone, gesture, reflectiveness probably the one that will be closest to me. If you still intend to dedicate it to me—forgiving my unforgivable silence—it will be a great lasting joy.

The Christmas period was hectic as usual, chiefly because of the number of students or former students who descended on New York. I saw Cal, found him rather stale, and I did not yet dare call Lizzy because he seemed so obviously impossible about the whole thing; I was afraid of her reaction and (squeezed in) in no mood to see her. The awkward side of the matter was that she had called me shortly before he arrived, had asked me to come to dinner with them, and then when he arrived he stayed at a friend's house and had changed his mind once more.

Bill: seems quite healthy; I don't know if he told you how extraordinarily kind and helpful he was with much needed advice. I have an offer for a distinguished professorship at one of the City University's colleges which I never had any intention to accept (this entre nous). Jonas[2] told the New School about it, explaining that I had no "pension" etc., whereupon the New School decided to solve my "problem." I called Bill who came immediately, chiefly in order to figure out what my "problem" actually would be in cold figures. I then did exactly as he told me, got a very good "solution" (according to Bill) which still has to be accepted by the Board of Trustees—probably will, the result would be that I am bound to go on teaching at the New School, cannot leave, which is entirely ok with me, but that at retirement (whose beginning is up to me) I would receive enough to live comfortably.

What are your plans? I cannot begin to tell you how much I miss you. Give me some hint when and where we shall see each other. I go to Chicago for one week, last week in February, and shall perhaps come to Europe in April/May—this time also to go to England for a few days (family). In June I must be back in New York—chiefly in order to arrange a number of things with Heinrich's students. (I have now all the old tapes from [Heinrich's] New School lectures transcribed and shall see then what to do with them. They read quite well.) Also, an honorary degree from Yale and a few other items. I have been busy—always with great difficulties—with my lectures on Judgment (Kant's Critique of Judgment) and shall now try out a few things in Chicago. In fall, I shall give a course on the Will.

Bill said something of you planning to go to China? The political scene here—too complicated for writing, too many details. Anyhow, Nixon is losing, the old credibility gap opening up, and I have some hopes for 1972—[Edmund] Muskie would not be bad. You know of course that all our war criminals are "not guilty," as far as I can see nobody cares much. Did you see Telford Taylor's little book [*Nuremberg and Vietnam: An American Tragedy*]? Far more important: Did you read Mrs. [Nadezhda] Mandelstam's Memoirs [*Hope Against Hope*]? About Speer another time. I now must have the apartment ready for the wreckers: New pipes, an awful nuisance. I escape to the office.

Much much love, dearest. You know of course that you can always stay here when you come to New York (Own bathroom, own telephone.)

Give Jim my love. Je vous embrasse tous les deux.

Hannah

1. *Winter Visitors*, the first chapter of *Birds of America*, was published in a limited edition, with an owl on the cover, as a New Year's greeting to friends of the author and publisher.
2. Hans Jonas, who taught philosophy and religion at the New School for Social Research, was an old friend of Arendt's from her student days at the University of Marburg.

141 rue de Rennes
Paris
February 10, 1971

Dearest Hannah:

It's I who should have written. I've been sunk in proof corrections and revisions. Now I have a few days hiatus. At first Bill *didn't* tell me that you'd liked the little owl book [*Winter Visitors*]—only that you'd found a mistake [unknown]. In a later conversation, he exclaimed "Didn't I *tell* you she liked it?" "No." I think the drugs he takes make him occasionally forgetful or is it the companies he's buying? Now one in Japan. In any case, I'm pleased to hear first hand that you did. Until recently there's been a rather unnerving silence on the subject. Few have written me from the U.S. It almost boils down to my dentist, Fred Dupee, and Sylvia Marlowe, all in rather guarded terms. Well, a charming letter from Jimmy Merrill, the poet. I began to feel that all the others thought it kinder not to speak of the poor little book. Here in Europe, now that a few owls have finally been sighted, it's better.

About the mistake. I don't think it matters there in Chapter One. At fifteen, Peter wouldn't know that. (I liked your remark, quoted by Bill, that you'd been a Jew for forty years without knowing that.) In Chapter Three, where he is nineteen, he has some reflections on the subject and decides that he would be a Jew in Nazi Germany, a Gentile in Israel, and God knows what in the Arab countries. . . .

It's too bad about the Lotte-Annchen squeeze. I wonder if women, liberated, would be better. Perhaps worse. They always seem more womanish when they're together, without men.

Of course I still intend to dedicate the book to you. In fact the deed is done. I've added as an epigraph something I found in Jaspers on Kant: ". . . to attempt to embody the Idea in an example, as one might embody the wise man in a novel, is unseemly . . . for our natural limitations, which persistently interfere with the perfection of the Idea, forbid all illusions about such an attempt . . ." If you know where that comes from or by chance know it in German, I'd be grateful to hear, to pass on to the German translator.

By the way, I've been having first-hand confirmation of what you say about the HBJ editors. The proofs scribbled over with idiotic queries, which demonstrate a total lack of the capacity to read, combined with zealousness. They have tried, through *two* sets of proofs, to correct that boy's grammar. E.g., "The Sorbonne was only interested in collecting the tuition." Editor's query: ". . . interested *only* in collected [sic] the tuition?" And sublimely assured misinformation: Editor, in the margin[:] "The *rouge-gorge* is *not* the American robin's cousin. American robins are members of the *thrush* family, while European robins are *warblers*." A statement like that drives one beserk [sic], since the mystery is how anyone who knows anything about birds could think the redbreast was a warbler. They are all of course thrushes. And someone I suspect of being the same idiot tells me that in Italy they don't have daylight saving time. So I start to ask myself, "Somebody is crazy here. Can it be me?" Then I run and ask someone to confirm the original statement, which was that they have it in the summer. Remember how it confused us, coming from Switzerland to visit Orta? Jim thinks I should tell Bill at some point as a public duty, and he could call his editorial staff together and give them a homily on how to read copy, i.e., for sense. It is as if these people's only purpose in life was to try to trip the author up. And just to write patiently "No . . No . . . No" to all that nonsense is bone-tiring, for one feels *no one* will understand, if these professionals don't. But perhaps that's the point. It's a professional deformation.

About China. I have rather cooled off on that idea. Mainly on account of Laos. In the first place, the latest U.S. exploit there makes it very unlikely the Chinese will give me a visa.[1] Second, if the Laos thing gets worse, I don't feel I belong in China wandering around recording "impressions" but somewhere closer to home, where the melee will be (I hope). Or even in Vietnam. But not simply out of the picture. Anyway, with these maddening proofs, I haven't had a minute to go to the Chinese Embassy.

I have another vague thought. Of covering the Medina trial.[2] That is, if he's ever tried and not just declared innocent at the outset and sent back to duty covered with flowers. . . . If he is tried, reporting it might be a fresh way of getting at the issues.

All this means that my plans are rather vague. I wish you were coming to Europe sooner than April/May. Sometimes I have an impulse to jump on a plane for New York, just like that. But I have work to do that will occupy me through March 11 or 12. And then Easter is drawing near. If Jim can get time off, I know he'd like to go somewhere for Easter. Back to Sicily, maybe, or the Auvergne or the Albigensian country. So even without China (or Medina) I remain uncertain. [. . .]

I am so pleased that you're getting the Yale doctorate. Have you heard about Bill's Alaska Commencement address? Divinely suitable. He thinks so too. I laughed when he told me, and so did he. So did Jim, when *he* heard it. Bill *is* Alaska.[3]

I did read the Mandelstam memoir, which I thought marvelous. I want to read it again. Quite often, during it, I thought of Cal. I've not heard from either him or Lizzie, which is slightly odd. One can't remain a friend of both, that seems clear (though he'd deny that), and perhaps, trying to, I've become the friend of neither.

Jim sends you much love and wants so much to see you. At worst, let us say, in April or May. Here. And not just a flying visit. We might take a little trip together if you'd like that. [. . .]

> All my tender love, my dearest Hannah,
> Mary

1. McCarthy had briefly contemplated a trip to China, until the stepped-up Vietnam bombing and the expansion of the war into Cambodia and Laos, in the early months of 1971, refocused her attention on Indochina.
2. After Lieutenant William C. Calley, Jr., was convicted for his part in the 1968 massacre

of noncombatants at My Lai, the army planned to court-martial Calley's immediate superior, Captain Ernest Medina, for the same crimes.

3. William Jovanovich, who was born in a Colorado coal camp, was the quintessential Westerner, in McCarthy's view. Many of the miners he knew as a boy, Montenegrin-born like his father, had prospected in Alaska, and he grew up charmed by their tales. The commencement address he delivered was at the University of Alaska, Fairbanks, where he was given an honorary degree.

[New York]
2/13/71

Dearest Mary: I just received your letter and am answering at once—just as I would answer if you were here. So delighted am I to have the letter and a little talk. [. . .]

Bill: Not the pills but the companies, including the ones he keeps make him forgetful. I have not the slightest idea of the Alaska-business—another company, which includes commencement speech? [. . .]

HBJ editors: This whole nonsense comes from their zeal to show how necessary they are, how well they worked and how much, etc.; plus, of course, sheer, undiluted stupidity with more than a bit of méchanceté [spitefulness]. The outrage is that they make us *work* to undo what they did, and each time they put one of their idiotic queries in the margin one rushes back to reference and God knows what. If we were compensated by the hour by the publisher for unnecessary work they would begin to be a bit more careful. Erich Heller left Knopf a number of years ago because of the state of the proofs. These people are not "professionals," they are actually unemployable people who have succeeded in landing a job which hardly exists to begin with.

China: You had not yet read the papers of today but probably are better informed than we are here.[1] The country is very quiet but by no means pro-Nixon—rather not knowing what to do now, nothing helps.[2]

I think it would be an excellent idea to cover the Medina trial—though he probably will also be acquitted. Did you see Telford Taylor's little book [*Nuremberg and Vietnam: An American Tragedy*]? The trouble is that the Nuremberg Trials can hardly be used as a paradigm, chiefly because of the sheer cowardice of the jurists to face facts.

Nathalie Sarraute was here and we had an absolutely lovely afternoon together, much favored by weather which has been abominable but decided to become sunny and spring-like in her honor so that we could go down to the Battery. She looked thinner and much younger than when I last saw her—ages ago—had been bored to distraction in Quebeck [sic] and exploited on top of it. One can laugh with her and one laughs about the same things—delightful.

Next week (the 18th) I'll go to Chicago where I'll stay till the 28th. I want to try out my "judging" business as I did last year with "thinking." But this time no lectures, only seminars. I had promised 3 with the success that the students scheduled 5, but I think we shall arrive at a compromise of 4. In the Fall, I shall give a lecture course and a seminar at the New School on the Will. Then I shall have in rough outline the book—thinking-willing-judging. Right now, I am reading students' papers, one or two surprisingly good.

You see, I am half-way "all right," no longer so awfully tired. Perhaps you will decide to jump on a plane, just like that, and come here. For me it is difficult to come before April. Apart from everything else, I have the wreckers in the apartment, new pipes, an awful nuisance, and it would not be wise to go before they are half-way finished. I must be back in New York end of May at the latest: there will be a ceremony in Bard, initiated by the alumni (half of the present alumni are former students of Heinrich), for some post-humous honor on the 28th and I must be present, of course. The students come, one of them brilliant, already [a] professor, all eager to have those lectures of Heinrich which were taped (mostly from the fifties from the New School), transcribed and this is what I am now having done. In June, this should be finished, and then I want to be back anyhow. [. . .] I am eager to come to Paris, a little trip would be marvellous, but anyhow just to see you and talk. Let us try.

Give Jim my Love! De toute coeur
Hannah

1. President Nixon had just announced his decision to open a dialogue with China.
2. Arendt refers to the absence of significant demonstrations following the February 1971 escalation of U.S. bombing throughout Indochina.

141 rue de Rennes
Paris
March 15, 1971

Dearest Hannah:

Too bad about that awful connection. Whenever that happens I feel guilty, as though if I only used more *will power*, I could hear or be heard.

Dearest, I'm overjoyed about your coming to Sicily.[1] Jim too. And I very much hope that you can spend a few days with me in Paris first, so that we can talk, without even the beautiful distraction of Greek temples and Norman mosaics. About practical matters: we shall leave for Palermo the afternoon of Holy Thursday—April 8; change in Rome and arrive that night. Jim will book three seats from Paris to Palermo tomorrow. This has to be done early, because there'll be the usual mass rush out of Paris of those making the *pont* for the Easter weekend, Friday and Monday being holidays. He'll also reserve rooms for the three of us at the Villa Igeia in Palermo— a very comfortable and pleasant hotel just outside the city; I don't know if you know it but we've stayed there before. Our plan is to stay there from the 8th through probably the 13th (or perhaps the 12th), using it as a base for seeing Palermo and then making day trips to Erice, Segesta, etc. The hesitation between the 13th and the 12th is on account of Cefalù, on the north central coast: one could either see it by day, returning to sleep in Palermo, or stop there for the night on the way to Syracuse. Cefalù, we're told, has splendid mosaics, perhaps the best in Sicily and is marvelously situated. We'd plan to arrive in Syracuse the 14th or the 13th. In Syracuse three or four nights, returning to Paris via Rome, where we'd probably spend the night. We're not sure about airplane connections from Syracuse. One may have to go from Catania; there are a number of flights from there, one, I know, going to Milan direct. Jim will have to look all that up. The idea is to rent a Hertz car at some point in the Palermo stay and drive it across the island to Syracuse.

There's one complication. We've arranged to meet friends in Syracuse, an American couple called DuVivier[2] who live in London— he's a lawyer. They'd arrive in Syracuse the 13th, I think, from Genoa. I know you don't like group ingatherings but think you could manage a day or two of it. And if you have to be in Zurich the 15th, you could vanish. I can't remember whether you know Syracuse or not. I was passionately taken by it when we were there a couple of years ago; Jim too. But we saw only the medieval part— the Old City—and this time we want to see the classical part also. The hotel situation isn't too good there, but there's one old and rather simple one, I hear, on the port in the Old City, looking out to sea, that ought to be all right. In terms of comfort, the Jolly is rated the best, but it's in a rather ugly location. Anyway we shall have had comfort in the Villa Igeia.

Last time the Villa Igeia made us a picnic for our trip, and it lasted three days. . . . I'm rather hoping for a repetition of this. Eating lunches by the roadside. But three days is perhaps excessive.

Jim is greatly interested in the Normans. He has been reading about them in an English half-history, half-guide called *The Kingdom in the Sun*. I'm going to write to my London bookshop to send it to you air mail, so that you can catch up with him. We thought that this time, in the interest of the Normans, we might skip Selinunte and Agrigento and just revisit Segesta while in Palermo. But that could be modified. Or you and I might do one of those separately if you want. Selinunte can be combined with Segesta perhaps. After some hesitation, we also thought we might skip Piazza Armorina [sic] this time. We saw it under such beautiful conditions, in the morning dew, that it seems a mistake ever to go back and shatter the crystal memory. But again that might be revised.

There's supposed to be a fantastic Easter celebration in a little town or village just a few kilometers from Palermo. That I'd like to go to and I'm eager to see Erice, which we missed before. Some people recommend Trapani. There's also a rococo sculptor, Serpotta (in Palermo and one convent in the town of Agrigento), whom I love and want to show you.

This is more like a travel brochure than a letter but reflects my excitement about the trip and your being with us. I've been very tired and longing for a vacation, fresh sights, and sun. When you called, I'd just got back from London, where I did a BBC lecture (at the Royal Institution, under simulated university conditions) and a talk in the House of Commons restaurant, on behalf of medical aid to North Vietnam—a press thing. I'd been hoping to reward myself by some gallery and museum-visiting, but an ancient waitress in the House of Commons turned over a huge wooden Gothic chair on my left big toe, which left me unable to walk or even, at first, get a shoe on. It turned out to be just a very bad bruise and is much better now.

To go back to Sicily: the weather. It ought to be quite warm but bring a coat, of course, and a sweater. On the other hand, bring a bathing suit. And a raincoat. In short prepare for all eventualities.

I don't know what made me think I'd be in New York in May. Perhaps Bill and publication date.[3] But now I'm disinclined and in fact would like to be as far as possible from that event. Already photographers and interviewers have got wind of it here. Two interviews and three photographers, and one photographer and two interviews declined. . . . I mean, I declined.

About China I feel more and more lukewarm. A journalist I know has just gone to Peking and promised to put in a word for me. In the meantime, he said, *don't* apply for a visa. I'm grateful for postponing the thought. Shawn has cabled that he'd be pleased to have me do the Medina trial. But God knows when that will happen. Not, I hope, in August.

How did the "judging" go at Chicago? I look forward to talking together about that in Paris. And other things. In Sicily let's not think about U.S. politics. Let's have pure escapism. I am convinced we are going to be bombing North Vietnam very soon again. I mean in a massive way, far beyond Johnson's war-of-destruction. And how will the country (ours) react and Nixon react to the reaction? The land-invasion talk is a red herring, I'm sure, originating in Washington and designed less to scare the North Vietnamese than to scare America. So that, after that, bombing Haiphong harbor will seem a lesser evil—almost a relief: no ground troops.

I saw Cal in London, by the way. We'll talk about that too. He seems calmer and saner than in some time. But (or is it "and") Caroline is pregnant. He seems pleased but is perhaps secretly daunted.

Now I have to stop. Please write that the aforegoing plans are OK. I am so elated about seeing you.

All my love,
Mary

[. . .]

1. Arendt had agreed by phone to join McCarthy and West on a holiday tour of Sicily, planned in honor of the Wests' tenth wedding anniversary.
2. David and Eleanor DuVivier.
3. *Birds of America* was scheduled for publication on May 19.

[New York]
March 19, 1971

Dearest Mary:

I confirm all plans with great happiness. I know Sicily but very little of the Norman side of it, and I shall try to learn as much as I

285

can—not much time—to be able to follow Jim. If it is all right with you, I'd come to Paris on the 5th, taking the plane here on the 4th—Sunday and Easter when certainly no one will turn up except me. I changed my Zurich plans so that I can stay until the 18th or so. To fly back from Catania would not be so bad anyhow because the Ursino Castel (the Museum in Catania) is one of the best which Frederick of Hohenstaufen built. Otherwise Catania is a bore. But I was so overjoyed that you too like Syracuse so much. Heinrich and I were so charmed with it that we stayed there for a whole week. The classical part—a very good Greek theater, interesting fortifications, a good Roman arena. I don't care for either Agrigento or Selinunte (the very interesting sculpture is anyhow in Palermo with its marvelous museum). Erice I don't know but I was quite disappointed that we could not go to Cefalù. Segesta I am not very fond of, I thought it is kind of a fraud, but what I must see, Normans or no Normans, that is, see again, is Monreale. And don't worry about the friends in Syracuse; I can easily disappear if you wish me to or not disappear if we decide it that way. I am very much for skipping Piazza Armorina [sic] where we (Lotte [Beradt] and I) dragged Heinrich along because of its great fame; he had seen the mosaics in a book and decided that this was very "provincial," how rich or rather nouveau-rich [sic] Romans liked to show off and [he] went around the sights murmuring to himself—"diese Ganse" [these geese], Lotte and myself. But about 5 km out of Syracuse on the way to Piazza Armorina, there is a very lovely small Greek theatre whose name escapes me, with very interesting Demeter figures in the surrounding. It also has an agora, bench for judges, etc. When we were there, in 1963, it was not yet quite excavated; perhaps we could see that.

You see, I too am all excited. I have only one problem—baggage. I must pack for about 6 weeks. But we shall manage somehow. Mary, JIM, remember: I join you and everything is going to be divided by three, car, etc.

Also: How about a hotel in Paris? Can you reserve a room perhaps in the one near the rue du Bac or even the better one next door? I shall be tired and confused because of the time difference. And shall try to see a few people. [. . .] So, let me know where you can get a room and don't come to the airport; these planes arrive at a beastly hour. And let me know if it is all right that I book for the 4th, arrive the fifth. I would like to see Natallie [sic] if it is conve-

nient, and also Nina Gourfinkel[1]—she knows her and probably has
her latest address. Could you find out?

Much love to both of you.   Hannah

1. Nina Gourfinkel, a friend of Arendt's in Paris, was active in Jewish organizations.

141 rue de Rennes
Paris
March 24, 1971

Dearest Hannah:

Splendid! The reservations are made. Yours at the Montalembert,
from the 4th to the 8th. Ours, all three, in Palermo, from the 8th
through the 12th. The 13th at the Piazza Armerina, and the 14th
through the 16th in Siracusa. The Piazza Armerina booking is because it looks doubtful whether we can leave Palermo, visit Cefalù,
and reach Siracusa that evening without feeling too pressured. If it
works out differently, we can cancel that booking and go straight
to Siracusa. In any case, we shan't visit the Roman villa but content
ourselves, maybe, with another look at the cathedral in the square,
which we liked. We hesitated between breaking the trip at Enna
and at Piazza Armerina, but the hotel situation in Enna seems un-
promising and also it's farther from Siracusa. We might stay the
17th too in Siracusa; that depends a bit on plane schedules Catania–Paris. Jim doesn't want to arrive in Paris very late Sunday
when he has to be back at work Monday morning. Or, as you suggest, we might sleep in Catania the 17th and look at the museum.
Let's leave that open.

I think I know what small Greek temple you mean and we can
visit it en route to Siracusa. Monreale *is* Norman. All that mosaic
work in and around Palermo by Byzantine craftsmen and their Italian pupils is Norman, appearances to the contrary.

I'll get Nina Gourfinkel's address from Nathalie.

About Nathalie herself, you'd probably like to see her alone once,
but I've thought, besides that, of asking her and Raymond [Sar-
raute's husband] to dinner here with you one night. It's quite a while
since we've seen Raymond, whom we like very much. I hope it's
OK if I go ahead and arrange this, assuming I can.

It looks too as if the Chiaromontes were going to be here during
your stay. Unless they change their reservations (which they tend
to do), they arrive March 27, as I learned the other night from the
Lévis. But Nicola and Nathalie are not a happy combination (as we

discovered once during a chance meeting at the airport; they also clashed during a literary conference in Madrid). I think it is Nicola's fault. Some demon seizes him when he's in the company of women he considers brainy. Which must mean he looks on *me* fondly as rather dumb. . . . Anyway, I know Jim will tell me not to try to insert the Chiaromontes into that evening with Nathalie and Raymond. And I will obey.

About meeting you at the airport, we'll see. Jim probably not, since it's a Monday a.m. But if it's not too insanely early, I'd like to come. Please furnish your flight number and arrival time. I picked the Montalembert over the Pont Royal because when I was last able to make a comparison the Montalembert was better; Kevin [McCarthy] and his girl friend recently had a ghastly depressing room, expensive, at the Pont Royal. Some time you may want to try the Hotel Victoria Palace just around the corner from us—rather expensive but said to be very comfortable. I didn't take the liberty of putting you there because, though it's convenient to us, it's not so convenient to the Seine, the Louvre, the St. Germain cafes, etc. . . .

Now I must stop. All my love, dear Hannah. We are both overjoyed.

Mary

P.S. Our friends [the DuViviers] arrive in Siracusa the 14th. I hope you will find them bearable. The husband is pleasant (a rather old-fashioned New York type of well-mannered, cultivated lawyer), and the wife is a real goose, whom I'm fond of. She lived a long time in Princeton, was a friend of Blackmer [*sic*], Ed Cohn,[1] and others. She admires you, of course, intensely, feels already humble, fearful, etc., at the prospect of meeting you. . . . That is part of her problem.

1. The critic R. P. Blackmur taught at Princeton in the 1940s and 50s, as did Edward Cohn, who was a professor of music.

New York, N.Y.
April/March (?) 1971[1]

ARRIVE SUNDAY AIRFRANCE FLIGHT 010 AT 1040 PM PLEASE INFORM HOTEL LOVE

HANNAH

1. Dated in McCarthy's handwriting.

Dearest Hannah:

Just a word. I'm feeling tired and harassed, with a slight case of persecution mania. Overrun by interviewers, photographers, and miscellaneous strangers with requests of one kind or another. We had a girl here from *Time*, flown in from New York for three days to do a piece. At the same time, the OECD social season is reaching flood-tide, e.g., yesterday a Finnish economic party and the Emperor of Japan's birtuday. . . .

Here is the confirmation from the Stafford[1] and your Montalembert bill. I finally got my money back from them, but it took two visits and they were rather unpleasant about it. I hope you like the Stafford; I always feel comfortable there. One point, for your convenience. There's a short cut entrance from St. James [*sic*] Street to the back of the hotel—the bar. You turn right off St. James Street into a mews called Blue Bell Yard. For pedestrians only; it saves a few steps. I still advise tea for your breakfast; it's strong, good, and restorative. Then you can descend for coffee. The Italian coffee bar I was thinking of is called Mokaris and is on Jermyn Street; it used to have decent coffee. The Stafford restaurant, by the way, is good and not expensive, and the lounge is a pleasant place to meet people you have to see for tea or a drink. There are bells in the wall to get a waiter. The hall porter is nice, and helpful. For walking, you will be near St. James Park and also Green Park. There's another short cut, apropos that, which leads from the end of St. James Place (the little street the hotel is on) up through Green Park to Piccadilly and the Ritz. Closed at sundown, though.

Do call Stephen Spender. [. . .]

Bill Jovanovich telephoned a few nights ago and talked for a long time. He sounded rather tired, I thought—was home, writing an essay. He mentioned in that plaintive, boyish voice he sometimes has that you had not written him. Perhaps you should send him a card.

As I told you, Jim has some splendid Sicily photographs. The best are you and me in the cloister at Monreale, Segesta with emphasis on the wildflowers, and the little Greek theatre. He will be having copies made to send you. Unfortunately there aren't any of the Martorana, unless there are still some rolls undeveloped. I wish we still had the trip to do over—ahead of us, instead of behind. Yet I know it was painful for you to revisit so many of the places you had been with Heinrich. That has never happened to me, to *repeat* an experience, with different people, that I'd shared with someone now lost, so that I can only try to imagine the effect of an overlay of fresh impressions on the first. I can only hope the good outweighed the disagreeable or discordant.

Last night I had a vivid dream about Heinrich. He had risen from the grave, literally a resurrection. He came out of his grave very merrily, dressed in outdoor clothes and wearing a little checked cap. It turned out that, though he'd been buried, he'd been alive all the time, just playing possum; it was a little joke he'd played on us. I was very much surprised and noticed that you weren't and said to myself, "Hannah has known all along." Yet I didn't dare ask you about this, as if it were a secret. Instead, I asked Heinrich how he had managed, underground, to keep breathing, and he explained that it was easy. But now I forget his explanation. It was a gay, lively dream, naturally.

When can you come to Castine? My own arrival plans aren't clear yet but I ought to have the information I need to make them in a few days and will let you know. Probably early in July. Jim late in July or on the first of August. Maria will come with me, and the best, I think, would be for you to let us have a couple of days to clean the house and get the dust sheets off the furniture and the curtains up before you follow. We won't have a car till Jim comes, but that doesn't matter. There's a town taxi driver and friends are helpful about trips to the supermarket. Last year Maria and I and Jonny lived without a car for nearly a month. Lizzie will be there, for which I'm glad. I think you can be as free as you want and yet have companionship. The apartment has been considerably fixed up since you were there. It still needs a good-sized table (as Marcia Wilson pointed out when staying there), and I shall try to find some way of getting one—maybe from Bloomingdale's. And some shelves for your books.

Now I must stop. A man from the Nice Festival du Livre will ring the bell any minute. They want to have me on a jury that awards a prize at the end of May. According to the prospectus, Stephen Spender will be on it too. I rather like those festivals as a way of seeing friends and occasionally making a new one. You don't, I know. Also I've never seen Nice.

I'll write again and call. Keep well, my dear.

Much, much love,
Mary

1. McCarthy had booked Arendt at the Stafford Hotel in London, where Arendt was scheduled to deliver some lectures.

141 rue de Rennes
Paris
May 18, 1971

Dearest Hannah: Here it is.[1] I've included the interview (which starts on the back of page 1), to give you an idea of the coverage. Could you send it back? The two other bad reviews (so far) were also weirdly *personal*.

Your call did me a lot of good. Hope you like Sir John Soan's [sic] house.[2] Also, if you haven't seen it, the Poets' Corner in Westminster Abbey gives a very good sense of the English character.

Much love,
Mary

1. Helen Vendler's front-page review of *Birds of America* in *The New York Times Book Review*, May 16, 1971, was headlined: "Mary McCarthy again her own heroine—frozen foods a new villain." The accompanying interview, "Mary McCarthy Explains," was conducted by Jean-François Revel. Vendler's was the most influential of the hostile reviews that greeted McCarthy's fifth novel.
2. Sir John Soane (1753–1837) was an architect and art collector whose London house is now a museum.

Stafford Hotel
St. James's Place
London, S.W. 1
Thursday May 1971 (?)[1]

Dearest Mary:

I tried in vain today to call you; shall try again. The review: the old malice compounded by the super-malice of (the editor's?!) title. Also, of course, sheer stupidity. The interview: Very good, very interesting. I took notes and shall write as soon as I can get a typewriter and 30 minutes alone. The interview will cancel out the review—I think, am not sure.

This only because I want to return the enclosed [clippings] as quickly as possible.

Don't let this get you down. It won't last.

Love
Hannah

1. The date is in McCarthy's handwriting.

New York
May 28, 1971

Dearest Mary,

I am late in writing this letter but there was neither typewriter nor that quiet hour available in England to sit down and write. Meanwhile I read as many of the reviews [as] I could lay my hands on and I am still rather speechless.* There is on the other hand the spontaneous warmth and admiration of just readers. ([Hans] Jonas, f.i., told me how delighted he was and also how baffled by the so-called critical response.) Some of the reasons [for] the reaction are clear—no one ever expected you to write this kind of book and the amount of malice that is floating around here in literary circles is enormous;** you are an ideal object to crystallize it and this is an old story. The discrepancy between public image and actual person is greater in your case than in any other I know of. And in this book it is your whole person that speaks as the author. But all this does not explain what really happened. This is in a sense an old-fashioned book (in a sense), that is, it goes against the grain of very many people, and most of all of the intelligentsia.

But I wanted to write about the interview around which Jovano-vich should center his ads.*** Perhaps he could print it as a small paper and send it out to booksellers etc. Anyhow here are a few remarks in shorthand—perhaps to be talked about when we see each other—soon thanks God [sic].

You speak of the *natural* life of the mind common to everybody: I wonder; the mind is precisely what always "transcends" nature and

---

[Notes marked by asterisks appear at top of first page of Arendt's letter.]
*I did not see Time or Life.
**For instance a very vicious personal attack on Morganthau in Commentary
***I saw no one: Have not yet seen him.

therefore does not belong to our natural equipment which we share with everybody in the same sense as our other equipment. Only to the extent that the mind is also part of our brain power is it true that it is "natural" and can be shared with everybody.

The aristocrats' love for the lower orders is not necessarily snobbism. Originally, that is, in the 19th century, the attacks against the bourgeoisie came from the "right" as well as from the left, and the arguments of the so-called conservatives were much the same as those from Marx, for instance, who has much in common with Lorenz von Stein.[1] The disgust with bourgeois values, style of life, etc. is exactly the same, as is the inclination to escape bourgeois society into the older orders of aristocrats on one side, ordinary people on the other. In other words, bourgeois society is really a hideous phenomenon, repellent to all "right-minded" people.

The apparent paradox: misanthropy plus love of solitude versus equality. The passion for equality says: I want to be like everybody else *out of pride*. To be superhuman would be monstrous. Nothing can be greater than to be truly human. The lover of equality actually says: I want everybody, literally everybody, to be like me, and whether this works out or not, I am going to live according to this assumption. Another kind of life would not be worthwhile. This is no paradox; it only comes into conflict with society.

I want to quarrel with your opposition of culture and nature. Culture is always cultivated nature—nature being tended and being taken care of by one of nature's products called man. If nature is dead culture will die too, together with all the artifacts of our civilization.

You speak about the hierarchical order of feudal society in the Middle Ages when one did not need to justify oneself and have a bad conscience if one belonged to the privileged classes: This is quite true but only because underlying this whole structure was the equality of all believers before God. And the accent of earthly life lay on this future equality. Therefore: no resentment on the side of the low, no bad conscience on the side of the high. In death which comes to all men you were stripped of all social distinctions.

May 31

This is how far I got Friday morning, then a sudden outburst of telephonitis and off I went to Bard. Irma Brandeis[2] sends you her warmest regards, she too is absolutely delighted with the Birds. In Bard, I got afflicted with Robert Gardiner of Gardiner's Island—you know better than I what that is, anyhow with white oaks and sea-eagles. Never heard anybody boast so openly and kind of innocently. Probably simply a case of stupidity. Very funny first, very tiresome when it turned out that it was nearly impossible to get rid of him.

And since we are with the social anyhow, Cal in London—I saw him also at Stephen Spender's as you know. I have the strong impression that he is shortly before another breakdown. The question of, Who is greater Caesar or Alexander? came up and, much worse and really pretty insufferable: His great lasting love for Hitler whom he likes "ever so much better than Napoleon" and who writes (again, again) such beautiful German. All this pretty much the same as usual—except that this time the antisemitic undertone was blatantly strong and very embarrassing. He succeeded in making any talk nearly impossible. For a few minutes or so I was sincerely sorry for him: this time he even *looked* mad, but then later I wondered. He brought me home: he talked about Lizzy, that his having deserted her would haunt him until his grave, that he would die soon, that he envied me Castine. And for the first time I did not like him.

Back to the interview: I love the passage about language, giving you messages, being a repository of everything on the verbal level that has been experienced by human beings. You say: on the verbal level. What other level is there? An experience makes its appearance only when it is being said. And unless it is said it is, so to speak, non-existent.

The same goes for your "submission to fate" or even chance. During the last months I have often thought of myself—free like a leaf in the wind. (It is a German idiom: frei wie ein Blatt im Winde.) And all the time I also thought: Don't do anything against this, that is the way it is, let no "autocratic will" interfere.

Then your Joyce experience: I had the same experience a few years back with Einstein whom I had to read for Stature of Man in the Age of Space, or something like that.[3] I often had tried when I was young, and certainly "sharper" than I am now, without success. And then suddenly, the whole business seemed "transparent"—so easy. Of course the same phenomenon.

Again major interruption! Now June 12.

I wish you would write about What it is in people that makes them want a story. The telling of tales. Ordinary life of ordinary people, Simenon-like.[4] One can't say how life is, how chance or fate deals with people, except by telling the tale. In general one can't say more than—yes, that is the way it goes. For better or worse, of course, but the worst certainly is what people used to tell you, especially in this country[:] Nothing ever happens to me. Think of the craze for operations in middle-aged women. We seem unable to live without events; life becomes an indifferent flux and we [are] hardly able to tell one day from the next. Life itself is full of tales. What made the tales disappear? The overpowering events of this century which made all ordinary events that concerned only you look too puny to be worth being told? Or this curious neurotic concern with the self which in analysis was shown to have nothing to tell but variations of identical experiences—the oedipus complex, as distinguished from the tale Sophocles had to tell—?

I found a few misprints. p. 93. line 2: little; p. 156, 1. 4 from bottom: prisunic?; p. 277, last line (unless the German is wrong in the original?) rechts Teufel or Teufeln, the first singular, the second plural; Teufels does not exist; p. 344, last word, Kind.

Also, on p. 148, last paragraph: I doubt the historical accuracy of Peter's discovery: the idea of equality, Jefferson's "lovely equality," probably was shipped to the Old World from the New World. But it does not matter.

Let me come back once more to the "leaf in the wind." It is of course only half true. For there is, on the other hand, the whole *weight* of the past (gravitas). And what Hölderlin once said in a beautiful line: Und vieles/ Wie auf den Schultern eine/ Last von Scheitern ist/ Zu behalten—And much/ as on your shoulders/ a burden of logs/ is to bear and keep. —In short: remembrance.

Much, much love.
Yours,
Hannah

[. . .]

1. Lorenz von Stein (1850–1890) was a German political economist and scholar of constitutional law.
2. Irma Brandeis taught literature at Bard and had been a colleague of Heinrich Blücher, and of McCarthy in 1945–46.
3. Arendt delivered a paper entitled "The Conquest of Space and the Stature of Man" at a Symposium on Space sponsored by the editors of *Great Ideas Today* in 1963. The essay is reprinted in her *Between Past and Future*.
4. As in the novels of Georges Simenon.

141 rue de Rennes
Paris
June 9, 1971

Dearest Hannah:

How nice to get your long letter. But first about your thinking
lecture. To me it seems all right for publication, though I feel there
are too many cuts. They're of two kinds: first, where you cut quali-
fying sentences or paragraphs: second, where you cut clarifying sentences or paragraphs. I would restore quite a few of the second
category. Otherwise it strikes me as too rapid and elliptical and
especially for what you're thinking of as "popularization." There are
moments when, precisely, because of the cuts the reader is unable
to follow the thought process of the author.

I have one objection to your vocabulary here. "Thoughtlessness."
It doesn't mean what you want it to mean in English, not any more;
the sense you are trying to impose on it is given in the big OED as
"Now Rare." And it seems to me a mistake to force a key word in
an essay to mean what it doesn't normally, even when the reader
understands what you are trying to say with it. Not to mention the
cases when the reader will fail to understand and read it as *heedlessness, neglect, forgetfulness,* etc. My suggestion would be to find not
a substitute—another abstract noun—but substitutes. E.g., in one
instance you yourself, page 2, come up with a synonym, which to
me is preferable, "inability to think."

But maybe *this* reader doesn't understand. On reflection, I see that
the difference between what you call thoughtlessness and what you
designate as stupidity isn't really evident to me. I would have said
that Eichmann was profoundly, egregiously stupid, and for me stupidity is not the same as having a low I.Q. Here I rather agree with
Kant (and always have, without knowing that Kant said it), that
stupidity is caused, not by brain failure, but by a wicked heart.
Insensitiveness, opacity, inability to make connections, often accompanied by low "animal" cunning. One cannot help feeling that
this mental oblivion is *chosen,* by the heart or the moral will—an
active preference, and that explains why one is so irritated by stupidity, which is not the case when one is dealing with a truly backward individual. A village idiot may be far less stupid than
Eichmann. Hence the old equation between "simplicity" and good-
ness of soul or heart. An idiot of course can be reflective; he *thinks,*

in your sense, probably quite a lot, maybe more than most people, since his other mental powers are deficient, and he "connects," which is somewhat different from making logical chains of ideas, though I would be hard put to say how the simple meditative associations of an idiot were distinguishable from the processes of normal logic.

In this context, I think your distinction between thinking and knowing is very illuminating, and if it goes back to Kant nevertheless carries the question much further. Using my own terms, I'd say that the thinking or meditation of a simpleton was at the opposite pole from the *reasoning* of a child (though on the surface they may resemble each other), in that the child is always seeking knowledge, clear definitions, answers, i.e., his mind is *acquisitive*. The simpleton too may acquire a few magpie trifles of certainty but on the whole he tends to play with them rather than put them to use.

This brings me—rather indirectly—to a final question or doubt. When you say, page 19, that we are "left with the conclusion that only people filled with this eros . . . are capable of thought," you infer that this excludes the mass of humanity from an elite of "noble natures" qualified for philosophizing. To me, this doesn't follow, whatever Plato opined. Surely the longing (or nostalgia) for beauty, wisdom, love, justice is just as much a natural need in human life, "an ever-present faculty in everybody" (see page 25) as the thinking-as-intercourse-with-oneself you describe. They aren't in contradiction (as the course of your argument seems to imply) but linked together. One has to assume that every man is a thinking reed and a noble nature, even if only part-time. If empirically this doesn't appear to be so, then one is thrown back on such a formulation as Stupidity is caused by a wicked heart to explain an Eichmann— or Man-is-inherently-good-but-corrupted-by-institutions. I prefer Kant's. Perhaps I'm dull-witted, but it seems to me that what you are saying is that an Eichmann lacks an inherent human quality: the capacity for thought, consciousness—conscience. But then isn't he a monster simply? If you allow him a wicked heart, then you leave him some freedom, which permits our condemnation.

But let us talk of all this in person. Since I started this letter (yesterday), I've learned that I'm coming to New York for a week, beginning June 23 or 24, to defend those poor *Birds* on television. Bill is urgent about it, Carmen is against, Nathalie ardently for, Jim uncertain but very faintly pro—. Anyway, I've decided. HBJ will find me a hotel—the San Carlos, if they haven't torn it down, or the Barclay. I'd love to stay with you, but with TV engagements virtually every night, plus, I suppose, radio and other interviews, it seems practical to be in midtown. As soon as I know which day I leave, I'll communicate and hope you will be free for dinner that night. And others. I long to be with you.

In view of this, I'll defer taking up many points in your letter. About the "natural life" of the mind, this, I guess relates to what I've been saying above and maybe we have a real disagreement. We'll see. About the "aristocrat's love for the lower orders," I'm in agreement already with you; the formulation came from Revel during our conversation and I weakly followed along. Your point about the misanthrope very taking; yes, out of pride. As for culture and nature, let's save that; *did* I oppose them? And we'll leave the tale-telling business; perhaps I shall write that next, if I ever start writing again. Anyway, it will be fun to talk about. And thanks for finding those misprints. But it is "Prisunic." "Monoprix" but "Prisunic." The *"recht"* and *"Teufels"* don't matter; those guides make horrible mistakes in whatever language they speak in to their flocks, except Italian, of course, but Italian groups tend not to have professional guides but rather a village priest or schoolteacher. But *"kind"*! I've already written HBJ to correct that, if there ever is another printing. [. . .]

I must stop and go out to lunch with James T. Farrell.[1]

All my love,
Mary

1. The author of the *Studs Lonigan* trilogy, James T. Farrell was an old friend of McCarthy's from New York in the mid-30s.

[After traveling to New Haven to receive an honorary degree from Yale, Hannah Arendt went up to Castine in July, where she stayed in the Wests' garage apartment long enough to finish a celebrated essay: "Lying in Politics: Reflections on the *Pentagon Papers*."

Published in *The New York Review of Books* on November 18, 1971, and delivered as a lecture at Haverford, Carleton, Notre Dame, and Harvard, "Lying in Politics" is a defiant critique of the American "crisis manager's" failure to learn from reality. It was a failure Arendt related to the substitution of theory for fact, and to a near chronic indifference in policy-making circles to the consequences of government action.

298

Mary McCarthy, meanwhile, set aside her disappointment over the poor reception of *Birds of America*, and traveled to Fort McPherson, Georgia, in August 1971 to cover the court-martial of Captain Medina for *The New Yorker*.]

[New York]
Sept. 23, 1971

Dearest Mary—

Where are you? How was London?[1] How is Paris? For I assume you went right back.

This only to send you the NY Times clippings *re* Medina.

I wish you would let me know how you are. I saw Bill who had removed the sideburns! [. . .]

I am constantly thinking of *Castine*.

Yours,
Hannah

1. McCarthy had gone to London to promote the British edition of *Birds of America*.

141 rue de Rennes
Paris 6ème
September 29, 1971

Dearest Hannah:

Thank you for the note and your file of clippings. The main reason you haven't heard from me is that Maria is off on a prenuptial honeymoon with her fiancé. She has just sent a postcard with the tomb of Philip the Bold on the verso, saying that she will extend it till next Monday. So I'm distracted by housework and putting my desk back in order after the vacation and being painted (the study, not me).

I did go to London and missed Medina on the stand, for which I hate myself, the media, and George Weidenfeld. But I'm going to do the piece anyway, started it day before yesterday.

Jim is fine, though acting as the target for some Woman's Lib poisoned arrows coming from me, owing to Maria's absence. [. . .]

We are having beautiful summer-like weather and I'm enjoying going to the street market Tuesdays and Fridays on the Boulevard Raspail with my *filets*. But it does take a lot of time.

I plan to come to New York October 22, which is a Friday. Do you still want to have me? The Vassar symposium[1] is Tuesday the

26th, and I will probably stay up there till Thursday night and return to Paris on Saturday. A letter from Lizzie suggests a dinner on Friday the 29th, with you, Bob, the Epsteins, etc. That sounds fine to me. OK?

When will Lying in Politics come out? I've been spreading word of it around.

Forgive this brevity, dear Hannah, but I must try to settle down to Medina.

Much love, Mary

1. The symposium at Vassar was entitled "The Artist as Social Critic."

141 rue de Rennes
Paris 6
November 24, 1971

Dearest Hannah:

Please forgive me for dictating this letter. I am still sunk in the Medina piece, a real quagmire, and seem to be immersed besides in various petty activities that keep me from writing you, Reuel, Bill, Chiaromonte—all my dear ones.

You asked to see reviews of B. of A., and Margo [Viscusi], my secretary, has collected some. Here they are. Those I'd like back sometime (unique copies) are marked with a red star. The others you can throw away.

Jim has been reading "Thinking and Moral Considerations"[1] with great enjoyment, respect and admiration. I haven't yet reread it but will soon. At the moment I'm reading concurrently the second volume of [Solzhenitsyn's] The Cancer Ward (partly because of work) and a long manuscript by Vassilikos, on which I promised to do Bill a report. But don't tell that to [Vassilikos's friend] Lotte [Beradt] since it would upset Vassilis, I think, if he knew Bill and I were, so to speak, talking about him in his absence. As a matter of fact, I like the book though it has some strange features and what I shall be trying to do is help Bill imagine it since he doesn't know French well enough to take time to read it himself.

Not much happening here. Tomorrow (Thanksgiving) we're having a lot of people for dinner. Among those you know are the Sarrautes, the Vassilikoses, Eileen Geist (plus her husband). Otherwise, life goes on about as usual; yesterday a Bengla Desh [sic] freedom fighter to tea, young and very handsome; he'd been sentenced to death for possessing explosives to blow up Karachi airport . . . today an Irish girl interviewing for London Harper's Bazaar.

We still have no clear Christmas plans. What about you? Will you stay in New York? How are your lectures going? And your health, my dear? I'll write a real letter soon. Many thanks for a wonderful, as always, stay with you.

Much love,
Mary

1. Hannah Arendt, "Thinking and Moral Considerations: A Lecture," *Social Research*, Fall 1971.

Paris
Dec. 7, 1971

Dearest Hannah:

[. . .] Our Christmas plans seem to be firming up. We're electing for the mad project of English Cathedral towns (chiefly northern: York, Lincoln, Durham—cold even in midsummer; and one in the southwest: Wells). It must be some notion of arctic romance. Or just novelty. I am still in that slough of despond with Medina, and Jim is deep in currency problems, complicated by a mild flu.

Tonight I will have dinner with Nathalie and Monique (Wittig) and a woman friend of Monique's to argue about Women's Lib. Three against one, and that one with a language handicap, isn't my idea of fun; being women, they can't be chivalrous either, I suppose. If it's amusing, I'll write you about it. What do you think about this "total war" between Mme. Gandhi and Ayub Khan?[1] There was a rather interesting interview with [Premier] Chou-en-Lai [*sic*] in the *Sunday Times*.

Love, Mary

1. In March 1971, East Pakistan (Bangladesh) tried to break away from West Pakistan, which sent troops to quell the revolt. India supported the move for independence and went to war in both East and West Pakistan. Indira Gandhi was then prime minister of India; General Muhammad Ayub Khan had been head of Pakistan, with dictatorial powers, until forced to resign over the 1968–69 troubles in Bangladesh.

New York
Dec. 8, 1971

Dearest Mary:

Thanks for the letter, the reviews (I return the red-marked ones by separate mail) and, alas so belatedly, for the wonderful flowers which cheered up the apartment for a whole week. (Incidentally, the matter with the reviews was a misunderstanding: I knew almost all of the American reviews, wanted to see some English ones, TLS, Guardian, etc. Never mind.)

Now that I want to write and even have the time to do it, I feel with a pang how awfully far Paris is. So that I don't know how to begin. Also, your letter sounded a trifle depressed, probably only because it was dictated. Still??? (This stands for questions.) I feel out of sorts; too much to do, the New School takes more of my time than ever. The lectures go well as far as the audience is concerned, not so well as far as I am concerned. The amount of quiet and time I need to do anything half-way well is really preposterous. And if I am quiet then all the thoughts of what I should have done and did not do intrude and overwhelm me. As f.i. call Lizzy, which I did not do. I never had much initiative in such matters, and now I have none. Also, my old, life-long difficulties with people, actually a form [of] hypochondria or something. Not important but unpleasant. Take f.i. a colleague of mine whom I have known for decades (you don't know him) and hence *know* that he is a pathological liar for no other reason than that he succumbs to every passing mood— gives false promises because he likes to be the bearer of good news, etc.,—no reason for me to feel that disgusted. Well, just overreaction, but difficult now to live with.

Otherwise: Nothing much new, mostly more of the same. My German restitution business came out all right,[1] all of a sudden when even my overoptimistic lawyer had all but given up. Decision of the [West German] Supreme Court. I don't yet know what this will mean in hard cash, probably more than I shall ever know what to do with. And also my angina-business is confirmed; or so my doctor believes. By no means bad enough to get excited about. But of course the usual talk—slow down, stop smoking, etc. Since I certainly am not going to live for my health, I'll do what I think is right—avoid everything which could bring me in an unpleasant situation, by which I mean a situation in which I am forced to make a fuss. Cut down on smoking or even cut it out if it does not bother me or prevent me from working. If that is not possible, tant pis. (This incidentally just among ourselves; here nobody knows about this.)

A couple of weeks ago I went to a party given by Partisan Review

for the old contributors. It was rather nice but sad. Not many people, hardly any "important" people. But William Phillips nice and
looking extraordinarily well. And Lionel Trilling with his Diana,
who is very fat now. Also, a reception at Dorothy Norman's for
Mrs. Ghandi [sic]—who is *very* good-looking, almost beautiful, very
charming, flirting with every man in the room, without chichi, and
entirely calm—she must have known already that she was going to
make war and probably enjoyed it even in a perverse way. The
toughness of these women once they have got what they wanted is
really something!

Next week, Christmas vacations start and I am very much looking
forward to a week of quiet. The last week of December is always
hectic with Conferences and people coming to New York.

Mary, what happened to the TREE?[2] Don't forget, I am kind of
rich now. And how is Medina going or rather coming? Give the
Sarraute's [sic] my very very best. As to Vassilikos, greetings if you
wish; you know I am not so very fond of them. Lotte [Beradt] is
back in New York and I am doing my best to get along. (My best
is not very good.) Where will you be for Christmas? And anyhow,
how are things?

Give Jim my love and all my love to you.

Hannah

1. After turning down her first application for restitution, in 1966, the West German government reversed itself and awarded Arendt a sizable pension, with back pay commensurate with
the salary she would have received as a full professor in a German university.
2. Arendt may have ordered a tree for the Wests' garden on the occasion of her July 1971
visit to Castine.

141 rue de Rennes
Paris
December 23, 1971

Dearest Hannah:

Not a letter, really, just a breathless word to say Merry Christmas
to you, dearest one, and a better New Year and to beg you to take
care of yourself and not to be despondent. The haste is because
we're leaving tonight for London (sleeper), and I have been working
up to almost the last minute, trying and failing to finish Medina. It
has got very long and lacks only about two paragraphs (I think) of
being done, but I know I shall not work on it while looking at
English cathedrals. Oh, well. It will be perhaps 25,000 words, and

it is only the rough draft I have been slaving over. Not for reasons of literary perfectionism, for I am striving to avoid anything "well written," even as much so as *Vietnam* and *Hanoi*. No poetry. Wrestling with the blocks of factual material has been the problem; times, distances, conflicting evidence.

We go down Christmas Eve to stay with Cal and Caroline and baby in Kent. The day after Christmas we start on the cathedral tour, going back to London by train and taking another train north to Newcastle-on-Tyne. We stay two nights in Northumberland (I love that name) and visit Durham, Hexam Abbey and the Roman wall. Then York and Lincoln. Then perhaps rent a self-drive car (too broke for a chauffeur) and drive across country to Gloucester and finally down to Wells. I wish you could be with us, even though it will be cold and probably gloomy and dark. But this trip will by no means finish the English cathedrals. So when we go back, you might join us.

Do think, Hannah, about planning a trip soon. There *is* something elating about travel. I feel it myself tonight and have watched the Lévis cheer up as they prepared to take off for Florence. Yes, I have been depressed, but a little less now that Medina seems to be coming to a close. I think the trip will do us both good.

Your angina report naturally perturbs me, though I do persist in thinking that it *may* have something to do with mourning. . . . In any case, do as the doctor tells you and keep to a healthy regime and don't overdo. And keep me informed.

My secretary, Margo Viscusi, has a little present for you that she brought with her very kindly when she left for three weeks in America with her husband and children. She will call and try to deliver it if she goes up to Columbia, which is likely. If not, perhaps *your* secretary could fetch it from her.

Financial stress has been taking its toll of us but that fortunately will be over January 3, when Harcourt disgorges the annual payment.[1] But we've had a rather (for us) reduced Christmas, which in fact has been good for my soul. Mainly books and things like an exchange of warm dressing gowns (those provincial English hotels) but also two very nice pocketbooks for me from Jim and he got a couple of additions to his masculine *argenterie*. A Georgian wine funnel, for one thing.

How extraordinary that you finally got the reparations! It's good to know that you won't have any more old age and security worries. (I don't think you needed to have them, but you did.)

I must terminate and close my suitcases. We'll be back the night of the 2nd.

> All my love, and Jim's too,
> and write soon,
> Mary

[. . .]

1. This was around $30,000 a year.

> 141 rue de Rennes
> Paris
> January 19, 1972

Dearest Hannah:

Nicola died yesterday. I tried last night to call you and tell you, but when there was a repeated no answer, I called Bob Silvers, who thought you were at that moment teaching at the New School and promised to pass it on. I thought you might want to send a word or a wire to Miriam.

It happened in an elevator in the Italian Radio building; he had just given a broadcast on the Revel book [*Without Marx or Jesus*] and was dead in a minute—no pain, or so one thinks. That morning he'd been well and in bright spirits. I talked to Miriam, who was in an extraordinary state of control and, yes, sweetness. Of course she must have been preparing herself for a long time—it's 11 years today, if I remember right, since he had his first coronary and someone called me from Rome. I remember it clearly—where I was standing.

That he's dead, though, is still unbelievable to me. I have not yet started missing him because he is still *there*. I suppose one had got used to his *not* dying for so long that one took him for eternal. I loved him so much.

Jim and I are going down this afternoon for the funeral (tomorrow). With Carmen, who happened to be here. The Lévis will be on the same plane. Anjo is very broken up (it was she who told me) and is saying that she can't go on, what can she do, and sobbing in a distracted way. I think of it as antique Jewish mourning, remembering my grandmother when she screamed at Aunt Rosie's death.

Miriam's composure is a contrast; she seems to be trying to console others, like a mother. To cut short the contagion of sobs.

I talked with Bob about people to tell. Dwight, Mike Stille,[1] Meyer Schapiro. Too late I thought of Tucci.

It's such a pity people can't have funerals in their lifetime. I think of all the friends who will be grieving for Nicola and wishing he could know they were there. But probably he would only be embarrassed and shy. And, like Heinrich, he knew, I suppose, all along and doesn't/wouldn't need the reassurance of a funeral to feel other people's love. He felt his own, that was it.

I'd just had a sweet letter from him when we got back from our vacation, which, alas, I hadn't yet answered. On account of the awful Medina and the fact that I was planning, when I finished it, to go to Rome. Now of course I don't feel like going, having lost the principal reason. I mean when the Medina piece is finished.

I must stop and get ready for departure. I feel dazed. As Jim said, it is *hateful*.

Much love to you, my dear. This grief makes me think doubly of you, triply perhaps. You will understand.

Mary

[. . .]

1. Ugo (Mike) Stille was for many years the New York correspondent for *Corriere della Sera;* later he became its editor.

New York

January 22, 1972—bad start,

1/25/72

Dearest Mary,

This letter is overdue. I couldn't be reached last week because of major trouble at the New School—a repeat performance of the Groves of Academe, as the Dean reminded me, somebody fired, i.e. denied tenure, because of incompetence and claiming an issue of academic freedom.[1] I did not call you because Bob could not reach me either, and when I received his wire I assumed, rightly of course, that you both were already in Rome. Then, when I just had sat down to write a few lines your letter arrived. Jim's "it is *hateful*" is what stopped me suddenly. It seems to me decisive but in the sense of being the decisive question. Maybe I should then have called. But transatlantic calls to debate this question?

Mary, look, I think I know how sad you are and how serious this loss is. (I sometimes find myself now going through New York and looking at all the houses which Death has emptied during the last years. And God knows I have some experience in the presence of absence, and can't bear the notion of ever leaving this apartment precisely because here this absence is there and alive in every corner and at every moment.) Still—if you just say "hateful" you will have to say hateful to many more things if you want to be consistent. One could look upon one's whole life as a being-given *and* being-taken away; that starts already with life itself, given at birth, taken away with death; and the whole time in-between could easily be looked at as standing under the same law.

As far as Anjo and Miriam are concerned (I sent Miriam a cable): Miriam is quite in tune with Jewish mourning. Women were not admitted to funerals according to orthodox rites *because* they were likely to scream. I looked up once more the Jewish death prayers: they, that is, the *kaddish*, are a single praise of God, the name of the dead one is not even mentioned: The underlying notion is what is inscribed on all Jewish funeral homes: The Lord hath given, the Lord hath taken away, blessed be the Lord. Or: Don't complain if something is taken away that was given you but which you did not necessarily *own*. And don't forget, to be taken away, it had first to be given. If you believed you owned, if you forgot that it was given, that is just too bad for you. Not that Anjo is not also quite Jewish. Jews are also one of the Mediterranean peoples, and that means they are expressive, demonstrative, and know how to lament. And lamentations (of which I am perhaps no longer capable) are what we owe the dead ones precisely because we go on living.

Last Friday was a party at William Philipps [*sic*]. Half the crowd completely unknown, and the other half the more or less senior citizens. Dwight was there, looking appalling, purple red face and neck, probably drunk, but the only one who mentioned Nicola immediately. I thought of the good old days when people would have cancelled the party. I went home with Lizzy who seems happy and content.

The term ended last week and I am now taking it easy. I wish you could be here and one could talk. I wish there were at least a memorial service for Nicola.

Love and yours—
Hannah

1. In McCarthy's novel *The Groves of Academe*, Henry Mulcahy, dismissed for incompetence from his teaching job at a progressive college, convinces his credulous colleagues that the president fired him because he once belonged to the Communist Party (he hadn't). The faculty mobilizes on his behalf and forces the president, a liberal, to resign.

141 rue de Rennes
Paris
April 5, 1972

Dearest Hannah:

It's such a long time since I've written. Forgive me. With that three-hour-a-day reading and writing limitation,[1] I couldn't do letters once my *Medina* proofs came. Then, when the doctor said all right, I went off to Rome for nine days, was back home and off again to Strasbourg with Jim for the Easter holiday, getting back late Monday night.

My eye is almost well. The only prohibitions now are traveling by air and going out in the sun without dark glasses. I have the strange feeling of having had almost a blackout in my experience during those nearly two months, which seem dim and hard to recall now, as if they'd dropped out of my calendar. But the only residue of the affliction (one can't call it an illness) is that I'm easily tired. Some mad chemist told Jim that laser beams cause an adrenalin drain and maybe it's so. I have to get back to work, to do an essay on Nicola, but shall have to force myself to do it.

Miriam is holding up quite well, though she has bad days and I suspect doesn't sleep much. But she is extraordinarily stoical, even cheerful sometimes. She has had a project, which keeps her attention occupied. A group of us has sent a letter to the Agnelli Foundation in Turin asking them to back a publications program of Nicola's uncollected writings and letters, also a book about him by friends. That letter went through as many variants as a long poem, getting more and more marmoreal as it was worked on by more and more hands, finishing with expressions like "lo Scomparso" (the Departed One). There was also the question of who should sign and who shouldn't and who would and who wouldn't—the criterion of the first being that the signer's name should be known to Gianni Agnelli and at the same time that he should be a friend of Nicola's. All this kept Miriam's phone busy with local and long-distance calls. Mine too. And the phone of a girl called Gaia[2] who [knew] Gianni Agnelli and was considered the final authority, though not, alas, on the text (hers, rather simple and impetuous, was the best). Anyway, it looks now as if the grant will come through, thanks probably to a command from Agnelli. But the Argentine kidnapping intruded, [3] as well as a political tempest surrounding the foundation head, who sounds like a rather sinister and disagreeable person—Miriam saw him while I was in Rome.

If the grant does come through, Miriam will have plenty to do. Nicola's publications and letters are in three languages, two of which she'll have to translate (with help) into Italian. There will be problems of selection and, with the letters, some benevolent censorship, since in his correspondence—at least with me—he was often frankly gossipy, sharp and very funny about some of the common friends. She has already started photocopying Nicola's reviews and essays, using the machine belonging to the Encyclopedia Britannica, Italian edition, where a young American we know works as editor. She is going to have her mother come over in May, perhaps permanently. The old lady lives on the upper West Side and is partly blind, being looked in on by a niece but doing her own work and being stubbornly independent. The consensus is that bringing her mother to Rome to live will be infinitely better than for Miriam to transfer to New York, under present conditions there. She will have to do one or the other, for, even before Nicola died, she was getting more and more anxious about her mother and had proposed bringing her to Rome then. I think her mother's refusal at that time may have been based on the fear of being in Nicola's way. Now that obstacle is gone. . . .

That is the gist of the Rome news. I stayed with Carmen, who is getting sadder and slightly stranger, thanks to Ernest ex-Meyerowitz, who is putting great pressure on her to move into an apartment with him. I fear she will cede and think it will be a mistake for both of them if she does since they've arrived at a *modus vivendi* which, though it may look bizarre, actually corresponds to the oddities of their relationship. Miriam agrees.

Strasbourg was nice. I'd never really seen it before. We went to the cathedral several times and to the museum and ate too much. The DuViviers came along, having been in Bâle first. We spent an hour in Colmar, visiting the museum again. As you know, the Schöngauer in the cathedral has been stolen, alas. [4] I am half-thinking of writing something about the figures of Ecclesia and Sinagoga (sp.?), which you see throughout that Rhenish country. There's a pair in Bamberg too, which we (Carmen and I) saw last June, and one—the first, I gather—in Rheims, which I don't remember. The idea seems to have been French. One guide says vaguely that it came from the "School" of Chartres, meaning, I assume, theologically, since there are no such figures in Chartres cathedral. Yet it strikes me as so *German* or, more precisely, northern. I don't mean as an anticipation of Hitler, though that thought is a typical Ernest idea and pronouncement. Of course there were a great many Jews— a big colony—along the Rhine in the Middle Ages. But there were a great many Jews in Venice. . . . Anyway, this might be a sort of opening into my long-dreamed-of plan about the Gothic. I find the Synagogue figure very poetic; she is almost always more beautiful in her melancholy than the Church, her sister. But as Peter Levi said, he was fond of hymns and carols that had Jews in them.

We went to Strasbourg, partly for me to see the cathedral and those figures, but partly to give Jim a brief change and respite [from problems with his ex-wife and eldest son]. [. . .]

I must stop and do a little cooking. Maria is in Provence with her husband for ten days. But before I go to the kitchen, I must tell you that I've read the *Esquire* article on the NYR[5] and I was proud of you. You are the only one who comes off well, and you are splendid. I loved your saying, as an explanation, that Bob is "broad-minded." How true, how simple, and none of those vulgar Peeping Toms would ever have thought of it. The writer sounds quite distasteful and I don't care for his "grandmotherly" vision of you, but still at hearing *you* I rejoiced.

All my love, my dear,

Mary

P.S. I did not cut off the end of my *Medina* but I changed it greatly. I did not like the sermonizing combined with a certain lack of traction in the arguments. It occurs to me that you were too kind to say this and instead suggested cutting. The surgical way. Instead, I applied band-aids and some verbal ointment.[6]

1. After mailing the Medina manuscript to *The New Yorker* in February, McCarthy checked into the American Hospital in Paris with a torn retina, which was treated by laser surgery.
2. Gaia Serviado (her professional name) was an Italian writer of whom Mary was very fond; she was married to a Scottish art dealer, William Mostyn-Owen.
3. On March 22, a Fiat executive was seized by leftist guerrillas in Buenos Aires. When the

Argentine government refused an appeal by Fiat (owned by Agnelli) and the Italian government to free imprisoned guerrillas and union leaders in exchange for the executive's release,
the man was shot.

4. This was the "Madonna of the Rosehedge," by the fifteenth-century German painter Martin Schöngauer. It was stolen from Colmar's Church of Saint Martin.

5. "Review of The New York Review of Books," by P. Nbile, Esquire, April 1972.

6. McCarthy blamed the army's failure to convict Captain Medina for his part in the My Lai
massacre on both the Nixon administration, for exonerating him, and the "counter-culture,"
for calling him a scapegoat. "Now any member of the armed forces in Indochina can, if he
so desires, slaughter a reasonable number of babies, confident that the public will acquit him,"
she argued in conclusion, "a) because they support the war and the Army or b) because they
don't." The Medina essay appeared in The New Yorker, June 10, 1972, was subsequently published by Harcourt Brace Jovanovich as Medina (1972), was reprinted in The Seventeenth Degree
(1974).

Chicago
May 15, 1972

Dearest Mary,

I just received your reminder—the beautiful card from Syracuse
[missing]—and am answering immediately precisely because there
is so much to do. I have a seminar this afternoon about Duns Scotus
and since I have high respect for the gentleman, I am properly
frightened. So, instead of preparing for class by just being afraid
(by far the best preparation) I sat down to the typewriter.

"What do we do now?" is the question most frequently asked, and
there is no answer. The reaction to the newest events[1] is by no
means as you read it in the newspapers. No one believes that the
reaction received in the White House is 4 to 1 for Nixon. But N. is
convinced that it really does not matter if you only say that it is
and no one can disprove it. You create the desired majority by pretending it exists. Just as you create the success of Vietnamization by
insisting that it is a big success.

I was pretty convinced from the beginning that no decisive reaction would come from either Moscow or Peking, and I believe that
both had been informed ahead of time and that Nixon [and] Kissinger [were] guaranteed a "mild" reaction. There is still a real possibility that the South Vietnamese will suffer a decisive defeat before
the end of the month, and the administration keeps telling the
American people that their own support is decisive; in other words,
if this should happen not the administration but the opposition will
be to blame. The trouble is that neither China nor Russia is interested in a victory of the North Vietnamese (as distinguished from
an infinite war in which America lets its resources go down the

drain); Russia pursues its old policy of killing all revolutions or liberation movements which are not directly dependent upon Moscow, and China seems also not over eager to have a kind of Tito-regime as their neighbor. Both enjoy the additional advantage of having America doing the dirty work for them (I am not so sure about Peking as I am about Moscow). The attraction and feeling of solidarity between the big powers *qua big powers* seem stronger than all political or ideological hostility.

The reaction here is not strong; there was a strike at the University but I think I was the only teacher not to cross the picket-line and my students—all of them of course against the government—did not care much so long as they could have their class. (We went to some private apartment.) All media and certainly the overwhelming majority are against the war, but the only reaction from the White House is to attack the press and the other media for reporting truthfully. We get a nice foretaste of what to expect if Nixon wins the election. In the same vein, the announcement of the Treasury Department that (I think) 80% of all tax returns prepared by accountants are "fraudulent"—announcing, I am afraid, harassment and persecution of the opposition in matters of taxes. You can imagine how unanimous the people here are on the war issue by noting that [presidential candidate George] Wallace has already come out for immediate peace. The only thing that could help would be if Congress would veto the money—and this is not likely to happen, though I really do not know why it is so unlikely. The second hope is that Nixon loses the election which also is not very likely though by no means impossible. God knows we could use somebody with a bit of "charisma"—although I hate that word.

I have a hope that you'll come in June—Bill said that this is a possibility. I very much long to see you and to speak with you. I am here for the Committee [on Social Thought] which is in very bad shape, but the students are quite good. I shall be back in New York on the 24th—go via Washington—and then stay there until July. You can stay with me—and this would be marvellous—except for a short week from June 4 to 11th. That is also the week when I have to go to Princeton (June 5th–6th) and Dartmouth (9th to 12th).

That is as far as I got yesterday when I learned that Wallace was shot and had to go to my class. And just now I read in the papers that Russia and America are preparing to go together, arm in arm, to Mars. The Wallace incident is of course pretty serious and changes the whole election picture.[2] He was a truly popular candidate and owed much of his success to the simple fact that he talked freely about things that are foremost in the mind of all but are not really talked about by other candidates—crime in the street, almost 100% black, in ever increasing proportions; the ruin of the public school system; the legitimate non-racist fear of low-income housing projects; and, though somewhat less urgent, inflation, taxes, etc. The question is of course, Who will get his votes? And I am afraid that the government will discover a "communist conspiracy," identify it with the opposition, and use this as a nice pretext for further undermining constitutional rights.

I suppose your Medina-piece has appeared—I have not seen it yet. It is almost impossible or rather time-consuming to get magazines here. The few news stands and book stores which sold magazines and papers in this neighbourhood have disappeared; there are no public means of transportation—you either walk for about 2 miles or grab a cab, not so easy either.

I think I wrote you my summer plans—you didn't write me yours. I shall come to Europe around July 15th, stay first in Zurich, go on August 1st to the Villa Serbelloni, Rockefeller Foundation, and on August 24th to Tegna until Sept. 18th, then go for a few days to Salzburg and home to New York. When and where do I see you? I may have to go also to Israel for a few days—family matters!

Nathalie, I suppose, reported our meeting. She seemed in high spirits and quite happy. I read with great pleasure "Vous les entendez?"[3] The Christian Gauss lectures were quite good—I hoped Bob [Silvers] would publish them—but the institution as such has lost much of its spirit and charm. I went together with Lizzy whom I have come to like very much. You know that Auden left—a sad affair and he himself in a queer and unshakable mood of "Nobody has been so lucky and happy as I," with an unbelievable complacency as façade, very difficult to get along with. Oh yes, and Eileen Geist: did she tell you that she tried in vain to get invited by me? I hope you will forgive me—I was busy and I really could not figure out what we possibly should be talking about. [. . .]

My dear, this is a long and *bad* letter. Don't get vindictive and write me nevertheless. Also, write me about the publication of Chiaramonte's [sic] essays. In New York—in connection with Nathalie—Paolo Milano suddenly appeared—looking very old and still completely the same. I had not seen him for ages. I also saw Dwight and was at a meeting of the PR people trying to imitate the Theatre of Ideas—complete failure. Also very sad. Well, I suppose it is simply getting old.

Excuse the bad typing—an unfamiliar typewriter!

Much much love—yours
Hannah

1. The United States had launched new bombing raids against Hanoi and mined Haiphong harbor.
2. Governor George C. Wallace of Alabama, a contender for the American Independent Party presidential nomination, was shot and partially paralyzed at a political rally and withdrew from the race.
3. Nathalie Sarraute's *Vous les entendez? [Do You Hear Them?]*, not a favorite of McCarthy's, became the occasion of a falling-out when Sarraute blamed her for an unfriendly review by someone else in *The New York Review of Books*.

141 rue de Rennes
Paris 6
May 17, 1972

Dear Hannah:

Forgive this hasty dictated letter. Melvin Hill of York University has been writing me about a conference on you and your work to be held in Toronto in the fall. I began by refusing. Something about his letter made a poor impression on me; it sounded as if he were planning an extremely academic get-together in which I wouldn't belong. But of course, instead of saying this, I told him that I did not expect to be in the United States during this period. So he now writes back and offers me my travel expenses, which was not the point.

I haven't yet answered his second letter and need your counsel. Is it something you would like to have me take part in and/or that I could somehow contribute to? I'm afraid I'm put off by the sort of memorial volume or Festschrift tone of his prospectus. I'm abysmal at writing that kind of essay. In fact I just can't. But if you think the conference might be open to an informal intervention or if my being there is important to you, of course I'll come.

By the way—did I tell you in my post card?—I'm arriving in

New York on the France, July 5th. I'm hoping you'll still be there and will now consult your schedule as you last gave it to me.

With love,
Mary

P. S. [. . .] Saw Klaus Piper [Arendt's German publisher] last night and we talked of you. I liked his wife.

x x x,
M.

[New York]
May 26, 1972

Dearest Mary,

I found your letter upon arrival from Washington; you should by now have received my letter from Chicago. I suppose you know that Bill was again in the hospital, is home again, I shall see him next week. Martha called; they seem both rather unhappy—naturally, he had been in very good form ever since Florida; no real heart attack but one of those very unpleasant reminders, and, what is rather worrying, without any provocation. This time, he really hadn't overdone anything.

Lottchen Kohler[1] just called—you remember? She had an operation of her knee last fall—and goes worse than she did before. She has come home from a visit to the surgeon who discovered a so-called "mouse" in the knee and wants to operate again! I wish I knew a first-rate physician who cares more about his patients than about his colleagues; I think I wish nothing more intensely and also furiously than that.

The Toronto-business:[2] Melvyn [sic] Hill is a former student of mine, very nice, quite intelligent, who had this brainstorm about which he wrote you. I have no idea how this will work out; I told him *not* to write you, *not* to write to Jovanovich, etc. —avec the succes qu'on connait. Bill was delighted and accepted and that, of course, encouraged him. I wonder whether you will not be tempted to take this as a pretext to come a bit to New York during the Winter. Expenses are being paid—he got a special grant for that. But under no circumstances should you write a paper; he also invited discussants. I thought for a moment that it may be fun—we go together, Bill, you and I. Sternberger[3] will probably also come. I

315

don't know much about it, told Hill that I am willing to come but not willing to lift a finger.

Klaus Piper—his wife is indeed very nice; he is so stingy that he can't walk straight.

Washington was rather interesting. Talked at length with [Marcus] Raskin and Richard Barnett [sic],[4] the latter a very intelligent guy who is just publishing an interesting book "The Roots of War" in which he tries to prove that war has become a permanent institution, that is, the kind of war we are waging in Vietnam. (Nuclear war seems indeed the most unlikely prospect.) This is quite possible. I also talked at length with Jack Blum who is one of those investigating senatorial assistants and busy with uncovering the housing scandals in the great urban centers. Most interesting the extent to which the banks with their mortgages are involved in the on-going deterioration, to the point where the security of the depositors' money is in jeopardy.

I wrote my time table. July 5th is fine with me! Am very much looking forward. A propos Washington: All those I talked with believe *now* that McGovern[5] has a real chance of winning the nomination and even the election!

Much love—
Hannah

1. Lotte Kohler became a friend of Arendt and her husband soon after her arrival in the United States from Germany in 1955. She and McCarthy were appointed co-executors in Arendt's will.
2. The Conference on the Work of Hannah Arendt, sponsored by the Toronto Society for the Study of Social and Political Thought at York University, was scheduled for October 1972. York professor Melvin Hill had studied under Arendt at the University of Chicago.
3. Arendt had known sociologist Dolf Sternberger in Frankfurt before the war.
4. Arendt had attended a political science conference, where she met Marcus Raskin and Richard Barnet, cofounders of the Institute for Policy Studies. Barnet's book was *Roots of War: The Men and Institutions Behind Foreign Policy* (1972).
5. South Dakota Senator George McGovern campaigned primarily on opposition to the war in Vietnam. He won the Democratic presidential nomination on the first ballot.

New York, N.Y.
June 21, 1972
[McCarthy's birthday]

60 WISHES EACH WITH LOVE YOUR PRESENT AWAITS YOU HERE

HANNAH

Villa Serbelloni
(Lago di Como)
August 22, 1972

Dearest Mary,

What great good luck that your card [missing] could overcome all the strange hazards of Italian mail and give me such a welcome whiff of Castine. Needless to say, many of my thoughts go back and forth to last year.[1] I had a good time in Zurich, including Basel (Frau Jaspers 94 years old and, alas, in good health apart from the senility: she receives me with a "we two who lost their men" and ten minutes later asks me "how is Heinrich?") and a very enjoyable visit in Freiburg. I then went for a week to Israel and had a good time with my family, saw Jerusalem again, always very impressive though not really beautiful.

This place is phantastic [sic] beyond expectation or imagination.[2] First of all: incredibly beautiful. A huge estate on a promontory which goes back to Roman times with a formal garden, also immense, and a villa which is like a castle. You feel as though you are suddenly lodged in a kind of Versailles. I am the proud temporary owner of a bedroom with large terrace on the lake and a studio, also with terrace into the garden. Now imagine this place filled, but by no means crowded, with a bunch of scholars, or rather professors, from all countries—France, Germany, Italy and the States, almost all of them rather mediocre (and this is putting it charitably) with their wives, some of them are plain nuts, others play the piano or type busily the non-masterworks of their husbands. The place has 53 servants, including the men who take care of the gardens and an abundance of flowers such as I never saw in my life. And then the olive trees, the cypresses, the cedars and palms together with centuries-old oaks, and every leaf-tree you ever saw, except, perhaps, birches. On top of the hill are ruins no one quite knows of what, and yesterday I discovered deep in a kind of grotto a little chapel which looked very old to me and which obviously is still used by the staff. This staff is presided over by a kind of head-waiter who dates from the time of the "principessa" and has face and manner of a great gentleman of fifteenth-century Florence. I forgot: beside my bed (and of course each bed of "residents" as distinguished from visitors who come for all kinds of Congresses) there are two bells, one for the chambermaid and the other for one of the innumerable footmen. I am happy to report we have three chefs in the kitchen and that the food as well as the cellar are excellent.

The director of the whole thing is a very nice and friendly American with a rather beautiful wife. We also had the visit of somebody high up in the Ford Foundation—competitors look each other over—; he as well as our own Dr. Olson took me aside and asked me if I *really* thought that this environment would serve to "inspire" people! (Roughly 4 weeks of inspiration for each.) The only "inspiration" I heard of is Saul Bellow who finished here Mr. Sammler's Planet.

This is all for today. Mary, write me a little if it is not too much bother. A bit [of] reasonable talk would do me lots of good. Morgenthau was here until day before yesterday, which was no great help, to tell the truth; I am here on good terms with everybody and enjoy a very civilized couple from Yale by the name of Lopez—he an Italian Jew (formerly Spanish, Marrano) and she, I think also Jewish, from Bruxelles.

I shall leave for Tegna day after tomorrow, a bit apprehensive because of Robert[3] in particular and too many "guests" in general. 'Too many' has its advantages; they will entertain each other. I have got to work, this much is sure. I am just on the point of finishing the first chapter—roughly 35 pages—and am already properly frightened when I think of the second chapter which, with some luck, I should be able to do there.[4]

You write about a "little work." What are you working on?

Many greetings to Jim. Remember me to everybody and especially to the French class.[5] Is Lizzy also there?

Much love
Hannah

1. Arendt had spent a month in Castine the previous summer.
2. The Villa Serbelloni is a Rockefeller Foundation retreat for scholars, writers, and artists.
3. Heinrich Blücher's friend, the German poet and songwriter Robert Gilbert, was a frequent visitor from nearby Locarno.
4. This was probably an early draft of *The Life of the Mind.*
5. McCarthy presided over an informal *cercle français* in Castine that read French classics.

Castine, Maine
Sept. 3, 1972

Dearest Hannah:

I was *so* pleased to have your letter and am hurrying to write so that the mail won't leave this morning at twelve without an answer from me. Monday is Labor Day, and there won't be a mail out of Castine between Saturday morning and Tuesday night—imagine. We've been cut down this year to one arrival and one departure per day exclusive of holidays and Sundays.

You sound lonesome; hence my haste. Your letter, by the way, took a week to get here, and I hope this will still catch you at Tegna. Here, as my postcard indicated, I have virtually sunk under the cargo of guests. Reuel and family were here for a week (a nice visit this time, much more relaxed on all sides), and the day they left Kevin and his two girls arrived for four days. The Sunday of *their* visit we had our annual lawn party (really on the lawn this year; the weather has been glorious): 42 people *seated*. Kevin and Jim moved practically every piece of furniture but the beds out onto the lawn. . . .

This week Jim has been in Washington and Alabama,[1] and I have been recuperating. I have only one little bit of writing to finish: an introduction to a catalogue for a Polish painter friend's[2] exhibition this fall in New York. Alabama. Incredible. He won his case *in toto*, except for one item: the court ordered him to pay Jonny's school costs this year in New York, which he was planning to do anyway. All her other demands were struck down, disallowed. Jim said (on the telephone) he felt sorry for her after it was all over: she looked awful, he said, tense and staring, and he was moved to give her and Jonny, whom she had crazily brought with her, a ride to Birmingham in his Hertz car—during which she passed out in the back seat. Then they went, all three, by plane together as far as Atlanta, where he gave them each a donation of money, and they separated. He says there's no question of her reopening the case; apparently she and her lawyer concurred in the decision. All this seems bizarre to me, considering the money spent on lawyers and travel there and her wild determination to inculpate him. But I shall learn the details when he gets back tonight. (Yesterday, when I didn't hear from him all day—he was supposed to call in the morning from Washington about his travel plans—I began to feel an eerie dread that she had murdered him in the Hertz car on some deserted Alabama back-country road!)

As you can imagine, this is the main news item. Otherwise nothing much is happening except anguished conversations about

McGovern. About two days ago, struggling with my civic conscience, I reached the point of deciding that I *couldn't* vote for him, out of sheer self-respect. This was after the Wall Street performance.[3] But then what? How to cast a protest vote? Dr. Spock is too much of a joke.[4] I'd rather vote for the Black Panther party if they were running a candidate, which I don't believe they are. Young Harriet Lowell says she'd vote for Gus Hall, the Communist candidate, while Lizzie (yes, she's here) looks excruciated and emits those whimpering sounds. The fact is there is *nobody* to vote for, even as a gesture; that tells the national story. And many people are saying this, particularly the young, though still not in public, so far as I know. I talked to William Phillips yesterday, and he confided "I've been saying I'd vote for a *dog* against Nixon, but now . . . I don't know." Then this morning I woke up early with new vacillations: maybe McGovern despite everything? As a half-joke to myself, I've been mentally saying "Should I send a telegram to Pham Van Dong, perhaps, and ask him what *he'd* like me to do?"[5] Of course this country is prone to waves of hysteria which are contagious: maybe nobody can be as much of a catastrophe as McGovern now seems to be to his adherents of less than two months ago. You and I never liked him much anyway, but that may be a good reason for keeping our heads now. . . .

I'm glad your first chapter got done and wish you much luck with the next at Tegna. It may even go better there. I've noticed that "ideal work circumstances" furnished by foundations such as the Villa Serbelloni are often a hindrance to serious application. Probably because of the unreality. My own "little work" was just that: a 9000 word review of the new Solzhenitsyn book.[6] Otherwise nothing. Nor do I have any plans for work. [. . .] *Are* you coming home via Paris? I do very much hope so. Meanwhile my mind is void of ideas and I say to myself that perhaps I won't write any more— what's the use? This must be partly the effect of depressing reviews of *Medina*. There's a limit to how much one can take of that. Especially if one feels, as I do, that the act of writing has something to do with communication.

Please give my warm greetings to Robert [Gilbert] and to the lady who runs Casa Barbati [sic] and whose name momentarily escapes me—Enid? No. Edith? No. But one of those, I think. And remember me to the place. I did love so much those days there [in 1970] with the cherry tree and the glow worms and I associate that spot particularly with Heinrich. How good that you both had found it.

Much, much love,
Mary

[. . .]

1. Margaret West had filed suit for increased child support and alimony in the Alabama court where she and James West got their divorce.
2. Probably Joseph Czapski.
3. Speaking on Wall Street in August 1972, Senator McGovern withdrew his earlier commitment to substantial defense cuts and an immediate withdrawal from Vietnam.
4. Benjamin Spock was the candidate of the People's Party.
5. McCarthy continued to exchange holiday greetings with North Vietnamese Prime Minister Pham Van Dong long after her 1968 trip to Hanoi.
6. Mary McCarthy, "The Tolstoy Connection," a review of Solzhenitsyn's *August 1914*, appeared in *Saturday Review* on September 16, 1972; it is reprinted in her *Occasional Prose* (1985).

141 rue de Rennes
Paris
October 20, 1972

Dearest Hannah:

Probably Annchen will send you the enclosed paeans,[1] but we can sometimes use two copies. The horrible and pious interview with Saul [Bellow] was in the same number. The other is part of my magpie hoard: I clipped it last week. J. P. Faye is or was one of the *Tel Quel* group—rather nice personally. If you think his book might interest you, I'll send it.

Jim and I were both very much pleased to see you spread out all over the Monde so reverently—yes, for the French it's sheer reverence. The drawing, though, makes you look quite French yourself and rather as if you were in the *haute couture*.

[Pierre] Vidal-Nacquet, among other things, is a Greek scholar, a great friend of a friend of ours. His position on Israel is somewhere near yours though slightly perhaps to the left of you (his Frenchness). I don't know what his reservations about the Dreyfus treatment in your book are but out of curiosity may try to find out, if I could do so easily.

Bob S. sent me the ad for Nixon taken out by [Sidney] Hook, [Oscar] Handlin, [Irving] Kristol, etc. I missed Podhoretz's name. And Saul's.

I am going to break down and vote for McGovern after all. My latest daydream was to write in Sen. [J. William] Fulbright, but I don't know his place of domicile, and you need that for a write-in.

We have the painter in the house (at present in the kitchen), and I am still not well.[2] Back on bismuth and other pills. It's a bore but I'm in circulation at least.

Much love to you,
Mary

P.S. Did you get some birthday flowers a week ago?

1. These were probably reviews of the French edition of Arendt's *Crises of the Republic* (1972), whose third essay, "On Violence," contains an interpretation of the Dreyfus affair that may have prompted the "reservations" McCarthy mentions later.
2. This may be a veiled reference to McCarthy's first bout with breast cancer; as is Arendt's question in the next letter about whether McCarthy, who received radiation treatments in Paris, "was now 'cured.' "

[New York]
October 22, 1972

Dearest Mary:

Last Sunday just when I lifted the receiver to call you my telephone went dead and was only repaired two days later—a record of rapidity as I was told. Today I have been trying since morning, but you were not home. So, much to my regret I have got to write. I wanted so much to hear you à vive voix.

Jim's and your flowers were absolutely beautiful, a fall assortment of dahlias and carnations in all the right colors. They lasted a full week. Since when do you know my birthday? Last year I went to Washington for the day and this year too, I was not in the mood of seeing people and had a good dinner and a very nice evening with the Jonases, Hans and I reminiscing about a nearly fifty-year-old friendship. It was important for me because I am more and more isolated by the necessity to work—nothing is more hateful than a deadline and the sudden panic which is likely to overcome me whenever I try just to live a bit. Also, and much more decisively, this awful and justified bleakness all around me. Things get worse from day to day; crime in the street [has] reached alarming proportions; people don't dare to come home by bus in the late evening hours because the Bus station is entirely unsafe, etc. etc. And then being told every morning that everything is fine and that the administration has succeeded in fighting crime in the street—quite apart from all the other things it has succeeded in, i.e. claims to—and hardly anybody who even raises an eye brow. I spent an evening with Bob Silvers, the Epsteins [Jason and Barbara] and Lizzy and got into trouble about the drug problem—which actually is no problem any more but a clear disaster. They took the "liberal" position and [. . .] did not see what possibly could be wrong with getting stoned except that these poor people had not enough money for their "habit," hence had to kill us. (I exaggerate of course.) Lizzy was in great good spirits; I think she now is positively glad to be rid of Cal. Whom, incidentally, I also saw, including Caroline. She made a much better impression than when I saw her, pregnant, in England; he struck me as quieter but also vaguer than usual. He was here for his divorce and eager to tell every detail about it, especially the money business. If he told the truth, Lizzy is very well off indeed. I also saw Auden before he left for England. For the first time he looks not only unhappy and neglected but sick. I hope it was only exhaustion from packing and leaving, but I doubt it. He looks as though something serious has happened to him, God knows what.

I wanted to call you also to know if you are now "cured" as your doctor had promised, and especially to talk—even if only for a few minutes—about your review of Solzhenitsin [sic]. The review is simply brilliant, especially your point about Tolstoy entirely right and so "clever." I think I am more bothered by the corniness which you mention en passant, and also about this Panslavistic [sic] chauvinism together with bigotry—Russia again, because of her suffering, the Christophorus among the nations.[1] I don't know how acquainted you are with Panslavist literature; this sounds to me like a phantastic da capo,[2] but on a much lower level. For instance, the dialogues between the Koljas [characters in *August 1914*] and the right-thinking sons of Mother Russia. God knows, Dostoevsky was on a different level though of pretty much the same persuasion with respect to these matters. I had the impression that this book, as distinguished from his earlier work, was written to prove a thesis; the military matters were probably adequately researched, though I am not sure, simply do not know, but the result is research and not the transformation into a story. On the other hand, I am pretty sure that this book and this position—Greek orthodoxy, anti-Western, anti-Peter the Great, and furiously chauvinistic (the only missing element from

19th century Panslavism is antisemitism)—are closer to the present mentality of Russians than almost anything else. And this after 50 years of revolution, fifty years like one day: Holy Russia on one side, drunkenness, corruption of the bureaucracy, and an ubiquitous incompetence on the other. Between them, again the narodniki and their insane belief in the "people"; and above them an extremely thin layer of first-rate mathematicians and scientists. No matter what happened, an unchanged and to me highly unpleasant national character. After reading your review, I tried to change my impression; but I can't help it. And you know of course that I read the book with the greatest expectations and all prejudices in its favor.

Now, come and we shall talk and see what happens. Here, all reviews were of course very laudatory, except yours. Also Rahv's though he seemed to have a few misgivings.

This is a chatty letter, too long.

Much love and yours,
Hannah

1. Christophorus, or St. Christopher, a legendary Christian martyr and a patron saint of travelers, is depicted in German and Dutch painting carrying the Christ child on his broad shoulders.
2. A fantastic repetition of Panslavic chauvinism.

141 rue de Rennes
Paris
January 15, 1973

Dearest Hannah:

This can't be a long letter, but I can't let more days pass without sending you my New Year's love. Nobody dares say Happy New Year on this one. Except the French. They offer *"meilleurs voeux"* without a second thought. Anyway, my *deep* affection and hopes for the book and the Gifford lectures.[1]

We weren't far from Scotland, though far from Aberdeen, on New Year's Eve, up near the Roman Wall, and walking briefly on the moors, I thought with envy of you in the spring. I have a strong love for the northern parts of the British Isles, so much so that it seems like an atavism, though so far as I know none of my primitive ancestors came from there. Again we had quite beautiful weather, warm and sunny on the whole (only one day of rain), and again roses were blooming in the dooryards of the stone cottages. It is all stone walls and sheep and brooks and occasional herds of cattle. At Durham, you're on the edge of the mining country and the invention of the railroad locomotive. Train country, with a nineteenth-century and early socialist flavor—moving to me. The people up there are more democratic than in the south of England, and we spent New Year's Eve in a pub called the Highlander Inn (not far from Newcastle of "coals to"), kissing and being kissed by locals of all ages and quite a few conditions, who were wishing everybody "All the best" in Northumbrian accents.

It would have been an ideal vacation if it hadn't been for the bombing,[2] even though up there it seemed farther away both in time and in space. Well, I won't write about that, because there is nothing to say that's suitable for words. Will he do it again? Maybe not or not soon. It looks as if some mournful concessions had been extorted from the North Vietnamese. I went to see them the other day at their delegation, and they were very sad and quiet. And so gentle. They commiserated with *me*. But they were also incredulous that there'd been so little reaction in the U.S. They could hardly take it in and asked me for an explanation. What can you tell them? They still wish to believe that *"le peuple américain, c'est un grand peuple."* I said that I was afraid that the American people had changed and felt cruel when I said it.

We've had some domestic woes. Maria's husband has been very sick; his gall bladder burst, and he was operated on. Successfully, but he seems to have nearly died. This happened during our absence. He's still in the hospital, of course, and she'll go on leave when he comes out, to look after him. She herself was very ill with flu, just before that happened, and afterwards had a relapse. Now she is well again, and he is rapidly getting better. But it's an ugly memory for her, and I feel somehow conscience-stricken about not having been here, though there was no way I could have guessed what was in store when we left. I ought to have telephoned sooner, but I didn't expect to be able to reach her, thinking she would be either in bed, convalescing, or out with him. When I did finally telephone, a day or so after Christmas, I got the house-painter, who told me only part of the story.

On the positive side, Jim's older boy, Danny (the one who's been in the mental hospital), suddenly and surprisingly, decided to come back to France with us. He stayed four nights and made his father extremely happy. He is a little shaky still—Danny—but much better and very open now in his conversation. I like him. He has gone back to London, with the idea of working as a chef's apprentice in order to learn to be a professional cook. It sounds odd, but a lot of young people from "good" families are doing it. Anyway, I hope it won't be too Orwellian behind the scenes.

Now I must rush out and get this in the evening mail. Jim sends you love too and talks about you and your book (yes) a lot.

Did you ever get a plant I ordered sent to you and was it all right? I kiss you, dear Hannah, and will write soon again.

Yours,
Mary

P. S. My German teacher is very much interested in what you think about practically everything.

1. Arendt had been asked to deliver the prestigious Gifford Lectures at Scotland's Aberdeen University beginning in April 1973. For her initial lecture she chose Thinking, the subject of the first volume of *The Life of the Mind*.
2. President Nixon had ordered massive B-52 raids against North Vietnam for December 15–30. The event left McCarthy more shaken than her letter suggests; she had briefly contemplated returning to Hanoi with a delegation of notables (Stephen Spender, Ramsay Clark, among others) who would, in effect, become hostages to U.S. bombs. It was an idea that met with little favor at the North Vietnamese Embassy in Paris when McCarthy presented it in December 1972.

Paris
Jan. 29, 1973
[Postcard]

Dearest Hannah: It was splendid to hear your voice. [. . .] And shall write you a real letter as soon as I enter my secluded state—Jim leaves tomorrow. I'm pleased too that you liked the Halberstam.[1] I was afraid that you wouldn't (or hadn't). And your voice sounded quite fond of "Thinking," indulgent, as if it were a newborn babe. I've started my Gothic book but can't feel as yet any tender emotions toward it.

Much love, Mary

P. S. My American panel is March 7–9.[2]

1. Mary McCarthy, "Sons of the Morning," an acerbic review of David Halberstam's *The Best and the Brightest*, published in *The New York Review of Books*, January 25, 1973; it is reprinted in *The Seventeenth Degree*.
2. McCarthy had been invited to speak at Washington and Lee University, in Lexington, Virginia.

New York
February 6, 1973

Dearest Mary:

Thanks for the letter, thanks for the card. How is your seclusion? What are you doing? How about the Chiaramonte [sic] biography? I think I forgot to tell you that I saw Dwight in an alarmingly bad physical and mental state of health. It was quite obvious for everybody but he as well as Gloria seemed quite unconcerned. Harold [Rosenberg] comes tonight. He is mentally quite unchanged, in very good form even, and quite admirable in his way of coping with his very bad arthritis.

I am writing because I want to explain about Martha [Jovanovich]. (Just tried to reach Bill to have the latest news. Could not get him, he is in a meeting, constantly expanding his empire.) Martha after a first very serious "relapse" after the operation—I told you that over the phone—recovered and was given radiation treatment. After a few treatments she relapsed again, not so serious, high temperature with nobody knowing the cause. The treatment was ceased; the temperature is down, but she is so weak that she could not even make it to the bathroom. What alarmed us (Helen [Wolff][1] and myself) was not only that none of the physicians could come up with a diagnosis (it could not be post-operational and apparently also not the consequence of radiation), but that they all said that she should go home and come back for treatment when she has recovered. God knows what that means, but you may know that this could signify that they have given up. This sending the patient home is almost routine in terminal cancer cases. What we are afraid of is of course the possibility of metastases, which would make the radiation treatment useless.

I also forgot to ask you if you can stay with me in March. I'd be very happy if you could.

The weather here today is nice and spring-like. I just sent you a few spring-flowers to greet the sun properly. We had here a huge welcome party to New York for Eugene Macarthy [sic]—kind of nice to watch all of New York but politically speaking I think rather a farewell party. He has been hired by the New School and I am going to see him at a small dinner party tomorrow. Kevin [McCarthy] was at the huge party and seemed in high spirits. Lizzy was very cheerful. [. . .] I also saw Bob Silvers who told me of the great success of your Halberstam review. The atmosphere here is rather scary with Number One [Nixon] in a very ugly mood. The reason why he finally did go back to negotiations is certainly the very strong opposition to the bombing policy plus the very high rate of losses. But no one, except Jonathan Schell in the New Yorker, points that out; so that Nixon can pretend that his policy worked and claim a big victory over his critics. Everyone is buying this imagery. Congress gave Kissinger a standing ovation!

This is about all. I better go back to work. I am a bit in trouble. The Gifford people demand a "syllabus" and sent me a few of their former lectures. I decided that a) I cannot do this, that b) I don't want to do it, that c) I thought this kind of summary simply nonsense. But I intended anyhow to write an introduction and now promised this instead of the summary. I wanted to write this as [the] last piece, but must do it now in a hurry. Hence—back to work.

Much, much love
Hannah

1. Helen and Kurt Wolff, noted German publishers before the war, started Pantheon Books in New York in the mid-1940s. Differences with investors later led them to retire to Locarno, Switzerland, but in 1960 they were persuaded by William Jovanovich to join Harcourt, Brace as co-publishers. After her husband's death in 1963, Helen Wolff, who died on March 28, 1994, continued the imprint.

141 rue de Rennes, Paris
February 10, 1973

Dearest Hannah:

Your letter this morning and two or three days ago those lovely flowers! Yes, a real greeting. And I was feeling a little wistful, in the empty apartment, with Jim and Maria gone and very gloomy weather. Thank you.

And thanks for telling me about Martha. As you know, I'm very ignorant about medicine. I had to look up metastases in the dictionary just now. It is certainly odd and disquieting. Yet if they sent her home, as a terminal case, surely they would have told Bill at least. Or have they and is he saying nothing? I wrote him right after you telephoned and I asked him to tell me how Martha was (not making this, though, the reason for my writing), but so far I've had no reply. I can well imagine his telling nobody.

I do hope you and Jonathan Schell are right about why Nixon went back to negotiations. That is what I thought and still want to think. But the North Vietnamese—did I tell you about my long talk with them?—were so extremely bitter about the lack of U.S. domestic reaction to the bombing that I understood them to be saying that *they* had been forced back to the table, not so much by the bombing itself as by the recognition that it was being accepted and would continue to be almost without protest by the American people. I said that there was going to be a demonstration on Inauguration Day. *"Mais c'est trop tard! C'est trop tard!"* their second man, Vy, cried in a voice like a wailing siren. I agreed. I don't see any other way to construe that exclamation than as meaning that they might have held out longer if they had only had help from us. They were betrayed, of course, all around, by the Russians, the Chinese, and finally by the U.S. anti-war movement, which did nothing or the next thing to it. Or so it appeared from here. I said people had sent so many telegrams to their senators, signed so many statements, marched and demonstrated so many times that they were tired, *"usés,"* and anyway nobody listened to them any more. He concurred. A sad talk, during which he would press my hand from time to time in sympathy. But perhaps I've written you all this.

Good luck, my dear, with your Gifford introduction. I am working like a snail on my Gothic book.

I'd love to stay with you when I come to New York. But I remember your saying something on the telephone about having to be somewhere on the 12th (?). My schedule is to arrive in New York Friday evening, the 9th, from Roanoke, Virginia, and leave either the 13th or the 14th for [a speaking engagement in] North Dakota. The Washington and Lee organizers (Lexington, Va.) are going to send me time-tables; apparently I shall be driven to Roanoke. Can you tell me your plans again? If you have to leave Sunday night, maybe I'd better stay at Kevin's, if he's there. Or stay two nights with you and then go to Kevin's or to a hotel? In any case, we'll have time to see each other and talk a lot.

All my love, dear Hannah, and à bientôt,
Mary

[New York]
February 16, 1973

Mary, my dear, there must have been a misunderstanding over the phone. I shall be in New York in March and the 9th is fine. Let me know in time when and where you arrive. And perhaps also if you want me to invite people. I thought you might like to meet Jonathan Schell and a few of the younger people—I half promised him an evening and they would of course be delighted to see you. We could also have Kevin and perhaps this nice daughter of his.

Martha: I have not heard from Bill. I called him and asked to tell him to call me back. This is the first time that he did not and I am kind of afraid to call again. Anyhow, Martha is back home but *after* they finished the treatment. This is encouraging. Perhaps they really do not know why she had these so-called "relapses." When I last spoke to him he told me that *he* had again some trouble and had to stay at home for a while. He is back in the office, but not on regular schedule.

The North Vietnamese: I am convinced that Nixon stopped the bombing under pressure; the trouble is only that no one says so openly (the lonely exception is Schell). There were some hidden news stories in the Times about the amount of protest wires, not to the President (this remains a well-guarded secret) but to Congressmen and Senators. Their mail ran very heavily in favor of immediate end of the war. I am no longer sure of the percentages. What does fail us now, apart from general weariness and despair, is the Democratic Party which does not capitalize on all this, does not crystallize the various issues and explain them, and also the press which is intimidated. Meanwhile we have the currency crisis, more serious than two years ago, and I am afraid that Congress will fight the money to reconstruct North Vietnam; and in the sad story of betrayals, this would be the last straw—it seems to me that this promise of 2½ billion, more than anything else, got them back to negotiations. Congress, incidentally, gave Kissinger a standing ovation!

You don't write what you are reading and lecturing about. Also: How was the talk with Auden? (Don't take the trouble of answering these questions. We shall have time here.) Today is the first day this curious winter when we have snow. Nice for a change.

This is all for today. I must go back to work—finish in a hurry the introduction to the lectures which they want ahead of time and I am late already. Also domestic difficulties. My Sallie had to leave because her brother died, and I have a dinner party here tonight— apartment to straighten up etc. She'll be back next week.

I hope Jim got rid of his poison ivy. Such a nuisance.

A bientôt—almost à toute à l'heure!

As ever,

Hannah

Paris
March 20, 1973

Dearest Hannah: The Stafford is putting you on the waiting list for April 18 and booking you definitely for the 19th and 20th—three nights—isn't that right?[1] I feel confident they'll manage a room for you on the 18th and have written them a letter confirming the reservation and telling them *who* you are. And I shall keep in touch with them. So so many thanks my dear. It made me very happy to be with you. Have just spent a day in bed recovering from my cold. All love, Mary

1. Arendt was stopping in London before delivering the first of the Gifford Lectures in Aberdeen.

141 rue de Rennes
Paris 75006
March 29, 1973

Dearest Hannah:

See enclosed.[1] So that is all right. Meanwhile Bill has called up (last night) and thrown me into a certain amount of confusion about dates. I had no idea that you finished at Aberdeen so soon. I thought you were there for six weeks. So this morning I've been trying to work out a schedule. My own dates have changed slightly since I was in New York. This is because Syracuse wants to give me an honorary degree on May 12. (Colby College, in Maine, is offering one in June.) I feel I must accept Syracuse because [poet] Philip Booth, our Castine neighbor who teaches there, has arranged it and is full of pride and pleasure in having done so. This led me to try to change my Berkeley lecture from April 23 to May 2; to my surprise there was no problem. Therefore I go to Minnesota first—April 26—for a lecture and overnight stay, then probably to visit the Dupees in Carmel, California, then Berkeley, then ten idle days before Syracuse. I can use them to get some dentistry done and some research in the library on my Gothic book. All that time you'll be lecturing in Aberdeen.

Study of the calendar, though, reveals a nice possibility. April 22 is Easter. Easter Monday, April 23, is a French holiday. Good Friday, April 20, is a French semi-holiday. All this means that Jim, if he's in France and not in Japan, may be able to fly with me to Scotland during Easter weekend. We could hear your first lecture, which my memory says is Monday the 23rd, after which he could return to Paris and I could fly the morning of the 25th to New York and spend the night and go to Minnesota the following morning. That would give you and me the day of the 24th to ourselves. (This assumes there'd be an Edinburgh–New York flight Wednesday morning, and that I could somehow get to Edinburgh from Aberdeen in time for it. Perhaps I'd have to spend the night of the 24th in Edinburgh. I must check air schedules.) If your first lecture, though, is NOT the 23rd, but the 24th, will you please quickly send me a cable (just "WESTWARD PARIS")? It should still be possible but more ticklish.

That is half the program. The other half would be to hear your last lecture, which, as I understand it, is Monday the 14th of May. Here again I must do some detective work on air schedules, but if I am able to leave Syracuse some time Sunday the 13th and get good connections in New York for London and in London for Edinburgh and in Edinburgh for Aberdeen, I can make it, though the time difference here works against me. If I'm a bit tired, it doesn't matter, because afterwards I can go home and collapse. I find it a very appealing thought to be present at the beginning and the end of your series; it has form.

No more time for letter-writing this morning. I am behind in everything, having developed a really awful bronchitis on my return [from the U.S.], as well as one blocked-up ear. Jim and Maria both consigned me to bed for two days, with a heavy anti-histamin [sic] supplied by Jim. This morning I've arisen, better but not totally freed of this wearisome congestion. At least today my mind is clear, since I stopped the anti-histamin last night.

Perhaps we should turn Norman Mailer loose on the common cold instead of on cancer.[2] I am convinced that these interminable colds, with affection of all your passages and conduits, are caused by modern technology. Not just air pollution, though that's part of it, but also probably the various vaccines and anti-biotics, which admittedly lead to the development of more ferocious viruses.

Has Bill talked to you about his idea of a magazine? If so, please tell me what you think is at the bottom of this. A tax loss? Prestige? A new kind of power? It can't be just a rehabilitation project for me once Jim's job terminates in Paris. I find all this rather alarming. Who needs a magazine at this point? And what *kind* of magazine is he really thinking of? I told him I didn't see how a literary magazine could compete with the *New York Review*. Nor really why one should. As for a general magazine, we already have the *New Yorker*, the *New Republic*, the *Atlantic*, etc. And I wouldn't trust Bill anywhere near the helm of a political organ.

My serious opinion is that the U.S. is badly under-informed outside New York and Washington both by newspapers and by TV. What's wanted are better newspapers, both in smaller cities and in towns and even villages (weeklies). But not another magazine, and above all not the kind that would reach an audience of intellectuals or consumers of intellectual fashions. Yet I can't picture a grass-roots magazine, though I can easily picture dozens of grass-roots newspapers, with emphasis, of course, on *local* matters. The point, obviously, is that a magazine can't be regional—all that have tried it have failed—and that we have enough national magazines (I think) right now. Bill may be thinking of something to take the place of the collapsing *Saturday Review*, but I doubt that the *Saturday Review* has a place any more. The kind of people who used to swear by it are dead or dying.

Now I must absolutely stop.

Much love, and, again, thanks,
Mary

1. Probably confirmation of Arendt's London hotel reservation.
2. For Norman Mailer in these years, cancer was a metaphor if not an actual manifestation of the modern malaise.

[Paris]
April 3, 1973
[Postcard]

Dearest Hannah: Pursuant to my letter: we leave Paris for Aberdeen Good Friday (April 20), arriving that night. I can get a plane from Aberdeen early Wednesday, the 25th, and reach New York that afternoon. Next day to Minnesota. Coming back, I think I can be there Monday, May 14. We'll book a hotel room from here by telephone; it will probably be crowded over Easter, but with the help of guide books we'll find something. And don't worry about us as encumbrances in your first days in Aberdeen; we are resourceful and will wear cloaks (plaid) of invisibility. Much love,
Mary

Dearest Mary—

Many, many thanks! I just confirmed your reservation for me at the Stafford and am rather relieved that I can have the room for the 18th. It means that I can take a day-flight.

I am looking forward to Easter. Connections with Aberdeen seem to be very good—6 flights per day. I am taking the 10:30 flight (BEA) [. . .] from London and shall arrive in Aberdeen around 12:30. Flights London–Aberdeen are not via Edinburgh but non-stop. Hence, no problems. With Good Friday you can perhaps come Friday to London and we can then fly together Saturday morning to Aberdeen. How about that? I cannot arrive in Aberdeen before the 21st because they could not find a hotel room for me in the Caledonian Hotel where I am supposed to stay.

As for the May plans: My last lecture is indeed the 14th of May (and the first the 23rd of April). That you come to the first and the last lecture impresses me very much—it does have "style"—except that they are probably the weakest of the lot. Tant pis. From your letter it looks as though you have nothing special after the May trip to Aberdeen. Perhaps you could stay a few days longer and we could go [sic] a bit sight-seeing. How about that? My schedule there is so tight—only weekends free—that I shall hardly have much chance before. Also, it would be fun only if we can do it together.

Congratulations [re] the honorary degrees. It is the least exhausting of all academic enterprises. They don't expect anything from you—just to be there. Give my best to Philip Booth. He sent me his poems and I did not answer as usually. I like some of the poems but don't remember now and have no time to look them up.

The magazine business: Bill told me of his plans. What he has in mind is a kind of Times Literary Supplement which indeed, if it could be done, would be worth while doing. "At the bottom of all this," however, is something else—to have you near him, I think, most of all. About the other motives we shall talk. He is physically in very good shape, but very restless, basically, I fear, bored by just publishing, interested not in books but in empire-building, depressed by Martha's sickness and his impotence to do something about it. But let us wait until we can talk.

334

Give my love to Jim and let me know where and when we meet. Try to get reservations in the Caledonian Hotel. [. . .]

Much love,
yours,
Hannah

Part Six

May 1973 – *November* 1975

[The Watergate revelations broke in April 1973, giving Mary McCarthy a subject whose primary elements—the break-in, the coverup, the free-floating paranoia of the Nixon administration, the confrontation the following year with Senator Sam J. Ervin, Jr., and his Select Committee—couldn't help but excite her. By June 1973, with the Senate hearings underway in the old marble-pillared Caucus Room, she had arrived in Washington and was covering them for *The Observer.* In expanded form, and augmented by stories written for *The New York Review of Books,* McCarthy's Watergate portraits are collected in *The Mask of State* (1974).

Hannah Arendt, too, was caught up in the spectacle of an administration caught red-handed in the act of spying and lying; though for her the unfolding scandals carried a more ominous portent: ". . . where all are guilty no one is," she observed; noting that if Nixon escaped punishment (which he did), it was not from innocence but because of the gravity of his crime. "Since Nixon actually behaved like a tyrant his downfall would be a kind of revolution," whose consequences, Arendt perceived, were too unpredictable for a loyal opposition to risk.]

141 rue de Rennes
Paris
May 27, 1973

Dearest Hannah:

[. . .] I hope Rhodes is nice.[1] How remote it must seem from

Watergate. I am a bit numb with that. There's a limit to what I can absorb of newsprint on the subject. But Nixon's recent 4000 word statement is perhaps the most revealing thing about the whole business. His appeal to "national security" is being taken by some commentators as a mere pitiful rallying cry; I think, though, that it expresses his true political aim—a police state, with rival security networks spying not only on citizens but on each other. When I read it, I immediately thought of *The Origins of T[otalitarianism]*. In this connection, the reactions of the CIA and the FBI are particularly interesting.

About my departure for Washington, I'm very much up in the air. I had thought of going June 11, but now it looks as if the "big" figures may be heard by the Committee earlier, so as to quicken interest in the proceedings, which seems to be waning. I've asked *The Observer* to query Washington about the likelihood of a revised schedule.

It's very hot here suddenly and quite pleasant. Bill went back to New York with a stomach upset and hospitalized himself but is now out again. I have this from one of Weidenfeld's associates whom he has hired away—just now—to run another part of the empire in New York, something parallel to Helen and Kurt Wolff books.

I must stop and put on a hen for Jim's dinner. He has been in London this weekend seeing Danny and will be back tonight. I think so often of our Highland stay, of the birds and sheep and am full of affection and thanks. By the way, I came across a quotation from Keats, where he talks of "our wide plains speckled with countless fleeces."

Carmen is here, still very much affected by her father's death. It looks as if she'll now decide to marry Ernest again. We've had slightly mournful, gentle meetings.

Please greet Morgenthau
And all my love, Mary

1. Arendt was planning a two-week trip to the island of Rhodes with former University of Chicago colleague Hans Morgenthau.

141 rue de Rennes
Paris
June 6, 1973

Dearest Hannah:

[. . .] By the time you get this, I shall be gone. I arrive in

Washington, via London, Monday the 11th, and shall be staying at the Watergate (hotel). For nearly three weeks. I've agreed to do three successive pieces for the *Observer*, the first to appear the 17th. Dean[1] is expected to be heard the 12th by the Ervin committee. I am quite excited by the prospect.

And yet I hate to leave Paris, Jim, and our apartment and have just finished pouring ten watering cans full of water on the plants on the front balcony and three on the back window-boxes. At least I hope to be back here by the first of July. Then I'll turn around and leave for Castine probably the 14th. Jim is up to his neck in the annual Ministerial meeting (25 Ministers of Finance from 25 countries). He did not come home for dinner tonight and fears he may have to work tomorrow night till five in the morning helping draft the concluding statement. The uncertain gold-and-dollar situation lends much tension to the occasion. At the same time we're trying to finish our income tax return before my departure. (A friend who's been in America tells me that Watergate has made everybody especially honest—or timorous—this year about their tax returns.)

Otherwise all is quiet here. Cal's new books of poetry (three)[2] have arrived, and I wonder what you'll think of them. Only one (*The Dolphin*) is really new, and it is full of pain or wretchedness, as well as being, at least to me, the most obscure of all his works.

I must go to bed. As you can see from this ragged typing, I am tired. It's eleven o'clock, and Jim still isn't back from the office.

> Much love, my dear,
> Mary

[. . .]

1. John Dean, who had been legal counsel to the President and was privy to the coverup, was the first White House staff member to break ranks and testify against Nixon.
2. Robert Lowell's new books were *For Lizzie and Harriet*, *History*, and *The Dolphin*.

> Tegna. [Switzerland]
> [June 21, 1973]

CONGRATULATIONS BIRTHD/.Y AND OBSERVER LOVE

> HANNA[H]

> [Washington, D.C.]
> June 21, 1973

Darling Hannah: The Flowers! Beautiful erect African daisies. And the cable! You have really lifted my spirits, which were low. The loneliness I experience in this (to me) hostile city. Thought of you in the Royal Caledonian—the Watergate food is not dissimilar. But now Everything looks suddenly brighter.

Thank you, dear, for your friendship.

Love,
Mary

Castine, Maine 04421
August 10, 1973

Dearest Hannah:

Just a few words to greet you. I was a bit worried at not having heard from you (not that I'd written myself), but Bill on the telephone this week reassured me.

I came up here finally a week ago today, having decided to miss the last three days of the Ervin panel—no great loss, it turned out. Perhaps I'll go back very briefly when they resume on September 10. [She didn't.] I want to see Colson.[1] To me, it's not the same on TV, at least if one's going to write a piece. The public is part of the story, and the reporters in the room with their speculations and running commentary. By the way, I met one, who often sat next to me, a young man, Ross Munro of the Toronto Globe, quite intelligent and much respected in Canada. He told [me] that reading *The Origins of T.*, when he was twenty-one or -two, had changed his life.

Of course there's the great TV public outside. The Ervin show became a tremendous success. Here the plumber's wife had it on all day long in the shop and she tells me that now she misses it. Her remark, that it has been an education, is often heard, I understand. Also it has been entertainment; I don't know how to judge that, and it's probably too soon to try to do so. She wrote me a note—about housewives: their soap operas, she said, had trained them to tell the good characters from the bad characters. . . .

Here it is very hot and damp—unusual for Castine. But the house is beautiful and tranquil, and the garden productive. Jim has taken up masonry, building or rather rebuilding a low brick circle round an abandoned windmill back near the vegetable garden that turned out to be part of our property. We've extended the garden back there (Jim bought an extra bit of land), planted grass, put up a sort of wattled fence, and I've planted hollyhocks and Canterbury bells against it; today, if the sun comes out, I'll plant foxglove (digitalis) and columbine.

Nothing but gardening, a little cooking, and reading. I am a judge for an English literary prize in September and have about thirty novels to read. No writing. I was awfully tired when I got up here from Washington and took a vow to do no work for two weeks; I mean literary work.

Bill thinks you are writing very furiously. I had come to the same conclusion. He is very enthusiastic about the book [*The Life of the Mind*] and talked of its spontaneity and gayety or perhaps he said naturalness. Does this mean he has seen it all—the thinking part? I envy you the task, having no project myself and rather low energy for the moment.

Jim is in poor spirits and has been for the last couple of months. I hope Castine can restore him. He's suffering from general loss of affect—the children, of course, and leaving or being forcibly retired from the State department, which he takes very hard, though there's no material loss—in fact a gain. [2]

Are you going to be able to come up here? I do count on it, if it's at all possible for you. The contrast between Castine and the rest of the world gets more striking every year, though, coming from Tegna, you wouldn't feel it as much as I did coming from Washington.

The people are all about the same, rather flourishing; one marriage has broken up, and the old Episcopal bishop, friend of Mrs. Roosevelt, has died, alas. [3] Lizzie will come up briefly in the fall; she's now at Villa Serbelloni. She has sold her house on the green and is doing over the barn. Our Cercle Français is reduced to four this summer; we're going to read Chateaubriand, but the books haven't come yet. Eileen and Tom Finletter are back in Bar Harbor and have had Bowden staying with them.

Now I must stop and get this in the mail. There's a hiatus between Saturday noon and Monday at five p.m. during which no mail leaves.

> Much love to you, my dear. Send me a little postcard.
> Mary

1. Charles Colson, counselor to the President and "the master of dirty tricks," in McCarthy's view, was directly implicated in the Watergate break-in and the burglary of Ellsberg's psychiatrist, but was never called to testify before the Senate committee outside executive sessions.
2. After West's retirement from the Foreign Service, he was invited to remain at the OECD, which agreed to cover the portion of his salary formerly paid by the State Department.
3. This was Will Scarlett, to whom McCarthy dedicated *Cannibals and Missionaries* in 1979.

Dearest Mary,

God knows why I did not write earlier, thinking of you all the time and reading the Observer, especially the Haldeman-Article, with the greatest admiration. It was the only article which explained and clarified things. I was very grateful. I did not write because I was kind of depressed about the whole affair. I had the impression that Nixon would actually emerge as victor in the guise of savior of the nation from Watergate, to be blamed not on him or the White House but on Congress. But I just read excerpts of his speech and a few comments on the reaction and I am reassured. He seems to have been again on the defensive without answering in detail—which, of course, he cannot do anyhow—and to me the whole thing sounded as though he was afraid. The main fact remains that only 31% (?) support him but that no one wants him impeached. In other words, no one really minds about this massive invasion of crime into the political process. Or, more likely, people are mortally frightened of what might happen if anything is actually done about it. And this I can understand. Since Nixon actually behaved like a tyrant his downfall would be a kind of revolution. I too feel that the consequence would be quite unpredictable and possibly of great magnitude. It is evidently true that the one who started a veritable "revolution" was Nixon himself; up to now, it was abortive, but the last word has not yet been spoken. Did you see the latest Gallup poll—if Nixon and McGovern were to run today, M. would defeat Nixon by 51 to 49. Well, perhaps. But I don't see any sign that the Democrats are using their chance. They believe that the Republicans will hang themselves and they can afford to do nothing. Which is a great mistake.

You see, Watergate has eaten rather deeply and sharply into my time and my attention. The overwhelming number of scandals which come to light is in a way self-defeating. Everybody, so it must *seem*, did more or less what Nixon did, and where all are guilty no one is.

We have here a very enjoyable summer weatherwise; but I am not writing "furiously"—partly because of Watergate and partly because I found new things about the Will. I have been working "furiously"—reading, taking notes, revising. To write about Willing is for me much more problematic than about Thinking where I always thought I could simply trust my instinct and my own experience. (Before I forget: my very able assistant (not the secretary) at the New School wrote: "The single most searching and suggestive article on Watergate that I have seen is Mary McCarthy's in the New York Review, 19 July.")[1]

I'll come home on September 5—at least that is the way I booked. I cannot say that I am looking forward to it. Things at the New School are in a mess, and I am afraid that my very real fear for the country will interfere with anything I'll do. I do not think that I can come to Castine. I have a number of things which I have got to take care of right away—Buy my apartment, prepare my seminars, take care of my long neglected mail, etc. Also: You will go to Washington on the 10th or—as I found in some newspaper— the 15th. *Can't you come and stay with me in New York before you go to Washington?*

It was good to have news from Castine. I am really quite sorry that I can't make it this year. Give my warmest regards to all who remember me. And give my love to Jim. I envy you your gardening and admire Jim's building skill. Maybe we should all have become gardeners or something of the sort. I often think of an ancient joke I found in Augustine: To the question: What did God do before he created Heaven & earth? the answer is: He prepared Hell for those who ask such questions.

What are you going to do with the Watergate articles? Make it into a book? Or into an Epilogue to the Vietnam-Book? Or what? I spoke here with Bob Silvers over the phone. He seemed also to suspect Nixon of being the true source of Agnew's troubles.[2] Could not Nixon have taken this complete unknown as his Vice President because he knew about his potential difficulties? and then, when the going gets a little rough, he of all people presents himself as Mr. Clean and prepares everything for the succession. Must be infuriating.

Have a good rest, my dear.

Much love and yours,
Hannah

1. This must have been "A Steady Dosage of Lies," reprinted from *The Observer* of July 15, 1973.
2. Spiro T. Agnew, Nixon's vice-president since 1969, was accused of having accepted pay-offs from building contractors while he was governor of Maryland. He resigned October 10, 1973.

[Castine]
Aug. 21, 1973
[Postcard]

Dearest Hannah: It worries me not to hear from you. Did you get my letter? I know you are all right because Bob Silvers says he talked at length to you. So . . . End of summer is approaching. I go back to Washington probably Sept. 9, then Paris.

Love, Mary

Tegna
8/28/73
[Postcard]

Dearest Mary, I wrote you a long letter and assume you received it meanwhile. I just got your card. Anyhow, I return next Wednesday, September 5th, from Zurich, shall call you either Wednesday or Thursday. Can you come [to New York] before Washington?

Love—
Hannah

[. . .]

[On September 28, 1973, W. H. Auden died, and his death, together with the "misery of his life," as Hannah Arendt saw his final years, prompted in her a painful reflection on the tie between suffering and poetic song. At the memorial service at St. John the Divine in New York City, she inscribed a couplet from Auden's poetry on her program: "Sing of human unsuccess/ In a rapture of distress."

At the New School, Arendt's students were struck by her agitation after this death, so different from the reserve she displayed after the death of her husband.]

[New York]
September 30, 1973

Dearest Mary—

Your call was a real *Lichtblick* [lift for my spirits] and so surprising that I forgot to thank you for the marvellous flowers which still greet me from everywhere in the apartment. I still am thinking of Wystan, naturally, and of the misery of his life, and that I refused to take care of him when he came and asked for shelter. Homer said that the gods spin ruin to men that there might be song and remembrance. Helen said in the Iliad: Zeus brought evil on her and Paris "so that in days to come we shall be a song for men yet to be"

343

and Hecuba (in Euripides) about to be carried off into slavery, says—consoles herself?—without this disaster "we would be unfamed, unsung, not something to be remembered by mortals in the future." Well, he was both the singer and the tale. But God knows, the price is too high and no one in his right mind could be willing to pay it knowingly. And the worst perhaps, at least for me, this desperate attempt of the last years to pretend to have been "lucky."

Watergate: Hunt[1] acted and looked pretty much like Eichmann—down to details, the same nose and such. Buchanan[2]—enormously aggressive, self-assured, smarter than anybody on the Committee, attacking the tax-free foundations and stressing that nothing unprecedented had happened.

Meanwhile: Bob called—if I want to write something about Wystan, and Shawn called, out of kindness, and do I plan to write anything about Watergate to be "considered" by them[?] The latter struck me as considerably less enthusiastic (wrong word) than his usual invitations. Also: I was reading some of the later "Talks of the Town" on Watergate—very feeble and hesitant. I am looking forward to Thanksgiving. One more detail: I told Morgenthau of Auden's death, and he immediately replied: Who is next? What did you decide to do?[3]

Much love.
Yours,
Hannah

1. Former White House aide E. Howard Hunt, Jr., had just appeared before the Senate Watergate committee. With G. Gordon Liddy, counsel to the Committee to Reelect the President, Hunt was implicated in the break-in of Democratic National Committee Headquarters at Watergate.
2. For many observers, White House speechwriter Patrick Buchanan's ridicule of the Senate Committee marked a low point in the Watergate hearings.
3. The question refers either to the disposition of McCarthy's Watergate reports, eventually collected in her book *The Mask of State*, or to the "Watergate Yearbook" mentioned in the next letter.

141 rue de Rennes
Paris 75006
October 4, 1973

Dearest Hannah:

You see, they're talking about your ideas here. See the enclosed (Jacques Thibau).[1] The piece by Marcelle Auclair is also worth reading—gossipy and *mondain*, but, like a lot of gossip, it tells you rather revealing things that the "serious" journalists don't know about or don't think worth mentioning. What she says about the low social position of the [Chilean] Army throws light in fact on Thibau's thesis, that this is a totalitarian enterprise. But is it? Certainly some of the criteria are there, but, in your view, isn't Chile too small and weak to turn itself into a totalitarian regime? How horrible all this is, and one of the depressing features is the impotence of liberals and leftists outside to do anything even to save endangered lives. There are meetings going on here all the time, at the Mutualité and elsewhere, "Soutien pour le peuple chilien!" but it makes you want to weep or laugh (both), because what support do they have to offer? If there were a civil war going on, at least they could send arms and medical supplies, but that is not the situation.

In another item in the same paper there's a story about an appeal by some French Catholic prior to the Chilean cardinal, asking him, in the name of Christ and the Church, to do something to save the life of the head of the Chilean C. P. But I cannot think that will be very useful either. Also an appeal by the British Labor Party to [Prime Minister] Heath to get him to intervene for this same Communist leader. But Chile and those generals are so remote that "world opinion," I imagine, can hardly reach or concern them. Of course the U.S. could do something and might have, even in Johnson's time, that is, put some pressure on the junta to tone down the slaughter a little, spare prominent figures, etc. The idea of showing concern for human rights, even a false concern, which used to be rather typically American, obviously doesn't enter Nixon's head. He has never heard of such a sentiment.

I have had a letter from a woman activist here, American and quite stupid, in my opinion, asking my help in raising $10,000 to support an underground railroad in Chile to help get people out with false papers, etc. She asks me to keep it a secret, so I won't say more. Normally I'd say yes and try to do something, but I mistrust this woman's judgment almost totally, though I suppose the connections she has there can't do any positive harm, and if they get caught, that won't make matters worse necessarily for those they're trying to rescue. Or will it? I wish you were here and could give me your counsel. I am rather torn up about it. It's the old story: if a contribution from me could save a life . . . ? Even one?

What a wonderful letter from you yesterday, my dear. So beautiful, those words from Homer, and fearsome too. I hope you are not reviling yourself for not having taken Wystan in and think it's not in your character to have that sort of regret or stab of conscience. It is always a false regret, I suspect, being given to it sometimes myself while knowing that if I had it to do over it would be the same. And in Auden's case, to wish things could have been otherwise would be to wish that he had been a different person. Not just you. He.

About Watergate, I've just about made a decision. To try to do the Watergate Yearbook I imagined, starting June 17, 1972 [the date of the break-in] and going up to June 17, 1973 (by coincidence the dateline of my first Watergate piece, I've discovered), making a sort of montage of my own private life (also my public one), world events, and Watergate developments. Like one of those Histomaps they had in schools in Reuel's day, where historical streams of different colors—Egypt, say, yellow; Greece, pink—were shown running parallel, widening and narrowing as each civilization grew and then declined. If I kept a diary, it would be easier. At the moment, without consulting last year's engagement book, I have no idea what I was doing on June 17. Except that I was in Paris and that in a few days it would be my sixtieth birthday and Jim would give his giant party at Prunier's. In my head somewhere was McGovern.

The idea is awfully ambitious and I am not sure I have the energy for it. I am not worried, though, about the immodesty of paralleling my little life with big events, many of which of course were miserably small and low. I'd simply be taking myself as a sample of anybody or everybody American and more or less on the "right" side— a quite humble notion really. The first sentence might be addressed to the reader: "Where were *you* on June 17, 1972?" Such questions actually came up during [John] Dean's testimony. Some senator— perhaps Baker[2]—said if you asked him *he* wouldn't know for the life of him what he had been doing on some of those dates. He wondered at *Dean's* power of recall.

Of course what I shall be trying to say through this juxtaposition is something else. I'm not sure yet. I get glimmers but no clear light. It is not the Christian idea: "We are members one of another." Or is it? Applied to the body politic (as against Christ's body), it might be more true than I care to think.[3]

Well, enough of that for the moment. I must stop and take a walk. I've made a resolve to walk at least half an hour every day. Unless it is pouring rain. Yesterday the Luxembourg Garden was so beautiful. Late flowers, men playing *boules*, the smell of fresh-cut grass, shade trees starting to turn their leaves, and pear and apple trees espaliered in charming patterns with each pear and each apple wrapped in paper or plastic, giving a Christmas tree effect. I looked at the bust of Baudelaire.

Thank you for saying yes to Thanksgiving.[4] And for my stay, which quite uplifted me.[5]

All my love,
Mary

1. The enclosure probably quotes from *The Origins of Totalitarianism.* Thibau and others were discussing the military junta which took power in Chile after a bloody coup that had led to the death of President Salvador Allende in September.
2. Committee member Howard Baker, Jr., was the Republican senator from Tennessee.
3. This curious project was never undertaken.
4. Arendt had been invited to celebrate Thanksgiving with the Wests in Castine, after McCarthy delivered a series of lectures in Philadelphia and in Lawrence, Kansas, earlier in November.
5. McCarthy had visited Arendt on her way from Castine to Washington in August.

141 rue de Rennes
Paris 75006
October 11, 1973

Dearest Hannah:

Jim had the enclosed photostatted for you. The obituary [of Auden], I feel sure, is by Spender. In the TLS of October 5, there is a splendid and very moving appreciation by Geoffrey Grigson, a strict and normally acidulous writer (who banished Cal, by the way, to outer darkness). He is an English moralist, as you will see, and yet I think his view of Auden is not far from yours.[1] If you haven't seen it, please drop me a line, and I will clip it. In general, I keep a file of the TLS intact; hence I haven't clipped it now for you but can, if need be.

About the Chilean business, I've decided to give them some money—$750—and Jim, on his own hook, has contributed $250. The woman I wrote you about came to see me yesterday, at my suggestion, and brought a young Frenchman who was in Chile last summer and supplied more particulars. Basically this is a Trotskyite effort, as I got the picture. They say that the CP, as usual, is taking care of its own and indeed is moving to take over the whole Allende cause in the outside world. The usual story. Hence the concerted outcry about Corvalan.[2] These people—the ones I'm in touch with—want to concentrate, first of all, on getting out two Socialist leaders who are in hiding: [Carlos] Altamirano, who is well known, and one they preferred not to name. Their next objective is to save some left-wing Christian Democrats, in hiding too, and some members of the MIR (?), the far left movement outside the Allende coalition.[3] The chief agent in the transmission belt is a Greek and old friend of Trotsky's who lives in Argentina and has connections with all these old Socialists. They claim he is level-headed and will not take unnecessary risks. The American woman has known him a long time. They have been told, recently, that Amnesty International, in London, with whom they're in contact, is going to give them some money for the rescue work. I hope so, because, aside from anything else, this is a sort of guarantee of the practicality of the enterprise.

At bottom, as I told the two yesterday, I am pessimistic about the result. All these people in hiding have large prices on their heads, and some, evidently (but these seem to be chiefly CP), have already been betrayed. But since I know of no sure-fire way of doing anything for them, I can't say no to this appeal. The alternative would be to do nothing. So I told them I'd give them some money and try to raise some more. They estimate they would need from $10,000 to $12,000, for false papers, getaway cars, etc. Would you be inclined to help them, my dear? If so, you can just send me a check. I am trying to think of others in the U.S. (and here too) who might agree and also agree to keep their mouths shut. There is no point in trying to get $25 contributions. There is not enough time, and the more people you ask the more gossip you risk. I said I thought I'd ask nobody who wasn't good for at least $100. I am running over names in my mind. This isn't Bill's pigeon, I think. Do any names occur to you? Lizzie? Well, maybe $100, but she *is* so garrulous. I am going to write Bob today and ask his advice. Maybe there is some parallel effort going on in New York; if so, he'd surely know about it. I shall also ask Spender for a contribution. When you think of the millions being raised for Israel, the sum here is certainly modest. Let us not talk about the Israeli-Arab war. Or— today—even about Agnew.[4]

A final note. I asked the young Frenchman for a policy statement on how the money would be used—not for myself, but for any appeal I'd make to friends. On Communists: saving them is not the objective, but of course if they came across a Communist in hiding needing help, they would help him. I agree. And the money would be used for purely humanitarian purposes—not to organize a resistance movement or spirit in weapons. I said I personally would be most unwilling to help finance a resistance movement, which in my view was suicidal.

Now I must stop. It turns out I shall not be meeting Bill in Frankfurt [at the Book Fair] after all (his decision). Instead, Jim and I will go to Laon on Saturday. Have you ever been there? It's almost my favorite cathedral. Architecturally, in my heart, its only competitor is Bourges. It's the one with oxen on the top. You see these oxen again in Bamberg—though less impressive. It's thought that masters from Laon worked in Bamberg.

All my love,
Mary

1. Arendt's appreciation, "Remembering Wystan H. Auden," was published in *The New Yorker*, January 20, 1975, and reprinted in *W. H. Auden: A Tribute* (1974/75).
2. Luis Corvalan Lepe was head of the Chilean Communist Party.
3. The Movimiento de la Izquierda Revolucionaria (Movement of the Revolutionary Left), which had pushed for faster nationalizations and tougher police action against the rightist opposition, was part of Allende's Unidad Popular, and thus within the coalition.
4. The Justice Department had dropped corruption charges against Vice-President Agnew and permitted him to plead *nolo contendere* to a lesser charge of income-tax evasion.

[New York]
October 16, 1973

Dearest Mary,

your letter arrived together with the news of WQXR—every hour on the hour—the rather frightening news from Israel,[1] the absurdity of the Nobel Prize for Peace[2] and a number of other unpleasant signs of what one calls World-history.[3] Many thanks for the Auden obituary; I did not see the TLS but don't bother; I can buy here a copy very easily. I am enclosing two checks. Lotte [Klenbort] is Channan's [*sic*] German wife and she is entirely reliable; I could not talk with him, it is really difficult to touch Jews at this moment. He has his brother in Israel; his kibbutz was shelled in the neighborhood of the Golan heights [*sic*] and he wrote that no one had warned them even though they often have been warned before and though the Israeli[s] pretend that they knew all about a forthcoming attack. This is but one small riddle in this whole affair, there are many more. I saw the first [U.N.] Security Council meeting, the one which Malik walked out from,[4] and I must confess that

I was flabbergasted by the amount of sheer hatred and the complete isolation of the poor and rather incompetent Israeli delegate. The American delegate was in no way different from the others. Your letter incidentally came just in time; I was anyhow about to give some extra money to Amnesty International because of the Chile business.

I am in the process of recovering from the French television interview—in my opinion an unmitigated disaster and very exhausting.[5] Not that it matters. I have some trouble to get back into work, chiefly of course because of this unexpected outbreak of "history" but partly also because of becoming involved in sheer nonsense. I envy you the trip to Laon which I don't know; it is precisely the kind of relaxation (even though for you it is also work) one cannot have in this country.

I must stop to get the checks in the mail.

De tout coeur—

Hannah

1. Egyptians and Syrians had attacked Israel on October 6, inflicting major casualties and regaining some territory lost in the Six-Day War of 1967. When Arendt wrote, an unstable ceasefire was in effect.
2. After negotiating a ceasefire in Vietnam, Nixon's National Security Advisor, Henry Kissinger, and his North Vietnamese counterpart, Le Duc Tho, were awarded the 1973 Nobel Peace Prize. Le Duc Tho refused his, asserting that the United States was still abetting the war between North and South Vietnam.
3. An outbreak of "World-history"—a favorite term of both Arendt's and Blücher's—occurred whenever international events invaded private life, thereby redefining, if only temporarily, one's commitments to work and action.
4. At the first Security Council meeting during the "Yom Kippur War," Yakov Malik, the Soviet Ambassador to the U.N., called Israeli Prime Minister Golda Meir and Defense Minister Moshe Dayan "international criminals," then walked out while the Israeli Ambassador, Y. Tekoah, was speaking.
5. Arendt may have regretted the interview she gave Roger Ererra for French television in October 1973 because it violated a ban she had put on television appearances in the United States, or, more likely, because it recorded her panic over the invasion of Israel.

Paris

Nov. 10, 1973

[Postcard]

Dearest Hannah: [. . .] Engrossed in work—way behind in everything thanks to Maria's month of vacation (now terminated). See you for Thanksgiving. I am booked to arrive Monday evening, but with the fuel shortage, who knows?[1] Try to come Tuesday.[2]

Love, Mary

1. In retaliation for Washington's aid to Israel, the Arab oil-producing nations cut back shipments of petroleum to the United States throughout the winter of 1973–74.
2. Arendt was expected in Castine on the Tuesday before Thanksgiving.

141 rue de Rennes

Paris 6

November 19, 1973

CONFIDENTIAL

Dearest Hannah:

Here is a small progress report on the Chilean rescue project. Thanks to this particular effort one leading figure is now out of Chile. Two others are in safe foreign embassies. Still a fourth is out and in Mexico, but it is as yet uncertain whether this was not effected by some other group.

Money is being spent for false papers, for radio receivers and transmitters and, in some cases, for maintenance of fugitives.

It's unwise to be more specific than this in a letter, but names (I have these, also affiliations, former posts held in the Allende government) will, I expect, be in the newspapers pretty soon. As soon, that is, as these people are safely out of the South American continent.

With thanks again.

Love,

Mary

P.S. This letter being sent to all the people who responded.

141 rue de Rennes

Paris 6

December 12, 1973

Dear Hannah:

Latest news on the Chile situation: part of the funds collected have been used to help people who wish to remain in Chile under extremely difficult conditions. Since prices have gone up nearly 1000 per cent and most leftists who are not in prison have been dismissed from their jobs, these people need help just to subsist.

In addition, several people have been transferred from their hiding places into foreign embassies—this is a measure to gain time.

Finally, Jorge McGinty, former Under-Secretary of Health in the

Allende Government, and number two leader of the Socialist Party (after Carlos Altamirano), has been helped to leave the country with several of his comrades. He is now on his way to Europe. A photocopy of a letter of thanks written by Jorge McGinty is enclosed. You will note that owing to the circumstances (he wrote it while in transit in an unfriendly South American country) the letter is not signed but only initialed.

Love,
Mary

P.S. This is a form letter. I'll write a real one soon. I'm just trying to recover from Holland and Sweden. The Gothic lecture was *horrible*.[1]

M.

1. McCarthy's visit to Holland was an early fact-finding trip for her next, and last, novel, *Cannibals and Missionaries* (1979). She delivered a lecture on December 7 in Leyden, Holland.

[Philip Rahv was found dead in his Cambridge, Massachusetts, apartment on December 23, 1973. Because a police investigation was ordered, Elizabeth Hardwick and others suspected a fatal combination of alcohol and pills, even suicide; but no definitive findings were made public. Rahv's death, at sixty-five, hit Mary McCarthy especially hard.]

[New York]
December 23, 1973

Dearest Mary,

Bill told me that you were not feeling well and I therefore tried today twice to reach you by phone. I suppose you are in Italy since there was no answer. Meanwhile Lizzi [*sic*] called; you probably received her cable with Rahv's death. She leaves tomorrow for Brandeis for the funeral and promised to write you a long explanatory letter. I must admit that I mind this relentless defoliation (or deforestation) process. As though to grow old does not mean, as Goethe said, "gradual withdrawal from appearance"—which I do not mind—but the gradual (rather sudden) transformation of a world with familiar faces (no matter, foe or friend) into a kind of desert, populated by strange faces. In other words, it is not me who withdraws but the world that dissolves—an altogether different proposition. I leave all details to Lizzi.

Had a very good time with Bill; he insisted on a talk about the Will and I was again pleased with his quick intelligence. [. . .] [A]m in the process of writing, slowly, the final (provisionally final) draft [of the lectures on Willing], and begin to enjoy it.

What went wrong with the gothic lecture? Please, answer or I shall believe that you [have] become a hypochondriac. And please, please take care of yourself and don't overdo it.

Love—
Hannah

[New York]
February 25, 1974

Dearest Mary,

I saw Lizzi yesterday and it suddenly occurred to me that I did not write you about the Rahv essay[1]—so beautiful, so tender, so absolutely convincing in every memorable detail—i.e. every detail that deserves to be remembered. And nice that the NY Times put it on the frontpage [sic]. The photo is abominable. Either he had changed beyond recognition since I last saw him—many years past—or just one of those snapshots which are always wrong.

Otherwise nothing special. I have been reading Master Eckhart, partly with great pleasure. Curiously, how unaware I was that the so-called late Heidegger is entirely influenced by him. I met a few days ago Robert Fizdale;[2] he told me about Carmen at great length. You must know him well; I liked him a great deal. Heard him play yesterday, very beautiful, without any chichi, très sympathique. Also met Tom Finletter and his wife [the former Eileen Geist], both in good form, he very much changed and very much to the better. He says: Eileen takes very good care of me, and this, surprisingly, seems indeed to be the case.

I am not in a letter-writing mood. Have a running nose. People here are in a rather bleak mood, and Jason Epstein seems to be even more pessimistic than I am. Bob as usual but also rather worried. Jovanovich is back from vacation but did not call. He gives a party for some Yugoslav fellow whose book, which I just looked at, apparently is pretty much the opposite of what Djilas has to say.[3] It also is not good. Am wondering what is going on there.

Shall now [be] returning my running nose to the grindstone.

Much love and yours,
Hannah

1. Mary McCarthy, "Philip Rahv (1908–1973)," *The New York Times Book Review*, February 17, 1974; it was reprinted in *Occasional Prose*.
2. Robert Fizdale was a pianist well known for his concerts and recordings with pianist Arthur Gold.
3. The Yugoslav author mentioned here was Ilija Jukić, whose book *The Fall of Yugoslavia* was published by Harcourt Brace Jovanovich in 1974. Milovan Djilas was the author of an influential study of Communist oligarchies, *The New Class* (1957).

141 rue de Rennes
Paris 75006
March 1, 1974

Dearest Hannah:

Your letter came this morning—on the day, finally, that I was about to write to you—my first free day since I can't think when, well, since we got back from Rome. Watergate is finished, except for reading page proofs and, on the last chapter, galleys. The Vietnam omnibus [*The Seventeenth Degree*] is at the binder's. I have a little interlude before I have to start on a preface to Nicola's theatre pieces and write my Pittsburgh lecture. And then the Aberdeen lecture—I can't think what to talk about to those Scots. [1]

Thank you for liking the piece on Philip, and, yes, the photo was abominable. We sent them a much nicer one, taken in the boat in Penobscot Bay, when he visited us in Castine; I don't know why they didn't use it. That was the last time I saw him, in the fall of 1970. Perhaps he did change after that but surely he didn't become *unrecognizable*. I had a nice letter from Frankie FitzGerald, who, with her boy friend, was with him, by coincidence, the night he died, and she says they had a marvelous evening. From her description of the things they talked about, it sounds as if he was very much the old Philip in his benign and confidential aspect. This leads me to doubt Lizzie's picture of his utter *"isolation,"* heavy drinking, sleeping drugs, total disintegration. [2] I had suspected her account anyway, so hysterical and insistent—a good deal of projection, I think, of her own assessment of her position onto him. Anyway she hadn't seen him for years, though they'd talked on the telephone.

I've had a great many letters thanking me for what I wrote about him; the last was from a Jesuit in Boston, somebody I'd never heard of and would never have guessed Philip knew. These compliments are as much or more compliments to Philip than to me and that pleases me; a lot of people must have been fond of him, more maybe than he guessed.

I find I miss him disproportionately. I can't bear to take his picture (in color) off my desk or file away his last two letters, which alas I never answered—he wanted me to write something for his magazine and I felt I couldn't. It's strange, but his death has hit me harder than anybody's, even Nicola's, though I was much closer to Nicola and saw him all the time. That I was in some way prepared for Nicola's death (having been ready for it to happen for eleven years) can't be the whole explanation. Maybe love, even such a long-ago one, gets at your vital center more than friendship and admiration. I realize that I *must* have loved him when we lived together and continued to do so, though unaware of it. Anyway his death hurts. Jim says maybe it's because I feel he had an incomplete, tentative sort of life. But does anybody have a complete life? Well, I suppose you could say it of Heinrich or Nicola, in comparison to Philip. A sign of that is that I'm interested in the survival and persistence of their thought but not really very much in the editions of Philip's unfinished and uncollected works now (it seems) projected. Philip's "ideas" weren't interesting, except as an expression of his personality. Though he certainly wasn't stupid and had a mental life, it didn't achieve independence, of the temporal, of *him*. That may be why that of all the friends who have died, I feel especially sorry that he couldn't have immortality, couldn't have gone to his own funeral and commented on it, followed the latest Watergate developments, had a crushing word for the newest marriage or divorce. . . .

Anyway Philip's death is the only event that has meant much to me in the last few months. Everything else is rather blah. Books, politics, social life. I am rather sick of the way Watergate is dragging on. I still think we'll get rid of Nixon but in some unsatisfactory way, I'm afraid. Of course it's he who has managed to prolong it by every conceivable trick, yet the fact that he wasn't removed, say, after the Saturday night massacre,[3] shows a general inertia and tonelessness of response that's alarming in itself.

We've been listening this morning to the English election results on the radio. Still inconclusive, but the good showing of the Liberals is encouraging in a small way; it indicates that there are quite a few people who refuse the either-or empty choice offered them.

But I don't see how it can develop into anything more political.

Now about April. I find that I had forgotten something—a promise I'd made to Canadian TV to do a long interview to be filmed at Vassar, on the campus. CBC writes that Vassar has agreed and suggests (CBC) that I go there straight from Pittsburgh, arriving the 18th or 19th. This looks good to me. I can then come down to New York when you'll be back from wherever you've gone, and if it's not too close to your Aberdeen departure[4] I can spend, say, a week. Jim and I meanwhile have decided about Easter: to drive to Germany Holy Thursday or the morning of Good Friday, stop in Trier again and in Aachen (where we've never been) and spend Easter Sunday in Cologne, in that hotel (the Excelsior) on the Domplatz, where we played chess looking out on the square one Easter—when was it? Perhaps five years ago. Then we'll come home, and I'll fly to Pittsburgh. Is the above approved by you, my dear?

Enough for now. I must write to Bill. Bob Silvers has just called (since I began this), very enthusiastic about the last Watergate chapter, which he wants to run immediately.

> So, hastily, warmly,
> All my love,
> Mary

1. "Living with Beautiful Things," delivered at the Carnegie Museum of Art in Pittsburgh on April 17, was also presented, slightly revised, in May 1974 in Aberdeen, Scotland, as "Art Values and the Value of Art." It is reprinted, under the first title, in *Occasional Prose*.
2. Elizabeth Hardwick wrote McCarthy a long and moving letter about Rahv on December 27, 1973, four days after his death.
3. The "Saturday night massacre" took place on October 20, 1973, after Archibald Cox, the Watergate special prosecutor, had ordered the White House to release all tapes of recorded conversations pertaining to the break-in and Nixon had instead offered an unacceptable compromise, refused by Cox. Attorney General Elliot Richardson and his then deputy William Ruckelshaus were ordered by Nixon to dismiss Cox. Both refused and resigned. Acting Attorney General Robert Bork fired Cox.
4. Arendt was going to deliver the second series of Gifford Lectures on "The Life of the Mind."

[New York]
March 11, 1974

Dear Mary,

This is only to fix dates. I'll go to Wisconsin on the 18th and shall be back on the 21st. From your letter I understand that you will be at Vassar on the 18th or 19th but it's not clear for how long.

Please let me know. I leave for England on the 28th and shall stay two days in London before I go to Aberdeen on May 1st.

Love,
Hannah

[. . .]

141 rue de Rennes
Paris 6
March 18, 1974

Dearest Hannah:

This is dictated and hurriedly. I expect to get to New York the evening of the 19th or, more likely, the 20th. I can get to your place then or, if that presents the slightest complication for you, wait till you get back. On Tuesday the 16th, on my way to Pittsburgh, I shall probably be passing through New York and I shall call you. Meanwhile, would you like me to book you a room at the Stafford or have you already done so?

Much love,
[Unsigned]

[New York]
April 3rd, 1974

Dear Mary,

Jim will have told you that I called last Sunday because I was delighted with your Watergate essay.[1] I'm writing today (rather dictating) because I had lost your note about dates which meanwhile showed up. So I know that you will be here either on the 19th or the 20th. Sally [Arendt's maid] will let you in. I leave for Milwaukee on the 18th in the late afternoon (6:20PM) and arrive on Saturday the 20th at the LaGuardia at 4:49PM. I should be home around 6PM.

I leave for London on the 28th and just wrote to the Stafford for reservations. I saw Nathalie Sarraute in a big party with rather non-big people, and Eileen [Finletter] informed me that she intends to give you a party. This only to keep you informed. That Natasha [Sarraute] has declared war on me plus Bob Silvers and Lizzie you know already.[2] We made up. Let's talk about it.

Yours,
[Unsigned]

[Dictated but not read]

1. Mary McCarthy, "Always That Doubt," *The New York Review of Books*, February 22, 1974; is reprinted in *The Mask of State*.
2. John Weightman's testy review of her *Vous les entendez*, "What's Going on Upstairs?" *The New York Review of Books*, April 19, 1973, enraged Sarraute. She blamed Arendt and Elizabeth Hardwick, as well as McCarthy, for not persuading Silvers to commission a sympathetic review, as might have happened in Paris.

[On May 5, 1974, in Aberdeen, Scotland, midway through the series of lectures on Willing, Hannah Arendt suffered a heart attack. William Jovanovich, who was staying at the same hotel, had been summoned by her early that morning; he found her standing but dazed. After checking her pulse and carotid arteries, he gave her some Demerol and called an ambulance and doctor.

Mary McCarthy came from Paris to be with her in the hospital, where Arendt was first placed in the intensive-care unit. After McCarthy returned to Paris, Lotte Kohler flew from New York to be with Arendt while she waited impatiently in the Aberdeen hotel for permission to travel to Tegna. McCarthy returned on May 27 to escort her to London; from there, Robert Gilbert's wife, Elke, accompanied her on the trip to Switzerland.]

Paris
May 11, 1974

My dearest
[. . .] I'm so glad you've finally got quiet and privacy.[1] Is the diet any better in the private sector? Naturally, since getting back (though I've been home only eighteen hours, nine of them consumed in sleeping), I have been swamped with telephoned sympathy and advice for you. Anjo Lévi, Eileen Finletter, Tom, and a friend you don't even know. The burden of the advice is what you already know from Dr. Finlayson: utmost care to be exercised during the first three months, then an adaption of some sort to meet the new circumstance. . . .

But I gather from my (to you) unknown friend, who has had two cardiac husbands, that intransigency, "misbehaving," obstinacy are so common as to be *symptoms* of heart disease. That is, after an attack. Her first question to me: "Has she been acting willful?"

Please, now, my dear, obey the doctor and direct your *will* to recuperation rather than to resistance. And enjoy at least the rest, enforced though it is. Once Lottchen comes, you will have less reason to be bored and hence restless.

Carmen is still here (with [her ex-husband] Ernest); I am lunching with her this noon. On the telephone, this morning, she foreclosed advice, while sending you much exquisite sympathy. But, since her father was a heart case (had a pacemaker) I suppose at lunch she *will* offer, gently, some fruits of experience. About the heart, I begin to feel like Berenson when he learned I had a Jewish grandmother: "Oh, dear, is *everybody* Jewish?" The thing about the heart, I suppose, really is that not only are heart attacks common but their pathology is rather simple and easily apprehended by the layman. . . . The rules, too, though they may differ in detail (some recommend coffee; some forbid it), are rather simple and uniform in broad outline: no doctor, I presume, would prescribe an agitated life, two packs of cigarettes a day, and running while carrying heavy objects.[2]

Now I must stop and dress. It makes me so happy to know that you are *there* and fairly intact physically after that frightening few hours. Now, as a philosopher, you should accept wisdom.

All my love,
Mary

1. After the oxygen tent was removed, Arendt recuperated in a private hospital room.
2. Arendt had been guilty of at least two of these infractions in the hospital: smoking was resumed as soon as the oxygen tent was removed, and resistance to the nurses kept her in a state of high agitation throughout her convalescence.

141 rue de Rennes
May 15, 1974

Dearest Hannah:

[. . .] Lottchen says you are sitting up, if this is per Dr. Finlayson's instructions, hurray! Elke called yesterday for details about you; she is lining up a limousine to take you both from Zurich to Tegna.

I am still feeling somewhat rotten—cold and cough—and a blood analysis done before I went to Aberdeen which got lost in the mail discloses too many white corpuscles, signifying an infection. My doctor believes it is sinus; I don't. But anyway he is sending me some penicillin, which ought to work on whatever is wrong.

Jim is fine and sends you much love.

I must go to work on that horrible Aberdeen lecture.

All my love,
Mary

[Tegna]
June 12, 1974

Mary, my dear, Since Monday I have been trying to call you. This morning I finally got your number—pas de réponse. I give up. I want to know how you are; anyhow, no longer home-bound.

The Black Prince [a novel by Iris Murdoch] just arrived. Many thanks. I read the Solshenitzin [sic], Archipelagus [sic], very important, very factual, somehow in clear contradiction to his awful letter and also the August 4 [sic] novel about the first world war.[1] Strange. I read it in German but suppose that the English translation is already available.

Doctor's report: Everything fine, no diuretic pills any more—I had stopped anyhow because I discovered that my nausea was caused by them, frequent reaction—, no digitalis, some very mild medication to get blood pressure a bit down and the rapid pulse, both not extraordinarily high, just back to what for me is normal. Very good doctor, wants to check me every ten days, I should continue to take it easy up to July 1st. No objection to moderate smoking, no diet—in short, let's forget about it apart from the obvious advantages.

I enclose the review of de Beauvoir, by far the best I ever read about her.[2] I hope you can understand it, am too lazy to translate.

I'll try again to call.

Much, much love
De tout coeur—
Hannah

1. Arendt refers first to Solzhenitsyn's *The Gulag Archipelago: 1918–1956*, published in the United States in 1974, and to his *August 1914*, an English translation of which appeared in the United States in 1972. The "awful letter" has not been identified.
2. This review, probably in German, has not been found.

Paris
July 2, 1974

Dearest Hannah:

Finally a nice review.[1] How amazing that Richard Goodwin should have come to my defense or, rather, rescue. Remembering [Sheldon] Wolin's review of *him* in the NYRB, I can't help but smile and remember Chesterton's picture of Don John of Austria in "Lepanto": "When, rising from a doubtful seat and half-attainted [?]

stall . . . *Viva la Hispania, Domino Gloria,* Don John of Austria is off to the crusade."

Well, it has done my soul some good. The DuViviers telephoned Sunday (just after you) from Princeton to tell us it was in the paper. We had no idea; not a word from Bill. Then, yesterday morning, the review itself arrived from some HBJ underling. Jim had photostats made in the office and has started a distribution. (Don't be alarmed at what looks like a skin disease on my face in the photo. That's just the stat.) One swallow doesn't make a summer, but this one has rather made mine. I felt so battered and sunk. [2]

We're in the middle of packing books to send to Maine (at the U.S. government's expense; Jim's severance), a tax review (9:30 a.m. tomorrow at the Embassy), getting me off to Hull [3] by plane and train, working dizzily with Anjo Lévi on the Watergate translation, seeing the house painter.

Now I just send love and wish you well. *Are* you coming to Castine?

Mary

1. *The Mask of State* was favorably reviewed by Richard Goodwin in "Watergate Observed," *The New York Times Book Review,* June 30, 1974.
2. McCarthy's Vietnam-era reporting had been harshly reviewed by James Fallows in "The Blinders She Wears," *Washington Monthly,* May 1974. Subsequent notices were lackluster.
3. McCarthy was to receive an honorary doctorate from the University of Hull, in England.

[Castine]
July 23, 1974
[Postcard]

Dearest: We are in Castine—very beautiful—and hope you are coming. Occupied chiefly with the garden and the kitchen (Maria arrives August 1) but last night had time to start *The Gulag Archipelago.* Yes, what a book. And that *furious* energy. All love, Mary

Tegna
July 31, 1974
[Postcard]

Dearest Mary, I just booked my return flight for August 15th. I then shall stay in New York for some dentist work, hence I cancelled the Colorado trip. I could come to Castine provided you are sure that this is convenient—around the end of the month for about 8 to ten days. You don't have to rush to tell me now; plenty of time when I am home again. With a bit of luck we should be able to celebrate Nixon's downfall together. [1]

Much love to both of you—

Hannah

1. On July 24, 1974, the Supreme Court held that Nixon must surrender White House tapes pertaining to Watergate for use in a criminal proceeding. Meanwhile, the House Judiciary Committee started closed hearings on May 9, 1974, and on July 27 recommended three articles of impeachment, which the House of Representatives voted on August 20 to support.

Castine, Maine
August 8, 1974

Dearest Hannah:

Right after I wrote you, your card came. It looks as if you'll be too late for us to celebrate Nixon's passing together. Today that appears to be a matter of hours, if not minutes. [1] Yet I am outraged at the thought of the deal that's being cooked up to facilitate his departure, and Jim says that American citizens ought to refuse to pay taxes if one cent goes to him and Pat. I don't understand exactly what the mechanism is (and the press so far hasn't been helpful) but doubt that Congress is obliged to accept his resignation, rather than hold him to impeachment and conviction, with attendant loss of perquisites. If we can find out swiftly, we'll dispatch some telegrams to Congressmen.

Dear Hannah, the end of the month of August isn't good for me. My uncle [Frank Preston] from Seattle arrives the 30th for a two-day visit ending September 1, and I feel this must be a family affair—he's bringing his second wife and his stepson. Either before or after would work out for us. It occurs to us that if your dental work is like ours there is generally a hiatus in the middle of it—while impressions are sent to the laboratory. Assuming this is so, couldn't you have your first appointment shortly after your arrival, then come to Castine, then return to New York for your last appointments. All of that would fit in neatly before my uncle, who is a nice man but interested in little outside his circle of friends and relations and is now eighty years old. (He does or did have strong anti-Nixon feelings, though he's an inveterate Republican, but is perhaps not eager to dwell on them except among close friends.) Or, if our view of your possible dentistry doesn't match reality, you could come up on Sunday, the 1st, after that group leaves. But this would make a shorter visit for you, because Jim and I too probably will be leaving the 8th or even the 7th, which means we'll start dismantling the house and packing a day or two before, which usually entails a certain amount of frenzy. For us, either choice you make is fine, and we want so much to have you here again, as do all the Castiners who knew you the last time. You can decide when you get to New York and let me know then. The only visitor we expect after August 15 is Alison, though she may bring a friend for a few days. Kevin may come back, but I doubt it. He and Jeanette [Bonnier] have broken up and he is feeling sad and at very loose ends and will probably go to Italy soon to see his younger daughter.

We have continued to have marvelous weather, and Castine has never seemed more idyllic. The momentous events reaching us by television and radio only accentuate this, lending poignancy.[1]

You don't mention your health in your postcard, and this must be a good sign. Carl Cori[2] takes a great medical interest in your recent history and will probably quiz you about it when you get here. He has become very sweet but also deafer and is very fond of you—indeed is fatherly to all of us.

The enclosed made me sit up sharply. Bill hadn't said a word of it to me. Had he to you? In fact I haven't heard from him since we talked in New York on my arrival, and I now think I perceive a connection: he had bigger matters on his mind.[3]

I must stop and do some household chores now.

> Much, much love, and from Jim too,
> Mary

1. Nixon announced on August 8 that he would resign, effective August 9.
2. Cori, a retired physicist, was a neighbor of the Wests in Castine.
3. The enclosed was no doubt a news report of a proposed merger between Harcourt Brace Jovanovich and Simon & Schuster, which eventually fell through.

> 141 rue de Rennes
> Paris 75006
> September 9, 1974

Dear Hannah:

[. . .] We got back yesterday morning, rather groggy; I hate those night flights, even though, this time, by mistake, we were put in first class, which made it slightly better. Here we found there had been a flood, from a roof leak, in my study ten days ago; the bookcases in that side of the room, the wallpaper, and some of the books have suffered badly, and the whole study will have to be repapered and repainted. Despite repeated telephone calls by the concierge and the inhabitants below, who were flooded too, the leak went unrepaired for a week, during which time it rained again. When Maria arrived Friday morning, the water was coming in "*en ruisseaux,*" and she and the concierge, with pails, couldn't keep pace with the inundation. The wallpaper is still wet, and books are piled on the floor. I cannot get the *syndic* on the telephone, to demand that somebody from the insurance company come to inspect the damage, so that I can get the painter and paperhanger in, to put the room back in shape. There are two workmen on the balcony outside my window who keep passing back and forth through the apartment, leaving a wet trail (though we've put newspapers down)—it is raining again, hard. Well, I guess it is better than being robbed.

This morning, on the BBC, we heard that [President Gerald] Ford had pardoned Nixon. I. e., the cover-up continues.

Thank you for coming up. It was sad to watch you go through the gate at the airport without turning back. Something is happening or has happened to our friendship, and I cannot think that in noticing this I am being over-sensitive or imagining things. The least I can conjecture is that I have got on your nerves. Not to say this, finally—I was aware of it already in Aberdeen but discounted it then—would put us, or at any rate me, in a false position.

But anyway, my dear, love,

Mary

[New York]
September 12, 1974

Mary, my dear,

I just come home and find your letter, and it is too late to call. Tomorrow morning I'll have to go to town, hence it will be too early to call. Therefore I write and still am—and probably will remain—speechless. The notion that you could ever go [*sic*] on my nerves never crossed my mind. I don't know why I did not turn back at the airport;[1] I was very sad, your notion of my splendid solitude notwithstanding, I am of course lonely as everybody would be in my situation. You may be right or wrong in being suspicious of your friends, but you could not very well be suspicious of *me* — or could you? And what have I done to provoke that? And of what were you aware in Aberdeen where I was so grateful for every minute of your presence[?] For heaven's sake, Mary, stop it, *please*. I say that of course for my own sake and because I love you, but I think I also may say it for your sake.

Friday

I waited a day to think about it, but there is absolutely nothing that could occur to me. What I do know is that I am not sensitive and rather obtuse in all purely psychological matters. But this you must have known for a long time.

Martha J[ovanovich] just came visiting. She seems entirely recovered, looks and acts very much alive. I tried to reach Bill: he was sick but no heart trouble. Something in his neck which presses on a nerve; unpleasant but not dangerous. I hope I'll see him soon. That he failed to get the deal with Simon & Schuster is probably a blessing in disguise. [. . .]

I must say I feel much better than a few days ago. It almost looks as though the cover-up of the cover-up will not succeed. But what saves us is again: Courts plus Journalists (the media which are outraged) plus (perhaps) Universities, but not the Congress. It seems that every representative, Congressman or Senator, is afraid somebody will discover a little something once an investigation has started. It is of course also possible that Nixon still has some blackmailing power left. This would explain the sudden turn in Mr. Ford—to leak a little something about Mr. Candor as he [Nixon] certainly leaked something on Mr. Clean [Arendt's names]. I heard Mr. Ford's speech of compassion. Again—Tartuffe.[2] The fact is that Nixon didn't admit a thing and his letter could very well be the first step in a campaign for 1976.

If all this is too phantastic to be true, I would propose as alternative explanation that Kissinger was behind the pardon business. His honeymoon with the media and public opinion is definitely over; he has probably more reason to fear further developments than anybody else.

I have let myself go; *quastschen ins Unreine* [twaddle or talk rot], let your German teacher translate it. I somehow hope that the disaster of inundation has made you forget your dark thoughts. Incidentally,

I am not so sure that I'd rather be inundated than be robbed. About the latter one can hardly do anything—which is always a relief.

All my love—

Hannah

1. William Jovanovich, who was often enlisted to intervene in misunderstandings between Arendt and McCarthy, recalls that "Mary believed Hannah was displeased, or worse, because she abruptly departed her and Jim at the Bangor airport, yet Hannah was merely being European in not lingering over goodbyes."

2. Molière's Tartuffe is a religious hypocrite and impostor who uses pious cant to impose on the credulity of the wealthy man who has befriended him.

141 rue de Rennes
Paris 75006
September 30, 1974

Dearest Hannah:

Forgive me if you become anxious at not getting an answer to your letter. It came while I was in Italy, and I hoped that Bob, when he called you [. . .] told you I was there. I was off on a trip through Apulia—six days—with Carmen and would have sent a postcard if the state of the Italian mails hadn't been a strong deterrent. In fact they're somewhat better but I suspect not for postcards.

The trip was quite extraordinary—wonderful, really—in that we saw such a fantastic amount and with such speed. We traversed and crisscrossed a part of the "boot" and the whole heel, leaving the hotel usually at eight-thirty in the morning and returning about eight in the evening. Over drinks, we then worked on the next day's itinerary. (Naturally we had a driver, supplied by Carmen.) Until we got to the deep south, we saw almost exclusively Norman, Swabian, and Angovin buildings—fortresses and cathedrals. In the south, unavoidably and sometimes with pleasure, we confronted the baroque. Even so, we did not finish; Frederick's[1] biggest castle, at Lagopiceno (which in fact isn't in Puglia but in Basilicata), we had to renounce the last day. But we did see the few stones which are all that remain of the castle where he died of dysentery—Castelfiorentino. It has left me with a strong impression of that time and those exploits; in fact it was more an historical than an esthetic trip. With the Norman and Angevin enterprises in Italy you feel a kind of grandiloquence—the scale of some of the constructions is enormous—that reminded me of the late Romans: Leptis Magna in Africa. As though the models were all Late Empire and provincial Late

Empire. This was literally true of a weird mosaic floor in the cathedral at Otranto (12th century), done by a monk, who surely must have visited Piazza Armorina in Sicily. A crude Christian imitation of an already coarse model.

Frederick was different. Nothing grandiose or grandiloquent—at least in what has survived—but, rather, strict, severe, compact almost to the point of being witty, like an epigram. We saw his stone table, at Lucera, his mint or treasury, ditto, a steep, dense polygon, remains of façades and castles and, again of course, Castel del Monte. Marvelous. I now see the appeal to him of the octagon. Do you remember the one in Syracuse? At any rate, he wasn't a barbarian. I kept thinking of our Normans in Sicily, and they were different too—Saracenized and Byzantinized. Most of the Norman work we saw in Apulia went back to their predecessors, Robert Guiscard and Bohémond, and of course there are Eastern influences in it, memories of the Crusades, but in a kind of savage medley with other memories. Fairy-tale building. They were fond of huge wheel windows and lions and griffins. Every now and then, mixed up with Moslem influences, you would see the Norman zigzag. A few of their churches are beautiful, though, particularly one at Molfetta (not far from Bari), all white and right on the sea, like a fortress. But often more strange than beautiful.

The trip was my vacation, which I'm enjoying more in retrospect than at the time I did because it was quite exhausting (we didn't have a single coffee-break) and because I had been bitten by what seems to have been a spider or spiders, back in France, and came out with ferocious pustules that itched and burned and swelled alarmingly—one, which finally lanced itself in my sleep, was the size of a large cranberry or small cherry. Thanks to this affliction (I felt like Job with eleven of them up and down my arms), I ran a slight temperature for the first three days. When I came home, I found that Jim had them too but in a milder form and not so many, and it was he who fastened on a spider as the culprit: we had been marveling at some huge spider webs at a country lunch near Paris.

Your letter. Dear Hannah, I just thought you were cross with me about all sorts of minutiae, as though whatever I did or suggested doing rubbed you the wrong way. I'm glad to be mistaken, and it's true that I was/am in a sensitized state and perhaps notice things which are either not there or not worth noticing. As for Aberdeen,

I *know* you were cross with me some times (for instance when I brought you some fruit paste candies from Paris), but I attributed it to normal convalescent irritability and not to any special reaction to myself. Then in Castine, feeling that I was on your nerves again, I wondered about that. I have since learned, by chance, talking to Miriam re Nicola, that irritability is a cardiac symptom. In fact I hadn't noticed it in him, except that sometimes he would get utterly enraged, which I knew was not supposed to be good for him, and once or twice some "leftist" opinion of mine was the cause. But it's easy to repress an opinion ("Don't tell Nicola again that Italy would be an ideal country for a revolution!"), but not so easy to know what little actions or gestures of one's own are likely to be provoking to someone you love.

Second. No, I am not suspicious of my friends. What an idea. It isn't a suspicion but a certainty, an objective fact, that when I got some very rough treatment in the press this late spring and summer, not a soul came to my defense. Or, rather, two strangers did, and neither of their refutations was printed. My sense of hurt is generalized rather than particular. It is not that I think A or B should have come to my support; what astonishes me is that no one did. And I can't help feeling, though I shouldn't, that if one of my friends had been in *my* place, *I* would [have] raised my voice. This leads to the conclusion that I am peculiar, in some way that I cannot make out; *indefensible*, at least for my friends. They are fond of me but with reservations. In any case, none of this involves you, because you were in the hospital and then recovering when it happened, because you weren't in the U.S. and didn't see those unpleasant pieces and because, finally, even if you had been on Riverside Drive and in the peak of condition, you *couldn't* have helped since people would have said that you were repaying the Eichmann debt, that we had dedicated books to each other, etc., etc. In other words, that you were a tainted witness. I guess I expected help to come from somewhere in the middle distance—not from my nearest and dearest. Though I must admit that if *Jim* had picked up his pen, I would have rejoiced, even though it would have been a foolish thing for him to do. Or my brother Kevin. This shows, obviously, that I am no feminist.

You don't understand why I should mind being on the receiving end of so much hostility. Well, it would be better, clearly, if I didn't mind, but I do and I find it deeply discouraging. The sense that one is not "getting through" to one's imagined listeners; it is like making a transatlantic telephone call with a bad connection. The fact that this *keeps* happening to me (the worst probably was *Birds of America*, which nearly "cured" me of writing novels) adds a ghostly element of repetition, as though I were condemned to this punishment throughout eternity. . . . And the punishment is somehow mysteriously, arcanely, related to my eternal self: the bars of the cell are, so to speak, my own ribs.

Actually, for some reason, I am now in better spirits. Maybe the beautiful summer "took," but slowly. And Jim has come back extremely happy, even content with his job. Of course this makes things look brighter to me.

Anyway, my dear, thank you for responding as you did. That too has lightened my heart. I'll write again soon, about public preoccupations, when I have a little more time. I am working on my preface to Nicola. [2]

All my love,
Mary

1. Frederick II of Hohenstaufen (1194–1250), King of Sicily and Holy Roman Emperor.
2. Mary McCarthy, "The 'Place' of Nicola Chiaromonte (1905–1972)," *The New York Review of Books*, February 20, 1975. ("Place" in medieval theatre was the central acting arena around which were grouped the various pageants.)

Paris
November 20, 1974

Dearest Hannah:

Carl and Anne Cori, who leave for England tomorrow (he is to talk on euthanasia at a scientific congress) are taking some letters for me. [1] [. . .]

All well here. I had a lovely time with you, my dear. [2] And guess who called yesterday evening—Jonathan Schell, who is here with Elspeth and staying at the St. Simon. I asked them to come immediately for a drink, since I happened to be entertaining a few other people, some young. They did, and we talked very nicely—and fondly—of you and of the dinner party they missed. He's such a good and intelligent young man and, by the way, getting better-looking every minute. He'll be here about ten days and plans to do a Talk of the Town piece on Paris. One wishes him luck; the situation is murky. There was a general strike yesterday, which didn't amount to much—in our apartment, we didn't have even a momentary shut-off of heating, cooking gas, or light. My impression is that the unions aren't eager for a real confrontation, and that Giscard [d'Estaing] is trying to push them into one. Chirac[3] gave a very ugly speech on television Monday. If Giscard is counting on producing a smashing victory over the left by these provocation tactics, I think he may win in the short run and fail in the long, since the grievances are genuine and most people know it. It also seems obvious that a compromise with the postal sorters could have been worked out, with some needed benefits for them, had he not decided to play the confrontation game. Some reports say that he is counting on mass unemployment to reduce inflation. But there's also a rumor, recounted to us yesterday, that he has no plan, deep-laid or otherwise, that he is in a state of confusion and torpor and half the time appears to be absent, unaware of what's going on. The distancing from reality that visits heads of state nowadays. Perhaps there could be a little of both. A plan and inattentiveness.

One of our friends, an old Polish painter, went to Solzhenitsyn's press conference in Zurich. A truly extraordinary man, he said, both morally and physically. Built like a bison. Makes a powerful impression when he speaks because of his total sincere conviction. [Joseph] Czapski (the painter) said that if he had read some of those things he was hearing in a newspaper, he would have thought them mad. But, as pronounced, they carried authority. At this press conference, S. announced that the devil was not Stalinism or Leninism but socialism in its entirety. Yet, as another Polish friend said, in fact he himself sounds like a socialist of some sort—the Christian kind. He is on a single track, they say, and indifferent to any errors in the transmission of his message that might be caused by differences of vocabulary. Meanwhile another book from the camps has come out—[Andrey] Sinyavsky's *Une Voix dans le Choeur.* It had a wonderful review from still another Pole in the *Monde.* I shall get it and let you know my reaction.

Don't tell Bill yet, but I think I'll forgo the autobiography for the moment and do a novel.[4] In fact I've started it. I want to get enough into it to establish the tone (the old one, if I can manage it, of the omniscient author) before telling him. Of course it's much harder to do than the autobiography would be (I wrote down a few notes on that too), and, being a perverse creature, I've been seduced by the temptation of difficulty. If it is a moral temptation, then I am making a mistake, but if it's an aesthetic one, maybe I am not.

I meant to write only a word, and now look! When Jonathan Schell goes home, if there's still no mail, I'll try to send another communication. We were out all day Sunday; hence no telephone call.

All my love to you and my thanks, dear,
Mary

P.S. Don't be mystified by the London return address. I've heard that the English post-office may not accept mail now with a French one.

1. French postal workers were on strike.
2. McCarthy had visited Arendt in New York earlier in November, and Arendt had given a large dinner party for her.
3. Jacques Chirac, prime minister under President Giscard d'Estaing, was a conservative who defeated the leftist candidate, François Mitterand, on May 19, 1974.
4. Jovanovich had proposed an "intellectual autobiography" as McCarthy's next work; the novel she was starting instead was *Cannibals and Missionaries*.

December 1974(?) [1]

ARRIVE MONDAY DEC 23RD 10PM FLIGHT 200 LOVE

HANNAH

1. Date and question mark were added by McCarthy.

[Hannah Arendt spent Christmas 1974 with the Wests in Paris. Back in New York, she received a letter from Thor A. Bak, Rector of the University of Copenhagen, informing her that she had been awarded the Sonning Prize for "meritorious work for European civilization." She was invited to Denmark to accept it.

Before leaving for Copenhagen in the spring, Arendt found herself immersed in a strike at the New School. Mary McCarthy, meanwhile, was at work on *Cannibals and Missionaries*.]

141 rue de Rennes, Paris
February 17, 1975

Dearest Hannah:

I wish I hadn't been in the middle of a delicate cooking operation yesterday when you called. Not that the call was ill timed—it came during the ten-minute idle interval between Step 3 and Step 4—but

I should have liked to talk longer. We'd been thinking of you and thinking, by coincidence, of calling *you* at some point during the evening. . . .

I wanted to hear more about the New School. Who was striking? Malcontents in the faculty, I assume.[1] Al Copley,[2] who was here, told me that you were very much involved in goings on at the New School, but his information wasn't very recent.

As for me, as I said, I had just finished the long first chapter of my new novel, and Jim had declared a holiday in reward. We went down to the center of France, the Allier, and explored various churches and gastronomic points. We had Eleanor Perényi[3] (you remember) and her cat along—she a trying passenger but the cat as good as gold. She suffers from acute anxieties of every description; no sooner is one allayed than another erupts. What a capacity for *worrying* a subject from every conceivable angle! [. . .] It struck me that I have a whole collection of neurotically afflicted friends, mostly female, e.g., Lizzie and Anjo Lévi, who are actually crippled by these symptoms while being at the same time almost abnormally rational, at the other pole from genuinely mad people. Travel affects most of them badly; they fall apart when outside their own controlled environment. Eleanor, for instance, imagines that she has a passion for France and Paris, yet, having moved in for three months to an apartment here, complains incessantly about the marketing— she is used to having her groceries delivered—claiming that it takes her "whole day," though she is only one person and, so far as I know, has had no guests. . . . I fear she won't last out her so long coveted stay but get sick and retreat to Stonington, [Connecticut]. She also vociferously hates air travel but when I say "Well, take the boat back," she at once finds so many arguments against boats, starting with "They take too long," that I feel I am loony to be booked on the Queen Elizabeth July 1.

Oh, my dear, sorry, I didn't start out to write about Eleanor, but since yesterday, after a weekend of restraint on our parts, she has been prominent in our thoughts. Last night I arrived at the formulation that her problem was that she is a soured hedonist. She assumes I am a hedonist too, likening Jim and me to Scott Fitzgerald's friends the Murphys (*Tender Is the Night*) with their "gift for living." I decided that any attempt at correction here would be invidious and let it go.

My work. I've been fairly well buried in this novel and alternate between exhilaration and despondency, with unusual highs and lows. Jim has read the just finished chapter and is enthusiastic. The chief figure—don't tell anybody—is an Episcopal minister, no hedonist he. I hope I am doing something new, for me anyway, but then I find I am steering down a channel with some very familiar landscape on either side. On the one hand he keeps sounding like the girls in *The Group* and on the other like Peter Levi [in *Birds of America*]. Scylla and Charybdis. It is sad to realize that one's fictions, i.e., one's "creative" side, cannot learn anything. *I* have learned, I think, but they, or it, haven't. The reason for this would be interesting to discover, if only one had the time. Those confining boundaries, I suppose, are set by my life-experience, which lies in vaguely upper-middle-class territory lying between those girls and Peter. My mental experience is broader, but that doesn't seem to count for the imagination. And if I went and worked in a factory, would the "hands" in a novel I wrote afterwards think like Vassar B-minus students of forty years ago or else be half-Jewish, thoughtful, and given to humor? I am going to have a Jewish character, a young woman, in this novel, and already I am feeling the temptation to make her *half*-Jewish, in the belief that I cannot fully imagine, from the *inside*, the outlook of a Jewish girl. It all leads to the awful recognition that one *is* one's life; God is not mocked.

I'm glad you've heard good things about the Chiaromonte preface. As you know, I guess, Bill is going to do a collection of his writings that Miriam is putting together. I learn to my horror that they're expecting me to do a preface for *that*. I must have agreed a long time ago and forgotten. It seems to me that it would be a bad mistake, from a publishing point of view, for me to take this on. As I wrote to Miriam, I would feel like Max Brod.[4] And to anyone who was aware of the NYRB preface, it would look like an egregious case of log-rolling. Yet Nicola does need introducing. Do you think Dwight could do it? Meyer Schapiro, a close friend of his, is another possibility, but I doubt whether he's available to do such a presentation.

I'll take this up with Bill when he gets back from his vacation.[5] I have a number of things to take up with him, the foremost being that they have let my Florence book, the illustrated hard-cover one [*The Stones of Florence*], go out of print. Without telling me. They have known this was going to happen since 1970! Having found it out by accident, I'm distressed and angry. It emerges that the Swiss printer was unwilling to print less than 5000 copies. So then Bill and Julian Muller [HBJ editor-in-chief] sounded out Heinemann, who had done the English publication, on taking a share of that. Failing to excite any interest, they quit. No thought, apparently, of trying Weidenfeld, who loves doing art books, or any of my French, German, or Italian publishers. Now, five years later, in the middle of a recession, that will not be as easy as it might have been then. Still, I'm determined to try. I can't understand Bill's concealing this from me for all this time. Or perhaps I can: he was afraid I'd push him into making further efforts.

Outside these self-centered arenas I have no news. In fact not much is happening, to judge by the newspapers. A lull. And what the French papers characterize as *"un drôle de récession."* Factory lay-offs, unemployment, in the midst of what looks like full prosperity: stores full, roads jammed with traffic to and from ski resorts during the recent ten-day school vacation, and the cars are cheap cars packed with families carrying their skis on top. . . . A mystery. The "last spree" explanation, which has been given since Christmas, doesn't seem to fit any more. The classified columns in the papers, which ought to be an index, show no change. Practically no "Domestic Situations Wanted"—there's one boy in the *Herald Tribune* who has been offering himself as an "apartment sitter". . . . Real-estate prices haven't fallen, though I hear they have in England.

Jim's office was wildly busy two weeks ago with the new energy committee that has been inserted in the OECD structure. Now all quiet, as if forgotten.

We have no plans beyond a few days in London for me next month, when George Weidenfeld is giving a party for *The Seventeenth Degree.* The DuViviers have arrived there for a month or six weeks. You *must* tell me about the weekend you spent with them in Princeton. I know from Ellie [DuVivier] only that it happened and find it almost impossible to picture you in that Aladdin's lamp house which sits so strangely in Princeton as though it had been deposited, with all its little treasures, by a magic carpet. Poor Ellie—she is another of my frenzied females but different because she isn't bright and knows it and has transferred her small aggressive sense of authority (also her anxiety) to her objects, which she then turns on angrily as if they were false friends.

This letter has turned out much longer than I intended. I wish we could talk a long time. I miss you tremendously.

Much love,
Mary

1. The strikers were clerical workers, newly organized by the Teamsters union.
2. Dr. Alfred L. Copley, a physician, was also a painter known as Alcopley. A German émigré, he was a member of the circle with whom Blücher and Arendt regularly gathered on New Year's Eve.
3. The writer Eleanor Perényi (1918–) was a friend of Mary McCarthy's from Stonington, Connecticut.
4. Max Brod, Kafka's close friend and executor, edited and published his unfinished writings and his diaries, presumably against Kafka's will; he also wrote his biography.
5. An abbreviated version of McCarthy's preface in *The New York Review of Books* was used to introduce Chiaromonte's *The Worm of Consciousness and Other Essays* (1974).

141 rue de Rennes
Paris 6
February 28, 1975

Dearest Hannah:

I've been rather hoping to hear from you but bravely contained myself. [. . .]

I'm dictating this letter in a hurry, but must add that our friend Eleanor Perényi in fact came down the same day I wrote you with acute appendicitis and was operated on at midnight that night in the American Hospital. It turned out that she had pus in the abdominal cavity and a touch of peritonitis. She is still in the hospital— getting out tomorrow—and we have her cat, a beautiful animal and sweet but unhappy about the absence of his mistress. Something he makes known to us regularly during the small hours of the night.

Much love,
Mary

New School for Social Research
66 West 12th St.
New York, N.Y. 10011
March 10, 1975

Dearest Mary:

This is a dictated letter—please forgive me. [. . .] I'm relieved to hear that everything finally turned out alright with Eleanor Perényi. I hope you are now reasonably free of visitors. I wish we could talk about the novel; I always believed that "one *is* one's life."

I'm writing today for a number of reasons. 1) I bought the dress.[1] 2) I wrote to Copenhagen that Jovanovich will come and perhaps you too. I asked them to tell me the hotel but did not suggest the Terminus because I had a hunch it would be wiser to leave it to the people concerned. Yesterday there was a short notice of the prize in the New York Times and now people begin to call up, but it's not too bad. My second reason for writing today is that Elizabeth (Elke) Gilbert—you remember her from Zurich—who translated Yeats's prose writings into German and got a translator prize for it wants very badly to translate your essay about Chiaromonte as well as his own essay about Pirandello from your English translation. She is really very good, very committed, and since she doesn't need the money, she can spend much more time than the usual German translators which are usually awful. What she would like is that you tell your agent or whoever it may be that you recommend her as translator. Do it only if it can be done without any fuss and feathers.

I had hoped to see Jovanovich today but didn't. [. . .] It seems now that he will be in Copenhagen on the 18th with the night flight from New York, arriving at 7:20 am and stay until Sunday. I shall be in Copenhagen on the 17th with the same flight and go home on Sunday at 12:30 pm which arrives in New York around 4:00 pm. Mary, believe me the whole thing is a nuisance.

I talked to Bill about the Florence book and I think he was really innocent. About the DuViviers I'll tell you when we see each other.

Much love to Jim and yourself,

Yours,
Hannah

1. McCarthy had urged Arendt to buy a new dress for the Sonning Prize award ceremony on April 18.

[In the spring of 1975, Hannah Arendt also accepted an invitation from Mayor Kevin White, of Boston, to speak at an early Bicentennial ceremony at the Boston Forum on May 20. Arendt's "Home to Roost" address, as it was called, mourned the recent "years of aberration": the Vietnam War, which had finally ground to a chaotic end; Watergate and the coverup; Ford's blanket pardon of Nixon. Together, these events signaled a "decline of the Republic's power," Arendt maintained, in a speech that was widely discussed throughout the United States.

After Boston, she went to Germany to deliver a lecture in Cologne, and then to the German Literary Archive in Marbach to deposit a collection of her letters to and from Karl Jaspers, Kurt Blumenfeld, and Erwin Loewenson (an old friend from Berlin). In her capacity as co-executor of Jaspers's literary estate, she stayed on in Marbach several weeks to sort and organize his correspondence for eventual publication. Mary McCarthy visited her there toward the end of June.]

Paris
May 26, 1975

Dearest Hannah: How happy I've been all day, with the sound of your voice so near. It nearly gave rise to the mad project of driving to Cologne this Saturday. But then we looked at your schedule and saw you would be gone—Friday. [. . .] So much love,

Mary

Cologne
5/29/75

Dearest Mary—enclosed the promised Xerox copy.[1] I just read your participation in the Symposium.[2] *Very* good. I also enclose a quotation of yours in German on [Adalbert] Stifter with which my friend here—Johannes Filkens—wishes to quarrel. I can't quite understand why; but here it is [missing].

New York is millions of miles away. Tomorrow I leave for Marbach. Köln [Cologne] was *very* nice this time. Anyhow I am looking forward to the 15th![3] I'll call you as soon as I have my own telephone.

Best of luck for the novel. Give Jim my love.

Je t'embrasse—
Hannah

1. This was the New School's "summer and fall itinerary of Hannah Arendt," which listed her projected travels from May 23, Cologne, through October 25, Aberdeen.
2. Arendt could be referring to "Living with Beautiful Things," presented as part of a lecture series in Pittsburgh in April 1974 and, as "Art Values and the Value of Art," in Aberdeen in May. It impressed Arendt by its insight into the psychology of collectors, and she had proposed that McCarthy make use of it in a novel—which she did, in *Cannibals and Missionaries*.
3. McCarthy was coming to Marbach for a visit.

141 rue de Rennes
Paris
June 24, 1975

Dearest Hannah:

Here is the [Daniel] Cohn-Bendit clipping. Thank you for everything.[1] How is the weather there? Here it is horrible. Rumor says that the only good weather in Europe is in, of all places, Brittany. . . .

Jim gave me a splendid surprise [birthday] party—at the house of friends, with about thirty people, including, to my amazement, Alison [West] and our Dutch friend [the writer Cees] Nooteboom.

It has all been constant festivity—Carmen and Ernest too and last night a grand dinner given in a restaurant by J. F. Revel at which, alas, I broke a bridge (the dental kind) on a piece of toast liberally spread with caviar. This is tiresome and may eliminate Stonington from my itinerary[2]—if I have to have a new bridge made by my dentist in New York. . . . Tomorrow I consult my Paris dentist for his opinion.

Much talk about Portugal. Soares telephoned Revel yesterday from Lisbon to say he would no longer be permitted to leave the country. It appears that General Carvalho attempted a coup ("Idi Amin style") and failed, with the result that, in some fashion, he has been kicked upstairs. But it is all still very murky and ominous.[3] [. . .]

Take care of yourself, my dear. Don't do too much. I think it will be a great joy for you to be in Tegna and taken care of. You deserve that.

> Much love (and in slight haste),
> Mary

1. E.g., Arendt's hospitality in Marbach.
2. McCarthy planned to visit Eleanor Perényi in Stonington, Connecticut, before going to Castine later that summer.
3. After a bloodless coup overthrew the Portuguese dictatorship in 1974, the new government, led by young military officers, promulgated a constitution giving essential power to the armed forces. Mario Soares was a Socialist who became premier in 1976. General Otelo Saraiva de Carvalho was head of security forces under the left-wing military government. McCarthy followed Portuguese events closely.

> Castine
> July 20, 1975

Dearest Hannah:

Castine. We are having a heat wave—unusual. I've been here nine days. The other night, summoned by Philip Booth, we saw the Apollo-Soyuz from the back lawn, Maria and I. Its speed was like a 747's, only more so. Since I was three days behind in reading the newspapers and hadn't turned on television, I had no idea what it was we were supposed to be witnessing. *"Les Russes,"* I said, vaguely, to Maria.

Intellectual life practically zero, except for what is self-generated, in one's head. Lizzie's tongue rattles, like a child's toy, sometimes making amusing sounds. I work a bit in the garden, weeding and setting out what I hope will be nice flowers, read, and have started on the third chapter of my novel, the remote action of which still seems a little unreal. Today I went to lunch at the Tolmans [Lee and Sally], where we had martinis, lobster salad, pot de crème au chocolat, and some aged Stalinists, house guests, whom Joe McCarthy seems to have overlooked in the State Department—too dull, Lizzie said, to have claimed attention. They had just been on a tour of Russia and were thrilled by the progress they saw. Jews on their tour, they claimed, were able to see their relatives freely. It was true, said the husband, that Jewish emigration was discouraged, but then *all* emigration was discouraged, so there was no discrimination. . . .

At the end, we got into a slight fight about Solzhenitsyn, regarded by people like that as now the main enemy of mankind. I feel so stricken by what he is doing and saying here, but of course philistines of all sorts are ecstatic in condemning him, so that I am driven to take his side, humanly, and express the hope that his intelligence and perceptiveness will eventually open his eyes to the quality of the people he is being used by—[George] Meany and Reagan and also our acquaintances Kristol and Podhoretz. No doubt he imagines that he is using *them*, to get his message across. An awful woman in Stonington, where I was staying with Grace Stone [Eleanor Perényi's mother] and Eleanor, said disdainfully "Well, of course, Solzhenitsyn is an *ass.*" If I weren't working on my novel, I would make an open letter of the imaginary letters I write him while falling asleep at night.

The Coris told of their visits to you.[1] You are reported very well, physically, as well as gay and full of energy. I trust Carl on these things but I do not wholly trust Annie, who also reported that you told her that you had never liked your mother.

I have seen them only once but am having dinner with them tonight. The wine got here safely, after its peripatetics. Jim, in Paris, seems to be well; we talked this morning. He is leading, except for the office, an even more solitary life than I am. Everyone I see wants to discuss his eventual retirement with me. Grace Stone strongly counseled against it; her own husband, she said, became extremely irritable.

Bill, in New York, seemed to be in good form. As you know, he's now in Mallorca—his last flight from home. I was touched by his melancholy about it. George [Boone, Jovanovich's driver] told me happily that "Mrs. Jovanovich is real well."

I'm reading Saul Bellow's book (novel) about Delmore [Schwartz].[2] Lizzie thinks it is awful, but I find it much better than *Mr. Sammler*, rather like a softer and more disarrayed *Herzog*, which was already mushy in parts. The Chicago sections, as usual, are good, I think, and the book seems to come from somewhere close to Saul's heart rather than from his schematic, paranoid brain. But it is certainly not a success (I mean artistically; it hasn't come out yet); in fact he seems to know that while writing it and the whole thing is haunted by a sense of failure and unresolved promise, both his own and Delmore's (I think he greatly overrates Delmore's "genius," but his own was real and still in evidence, like the traces of an overgrown garden). Practically everybody we know is in this novel, in ludicrous, childish disguise; Dwight, for instance, is "Orlando Huggins," identifiable by a short beard and a stammer. I haven't yet found you or me.

The humming-birds are back. I have seen one pair of goldfinches. It is as beautiful as ever here, and I suppose I could sink into what Rahv called "rural idiocy." But only for four months of a year.

Did you ever get the letter I sent to Marbach? Please write— just a postcard to say how you are. And how "Judgment" goes.[3] I miss you.

All my love,
Mary

[. . .]

1. Carl and Anne Cori had visited Arendt in Tegna.
2. Bellow's new novel, *Humboldt's Gift*, won the Pulitzer Prize for fiction in 1976.
3. Arendt's reflections on the faculty of Judgment were to be the subject of the third and final Gifford lecture.

CH 6652 Tegna, Ti[cino]
Casa Barbatè   1975[1]

Dearest Mary,

thanks for your letter, so good to have it. The Coris—it was nice

380

and I like him. Ann [sic] is really impossible but good natured (the business with my mother is of course sheer, well, imagination) and she takes well care of him. We have a radiantly beautiful summer here and I am grateful for so much sun without heat and without humidity. I am very well (physically) but work is so-so at best. After Marbach where I succeeded in finishing all business I got extremely lazy and am coming back to Judgment and Kant only now. I read the posthumous fragments. Partly very beautiful; strange that no one, apparently, has ever read through them and published a selection of aphorisms. As for instance that speculations about an afterlife could be likened to a caterpillar who knows that his true destiny is to become a butterfly.

I had a letter from Bill and am worried about this "last flight from home." He wrote he would call from London or Mallorca, but has not. He agreed to use your edited version of the bicentennial article instead of his, so perhaps he is offended or he is losing interest or what?[2] —I was very pleased with your remarks about Saul. It is so much better to think well of him after all those years when he really was unbearable. I had good reports about his new girl and his change from others.

I enclose a card [missing] about my "rural idiocy" marking my terrace where too robbins [sic] appear every morning to pick up the crumbs from my breakfast. Elke [Gilbert] is here and that is nice and relaxing for company. Tomorrow we shall go to the circus. Did you read the Sartre interview in the NY Review of Books?[3] It seems to me among his very best things. Genuine and honest and quite interesting.

Dear, I feel like calling for a little talk, but that seems really a bit extravagant since there is not even the shade of a pretext let alone a reason. Also, I am submerged in mail, partly still as a result of "Home to roost." I think I never had so many "fan" letters for anything I wrote. Strange, chiefly of course because of the Tom Wicker editorial [praising the speech in *The New York Times*]. The power of the press. Among these letters one greatly amusing—after the usual compliments the young man wrote that he heard that I was "going on in years" and he wanted me to know his opinions before I "pass on."

Much much love
yours,
Hannah

1. The date is in McCarthy's handwriting; probably late July.
2. Arendt's Bicentennial address, "Home to Roost," was reproduced by Sam Bass Warner, Jr., in *The American Experiment: Perspectives on 200 Years* (1976).
3. "Sartre at Seventy: An Interview," by Michel Contat, *The New York Review of Books*, August 7, 1975.

Castine, Maine 04421
August 5, 1975

Dearest Hannah:

I loved hearing from you. [. . .]

Things have been very quiet here until Jim's arrival August 1, which more or less coincided with a fearsome heat wave and a village political storm over a property tax voted by the state legislature for the purpose of equalizing Maine's education. It is a weird business. Castine has had sixteen minutes on national television (CBS); it has been in all the papers because it has voted to refuse to collect or pay the tax. The local people are fired with the Spirit of '76 and acting like a bunch of minute-men. Ten days ago a Superior Court judge in Portland (Maine) ordered the town officials to pay the tax or be held in contempt, so last night a town meeting was held to decide what action to take in view of the court order.

Everybody attended, some virtually in wheelchairs, with Bangor reporters and TV cameras watching. The point is that the legislation was designed to penalize the "rich coastal towns" with high property assessments to favor the poor parts of the state which don't raise enough money in property taxes to pay for their local schools. The coastal towns, naturally, are indignant and some have banded together to declare the law unconstitutional and fight it in the courts. On that point almost everybody here is in agreement; they believe the law is unjust, whether because of the principle involved (that the rich should be soaked for the poor) or because property assessments in the state vary widely, some being fixed too high (Castine's case) and some too low (a few towns like Camden that are full of millionaires and have property assessments that might be suitable for a trailer camp). But on what methods to be used to correct the inequity, there is heated disagreement. The other coastal towns that have joined the legal battle have levied the tax and either paid it over provisionally to the state or are holding it in escrow until the Supreme Court (state) hands down a decision. Castine, however, stands alone in its mutinous attitude and the five town officials risk going to jail or paying a whacking fine. Last night's town meeting

382

was held to decide whether to persist in this open rebellion or pay up temporarily and remain within the law.

The moderate or law-abiding party includes most of our friends and us; Phil Booth has emerged as a leader. Whereas the immoderates include most of the natives and some transplants like the local retired military (Col. Dodge up the street, Gen. Gillette, who sold us our house). The situation thus is paradoxical, with the richer, i.e., more educated residents—those who stand to suffer most from the new law—urging compliance, while the poorer—the bulk of the population—are up in arms. In general the moderate party are liberals, and the few liberals among the natives have either been converted to our view or are trying to stay out of it—especially, as you can imagine, the shopkeepers, anxious not to offend *anybody*—and have found various pretexts for not voting ("Well, you see, I don't think I *ought* to vote, because I'm on the school board"). Another complication is that the moderates are mostly summer residents and therefore can't vote; though they were allowed to speak last night, they weren't allowed to cast a ballot. At the same time they pay a high share of the property taxes. By a freak of circumstance, Jim and I are on the town rolls as residents and *can* vote.

I hope this isn't a bore to you. Last night was comical, also depressing, as an example of village democracy. I said to Jim at one point "I do hope the *polis* wasn't like this." The atmosphere was so inflamed that anybody who didn't want to see the town officials go to jail was treated as a public enemy, and this morning it was being said—by extreme elements—that Phil Booth was a "socialist," even a "communist." There have been numerous references to "Russia," now identified with Augusta, Maine. Of course the natives have good reason in a way to be angrier than we are, because they can't afford, many of them, to pay the additional tax, while we can. So that there *is* a class division, though the leadership elements of the locals are, naturally, the illiberal rich and propertied. It is easy to pick out, looking at the tense excited faces, the fascists in embryo in the village, who are carrying the more conservative and frightened innocents along with them. Well, it's a microcosm. And where "Russia" was much invoked by the minute-men, Watergate, though not mentioned by name, played an obvious part in swaying those natives who moved over to the moderate position, mentioning the necessity for "respect for the law" on the part of public officials. . . .

Among those who spoke that you know were Phil Booth, Tommy

Thomas, and I. And Lee Tolman—did you meet him?—a nice New York lawyer, now retired, and friend of David DuVivier. Lizzie held her peace, though not privately. The issues are as tangled in her mind as in most of the natives' and, like them, she has most of the facts insistently wrong. Her position, so far as it can be located, is that Castine ought to be soaked, because "it's just a retirement town!", and at the same time, somehow, that our property tax is infamous. She is fixated on Nelson Rockefeller's property, over on Mount Desert, and keeps comparing his situation with that of a poor mill worker in Portland who has to send his children to school—which is neither here nor there so far as the issues in Castine are concerned.

In the town meeting of course we lost but did much better than anybody expected—125 to 65. After it ended, at nine o'clock, we had some food and drink here for fourteen of the moderate persuasion. I have the feeling that despite the victory and the jubilation all is not over. There may be another town meeting, when people have started to notice that they will be paying heavy fines and legal costs as well as—probably—the jacked-up property tax in the long run. This prospect, quite realistic, I fear, was not even mentioned last night.

This morning, to cap the story, Jim and I saw a large tourist bus from Brunswick, Maine, drive down Main Street and pause to look at Emerson Hall, the scene of last night's action. A hankering for publicity has a good deal to do with last night's vote. The eye of television has hypnotized these poor people.

That is our news. But I'm glad to report that we played no part in the electioneering. Instead, I have been working, rather well, I hope, and with intense concentration. Now that Jim is here, and Reuel will be coming with his little boy, that period is over. Still, I shall be able to shut myself up for some part of the day, since few guests are expected.

I finished reading Jonathan Schell's pieces[1] and find them a good deal better than I thought when we were together. Much too wordy still, but the link he makes between the image business and "credibility" and the nuclear impasse is new, so far as I know. Nobody has thought to put the three things together before, though separately they were familiar. Where you go from there is something else, and he doesn't contemplate that, unfortunately.

On the other hand, I found Saul Bellow's book [*Humboldt's Gift*] much worse than I thought when I wrote you. The middle part is the best or the better. I shall be curious to see the reviews. Lizzie thinks they will be very laudatory, full of male *machismo*, as she puts it.

I miss you.

Much love,
Mary

1. Jonathan Schell, "Reflections: The Nixon Years," *The New Yorker*, June 2, 9, 16, 23, 30, and July 7, 1975.

Tegna
den 22, August 1975

Dearest Mary,

Your letter greeted me when I came back from a little trip. Annchen was here this week and just left. I am glad to have some quiet, hardly worked at all this month. I was very amused about the Castine turmoil, also proud that it got 20 minutes television time. Well, the polis was not quite like that for the simple reason that the Assembly did not vote on soaking the rich; if I remember rightly, that was done by the Executive directly to pay, not for the poor, but for processions, games and the theatre. It is unlikely that they (the rich) enjoyed it very much; there was no law, only a kind of noblesse oblige.

I was in Freiburg and came home very depressed. Heidegger is now suddenly really very old, very changed from last year, very deaf and remote, unapproachable as I never saw him before. I have been surrounded here for weeks by old people who suddenly got very old. I don't know if I told you that my first husband [Günther Anders] suddenly surfaced—in very bad shape. He now tells me that his present wife—an American woman, pianist—has left him. He sits in Vienna, I think completely alone. Rather ghastly. Then Morgenthau: called me up: he wants to come for a week. A few days later; he must cancel, he had a stroke. This turned out to be a mistake—probably a mixture of a severe case of hypochondria and incompetence of his physician. Annchen was also not well at all; high blood pressure etc. Then, Uwe Johnson[1] who was supposed to come here, writes that he had a coronary—of course much too young for such extravaganza. I am not even sure that this is true;

he drinks very heavily and probably does not want to admit a collapse. Elke is here now, thanks God [sic] completely unchanged; Pellegrini, my driver, calls her la bella donna. But Robert (Gilbert, do you remember?) has lost about 30 pounds, does not touch any alcohol or cigarette or coffee and is interested only in his various diseases which he does not even have. I suspect that all this would not touch me greatly if I were not so depressed about Heidegger.

We had a very beautiful summer here, weatherwise perhaps the best ever. Something actually funny happened a few days ago: I was selected as winner of the first award [the Lippincott Award] of the American Political Science Association (which had ignored me for more than 20 years) for The Human Condition "as the best work in political theory" that has survived at least 15 years since publication. It is not much money, but I don't have to come to the ceremony (name a stand-in) and don't have to sing. [James] Kirkpatrick, the very powerful Executive Secretary (with whom I had a terrific row a few years ago because of the Pentagon Papers, if I remember rightly) writes me a very cool letter. The nomination was done by a Committee and had to be submitted "no later than April 15"; it seems the gentleman hoped for a miracle before he could get himself to notify me. The whole thing is very amusing.

I did not receive Schell's last pieces and read only one review of Saul's book. The nicest thing about Tegna is that one is so far away from everything. I read a good article about Nixon in the Observer and enclose the clipping.

Finally: I got the invitation to the "International Symposium" in Paris about the Year 2000. The trouble is that it is not in Paris but in Jouy-en-Josas, about 30 km. away from Paris. That means I am much less tempted and not sure that I shall not cancel: To go there would mean to be imprisoned for 4 days in something which, after all, interests me only because of language.[2] When do you come back? Let me know.

All my love—give Jim my love and also many greetings for Phil Booth, and the Koris [sic] and of course Maria, Reuel.

yours,
Hannah

1. German novelist Uwe Johnson was a close friend of Arendt's.
2. In late September Arendt did attend the symposium, entitled "Terrors of the Year 2000," where she served as a critical commentator on a paper about the future of terrorism.

141 rue de Rennes
Paris 6
October 22, 1975

Dearest Hannah:

This is a hurried dictated note, written really at the instance of Miriam Chiaromonte. She wondered, by telephone, whether it would be all right to ask Harcourt to send you a copy of Nicola's book [*The Worm of Consciousness and Other Essays*] for comment. I told her to go ahead; I'm sure you'll want to see the book, and a comment of course would be nice for her and, I guess, for Bill too. A review would be wonderful, but I told Miriam that I thought you were doing no reviews on account of Willing and Judging. How I wish Nicola himself could read that book when it's finished. In many senses he was the ideal reader for it.

I am still in a rather low state physically but have found a new doctor, who of course could discover nothing wrong with me by doing the usual tapping, poking, and listening. But he's sending me for tests of the various organs and elements of the body, and perhaps something will show up. He thinks what he describes as my "fatigue" (it isn't that) might be a sequel to the grippe, which by general accord has been a particularly vicious type this year in Paris. Jim thinks it's anemia. We shall see.

I shall write a new and more intimate letter soon. With much love to you, and from Jim also.

Mary

[New York]
November 3rd 1975

Dearest Mary:

This too is hurried and dictated. Just to let you know immediately that it is alright to send me Nicola's book, though I can't promise I will comment. I will certainly read it carefully.

Please let me know about the physician's tests. Why don't you come? We will find a good doctor here.

Yours,
[Not read; signed in her absence]

New School for Social Research
66 West 12th Street
New York, N.Y. 10011
November 10th 1975

Dearest Mary:

You wanted to get your files [from] the Secret Service.[1] The enclosed tells you how to get it.[2]

Yours,
Much love
Hannah

I'll see Jovanovich tomorrow and shall write then.

H.

1. "the Secret Service" was added in Arendt's hand.
2. Probably instructions for obtaining copies of FBI and CIA files under the 1966 Freedom of Information Act.

141 rue de Rennes
Paris 6
November 12, 1975

Dearest Hannah:

Again by dictation. Just to tell you that I now have the results of the tests, which show nothing wrong except a surplus of white blood corpuscles, indicating an infection. That I had an infection I already knew. However, the doctor has proscribed [sic] some antibiotics to try to get rid of it—the bronchial cough, I mean.

Meanwhile I've perhaps stumbled on the source of the trouble. My dentist the other day found a quite large cyst or abscess in the bone above a dead tooth, has curetted it, and taken six or seven stitches in the gum. Jim and I and Margo [Viscusi] (you remember her) have instantly jumped to the conclusion that this has been the hidden reason for my feeling so unlike myself for such a long time. We shall see. In any case, my morale has shot up, which may only prove I'm suggestible.

How are you, my dear? And your work? As I think I told you, we have been in Holland, which was great fun except that we all had horrible colds—new ones. But I went to Parliament and had dinner with the Prime Minister. He and the Secretary of Defense gave me very pertinent advice about some of the technical problems of my novel [*Cannibals and Missionaries*] such as could the Dutch government borrow a helicopter capable of carrying thirty passengers from the German Nato forces. Very amusing and very nice people. The only fear is that, Holland being such a small country, everybody will soon know the plot of my story. We also visited a polder and inspected its landing facilities.

I'll write again soon a real letter. I miss you, and much love.

[Unsigned]

Epilogue

Hannah Arendt suffered another heart attack on December 4, 1975, and died instantly in her Riverside Drive apartment. She had returned exhausted from the summer in Europe, having decided to postpone the final Gifford Lectures until the following spring. Retired from the New School, she had resumed a round of dinners and excursions with friends and former students which had grown more frequent in the years since Heinrich Blücher's death. Every other Sunday she continued to talk by phone with Mary McCarthy in Paris. The night she died, she had served dinner to Jeannette and Salo Baron, old friends with whom she had worked for Jewish Cultural Reconstruction after the war.

In the days before her death, Arendt had finished "Willing," the second section of *The Life of the Mind*. Notes for "Judging" lay on her desk, and the first page was in the typewriter. It was blank except for the title and two quotations—"mottos," Arendt called such passages. The first—"The victorious cause pleased the gods, but the defeated one pleases Cato"—had already been used at the end of the "Thinking" manuscript. It is from Lucan's *Pharsalia*, the epic account of the civil war between Caesar and Pompey, and celebrates the anti-Caesar republicanism of Cato the Younger. (Arendt had mistakenly attributed it to "Old Cato.") The second quotation, from

Goethe's *Faust*, Part Two, might have served (with a change of pronoun) as her epitaph: "If I could rid my path of magic,/ could totally unlearn its incantations,/ confront you, Nature, simply as a man,/ to be a human being would then be worth the effort."

For Arendt, the faculty of Judgment was the linchpin in the mind's triad: without it, Thinking and Willing could not lead to moral action. Judgment informed the will with the wisdom of thought; of imagination, more precisely, for it was sympathetic participation in the experience of others that made judgment possible. Judgment was the heart of the mind's darkness, which Arendt, alone perhaps among contemporary thinkers, set out to map.

Arendt's funeral, like Blücher's, was a simple ceremony of remembrances. In a compromise reached over the question of whether Jewish prayers should be said, her Israeli niece read a psalm in Hebrew, which was then read in English by Chanan and Lotte Klenbort's son Daniel. Among the many reminiscences, including a moving portrait of Arendt as a student at Marburg fifty years before by Hans Jonas, were tributes by her former research assistant at the New School for Social Research, Jerome Kohn, and her publisher and friend, William Jovanovich, who said: "She was passionate in the way believers in justice can become and that believers in mercy must remain. [. . .] She followed wherever serious inquiry would take her, and if she made enemies it was never out of fear. [. . .] As for me," he ended, his voice breaking, "I loved her fiercely."

Mary McCarthy's valedictory, "Saying Good-bye to Hannah," published in *The New York Review of Books*, and reprinted in *Occasional Prose*, was remarkable for the vividness of the physical being it recalled. Before the hundreds of assembled mourners, which included a group in denim overalls wearing Farm Workers buttons, McCarthy spoke of a woman few perhaps had seen: "alluring, seductive, feminine [. . .] her eyes, so brilliant and sparkling, starry when she was happy or excited, but also deep, dark, remote, pools of inwardness."

This was the Hannah Arendt Mary McCarthy loved, who "had heard a voice such as spoke to the prophets," but who also had the touch of an actress in her. Remembering the first time she heard Arendt speak in public, thirty years before, McCarthy thought of "what Bernhardt must have been or Proust's Berma, a magnificent stage diva, which implies a goddess." Arendt wasn't an orator, she said; more a "mime, a thespian, enacting a drama of mind, that dialogue of me-and-myself she so often summons up in her writings. Watching her framed in the proscenium arch we were not far from the sacred origins of the theatre. What she projected was the human figure as actor and sufferer in the agon of consciousness and reflection, where there are always two, the one who says and the one who replies or questions."

A strange and wonderful note of Nietzsche's, unused in an unfinished essay published only posthumously, bears quoting here; for it, too, might stand as one of Arendt's mottos: "With thee, beloved voice, with thee, the last remembered breath of all human happiness, let me discourse, even if it is only for another hour. Because of thee, I delude myself as to my solitude and lie my way back to multiplicity and love, for my heart shies away from believing love is dead. It cannot bear the icy shivers of loneliest solitude. It compels me to speak as though I were Two."[1]

When Arendt died, McCarthy put down the half-finished manuscript of *Cannibals and Missionaries* to begin the arduous task of editing and annotating the Gifford Lectures for *The Life of the Mind*. It took her three years, and was "a heavy job," she remarks in her Editor's Postface, but one which "kept going an imaginary dialogue with her, verging sometimes, as in life, on debate. [. . .] I do not think I shall truly miss her, feel the pain in the amputated limb, till it is over. I am aware that she is dead," McCarthy continues, "but I am simultaneously aware of her as a distinct presence in this room, listening to my words as I write, possibly assenting with her musing nod, possibly stifling a yawn."

It is a sensation I feel myself, as I come to the end of these letters between friends. Their incorporation into a book was a charge laid on me a year before Mary McCarthy died in 1989. For me, this task, too, has kept a certain dialogue alive. But there's more to it than that, as Nietzsche understood. "No one converses with me besides myself," he observes, "and my voice reaches me as the voice of one dying."[2]

1. Friedrich Nietzsche, "Philosophy in the Tragic Age of the Greeks" (1873), quoted in James Miller's *The Passion of Michel Foucault* (1993), 11.
2. Ibid.

Works* by Hannah Arendt

The Origins of Totalitarianism. New York: Harcourt Brace & Co., 1951. Second, Enlarged Edition, New York: World Publishing Co., Meridian Books, 1958. Reprints, San Diego: Harcourt Brace/Harvest Books, 1973. Magnolia, Mass.: Peter Smith, 1983.

The Human Condition. Chicago: University of Chicago Press, 1958. Reprint, Chicago: University of Chicago Press, 1970.

Between Past and Future: Six Exercises in Political Thought. New York: Viking Press, 1961. Revised Edition, including two additional essays, New York: Viking Press, 1968.

Eichmann in Jerusalem: A Report on the Banality of Evil. New York: Viking Press, 1963. Revised and Enlarged Edition, New York: Viking Press, 1965. Reprint, New York: Viking Penguin, 1977.

On Revolution. New York: Viking Press, 1963. Reprint, New York: Greenwood, 1982. Revised Second Edition, New York: Viking Press, 1965. Reprint, New York: Viking Penguin, 1977.

Men in Dark Times. New York: Harcourt Brace & World, 1968. Reprint, San Diego: Harcourt Brace/Harvest Books, 1970.

---

*American editions.

Antisemitism. Original title: *The Origins of Totalitarianism,* Part 1. San Diego: Harcourt Brace/Harvest Books, 1968.

Imperialism. Original title: *The Origins of Totalitarianism,* Part 2. San Diego: Harcourt Brace/Harvest Books, 1968.

Totalitarianism. Original title: *The Origins of Totalitarianism,* Part 3. San Diego: Harcourt Brace/Harvest Books, 1968.

On Violence. New York: Harcourt, Brace & World, 1970. Reprint, San Diego: Harcourt Brace/Harvest Books, 1970.

Crises of the Republic. New York: Harcourt Brace Jovanovich, 1972.

Rahel Varnhagen: The Life of a Jewish Woman. New York: Harcourt Brace Jovanovich, 1974.

The Jew as Pariah: Jewish Identity and Politics in the Modern Age. Edited and with an introduction by Ron H. Feldman. New York: Grove Press, 1978.

The Life of the Mind. Vol. 1, *Thinking.* Vol. 2, *Willing.* Edited by Mary McCarthy. New York: Harcourt Brace Jovanovich, 1978. Reprint, San Diego: Harcourt Brace/Harvest Books, 1981.

Hannah Arendt, Karl Jaspers: Correspondence, 1926–1969. New York: Harcourt Brace & Co., 1992.

Essays in Understanding: 1930–1954. Edited by Jerome Kohn. New York: Harcourt Brace & Co., 1994.

Works by Mary McCarthy

The Company She Keeps. New York: Simon & Schuster, 1942. Reprint, San Diego: Harcourt Brace/Harvest Books, 1967.

The Oasis. New York: Random House, 1949.

Cast a Cold Eye. New York: New American Library, 1950. Reprint, San Diego: Harcourt Brace/Harvest Books, 1992.

A Charmed Life. New York: New American Library, 1955.

Venice Observed. New York: G. & R. Bernier, 1956. Reprint, San Diego: Harcourt Brace/Harvest Books, 1963.

Memories of a Catholic Girlhood. New York: Harcourt Brace & World, 1957. Reprint, San Diego: Harcourt Brace/Harvest Books, 1972.

The Stones of Florence. New York: Harcourt Brace & Co., 1959. Reprint, San Diego: Harcourt Brace/Harvest Books, 1963. Reissue, New York: Harcourt Brace Jovanovich, 1976.

On the Contrary. New York: Farrar, Straus and Cudahy, 1961. Reprint, New York: Hippocrene Books, 1976.

Mary McCarthy's Theatre Chronicles, 1937–1962. New York: Farrar, Straus & Giroux, 1963.

The Group. New York: Harcourt Brace & World, 1963. Reprints, New York: Avon, 1980; New York: Harcourt Brace Jovanovich, 1989; San Diego: Harcourt Brace/Harvest Books, 1991; New York: Buccaneer Books, 1991.

The Writing on the Wall and Other Literary Essays. New York: Harcourt Brace & World, 1970. Reprint, San Diego: Harcourt Brace/Harvest Books, 1971.

Birds of America. New York: Harcourt Brace Jovanovich, 1971. Reprint, San Diego: Harcourt Brace/Harvest Books, 1992.

The Seventeenth Degree. Includes *Vietnam, Hanoi, Medina,* and "Sons of the Morning." New York: Harcourt Brace Jovanovich, 1974.

The Mask of State: Watergate Portraits Including a Postscript on the Pardons. San Diego: Harcourt Brace/Harvest Books, 1974.

Cannibals and Missionaries. New York: Harcourt Brace Jovanovich, 1979. Reprint, San Diego: Harcourt Brace/Harvest Books, 1991.

Ideas and the Novel. New York: Harcourt Brace Jovanovich, 1980.

The Hounds of Summer and Other Stories. New York: Avon, 1981.

Occasional Prose. New York: Harcourt Brace Jovanovich, 1985.

How I Grew. New York: Harcourt Brace Jovanovich, 1987. Reprint, San Diego: Harcourt Brace/Harvest Books, 1988.

Intellectual Memoirs: New York 1936–1938. New York: Harcourt Brace & Co., 1992. Reprint, San Diego: Harcourt Brace/Harvest Books, 1993.

Index

Boldface page numbers indicate brief identification of persons appearing in the letters.